JOSEPH CONRAD

LONGMAN CRITICAL READERS

General Editor:
STAN SMITH, Professor of English, University of Dundee

Published titles:
K. M. NEWTON, *George Eliot*
MARY EAGLETON, *Feminist Literary Criticism*
GARY WALLER, *Shakespeare's Comedies*
JOHN DRAKAKIS, *Shakespearean Tragedy*
RICHARD WILSON AND RICHARD DUTTON, *New Historicism and Renaissance Drama*
PETER WIDDOWSON, *D. H. Lawrence*
PETER BROOKER, *Modernism/Postmodernism*
RACHEL BOWLBY, *Virginia Woolf*
FRANCIS MULHERN, *Contemporary Marxist Literary Criticism*
ANNABEL PATTERSON, *John Milton*
CYNTHIA CHASE, *Romanticism*
MICHAEL O'NEILL, *Shelley*
STEPHANIE TRIGG, *Medieval English Poetry*
ANTONY EASTHOPE, *Contemporary Film Theory*
TERRY EAGLETON, *Ideology*
MAUD ELLMANN, *Psychoanalytic Literary Criticism*
ANDREW BENNETT, *Readers and Reading*
MARK CURRIE, *Metafiction*
BREAN HAMMOND, *Pope*
LYN PYKETT, *Reading Fin de Siècle Fictions*
STEVEN CONNOR, *Charles Dickens*
REBECCA STOTT, *Tennyson*
SUSANA ONEGA AND JOSÉ ANGEL GARCÍA LANDA, *Narratology*
BART MOORE-GILBERT, GARETH STANTON and WILLY MALEY, *Postcolonial Criticism*
ANITA PACHECO, *Early Women Writers*
JOHN DRAKAKIS AND NAOMI CONN LIEBLER, *Tragedy*
ANDREW MICHAEL ROBERTS, *Joseph Conrad*
JOHN LUCAS, *William Blake*

JOSEPH CONRAD

Edited and Introduced by

ANDREW MICHAEL ROBERTS

LONDON AND NEW YORK

First published 1998 by Addison Wesley Longman Limited

Published 2013 by Routledge
2 Park Square, Milton Park, Abingdon, Oxfordshire OX14 4RN
711 Third Avenue, New York, NY 10017, USA

First issued in hardback 2014

Routledge is an imprint of the Taylor & Francis Group, an informa business

Copyright © 1998, Taylor & Francis.

**The right of Andrew Michael Roberts to be
identified as editor of this Work has been asserted
by him in accordance with the Copyright, Designs
and Patents Act 1988.**

All rights reserved. No part of this book may be reprinted or reproduced or utilised in
any form or by any electronic, mechanical, or other means, now known or hereafter
invented, including photocopying and recording, or in any information storage or re-
trieval system, without permission in writing from the publishers.

Notices
Knowledge and best practice in this field are constantly changing. As new research and
experience broaden our understanding, changes in research methods, professional
practices, or medical treatment may become necessary.

Practitioners and researchers must always rely on their own experience and knowledge in evaluating and using any information, methods, compounds, or experiments
described herein. In using such information or methods they should be mindful of
their own safety and the safety of others, including parties for whom they have a professional responsibility.

To the fullest extent of the law, neither the Publisher nor the authors, contributors, or
editors, assume any liability for any injury and/or damage to persons or property as a
matter of products liability, negligence or otherwise, or from any use or operation of
any methods, products, instructions, or ideas contained in the material herein.

ISBN 13: 978-1-138-83653-2 (hbk)

ISBN 13: 978-0-582-24598-3 (pbk)

British Library Cataloguing-in-Publication Data

A catalogue record for this book is available from the British Library

Library of Congress Cataloging-in-Publication Data

Joseph Conrad / edited and introduced by Andrew Michael Roberts.
    p.   cm. — (Longman critical readers)
    Includes bibliographical references and index.
    ISBN 0-582-24599-0 (CSD). — ISBN 0-582-24598-2 (PPR)
    1. Conrad, Joseph, 1857–1924 — Criticism and interpretation.
  I. Roberts, Andrew Michael, 1958– . II. Series.
  PR6005.04Z7498   1998
    823'.912—dc21   97–44495
                                                              CIP

Set by 35 in $9\frac{1}{2}$/$11\frac{1}{2}$pt Palatino

Contents

General Editors' Preface	vii
Preface	ix
Acknowledgements	x
Introduction	1
Narrative, textuality and interpretation	4
Imperialism	8
Gender and sexuality	12
Class and ideology	16
Modernity	20
Conclusion	24

PART ONE: CONRAD AND THE CRITICAL TRADITION

1	RAYMOND WILLIAMS Joseph Conrad	31
2	FRANCIS MULHERN English Reading (*Typhoon*)	37

PART TWO: NARRATIVE, TEXTUALITY AND INTERPRETATION

3	TERENCE CAVE Joseph Conrad: The Revenge of the Unknown (*Under Western Eyes*)	47
4	JEREMY HAWTHORN Seeing and Believing: Represented Thought and Speech in Conrad's Fiction (*Nostromo*)	71
5	MARK WOLLAEGER Skeptic Comedy and the Coercion of Character (*The Secret Agent*)	91

PART THREE: IMPERIALISM

6	CHINUA ACHEBE An Image of Africa: Racism in Conrad's *Heart of Darkness*	109
7	CHRIS BONGIE A Man of the Last Hour (*Almayer's Folly, An Outcast of the Islands, Tales of Unrest, The Nigger of the 'Narcissus'*)	124

PART FOUR: GENDER AND SEXUALITY

8	PADMINI MONGIA 'Ghosts of the Gothic': Spectral Women and Colonized Spaces in *Lord Jim*	155
9	NINA PELIKAN STRAUS The Exclusion of the Intended from Secret Sharing in Conrad's *Heart of Darkness*	171

Contents

10 WAYNE KOESTENBAUM Conrad's and Ford's Criminal
Romance (*Romance*) 189

PART FIVE: CLASS AND IDEOLOGY

11 FREDRIC JAMESON Romance and Reification:
Plot Construction and Ideological Closure in
Joseph Conrad (*Lord Jim*) 201

12 JIM REILLY Stasis, Signs and Speculation: *Nostromo* and
History 214

PART SIX: MODERNITY

13 ALLON WHITE Joseph Conrad and the Rhetoric of
Enigma (*Heart of Darkness*) 235

14 DAPHNA ERDINAST-VULCAN The Failure of Textuality
(*Victory*) 247

Notes on authors 270
Glossary of terms 272
Further reading 275
Index 279

General Editors' Preface

The outlines of contemporary critical theory are now often taught as a standard feature of a degree in literary studies. The development of particular theories has seen a thorough transformation of literary criticism. For example, Marxist and Foucauldian theories have revolutionised Shakespeare studies, and 'deconstruction' has led to a complete reassessment of Romantic poetry. Feminist criticism has left scarcely any period of literature unaffected by its searching critiques. Teachers of literary studies can no longer fall back on a standardised, received methodology.

Lecturers and teachers are now urgently looking for guidance in a rapidly changing critical environment. They need help in understanding the latest revisions in literary theory, and especially in grasping the practical effects of the new theories in the form of theoretically sensitised new readings. A number of volumes in the series anthologise important essays on particular theories. However, in order to grasp the full implications and possible uses of particular theories it is essential to see them put to work. This series provides substantial volumes of new readings, presented in an accessible form and with a significant amount of editorial guidance.

Each volume includes a substantial introduction which explores the theoretical issues and conflicts embodied in the essays selected and locates areas of disagreement between positions. The pluralism of theories has to be put on the agenda of literary studies. We can no longer pretend that we all tacitly accept the same practices in literary studies. Neither is a *laissez-faire* attitude any longer tenable. Literature departments need to go beyond the mere toleration of theoretical differences: it is not enough merely to agree to differ; they need actually to 'stage' the differences openly. The volumes in this series all attempt to dramatise the differences, not necessarily with a view to resolving them but in order to foreground the choices presented by different theories or to argue for a particular route through the impasses the differences present.

The theory 'revolution' has had real effects. It has loosened the grip of traditional empiricist and romantic assumptions about language and literature. It is not always clear what is being proposed as the new agenda for literary studies, and indeed the very notion of 'literature' is questioned by the post-structuralist strain in theory. However, the uncertainties and obscurities of

vii

Joseph Conrad

contemporary theories appear much less worrying when we see what the best critics have been able to do with them in practice. This series aims to disseminate the best of recent criticism and to show that it is possible to re-read the canonical texts of literature in new and challenging ways.

RAMAN SELDEN AND STAN SMITH

The Publishers and fellow Series Editor regret to record that Raman Selden died after a short illness in May 1991 at the age of fifty-three. Ray Selden was a fine scholar and a lovely man. All those he has worked with will remember him with much affection and respect.

Preface

In selecting articles and excerpts for this reader, I had three main aims in mind. The first was to pick criticism that was intrinsically interesting. The second, in accordance with the objectives of the series, was to represent a range of contemporary literary theory, applied tellingly and lucidly to Conrad's work. The third was to include criticism of a good proportion of Conrad's fiction so that, ideally, readers would be likely to find something of interest on whatever Conrad work they happened to be reading or studying. Given the limitations of space, there was bound to be some conflict between these aims, and, in particular, between the second and third. Criticism of Conrad has, for a long time, tended to focus on certain texts: *Heart of Darkness* above all, plus *Lord Jim, Nostromo,* sometimes *The Secret Agent* and *Under Western Eyes,* and perhaps some of the shorter fiction such as 'The Secret Sharer' and *The Shadow-Line.* Although, as I discuss in my Introduction (p. 3), there has been a recent move to study late Conrad, it remains true that a selection of classic examples of theoretically orientated Conrad criticism will tend to cluster around certain Conrad novels. Since these are also the novels which readers of this volume are most likely to be studying, I decided, with some regret, that I could not dedicate much space to Conrad's shorter works (although the extracts by Mulhern and Bongie deal with some of these), nor to Conrad's late work (although the extract by Erdinast-Vulcan discusses *Victory* in detail and other late works briefly). Otherwise, I tried to achieve a good spread: the table of contents identifies the main texts discussed in each piece.

The following referencing system has been used in the Introduction and in the headnotes at the start of each critical excerpt: page references given in brackets in the text, with no name or title attached, refer to the present volume; where the name of the critic is given in brackets in the text, the reference is to the original book or article. Terms which are included in the glossary are asterisked in the text at their first occurrence.

I would like to thank Stan Smith for his encouragement, Jakob Lothe, Jeremy Hawthorn and Robert Hampson for learned advice on matters Conradian, and the editorial team at Addison Wesley Longman for their good humour and patience.

ix

Acknowledgements

The publishers are grateful to the following for permission to reproduce copyright material:

The author Chinua Achebe for his essay 'An Image of Africa: Racism in Conrad's *Heart of Darkness*' in *Hopes and Impediments: Selected Essays 1965–1987* (Heinemann International, 1988) © Chinua Achebe; Hodder Headline Plc for extracts from *Joseph Conrad: Narrative Technique and Ideological Commitment* by Jeremy Hawthorn (1990), pp. 1–4, 14–16, 30–40; International Thomson Publishing Services for extracts from 'English Reading' by Francis Mulhern in *Nation and Narration* ed. Homi Bhabha (Routledge, 1990), pp. 250–2, 254–6, *The Political Unconscious: Narrative as a Socially Symbolic Act* by Fredric Jameson (Methuen & Co, 1981), pp. 206–19, *Double Talk: The Erotics of Male Literary Collaboration* by Wayne Koestenbaum (Routledge, 1989), pp. 166–73, *The Uses of Obscurity: The Fiction of Early Modernism* by Allon White (Routledge & Kegan Paul, 1981), pp. 110–17; International Thomson Publishing Services, and the literary executor Peter Reilly, for an extract from *Shadowtime: History and Representation in Hardy, Conrad and George Eliot* by Jim Reilly (Routledge, 1993), pp. 143–59; Novel Corp. for the article 'The Exclusion of the Intended from Secret Sharing in Conrad's *Heart of Darkness*' by Nina Pelikan Straus in *Novel: A Forum on Fiction*, Vol. 20, No. 2, Winter 1987, copyright © Novel Corp. 1987; Oxford University Press for extracts from *Recognitions: A Study in Poetics* by Terence Cave (1988), pp. 464–88 © Terence Cave 1988 and *Joseph Conrad and the Modern Temper* by Daphna Erdinast-Vulcan (1991), pp. 139–47 and 172–85 © Daphna Erdinast-Vulcan 1991; Random House UK Ltd for an extract from *The English Novel from Dickens to Lawrence* by Raymond Williams (Chatto & Windus, 1970), pp. 140–6; Editions Rodopi B. V. for the article '"Ghosts of the Gothic": Spectral Women and Colonized Spaces in *Lord Jim*' by Padmini Mongia in *Conrad and Gender* ed. Andrew Michael Roberts (1993); Stanford University Press for extracts from *Exotic Memories: Literature, Colonialism and the Fin De Siècle* by Chris Bongie (1991), pp. 4–5, 15, 17–18, 20, 22, 148–72 and *Joseph Conrad and the Fictions of Skepticism* by Mark A. Woolaeger (1990), pp. 142–55, Stanford University Press © 1990 and 1991 by the Board of Trustees of the Leland Stanford Junior University.

Introduction

Joseph Conrad's fiction raises questions of literary value with particular intensity.[1] As the section headings of this reader indicate, Conrad criticism has been involved with many of the most politically contentious areas of contemporary literary debate, including race, class and gender, as well as with philosophical and historical questions about interpretation and modernity. Basic questions about value underlie such debates. Why and how do we ascribe value to works of literature or the processes of writing and reading them? On what grounds do we value some works above others? Is there a single scale of value, from the 'great work' to the worthless, or are there different sorts of value which a literary text may possess? In this Introduction I shall discuss how questions of political, moral and aesthetic value are explored by critics of Conrad's work, before finally offering my own explanation as to why Conrad's fiction has proved such a productive field for critical debate.

F. R. Leavis, whose ideas dominated much English literary criticism from the 1930s until the arrival of the new literary theory in the 1960s, gave Conrad canonical status within what he termed the 'Great Tradition' of English fiction, describing him as 'unquestionably a constitutive part of the tradition, belonging in the full sense'.[2] Yet it could be argued that Conrad never belonged in the full sense to anything or anywhere. He was born a minor member of the Polish gentry, became a sailor and eventually a master in the British merchant navy, then changed career to become an admired, and eventually a popular, English novelist. Born in the Ukraine, legally a Russian citizen but the son of a Polish nationalist leader, he travelled to France when he was eighteen and learnt English, as his third language, only in his twenties, becoming a British citizen at the age of twenty-eight. His life and work are full of productive contradictions and tensions. A childhood victim of the Russian Empire and an adult servant of the British Empire, Conrad satirised the evils of imperialism while hinting at admiration for its ideals. He was a conservative whose scepticism called into question the

Joseph Conrad

basis of conservative values. If his work shows the influence of English novelists such as Dickens (most obviously in *The Secret Agent*), it is also crucially influenced by the French writers Flaubert, Maupassant and Anatole France and, despite Conrad's avowed dislike, by the great Russian novelist Dostoevsky.[3] Conrad's own account of his personality suggests contradiction. He famously commented that 'my point of view is English, from which the conclusion should not be drawn that I have become an Englishman. ... Homo duplex has in my case more than one meaning'.[4] Though he claimed that he had a 'natural talent' for idleness, he made himself ill through overwork.[5]

Leavis made absolute assertions of literary value central to literary criticism, linking them to ideas of cultural centrality. For Leavis the value of Conrad's work lies in its Englishness and in its espousing of essential human values. Against this, Francis Mulhern, in the second excerpt included here, sees Conrad as driven to write by anxieties about the stability of such values. For Mulhern, *Typhoon* is indicative of the tendency of narrative to unsettle essences and to reveal the repressed underside of ideologies and values (pp. 41–2). This approach offers us a far more centrifugal and hybrid Conrad than presented by Leavis, and this emphasis is shared by a number of other critics. The excerpts by Terence Cave and Mark Wollaeger share something of Mulhern's sense of the unsettling potentialities of narrative itself. Cave finds a 'revenge of the unknown' in *Under Western Eyes* (comparable to Mulhern's sense of the 'return of the repressed' in *Typhoon*) and Wollaeger celebrates the attempts of Conrad's characters to resist the coercive power of their author. Similarly, Fredric Jameson argues for a Conrad whose place is still 'unstable, undecidable, and his work unclassifiable' (p. 202), while Jim Reilly, in an earlier section of his book *Shadowtime*, suggests that 'firm ground under one's feet, a secure grasp of the real, a sense of personal solidity ... always eluded Conrad'.[6] Padmini Mongia's article in this collection shows a Conrad whose work crosses and mixes genres, whereas Leavis's account of Conrad focuses on his 'masterpieces' as high literature, downplaying elements of popular genres such as romance, detective fiction and adventure stories and deploring 'minor' works such as *The Arrow of Gold* and *The Rescue*, in which such genres were most evident.[7] Just as the complexity of Conrad's background raises issues of cultural value (is it better to 'belong' or to embrace hybridity?), so the generic complexity of his work raises issues of literary value. For instance, one possible narrative of Conrad's development as a writer is in terms of a hierarchy of literary genres (an assumption of the superior literary value of high art techniques such as symbolism over popular genres

Introduction

such as the detective story, the adventure story and the romance).
According to this account, Conrad took elements of the adventure
story and exotic romance (strongly present in early works such as
Almayer's Folly or 'Karain: A Memory'), and progressively transformed these through 'high' modernist strategies of impressionism,
ambiguity, narrative complexity and symbolism to create 'major'
works such as *Lord Jim, The Secret Agent, Heart of Darkness* and
Nostromo. This, so the argument goes, was followed by a decline
into more limited romances such as *Chance* and *The Arrow of Gold*.
This narrative has some plausibility. However, Conrad's later works
have recently been revalued by a number of critics, who have
pointed to their attention to issues of gender.[8] The traditional low
valuation of 'popular' or mass genres such as the detective story
and the romance is political as well as aesthetic, reflecting as it does
class and gender relations (the romance is sometimes, though not
always, associated with women readers and women's interests).
It is also worth noticing that *The Secret Agent* is both symbolist
and a detective story and draws some of its originality from this
combination.

While the explicit values of the author are at issue, so too are
values which may reside in the unconscious of the author, or of
the text, values which readers find in the text and the processes of
reading, and values which critics seek to champion through their
analyses. There is, of course, no value-free critical or theoretical
position. Leavis's view of Conrad reflects his political, cultural and
aesthetic values, but the same is true of Mulhern's championing of
the value of hybridity and the unsettling of hierarchies of nation,
class and gender. In this Mulhern typifies general tendencies of
post-1960s literary theory. Such theory tends to value multiplicity,
scepticism, uncertainty, hybridity, the marginal and the oppressed
and to take a critical view of centrality, authority, certainty and
unity. Steven Connor, in his book *Theory and Cultural Value*, points
out a paradox. Literary theory, he argues, has turned away from
evaluation (especially the Leavisite claim that literature inculcates
social and humane values) towards 'a concern with interpretation'.
Yet such theory focuses on questions which inescapably involve
issues of value. These include 'the politics of interpretation and
representation, the prejudiced representation of minority groups in
literature and art, the violent effects of discourse and the question
of the social effects and functions of cultural practices of all kinds'.
Connor suggests that value and evaluation have been 'driven into
the critical unconscious, where they continue to exercise force but
without being available for analytic scrutiny'.[9] That is, contemporary
literary theory is concerned with issues of value, but rarely asks

3

Joseph Conrad

itself what value is or how it functions. Both Daphna Erdinast-Vulcan and Jeremy Hawthorn, in the books excerpted here, make use of literary theory (deconstruction and narratology respectively), but both stress the importance, for their reading of Conrad, of his moral values. This Introduction, by posing questions of value in relation to Conrad's texts and in relation to the critical passages here reproduced, will seek to illuminate both fiction and criticism.

It is indicative of the richness of the readings collected here that almost all could have been included under several of the headings, as well as under other possible headings not used: for example Jameson addresses questions of modernity as well as those of politics and ideology, Mongia analyses constructions of race and imperialism as well as gender, and both critics draw on psycho-analytical theory and concepts of space. Indeed, it could be argued that the direction of literary theory since the 1980s (all but one of the pieces are post-1980) is best defined by the synthesis, dialogue or dialectic of different theoretical methodologies, as opposed to the predominance, in the 1960s and 1970s, of critical writing squarely adhering to one methodology: structuralist, psychoanalytical, feminist, etc. For this reason, the categorisation of texts in this reader is less by methodology (feminism, post-colonial theory, Marxism) than by the theoretical issue addressed (gender and sexuality, imperialism, class and ideology). Within categories, methodological contrasts emerge: Achebe and Bongie both write about Conrad's relationship to imperialism, but one from the standpoint of identity politics and the black critique of European racism and the other on the basis of postmodern theories of knowledge and history. White and Erdinast-Vulcan consider Conrad as a modern writer, but White in stylistic, hermeneutic and structuralist terms, while Erdinast-Vulcan bases her argument on the philosophical scepticism characteristic of modernity. Similarly, in the section entitled 'Narrative, textuality and interpretation', Terence Cave juxtaposes contemporary narratology with classical Aristotelian analysis of rhetoric, while Mark Wollaeger's account of the modes and motivations of narrative draws on Bakhtin's theory of the novel and Foucauldian conceptions of the body.

Narrative, textuality and interpretation

Most critics would agree that the sophistication of Conrad's narrative technique and the wealth of meanings which this helps to create are crucial to the value of his work. Narrative structures and the generation of meaning are particular concerns of the approach

4

Introduction

known as structuralism, which became influential from the 1960s onwards. Early structuralism aimed to show *how* texts mean rather that *what* they mean, and tended to analyse texts in terms of fixed structures. This produced a relatively stable conception of meaning. When applied to fiction, structuralist analysis seemed to offer an exhaustive mapping of the modes and forms of narrative in such a way as to pin down all the possible interpretations. However, two related factors carried the analysis of narrative in a different direction. One is the fact that analysing fiction using the grid of narratological terms is often most interesting precisely at the moment when the narrative eludes or transgresses the grid. As Gérard Genette puts it, 'the analyst's curiosity and predilection went regularly to the most *deviant* aspects of . . . narrative, the specific transgressions or beginnings of a future development'.[10] Several such aspects of Conrad's narrative technique are identified in *Under Western Eyes* by Terence Cave, in the chapter included here. He points, for example, to the conflict of narrative levels involved when we read Razumov's own narrative as more 'authentic' than the account provided by the language-teacher, yet have access to the former only though the latter, so that we rely on the inauthentic or limited narration to convey to us the authenticity which it cannot itself attain. Significantly, Genette goes on to associate narrative transgressions with Roland Barthes's concept of the 'writerly' text in *S/Z*. Here Barthes defines the writerly text (which allows the reader to create meanings in the process of reading) as 'ourselves writing, before the infinite play of the world . . . is traversed, intersected, stopped, plasticized by some singular system'.[11] In this celebration of a play of meanings which exceeds system and structure, *S/Z* marks a shift from structuralism to post-structuralism, a shift which brings us to the second factor in the development of narrative analysis. This is best summed up by the Derridean concept of *différance*, an invented word which combines 'difference' and 'deferral' in order to suggest that a finality of meaning is never reached. While structuralist 'difference' offered a static mapping of narrative structure, post-structuralist or deconstructive *différance* emphasises meaning as unending process; in his essay 'Force and Signification' Derrida criticises 'the stasis of a form whose completion appears to liberate it from work' and attacks the very notion of structure when it is allowed to become 'the object itself, the literary thing itself'.[12] This approach is reflected, for example, in Mulhern's idea of narrative as a 'work' of change: 'the work of narrativity is always an opening and closing' (p. 42).

There is then a tendency in post-structuralist criticism implicitly to ascribe value to the process of interpretation itself. The possibility

5

Joseph Conrad

of multiple interpretation (that is, ambiguity) has been accorded aesthetic value by modern criticism at least since the work of the New Critics, a school which had its roots in Britain in the 1920s in the critical writings of I. A. Richards and T. S. Eliot but became strongly established in America by the 1950s. While the New Critics tended to privilege poetry, their influence encouraged the celebration of ambiguity, complexity and irony in literature. Since Conrad's narrative techniques and style allow multiple inter-pretations, and since he is one of the greatest of modern ironists (particularly in *The Secret Agent*), this contributed to the high valuation of Conrad's work following what Robert Hampson describes as 'the rediscovery of Conrad in the 1940s'.[13] In the late 1940s F. R. Leavis had sharply distinguished between 'Conrad's art at its best', which created a moral atmosphere through concrete particulars, and an element in Conrad's writing which Leavis deplored: the vague evocation of mystery and profundity (in *Heart of Darkness*) by means of 'an adjectival and worse than supererogatory insistence on "unspeakable rites", "unspeakable secrets", "monstrous passions", "inconceivable mystery" and so on'.[14] Albert Guerard, whose book *Conrad the Novelist* initiated a wave of serious scholarly studies of Conrad in the 1950s and 1960s, defended such effects on grounds, derived from Freudian psychoanalysis, which involved a valuation of complexity and conflict in literature: 'it may be the groping, fumbling "Heart of Darkness" takes us into a deeper region of the mind'. For Guerard, Conrad's achievement lay in 'his creation of conflict in the reader, and his fine control of that conflict'.[15] However, following the rise of structuralist, post-structuralist and Marxist literary theory from the 1960s on, attention shifted away from the author and morality and towards the text and politics. Complexity and multiplicity continued to be valued, but in new ways. Interpretation as an activity, and more specifically freedom of intepretation, has been given political value at least since Roland Barthes's essay 'The Death of the Author' (1968).[16] In that essay, and in *S/Z*, Barthes sees a democratising and even subversive freedom in the ability of the reader to 'write' the text: to interpret it, to produce its meaning. The work of Mikhail Bakhtin (translated into English from the late 1960s onwards) had already made a comparable claim for diversity of meaning within the text, finding moral and political value in the principal of the 'dialogic',* in which the texts allow room and authority to different voices. Underlying such theories is a wish to weaken or subvert the authority of the god-like author.

These themes are addressed most explicitly in the present collec-tion by Mark Wollaeger. He gives a distinctive twist to the question

Introduction

of whether the value and meaning of a text are controlled by the author, when he envisages characters resisting the narrative design.[17] Using Bakhtin's categories of the monologic* and dialogic, Wollaeger argues that, in the absence of a mediating character-narrator such as Marlow, Conrad's scepticism leads him towards a monological domination over his characters. However, he suggests that in *Nostromo* not only do the characters struggle to maintain their autonomy, but Conrad's thematisation of such struggles (between characters and between characters and narrators) amounts to a reflexive critique on Conrad's part of his own complicity. In *The Secret Agent*, on the other hand, characters' resistance is expressed only via futile 'resentment and indignation' and the author seems unself-critical about his own 'love of domination'.[18] Wollaeger draws on Foucault's theorisation of the body as a site of inscription and power for his account of how the author of *The Secret Agent* 'violently processes characters into expressions of themes'.[19] So, whereas Jeremy Hawthorn values clarity of authorial intention, Mark Wollaeger values resistance to authorial intention. Wollaeger does make the point that, in Bakhtin's scheme, authorial intention still remains the ultimate horizon, even within a fully dialogic work, although the 'author' in this context can only be what Bakhtin calls the 'secondary author': '"the image of the author" created within the text by the "primary" or historical author'.[20] Jakob Lothe, whose book *Conrad's Narrative Method* represents the most detailed and rigorous analysis of Conrad's narrative techniques, also offers a subtle approach to the vexed question of authorial intention, arguing that there is 'an insistent and forceful "Conradian voice" in Conrad's fiction', a voice which, while founded upon the author's experiences and awareness, is also a product of his narrative method. Thus Lothe argues that we should see narrative technique, not simply as a reflection of pre-existing intentions, but as 'a constituent aspect of Conrad's fiction'.[21] Where Wollaeger is influenced by Bakhtin and by deconstruction, Jeremy Hawthorn's approach to narrative is Marxist and humanist, a combination which may seem surprising on the face of it, but belongs to a certain tradition in British criticism, including most notably Raymond Williams and Arnold Kettle. Hawthorn is Marxist in his sense of the economic basis of injustice and inequality but humanist in his moral response to such injustice. So, whereas a deconstructive Marxist such as Mulhern is inclined to celebrate the 'unsettling' of fixed meaning as valuable *in itself* (because it resists authority and totality), Hawthorn, retaining more links to the Leavisite tradition of moral humanism, distinguishes between 'productive' and 'unproductive' ambiguity in Conrad's work, and rests this

Joseph Conrad

distinction on the certainty of the author's underlying moral and ideological values. To this extent the value of the work, for Hawthorn, continues to be centred in the author, whereas for many post-structuralist critics it is centred (or rather, de-centred) in the reading process itself.

Mulhern's idea of narrativity as work and as open to the 'return of the repressed' is influenced by Freud's idea of the 'dream-work' – the process by which the unconscious mind transforms repressed desires into the coded symbolic narrative structure of dreams. Freudian theory also contributed to Roland Barthes's emphasis on pleasure and sexuality in relation to narrative in *The Pleasure of the Text*.[22] Barthes's work introduced the concept of narrative desire into the discussion of the novel. So Terence Cave, in the chapter from *Recognitions* included here, sees narrative desire as an important motivation for the author (p. 48), for a character-narrator, and for the reader (p. 55), and cites Conrad's delusory conversations with the characters of *Under Western Eyes* as evidence of the 'insatiability' of such desire: the story is never ended. Cave, like Mulhern, values the way in which narrative eludes resolution and finality: for him, seeming inconsistencies and incoherences within the narrative structure of *Under Western Eyes* are not technical problems so much as sites of philosophical meaning, indicative of the insight that 'the whole truth is precisely not narratable' (p. 57). Much of Conrad's fiction might be seen as a continuing engagement between the desire to tell stories which reveal the truth and this sense that aspects of truth always elude narration.

Imperialism

Conrad both lived in and wrote about a world in which the empire-building of the European states was a crucial economic and political force. Pre-theoretical writing about Conrad often treated imperialism as merely a 'setting' within which existential or moral issues were worked out: for example, *Heart of Darkness*, though it describes a brutal and wasteful policy of colonial exploitation in the Belgian Congo, was often read by critics as a symbolic journey of self-discovery by its protagonist and narrator Marlow.[23] However, the somewhat inert text/context model of literature's relationship to history has been largely superseded by a discourse-based model according to which, in Foucault's terms, 'discourse is not simply that which translates struggles or systems of domination, but is the thing for which and by which there is struggle, discourse is the power which is to be seized'.[24] On the basis of such a theoretical

8

Introduction

approach, nineteenth-century fiction of colonial adventure is seen as part of colonialism not a reflection of it. That is to say, the fictions of empire did not merely reflect what was going on in 'reality', but helped to authorise it, to give it shape in the popular imagination and in the minds of policy-makers, to motivate its continuance (or resistance to it). Conrad's writing can then be seen in terms of the discourse of colonialism, and the two pieces in this section assess, in different ways, the extent of his work's complicity with that discourse.

Chinua Achebe's article accuses Conrad, primarily on the basis of his representation of Africa and Africans in *Heart of Darkness*, of being a 'thoroughgoing' racist (p. 117). This has prompted a continuing debate over questions of racism in Conrad's work: a debate over political and moral value. When a critic deals with the question of racism, he or she often tends to elide author and text. It is difficult, if theoretically possible, to condemn the author and accept the text, or vice versa. Strangely, *Heart of Darkness* has been defended, both on the grounds that it is realistic (that the attitudes it shows are accurate for the period) and on the grounds that it is not realist (that it is a symbolic narrative, not a realist presentation of Africa).[25] Other grounds of defence have been the distinction between Conrad and his narrators, his use of irony and ambiguity, his overt criticism of European cruelty, his symbolic linking of Europe and Africa and his relatively progressive attitude to empire when set against others of his period. However, some critics have agreed with Achebe, often with refinements: Patrick Brantlinger sees *Heart of Darkness* as a 'schizophrenic' text , with an 'anti-imperialist message . . . undercut both by its racism and by its impressionism'.[26] Conrad's critical stance towards European 'civilisation' and the behaviour of its representatives is perhaps the strongest argument in his favour, but this defence is powerfully countered by Terry Eagleton's point that the novella shows Western civilisation to be 'as barbarous as African society – a viewpoint which disturbs imperialist assumptions to the precise degree that it reinforces them'.[27] That is, in showing London as also a 'heart of darkness', Conrad presupposes the 'darkness' or 'savagery' of Africa. Furthermore, the association of the heart of darkness which Marlow finds in Africa with absence, horror and negation is in a tradition of racist discourse; as Henry Louis Gates points out, 'The trope of blackness in Western discourse has signified absence at least since Plato'.[28]

Achebe begins his article by commenting on ignorance of Africa in American educational institutions. And he rejects a positive conclusion because of the continuing 'grip and pervasiveness' of the 'stereotype image' of Africa in the West (p. 121). It is, then,

9

Joseph Conrad

the extraordinary status of *Heart of Darkness* as canonical work of modernism, as a famous 'masterpiece', as set text on thousands of university and college courses round the world, that makes its value such a political issue. Whatever its merits, it is a text which tells us almost nothing about the vast and culturally rich continent of Africa, except the fact that the Congo was subject to brutal European exploitation. What does it mean to have as one of the best-known and most influential texts about Africa a work from which African history, culture, language, art, customs, ideas and religions are wholly absent?

Chris Bongie suggests reasons why nineteenth-century European society might have needed Africa, or the Far East of Conrad's earlier novels, as an 'Other' and why contemporary Western society might persist in such a tendency, even though for Bongie such a fantasy of otherness was already becoming untenable in Conrad's time, given the advance of global modernity which tends to create a homogeneous world. It is crucial to bear in mind here the close connection between otherness and sameness, pointed out by many post-colonial and feminist theorists. My 'Other' is my imagined opposite, which confirms me in my sense of my own identity (imagined as an essence). For the white, male colonialist, the supposed otherness of African or Malayan people, and in different ways the supposed otherness of women, confirm his identity as universal human subject. *Heart of Darkness* stresses the otherness of Africa (seen as primitive and primeval) but recuperates this as sameness, via such moments as Marlow's sense of kinship with the African dancing and his comments on London as having also been 'one of the dark places of the earth' (*Heart of Darkness*, p. 48). This liberal gesture of self-critique remains within the Same–Other dichotomy, and does not allow room for difference or hybridity. Bongie explains this desire for the Other in terms of a quest for values of authenticity which seem to have been lost by modern 'civilisation'. In a sense, then, he sees the *motivation* of *Heart of Darkness* as the inverse of what its story might seem to suggest. If the story is about confronting otherness (the remote and 'primitive') and finding sameness (the darkness within), its motive, according to Bongie's theory of *fin-de-siècle* exoticism, is a fear of sameness (global homogenisation) creating a desire for otherness. The structure of the novella would seem to support this claim. If we invoke the narratological distinction between story (the events in chronological order) and plot (the events as arranged in the text), then it is striking that the plot begins and ends in darkness (on the Thames) with a journey to darkness (up the Congo) in the middle. Chronologically Marlow may have begun with a sense of Africa as

Introduction

unwritten otherness (the white space on the map), but textually, London and Africa are always already part of the Same. Bongie claims that the requisite condition for exoticism is the 'autonomy of alternative cultures and territories, their fundamental difference from what we might call "the realm of the Same"' (p. 126). This is, however, a claim which would be contested by many post-colonial theorists, who would see exoticism as epitomising the realm of the Same, in that it projects the needs and fantasies of the West onto other cultures.[29] Indeed, Bongie's whole approach might itself be accused of complicity with the colonial appropriation of the Other. In postmodernist style he acknowledges this complicity as inevitable: 'I will not be describing the exoticist project from some putatively neutral observation post: the story of loss that generates exoticism is also the story of this book, a study that to a certain extent participates in what it purports to analyze'.[30] Bongie asserts the 'ethico-political' value of a continuing attachment to a lost cause, a continuing longing for an alternative space of the exotic which one knows does not exist, and perhaps never did exist (since the exotic is always a fantasy). This may seem a very perverse set of values, especially since it is predicated upon a view of late capitalist society as marked by 'the *definitive* loss of value(s) and a *real* absence of alternative worlds'.[31] Bongie's approach relies upon a postmodernist belief in living with paradox, a claim that in 'conserving this unreal alterity' Conrad and other writers create a space between the lost past and the inescapable present, and that 'To inhabit this space is, finally, to put oneself in the place of the Other: to take as one's own the burden of an emptiness that can never be possessed'.[32]

There is therefore a conflict of values here. On the one hand we have a post-colonial criticism (exemplified in Achebe's article) which attacks the whole rhetoric of Same and Other, and champions the value of hybridity.[33] On the other there is a postmodern philosophy which denies the possibility of genuine escape from the sameness of the modern world, and sees hope only in living within the knowledge that such an escape would be fantasy. Achebe's piece seems to me crucial in challenging complacent assumptions which are sometimes still made, even if some of its own assumptions can be challenged in turn. Bongie's history of the idea of the exotic can be accused of yielding too easily to Eurocentrism, but it does offer a strong account of the development of Conrad's work, from the start of his writing career up to *Lord Jim*, outlined on pp. 130–1.

It would be arrogant to attempt here some arbitration between the views of Achebe and Bongie, which are anyway only two among many discussions of imperialism in Conrad's work (see Further reading). Such arbitration is particularly dubious in the context of

11

Joseph Conrad

post-colonial criticism, where it is precisely difference in cultural perspective that is at issue, and where critiques have often been made of Western or 'first-world' 'discursive colonisation', when Western critics arrogate the authority to judge on cross-cultural issues.[34] It is important to recognise the heterogeneity of critical perspectives: the fact that they may have different sorts of value not necessarily assessable in each other's terms. What can be said is that Conrad's writing operates within the discourses of his time and context, and is shot through by the specific historical configurations of empire and 'race', even when not addressing these matters explicitly. So *The Secret Agent*, set in London and almost entirely concerned with European characters, nevertheless invokes the context of empire and ideas of race, foreignness and otherness: Verloc 'generally arrived in London (like the influenza) from the Continent' (*The Secret Agent*, p. 11); the Assistant Commissioner longs for the relative satisfaction of police work in the colonies (*The Secret Agent*, p. 89) and associates Inspector Heat with 'a certain old fat and wealthy native chief' (*The Secret Agent*, p. 93), and the Russian First Secretary Mr Vladimir is associated with the 'oriental' (*The Secret Agent*, p. 171). Most crucially, Winnie Verloc and Stevie are surrounded with the rhetoric of racial degeneracy and otherness. As Rebecca Stott has argued, Winnie 'carries some of the iconographic traces of Conrad's early native women as an atavistic murderess and agent of death'.[35] Winnie, who is presumably English, comes to be symbolically 'black' (the black of the body, of darkness, of otherness), in a way which reveals that 'race' is a symbolic construction, not a material reality.

Conrad's undoubted genius did not allow him to stand outside his time. It is when we imagine that he could – when, for example, we want to read *Heart of Darkness* as embodying universal existential truth – that we risk producing a 'racist' Conradian text. To recognise Conrad's historical placement and conceptual limitations (provided, of course, we remember our own) is not to deny him the distinctiveness of his understanding, nor his crucial ability to analyse and criticise those configurations from within.

Gender and sexuality

Many first-time readers of Conrad express the view that he is a man's author. A traditional critical response to such an objection might be to defend the value of his work, either by maintaining the complexity and interest of certain of his female characters, or by

Introduction

acknowledging the masculinist bias arising out of his biographical and cultural context, while claiming that the semantic richness, philosophical and political depth and literary innovations of his works transcend this limitation. An alternative and perhaps more satisfying response (more responsive to the experience of women readers) takes value itself, and hence the ways in which fiction is valued, as a topic of enquiry rather than as a ground to be defended. So Nina Pelikan Straus, in the article in this collection, considers how the needs, desires and fantasies of the male reader are implicated in the symbolic structure of *Heart of Darkness*, tending to exclude the female reader. In this way she offers a critique of much existing criticism of the text, protesting in particular against the continuing 'romanticization' of *Heart of Darkness* (p. 186). Just as Achebe sees it as a 'racist' text, she sees it as 'brutally sexist' (p. 173), but like Achebe her concern is not to dismiss the novella but to argue for an oppositional reading of certain elements of its ideology. If one agrees with such political judgements about the text it is bound to affect one's sense of its aesthetic and philosophical value, but I would argue that it by no means destroys such value. Rather it places that value historically and makes one, as reader, self-conscious about one's distance from the text: it can speak to our own lives and experience but does so from a distinct cultural and ideological position, not from a transcendent point outside history. This might imply what Edward Said terms 'contrapuntal reading', which opens a text out 'both to what went into it and to what its author excluded'.[36]

One long-standing view of gender and sexuality in Conrad has been that he was simply not very good at portraying either sexuality or women: thus Albert Guerard, in his book *Conrad the Novelist*, comments on Conrad's 'clumsiness and evasion' in approaching what he termed Conrad's 'least congenial subject', that of sexual attraction.[37] The greater focus on women and on sexual relationships in Conrad's later work has been associated by some with a supposed decline in that work.[38] For example, Guerard lists and analyses in detail three 'gross characteristics' of Conrad's literary decline: 'the sentimental ethic'; 'the narrator or central consciousness as dullard'; 'failure of imaginative power and imaginative common sense'.[39] Many of his arguments are telling, but they are also shot through with an unthinking masculinist bias and assumptions of the inferiority of women. The behaviour of Ricardo in *Victory* is judged ridiculous because of the 'effeminacy' of his way of talking; Peyrol in *The Rover* is no longer really interesting because he is 'emasculated' by lack of heroic action; Conrad's portrayal of the oppressive dependence of young women in *Chance* is dismissed as

13

Joseph Conrad

exploitation of 'a staple sentimental plot of popular fiction', and what for Guerard is missing from these later works is Conrad's 'tragic sense of individual moral failure in a world of men': a comment which forgets the importance of women in *Heart of Darkness, Nostromo* and *The Secret Agent*. Dismissing portraits of vulnerable women as 'sentimental', Guerard seems no happier when they acquire some strength: 'These are then women to be pitied, protected, saved – though now and then they seem alarmingly able to take care of themselves'.[40]

Many of the features Guerard identifies as weaknesses, such as Marlow's tendency to odd rambling in *Chance*, have been reinterpreted by critics interested in issues of gender as *different* techniques from those of Conrad's better-known novels, rather than simply a falling-off of technique. I have elsewhere interpreted Marlow's contradictory comments on women in this novel as an exploration of some of the uncertainties of masculinity, and as a staging of competition between men for 'the knowledge and, symbolically, for the sexual possession of women'.[41] Feminist critics and criticism came relatively late to Conrad, presumably because his works seemed at first sight unpromising material. D. H. Lawrence and T. S. Eliot were seen as cultural icons or authority figures whose misogyny needed to be revealed and attacked, but many feminists tended to assume that Conrad was just not very interesting on the subject of gender.[42] The first book on gender issues in Conrad, Ruth Nadelhaft's *Joseph Conrad*, is critical of earlier work which identifies male and female roles rather than analysing the underlying structure of gender.[43] However, Nadelhaft herself tends to drift towards an essentialism in which women characters are intuitive, open to cultural difference and in touch with 'gritty' reality, while men characters are stupid, imperialistic and unable to face reality. She then valorises Conrad's work in terms of his positive representation of strong women characters and his (only partly conscious) use of them to 'embody the criticism and the alternatives to white, male, European self-centredness'.[44] More sophisticated feminist work on Conrad has tended, ironically enough, to arise in conjunction with the increasing attention to masculinity in literature. I refer here, not to the reactionary 'backlash' of male writers claiming victimhood, but to feminist critics, both female and male, who have seen analysis of the construction of masculinity as a complementary project to feminism. Padmini Mongia's article on *Lord Jim* in this collection illustrates this complementarity, beginning as it does with the figures of Jewel and her mother as 'spectral' presences within the narrative of male adventure, before going on

14

Introduction

to identify a Gothic subtext in the novel. Within the psychic and geographical spaces mapped out by this Gothic subtext, female identity is explored in terms which can be explicated psycho-analytically, while the male protagonist Jim is feminised. Gender and genre are closely interwoven. Masculinity is unsettled by the Gothic, but is seemingly bolstered by a return to the adventure genre at the end of the novel. However, this conclusion leaves residues expressive of anxiety about masculinity. Such an approach gets away from the limiting debate around authorial 'insight' and intention (conscious or otherwise) by looking at literary structures such as genre and at cultural factors such as imperialism and the *fin-de-siècle* mood. Mongia's article neither defends nor attacks Conrad but relates the ambivalence of his texts to psychological, historical and social factors in a way which enhances the richness of our reading.

The development of gay or queer studies (terminology here tends to be fast-changing and politically loaded) is both cause and result of increased attention to masculinity. Like feminist criticism, gay theory seeks to displace normative masculinity from its position of assumed cultural centrality. Wayne Koestenbaum's discussion of Conrad's collaboration with Ford Madox Ford (included here) attends to the marginal in several ways. Mainstream literary criticism has a tendency to marginalise collaboration itself because of the continuing investment of our culture in the idea of individual genius. Popular genres such as the romance are often treated as marginal to the work of a major and 'serious' author such as Conrad. Biographical information has an odd status: despite its immense popularity and even dominance in media accounts of literature, much literary theory has wanted to exclude or margin-alise biography, in reaction against its reductive use to explain the meaning of texts. Koestenbaum ignores such earnest methodological arguments and freely weaves together autobiographical texts and remarks with passages from *Romance* and the circumstances of the authors' lives. He also makes free play with the contemporary connotations of words such as 'queer', 'gay' and 'fagot', implying a possible ambivalence in their use by Conrad and Ford, though without claiming any explicit 'code'. However, he also historicises his account in a way which connects to Mongia's sense of the *fin-de-siècle* as a period of male anxiety, since the 'specter of Wilde' (p. 196), which Koestenbaum finds invoked in the court scene of *Romance*, was the defining figure of that crisis of masculinity. This was a crisis to which Conrad (though himself a most un-Wildean figure) was by no means immune.

15

Joseph Conrad

Class and ideology

Conrad's political opinions have long been a matter for debate. In his 1967 book, Avrom Fleishman objects to the view of Conrad as a reactionary who used his novels to attack liberal and humanitarian principles. Fleishman, who claims that Conrad gradually escaped from his early prejudices and evolved 'a grand vision of social community', reads *Nostromo*, *The Secret Agent* and *Under Western Eyes* as novels which express 'a complex political imagination . . . not reducible to political ideology'.[45] However, as Fleishman is obliged to acknowledge, some of Conrad's most explicit comments on politics (at least from early in his career) strongly support the idea of him as a political reactionary. In letters of 1885 and 1899 he attacks 'social-democratic ideas' and 'fraternity', denies that he is a 'democrat' and, in what seems a hysterical response to a widening of the franchise in the 1885 British general election, claims that:

> the International Socialist Association are triumphant, and every disreputable ragamuffin in Europe feels that the day of universal brotherhood, despoilation and disorder is coming apace, and nurses day dreams of well-plenished pockets among the ruins of all that is respectable, venerable and holy.[46]

There are echoes of such views in Conrad's later portraits of revolutionaries or those who claim to represent the rights of working people. As Jim Reilly notes in the excerpt included here, Conrad's narrative directs 'absurd, spluttering invective' (p. 218) and physical loathing at characters such as Donkin in *The Nigger of the 'Narcissus'*, the revolutionary photographer in *Nostromo* and the anarchists in *The Secret Agent*. Like many other commentators, however, Reilly sees this as indicative of an inner conflict in Conrad, rather than a programmatic position.

Many critics have drawn attention to the importance of Conrad's personal and family history, involving distinctively Polish political alignments which are likely to be very unfamiliar to British and American readers. Conrad's father was a nationalist revolutionary leader, involved in the run-up to the 1863 uprising against Russian rule in the eastern half of Poland. This involvement led to his imprisonment and later the exile of the family in Russia and the early death of both Conrad's parents. Apollo Korzeniowski was, however, a member of the *szlachta* or Polish gentry, and not inclined to support land reform in favour of the Ukrainian majority in the area where he lived, who were serfs of Polish landlords. So Conrad's father could be seen as a model for resistance to (Russian)

Introduction

imperialism, or as a supporter of the quasi-colonialist prerogatives of the Polish landowners. In either event his politics do not map easily onto the conventional left–right divide of modern Western debates. Furthermore, two of Conrad's uncles took different positions in the Polish politics of the time. There is not room here to survey the complexities of the history involved, nor to consider in any detail the possible psychology of Conrad's reactions to this legacy. These reactions may have included guilt at leaving Poland, loyalty combined with resentment or denial in relation to his father's idealistic and mystical nationalism, and a conflict of influences involving his father and the more pragmatic uncle, Tadeusz Bobrowski, who became Conrad's guardian after the death of his father.[47] It is, however, worth bearing in mind that when Conrad rejects 'fraternity' as a threat to 'national sentiment' or takes a bleakly pessimistic view of revolutionary idealism, his attitudes are informed by the situation of Poland and his own tragic family history.

This is an area of debate in which the allegiance of the critic is likely to condition the argument. Terry Eagleton, in his 1976 book *Criticism and Ideology*, agrees with Fleishman in seeing the ideal of organic community as central to Conrad's politics, but for Eagleton this is symptomatic, not of Conrad's mature move away from early conservative prejudices, but of his continuing attachment to a hierarchic ideal from the past, 'the organicist tradition of nineteenth-century Romantic humanism'.[48] Where Fleishman is a liberal humanist critic, Eagleton is a Marxist, and liberal humanism, which sees itself as liberal and progressive, has been seen by radical literary theory as complicit with the world-view of the affluent Western middle classes. It has been suggested that humanism's tendency to privilege the aesthetic over the political (evident in Fleishman's claim that Conrad's political art transcends the political) serves to maintain the status quo. Marxist criticism now finds itself in an odd position. Associated in the minds of many with a discredited communism, it remains a powerful though troubled intellectual tradition, offering a theory of history and economic change, and a critique of the tendency of capitalist powers to pursue destructive economic self-interest under the guise of protecting democracy.

Conrad's relationship to Marxist thought is an intriguing one. Despite his conservative allegiances and instincts, and his humanistic interest in ideals, psychology and human nature (which are inimical to the economic and social determinism of Marxism), Marxist literary criticism has found Conrad's fiction a productive site of debate because that fiction engages powerfully with the role of economic forces in shaping history and consciousness. This is

17

Joseph Conrad

most explicit in *Nostromo*, where the power of 'material interests' to determine human lives is a major theme. Such an engagement is suppressed rather than explicit in a work such as *Lord Jim*, where the economic basis of the work of merchant seamen and other agents of colonial trade is partly effaced by a concern with moral issues. It is claimed that morality transcends the economic: 'the prosaic severity of the daily task that gives bread – but whose only reward is in the perfect love of the work' (*Lord Jim*, p. 10). The two excerpts included in this section are taken from longer chapters, but indicate both the theoretical methodology of contemporary Marxism and its bearing on Conrad. Jim Reilly, recognising Conrad's humanism, nevertheless argues, in an earlier section of his book, that Conrad 'reaches a Marxist conclusion through non-Marxist premisses'. The Marxist conclusion is that history consists of relentless struggle, and that 'individual psychology is itself correspondingly riven with contradiction'; the non-Marxist premise is the priority which Conrad accords to human nature, since for Conrad it is the duality of that nature which produces historical conflict, not vice versa.[49] This is a crucial philosophical difference between Marxism and humanism: the former takes human consciousness, including human beliefs, to be the product of economic and historical forces, not the cause of economic and historical change. It is therefore not surprising that a critic like Reilly, strongly influenced by Marxism, should be drawn to *Nostromo*, which repeatedly shows characters imagining that they can shape history, but realising too late that they have been controlled by larger forces and have fitted unwittingly into larger patterns. In particular, Charles Gould and Nostromo, acclaimed by themselves and others as leaders and heroes with the power crucially to influence events, realise that they are the slaves of 'material interests'. Is Reilly right to claim that Conrad gives causal priority to human nature? The case can certainly be made, since Conrad tends to stress the personal and psychological aspects of the process by which characters realise their lack of autonomy. For example, Gould's actions and his illusions of moral autonomy are shown to be a reaction to the life and death of his father. Nevetheless, part of the fascination of the novel is the way in which it seems poised between historical determinism and an ethical stress on individual choice and responsibility.

Ironically enough, Reilly's reading of *Nostromo* involves an element of psychological speculation about its author, since he links Conrad's accounts of his own psychic stresses and conflicts to unresolved tensions within the novel, produced by its critique of capitalism, a system to which it nevertheless admits no viable

Introduction

alternative. The much-criticised ending of the novel slides away from its political insights; as I have argued elsewhere,

> If *Nostromo* sees history as transcending the individual will, it also ultimately sees the mystery of an impersonal universe as transcending human history. Occasionally, as in the last sentence of the novel, Conrad gestures towards a romantic position in which the individual, at moments of intensity, is perceived as standing outside history and in direct relation to the unknowable.[50]

Just as *Lord Jim*, by returning to the adventure mode at the end, reinstates a heroic masculinity which it has previously destabilised (see Mongia), so *Nostromo* shifts in its last paragraphs into a romantic mode which seeks to reinstate the tragic heroism of Nostromo himself, a heroism which the novel has arguably revealed to be an illusory denial of historical reality. If Marxism accuses liberal humanism of obscuring political and economic realities, humanism in return accuses Marxists of programmatically imposing a preconceived political theory onto the text. The second excerpt in this section is drawn from Jameson's *The Political Unconscious*. In a sustained critique of Jameson's influential study, Jacques Berthoud claims that 'By identifying consciousness with ideology, Jameson renders himself completely incapable of acknowledging Conrad's text as offering, like his own, a responsible interpretation of the world'.[51] Certainly Marxist theory is very much a 'grand narrative', claiming to subsume, judge and incorporate all other perspectives. Jameson offers a (useful) listing of the many possible critical approaches to Conrad (see pp. 203–4), and sees his own account as a 'metacommentary' which can embrace and account for all these approaches. Indeed, Jameson explicitly claims that Marxism should be seen as an 'untranscendable horizon'.[52] Jameson is a more programmatic Marxist than Reilly, though he is also a highly sophisticated one. Such sophistication is part of the development of Marxist criticism away from so-called 'vulgar Marxism' (which saw culture as merely a secondary effect of economic structures) towards a new and less reductive account of aesthetic value which nevertheless remains true to the principles of Marxism. Like Reilly (who alludes to Conrad's well-known characterisation of himself as 'homo duplex'), and like many other critics, Jameson sees Conrad in terms of a division. Not, however, a psychological division, but a cultural, discursive and historical one. For Jameson the generic shift within *Lord Jim* is symptomatic of a 'fault line' (p. 202) as modernism and commercialised 'mass' culture evolved alongside

Joseph Conrad

each other. This brings us to the question of Conrad's position in relation to modernism and modernity.

Modernity

Modernity as a social, cultural and economic condition can be distinguished from modernism, a movement in the arts generally associated with innovation in technique and radical change in the conception of art's role and function. Modernity and modernism are of course closely linked: modernism is arguably a response to the condition of modernity, a condition in which urbanisation, technological change, imperialism and war produced rapid changes in social structures, ways of life and patterns of belief and behaviour. This response by writers, painters, musicians, dancers, architects, sculptors, etc. may be affirmative, celebrating the exhilaration of the modern world, or it may express alienation and fear of cultural crisis. So it is not really a paradox to state that Conrad was a major modernist writer who was temperamentally and ideologically opposed to many aspects of modernity. For example, in his essays 'Ocean Travel' and 'Travel' Conrad mourned the displacement of sail by steam, and the ending of 'the days of heroic travel'[53] (a nostalgia which is discussed by Bongie; see pp. 127–8). Conrad associated modernity with the decline of the values epitomised by a figure such as Singleton, in *The Nigger of the 'Narcissus'*, an old sailor of few words whose life has been dominated by hard work and unquestioning loyalty to his duty. Conrad wrote of himself that:

> Those who know me know my conviction that the world, the temporal world, rests on a few very simple ideas; so simple that they must be as old as the hills. It rests notably, among others, on the idea of Fidelity.[54]

Michael Levenson, in his book *A Genealogy of Modernism*, sees Conrad as typical of 'the agon of modernism . . . the struggle between its values and its forms': values favouring order, solidarity and authority in conflict with forms which reflect individuality and the belief that only consciousness can give meaning to the world.[55] This somewhat resembles Daphna Erdinast-Vulcan's idea of Conrad as divided between corroding scepticism and relativity on one hand, and the transcendental authority of myth and religion on the other, though she sees this as a conflict between modern and pre-modern philosophies, rather than as a conflict between values and forms

20

Introduction

within modernity itself. Erdinast-Vulcan's account of Conrad's work as a 'foredoomed rejection of modernity' is a powerful one, yielding a strong developmental account.[56] However, it is arguably too locked into a binary opposition of the modern and the premodern. Levenson points out the tendency to such a dualism in the pronouncements of modernists like Eliot and Pound, and suggests that it conceals the 'suppressed transitions which unite all contrasts'.[57] A number of critics have argued that modernism inherits many of its problems and obsessions from a Romanticism which it claims to reject: in particular the problem of how the individual consciousness relates to the world and to the wider human community.[58] Unusually amongst modernists, Conrad did not disavow his Romanticism, though he presented it as in need of checking:

> The romantic feeling of reality was in me an inborn faculty. This in itself may be a curse but when disciplined by a sense of personal responsibility and a recognition of the hard facts of existence shared with the rest of mankind becomes but a point of view from which the very shadows of life appear endowed with an internal glow.[59]

Here Conrad seeks to balance Romantic subjectivity with a classical emphasis on order and duty. The passage would accord well with Levenson's view of modernism as divided between radical individualism and traditional authority. As if such a blending of Romantic and modern were not confusing enough, Conrad's ideal of 'fidelity to an absolutely lost cause', which Erdinast-Vulcan reads as his 'foredoomed rejection of modernity', resurfaces in Bongie's account as a postmodernist 'politics of absence'.[60] The link is less surprising than it might seem, since Erdinast-Vulcan is emphasizing Conrad's conservative side, and Bongie is espousing a postmodern 'weak' conservatism, a 'fight for the conservation of [cultural alternatives which] no longer exist.[61] Furthermore, Bongie is aware of the Romantic underpinning of such a longing for the past, since he suggests that Conrad's resistance to the New Imperialism of the late nineteenth century was a result of his 'Romantic belief in the individual's sovereignty'.[62] We should perhaps see Romanticism, modernism and postmodernism as grappling with many of the same problems – questions of knowledge, truth and subjectivity – in a Western culture which lacks a theological consensus.

Ian Watt's book *Conrad in the Nineteenth Century* offers one of the most balanced and nuanced accounts of Conrad's relationship to modernity (though not a highly theorised one), stressing the effect

21

Joseph Conrad

of Conrad's personal experience and cultural background. Cultural dislocation, exile and alienation are central themes of modernist art, but, as Watt points out, Conrad experienced these in more extreme and less voluntary forms than most other modernists. Watt links Romanticism, modernism and (tentatively) postmodernism in Conrad's outlook: in his account Conrad's tragic family and national history meant that he felt modernism's alienation more directly than others and saw more clearly the need to escape from such alienation, drawing here on the patriotic solidarity of Polish Romanticism (with its dedication to lost causes):

> Conrad also knew that his sense of loss was not merely familial, social, and national; alienation was a much more universal condition, and one with deep roots in the romantic imagination ... Conrad may be said to have inherited much of his modernity – perhaps his post-modernity – from his Polish past.[63]

Watt's is the account of a Conrad enthusiast, and is itself a little in thrall to the Romantic-humanist dream of the visionary artist who alone sees the truth of his or her society's predicament. Nevertheless, its basic articulation of Conrad's position is convincing in its own terms and a useful reminder of the cultural variability which abstractions like 'Romanticism' and 'modernism' can sometimes efface.

Allon White shares with the critics already discussed a sense of the complexity of Conrad's relationship to the modern. White's book *The Uses of Obscurity*, from which the passage included here is taken, addresses obscurity and difficulty as features of literature which first acquired a positive value in early modernist writing, particularly the novels of George Meredith, Henry James and Conrad. In his Introduction, White notes that the difficulty of modernist writing is usually attributed to alienation or to 'the disruptive effects of the unconscious', but argues that such difficulty is best understood in relation to a new way of reading which he terms 'symptomatic reading' (see headnote to Jameson piece, p. 201).[64] Symptomatic reading 'treats a literary utterance as a surface sign of something that could not be said directly', and becomes dominant when, in the modern era, 'the idea of an unconscious replaces that of the soul'.[65] For White, then, the decline of religious faith and the influence of psychoanalysis and psychology leads both to 'symptomatic writing', which relies heavily on 'evasion, equivocations, enigmas and obliquities', and to a complementary 'symptomatic reading' which is always attempting to decode what lies hidden within or beyond the text.[66] This broad cultural theory

Introduction

of the significance of obscurity in modernist fiction gives White a new perspective on the question of Conrad's style, raised by F. R. Leavis, who objected to Conrad's overuse of words like 'inscrutable' and 'unspeakable' and claimed that Conrad was 'intent on making a virtue out of not knowing what he means'.[67] Apart from the issue of a masculine bias in Conrad's writing, this matter of the difficulty of his style is the most common objection to his work raised by new readers, such as students who have been asked to read *Heart of Darkness* and have either given up or not enjoyed the experience. A critical approach which makes sense of the use of such a style is therefore very useful. White sees a strong Romantic strain within Conrad's modernist obscurity, suggesting later in his chapter that Conrad belongs to the 'Romantic survival' in his inclination to see art in quasi-religious terms as a way of maintaining sacred mysteries. White is very critical of this impulse of 'romantic nostalgia' in Conrad, partly following Leavis when he states that 'The worst aspect of Conrad's fiction resides in this use of enigma as a way of artificially generating value'.[68] So, while White's initial focus is on style, his argument crucially involves questions of cultural value. He sees the modern age as generating ways of writing which, on the one hand express a certain longing for religious values, while on the other hand use obscurity of style to invite and resist a reading in terms of the psychological (the unconscious) rather than the spiritual (the soul). This leads us back to one of the points with which I began this section: the characteristic ambivalence of modernist writers about modernity. In the passage of White's book reproduced here, he suggests a very specific form of such ambivalence in Conrad's writing. Walter Benjamin's essay 'The Work of Art in the Age of Mechanical Reproduction' (1936) argues that modern technologies of reproduction erode the idea of authenticity, the idea of a work of art as a unique object, 'imbedded in the fabric of tradition'.[69] For example, any number of equally good prints can be made from a photographic negative, so that it makes no sense to ask which is the 'authentic' print, as one might ask for an 'original' painting as opposed to a copy. Benjamin, then, is linking changes in the conception of art to changes in technology, and he argues that once 'the criterion of authenticity ceases to be applicable to artistic production', art comes to be based on politics rather than ritual.[70] White makes a convincing case that Conrad's enigmatic style serves to preserve the 'aura' of the authentic work of art. That style, then, is a form of resistance to modernity, technology and politics; a clinging on to the values of religion and ritual. This connects to Erdinast-Vulcan's sense of Conrad as struggling against modern scepticism. Given the conventional association of 'ritual' with the

Joseph Conrad

supposedly 'primitive', White's argument also chimes with Chris Bongie's claim that Conrad's work shows a longing for a lost realm of the exotic. However, White, Bongie and Erdinast-Vulcan differ in the value which they attach to such harking back. White is critical of Conrad's preoccupation with the enigmatic and mystic, but he does see it as having some positive consequences. Specifically, it makes Conrad aware that finality is impossible and makes his work infinitely open to interpretation.

Conclusion

An Introduction such as this is inevitably a metacommentary, a discussion of texts which themselves discuss Conrad's texts. Furthermore, given the reflexive and self-conscious nature of much literary theory, this Introduction is frequently a metacommentary on texts which (explicitly in the case of Jameson's) are already meta-commentaries, already reflections on the processes of interpretation as well as acts of interpretation. In such a situation it is absurd to attempt a conclusive word, as if this Introduction somehow operated at a higher level of discourse than the excerpts which it surveys, and could subsume, synthesise or judge them. Nor is any conclusive statement about Conrad's texts plausible. If this Introduction assumes the tones of evaluation, that is a result of the inescapability of value to which Steven Connor points, when he writes that

> we cannot help but enter the play of value, even when we would wish to withdraw from or suspend it. The necessity of value is in this sense more like the necessity of breathing than, say, the necessity of earning one's living.[71]

Given such a necessity, I should perhaps return to the assertion with which I began – that Conrad's work raises questions of value with particular intensity – and offer my own explanation. I can best do so in terms of another of Connor's observations: that the operation of particular values is always potentially in conflict with the process of evaluation.[72] So long as we continue to make judgements we are liable to revise our values in the light of experience. Conrad's fiction, I would suggest, stages this conflict. It offers us values on various levels: values implied by the author, expressed by narrators and characters and embodied in actions and decisions. But it also subjects these values to revaluation. Marlow's faith in hard work is called into question by his fascination with Kurtz; the 'correct' behaviour for a captain seems overridden by

24

Introduction

more enigmatic imperatives in 'The Secret Sharer'; in *Nostromo* the values consciously held by Gould and Nostromo are revealed as subordinate to historical forces. This staging of evaluation as a process is apparent in Conrad's use of hermeneutic structures such as the inquiry (*Lord Jim*), the quest (*Heart of Darkness*), the mystery (*Under Western Eyes*). Because Conrad's work enacts the processes of evaluation rather than espousing fixed values, it retains, some hundred years later, its interest and its ability to stimulate continuing debate.

Notes

1. Conrad published some 16 novels, 7 novellas and 23 short stories. This includes 3 collaborative novels with Ford Madox Ford, but not Conrad's unfinished novel *The Sisters* (which is excluded from the Standard Edition). The distinctions between novellas and short stories on the one hand, and novellas and novels on the other, are not clear cut.

2. F. R. LEAVIS, *The Great Tradition* (1948; Harmondsworth: Penguin, 1972), p. 29.

3. On French influences on Conrad, see YVES HERVOUET, *The French Face of Joseph Conrad* (Cambridge: Cambridge University Press, 1990). On the relationship of *Under Western Eyes* to Dostoevsky's *Crime and Punishment*, see AARON FOGEL, *Coercion to Speak: Conrad's Poetics of Dialogue* (Cambridge, MA: Harvard University Press, 1985), pp. 196–207.

4. *The Collected Letters of Joseph Conrad*, ed. Frederick R. Karl and Laurence Davies, 5 vols. (Cambridge: Cambridge University Press, 1983–96), III, 89.

5. 'Author's Note' to *Victory* p. xv. All references to the works of Conrad in this Introduction are to the Dent Standard Edition in 22 vols. (London and Toronto: J. M. Dent & Sons Ltd, 1923–28), with the exception of those works which have now come out in the new Cambridge Edition: *The Secret Agent*, edited by Bruce Harkness and S. W. Reid, and *Almayer's Folly*, edited by David Leon Higdon and Floyd Eugene Eddleman (Cambridge: Cambridge University Press, 1990 and 1994). The page numbers of the Oxford University Press paperback editions are generally the same as the Dent edition, though the pagination of the author's notes does not correspond.

6. JIM REILLY, *Shadowtime: History and Representation in Hardy, Conrad, and George Eliot* (London: Routledge, 1993), p. 133.

7. LEAVIS, pp. 210–11, 215.

8. See *Conrad and Gender*, ed. Andrew Michael Roberts (Amsterdam and Atlanta, GA: Rodopi, 1993), especially SUSAN JONES, 'Representing Women: Conrad, Marguerite Poradowska, and *Chance*' (pp. 59–74); LAURENCE DAVIES, 'Conrad, *Chance* and Women Readers' (pp. 75–88); ANDREW MICHAEL ROBERTS, 'Action, Passivity and Gender in *Chance*' (pp. 89–104). Also ANDREW MICHAEL ROBERTS, 'The Gaze and the Dummy: Sexual Politics in Conrad's *The Arrow of Gold*', in *Joseph Conrad: Critical Assessments*, ed. Keith Carabine (Robertsbridge, East Sussex: Helm Information, 1992), pp. 528–50.

9. STEVEN CONNOR, *Theory and Cultural Value* (Oxford and Cambridge, MA: Blackwell, 1992), pp. 10, 13, 14.

Joseph Conrad

10. GÉRARD GENETTE, *Narrative Discourse*, trans. Jane E. Lewin (Oxford: Basil Blackwell, 1980), p. 265.

11. ROLAND BARTHES, *S/Z*, trans. Richard Miller (Oxford: Blackwell, 1990), p. 5.

12. JACQUES DERRIDA, *Writing and Difference*, trans. Alan Bass (1978; London: Routledge & Kegan Paul, 1981) pp. 14, 15.

13. ROBERT HAMPSON, *Joseph Conrad: Betrayal and Identity* (London: Macmillan, 1992), p. 1.

14. LEAVIS, p. 206.

15. ALBERT GUERARD, *Conrad the Novelist* (Cambridge, MA: Harvard University Press, 1966), pp. 42, 59.

16. ROLAND BARTHES, 'La Mort de l'auteur', *Mantéia* V, 1968, translated as 'The Death of the Author' in *Image, Music, Text*, essays selected and translated by Stephen Heath (London: Fontana, 1977).

17. MARK WOLLAEGER, *Joseph Conrad and the Fictions of Skepticism* (Stanford, CA: Stanford University Press, 1990), p. 122.

18. WOLLAEGER, pp. 146, 147.

19. WOLLAEGER, p. 149. See MICHEL FOUCAULT, *Discipline and Punish: The Birth of the Prison*, trans. Alan Sheridan (1977; Harmondsworth: Penguin, 1979).

20. WOLLAEGER, p. 131.

21. JAKOB LOTHE, *Conrad's Narrative Method* (Oxford: Clarendon Press, 1989), pp. 7, 2.

22. ROLAND BARTHES, *The Pleasure of the Text*, trans. Richard Miller (New York: Hill and Wang, 1975; London: Jonathan Cape, 1976).

23. For example GUERARD, in a chapter indicatively titled 'The Journey Within', pp. 33–48.

24. MICHEL FOUCAULT, 'The Order of Discourse', in *Untying the Text: A Post-Structuralist Reader*, ed. Robert Young (Boston and London: Routledge & Kegan Paul, 1981), pp. 52–3.

25. The first of these defences is put forward by CEDRIC WATTS, in '"A Bloody Racist": About Achebe's View of Conrad', *Yearbook of English Studies*, 1983, pp. 196–209 (p. 199).

26. PATRICK BRANTLINGER, '*Heart of Darkness*: Anti-Imperialism, Racism, or Impressionism?', *Criticism*, 27.4 (1985), pp. 363–85 (pp. 365, 383).

27. TERRY EAGLETON, *Criticism and Ideology: A Study in Marxist Literary Theory* (1976; London: Verso, 1978), p. 135.

28. HENRY LOUIS GATES JR, ed. *Black Literature and Theory* (London: Methuen, 1984), p. 315.

29. See for example TRINH T. MINH-HA's critique of the Western desire for the 'authentic' in *Woman, Native, Other: Writing Postcoloniality and Feminism* (Bloomington, Indianapolis: Indiana University Press, 1989), p. 89.

30. CHRIS BONGIE, *Exotic Memories: Literature, Colonialism and the Fin-de-Siècle* (Stanford, CA: Stanford University Press, 1991), p. 5.

31. BONGIE, p. 6.

32. BONGIE, p. 228.

Introduction

33. See HOMI K. BHABHA, *The Location of Culture* (London and New York: Routledge, 1994), pp. 66–84, 173, 207.

34. The idea of a 'discursive colonisation' of the third world by Western feminist writing is put forward by CHANDRA TALPADE MOHANTY, 'Under Western Eyes: Feminist Scholarship and Colonial Discourses', in *The Post-Colonial Studies Reader*, ed. Bill Ashcroft, Gareth Griffiths and Helen Tiffin (London and New York: Routledge, 1995), p. 260.

35. REBECCA STOTT, 'Race and Gender in *The Secret Agent*', in *Conrad and Gender*, p. 152.

36. EDWARD SAID, *Culture and Imperialism* (London: Chatto & Windus, 1993), p. 79.

37. GUERARD, p. 51.

38. See HAMPSON, pp. 2–3, 251 for a summary of differing views of Conrad's late fiction.

39. GUERARD, pp. 257–61.

40. GUERARD, pp. 261, 258, 261, 257.

41. ANDREW MICHAEL ROBERTS, 'Action, Passivity and Gender in *Chance*', in *Conrad and Gender*, p. 100.

42. See KATE MILLETT, *Sexual Politics* (1971; London: Virago, 1977) for an early polemical attack on Lawrence. MAUD ELLMANN discusses Eliot's misogyny in *The Poetics of Impersonality: T. S. Eliot and Ezra Pound* (Brighton: Harvester, 1987), pp. 98–107.

43. RUTH NADELHAFT, *Joseph Conrad* (Hemel Hempstead: Harvester Wheatsheaf, 1991), in the series 'Feminist Readings', p. 14.

44. NADELHAFT, p. 25.

45. AVROM FLEISHMAN, *Conrad's Politics: Community and Anarchy in the Fiction of Joseph Conrad* (Baltimore, MD: The Johns Hopkins Press, 1967), p. ix.

46. Letter of 19 December 1885 to Spiridion Kliszczewski, *The Collected Letters of Joseph Conrad: Volume 1 1861–1897*, ed. Frederick R. Karl and Laurence Davies (Cambridge: Cambridge University Press, 1983), p. 16.

47. See FLEISHMAN, pp. 3–20; ZDZISŁAW NAJDER, *Joseph Conrad: A Chronicle* (Cambridge: Cambridge University Press, 1983); ADDISON BROS, 'Apollo Korzeniowski's Mythic Vision: Poland and Muscovy, "Note A"', *The Conradian* 20.1–20.2 (Spring/Autumn 1995), pp. 77–102.

48. EAGLETON, p. 134.

49. REILLY, p. 135.

50. ANDREW ROBERTS, '*Nostromo* and History: Remarkable Individuality and Historical Inevitability', *The Conradian*, 12.1 (May 1987), p. 15.

51. J. A. BERTHOUD, 'Narrative and Ideology: A Critique of Fredric Jameson's *The Political Unconscious*', in *Narrative: From Malory to Motion Pictures*, ed. Jeremy Hawthorn (London: Edward Arnold, 1985), p. 113.

52. FREDRIC JAMESON, *The Political Unconscious: Narrative as a Socially Symbolic Act* (1981; London: Routledge, 1989), p. 10.

53. JOSEPH CONRAD, 'Ocean Travel'; 'Travel: A Preface to Richard Curle's "Into the East"', in *Tales of Hearsay and Last Essays* (London: Dent, 1928), pp. 35–38 and 84–92 (p. 89).

Joseph Conrad

54. JOSEPH CONRAD, *A Personal Record*, p. xix.

55. MICHAEL LEVENSON, *A Genealogy of Modernism: A Study of English Literary Doctrine 1908–1922* (Cambridge: Cambridge University Press, 1984), p. 36.

56. DAPHNA ERDINAST-VULCAN, *Joseph Conrad and the Modern Temper* (Oxford: Clarendon Press, 1991), p. 21.

57. LEVENSON, p. ix, quoting George Eliot.

58. See MATEI CALINESCU, *Five Faces of Modernity* (1977; Durham, NC: Duke University Press, 1987), pp. 35–58; Robert Langbaum, *The Poetry of Experience: The Dramatic Monologue in Modern Literary Tradition* (1957; Chicago and London: University of Chicago Press, 1985), pp. 9–37.

59. JOSEPH CONRAD, 'Author's Note' to *Within the Tides*, pp. v–vi.

60. ERDINAST-VULCAN, pp. 20, 21; BONGIE, p. 228.

61. BONGIE, p. 227.

62. BONGIE, p. 40.

63. IAN WATT, *Conrad in the Nineteenth Century* (London: Chatto & Windus, 1980), pp. 358–9.

64. ALLON WHITE, *The Uses of Obscurity: The Fictions of Early Modernism* (London, Boston and Henley: Routledge & Kegan Paul, 1981), p. 2.

65. WHITE, p. 4.

66. WHITE, p. 3.

67. Quoted in WHITE, p. 109.

68. WHITE, p. 122.

69. WALTER BENJAMIN, 'The Work of Art in the Age of Mechanical Reproduction', in *Illuminations*, trans. Harry Zohn (1970; London: Fontana, 1992), p. 217.

70. BENJAMIN, p. 218.

71. CONNOR, p. 8.

72. CONNOR, pp. 2–3.

Part One

Conrad and the critical tradition

1 Joseph Conrad*

RAYMOND WILLIAMS

This passage from Raymond Williams's book on *The English Novel* is the earliest piece in this collection and marks (somewhat ahead of its time) the transition from universalising existentialist readings of Conrad's work (which see it as a meditation on the human condition) to political readings (which emphasise its engagement with history, economic forces and the effects of power and ideology). Williams's emphasis on material realities, historical forces and socio-political issues presages the direction of much of the later criticism represented in this reader. Williams is not dismissive of all earlier criticism, but only of a one-sided tendency: he offers an explicit and trenchant critique of what he sees as a facile slip into 'metaphysics'. Before the growth of literary theory in the 1960s, much criticism appealed, explicitly or implicitly, to ideas of the 'universal' and the 'natural' as touchstones of literary value. Williams, with his idiosyncratic but influential blend of Leavisite moralism with Marxist cultural politics, recognises the importance of universalising abstractions in Conrad's fiction, but insists that we should not allow symbolic readings to obscure the specificity of the social and economic context.

Isolation and struggle. Man against Fate. These have been the common terms of descriptions of Conrad. And of course they are relevant. The novels raise those issues. But I want to look at the phrases and at the ideas behind them – turn them round and look at them – because I am far from sure that in the end with Conrad they help; at least in their simple rhetorical forms. There is isolation in Conrad of course. There is Man and there is Fate: the abstractions and others like them are a critical part of his style. And of course there is struggle of an intense kind: more intense, more practical, for many reasons, than in most other novelists in the language. But

---

* Reprinted from *The English Novel from Dickens to Lawrence* (London: Chattto & Windus; Toronto: Clarke, Irwin & Co., 1970), pp. 140–6.

Joseph Conrad

when we put the terms together, as in the ordinary account, are we still with Conrad in any central way? Is it quite that world, that metaphysical* world, that his novels compose?

We have to make discriminations between and within his work, if we are to answer that question. Take first, as he did, the stories of the sea and of ships. There if anywhere, we might say, are the physical instances of the metaphysical situation. There very clearly men can find themselves alone against overwhelming forces, natural forces. The sea can feel like an enemy: incomprehensible, implacable.

The ship trembled from trucks to keel; the sails kept on rattling like a discharge of musketry; the chain sheets and loose shackles jingled aloft in a thin peal; the gin blocks groaned. It was as if an invisible hand had given the ship an angry shake to recall the men that peopled her decks to the sense of reality, vigilance and duty.

'As if an invisible hand'. It is a way Conrad often writes.

The ship knew, and sometimes would correct the presumptuous human ignorance by the wholesome discipline of fear.

Yet this is never the only emphasis.

Singleton didn't stir. A long while after he said, with unmoved face: – 'Ship! . . . Ships are all right. It is the men in them.'

And the angry shake of the invisible hand, we remember, was to recall the men to a sense of 'reality, vigilance and duty'. To recall men, that is to say, to the fact of their existence as a ship's company, a working community.

Or take that famous case of isolation: the isolation of Lord Jim. What actually isolates him? What is he really struggling against? There is certainly the storm that threatens the *Patna*. But the central crisis is very human and social. Jim has been taught a code, a set of laws about sailing, and these are not only technical but in their essence moral – definitions of responsibility and of duty which are at once specific practical rules and general social laws. He is a part of a hierarchy – the officers of the ship – in which those laws are manifest or are supposed to be manifest. His moral conflict is not the product of isolation, of the lack of a society and of shared beliefs. It is that earlier kind of conflict, historically earlier, in which a man's strength is tested under pressure; in which others break the agreed rules and he goes along with this to his subsequent shame;

32

Joseph Conrad

in which, that is to say, what is really being looked at is *conduct*, within an agreed scheme of values.

The ship in Conrad has this special quality, which was no longer ordinarily available to most novelists. It is a knowable community of a transparent kind. The ship has in the main a clear and shared social purpose and an essentially unquestioned customary morality, expressed in fellow-feeling and in law. Within these terms Conrad can write with a simplicity and clarity of moral emphasis that may appear when taken outside this very specific community merely abstract or verbal.

No community of this kind is in fact without conflict. *The Nigger of the 'Narcissus'* is a struggling community in so many ways: the crew struggling against the sea, struggling with each other, and within all their active relationships failing to recognise the truth about the Nigger, which their roughness hides. Nevertheless:

> Haven't we, together and upon the immortal sea, wrung out a meaning from our sinful lives? Goodbye, brothers!

Like any active community the ship's company learns from experience and consequence. Even its heroes, like Captain MacWhirr in *Typhoon*, are a kind of consummation of this shared strength. The isolated man taking his ship through the typhoon is an instance, an heroic instance, of essentially shared values:

> Facing it – always facing it – that's the way to get through. You are a young sailor. Face it. That's enough for any man. Keep a cool head.

It is this that men have learned, face to face with natural forces:

> The hurricane, with its power to madden the seas, to sink ships, to uproot trees, to overturn strong walls and dash the very birds of the air to the ground, had found this taciturn man in its path, and, doing its utmost, had managed to wring out a few words.

The individual heroism is a clear social value, a way of living and sailing.

But of course even the close community of the ship is not really isolated. The strength and skill of seamanship, of the ship's company, are always necessary, but the purpose of the voyage, the seaworthiness of the vessel, responsibilities to families or to owners, begin and end on land, in a more complicated society. The conflicts of value which then inevitably occur involve different viewpoints and a different consciousness.

Joseph Conrad

He had attended faithfully, as by law a shipmaster is expected to do, to the conflicting interests of owners, charterers and underwriters. He had never lost a ship or consented to a shady transaction; and he had lasted well, outlasting in the end the conditions that had gone to the making of his name.

That is Captain Whalley in *The End of the Tether*. But it is not these known conflicts that wreck him. In his own capacity he has steered his life straight during fifty years at sea. But

he had buried his wife (in the Gulf of Petchili), had married off his daughter to the man of her unlucky choice, and had lost more than an ample competence in the crash of the notorious Travancore and Deccan Banking Corporation, whose downfall had shaken the East like an earthquake. And he was sixty-seven years old.

Whalley is going blind, but under pressure to send money to his daughter he tries to use his experience to continue in command. The ambitious, 'instinctively disloyal' Sterne discovers his secret and deliberately wrecks him. But he couldn't have done this if Whalley had not already broken the only law he has lived by: that responsibility which now another responsibility contradicts.

This necessity opened his eyes to the fundamental changes of the world.

Or again Lord Jim, after the crisis of the *Patna* where what is abandoned is not only a ship but the eight hundred 'unconscious pilgrims of an exacting belief', has to relive his choice of duty at the edge of the colonial world, in the complicated and peripheral society of merchants, brigands, native rulers, the interaction of economies and of cultures. Without leaving the world of the ship, but simply following its natural extensions in trade and its consequences, Conrad pushes towards what is in the end the heart of darkness. There is an immense regret, and an altered tone, as 'lawful trade' – the simple social definition to which the laws of seamanship could directly relate – is seen in its real complications. Over much of this seeing the simpler values still preside. A man who has known the crew of the *'Narcissus'* is not going to be surprised by the people around Patusan, and in the first instance he will know exactly how to describe them. But in *The Heart of Darkness* it is already more complicated: the brigands, the speculators, the dishonest traders are easier to see, easier to

34

Joseph Conrad

understand, than the system which now, in the Congo – in the organised ivory market – begins to be apparent. It is a world of darkness of many kinds that this voyage explores, but among these kinds – the reminder is still critically necessary – is the reality of colonial exploitation, the ambiguity of the 'civilising mission' into Africa. As he put it to his publisher:

> the criminality of inefficiency and pure selfishness when tackling the civilising work in Africa.

But of course notice those terms: the mission is accepted, the criminality is a contingent failing. Much of the pressure of *Heart of Darkness* is in that uneasy relation. The colonial system is directly evoked; in the opening reference to the Romans (with its profound historical irony); then in the gunboat 'firing into a continent'; and above all in the contrasted scenes of the African chain-gang and the company clerk who to keep his books right has to shut out 'the groans of this sick person'.

> Each had an iron collar on his neck, and all were connected together with a chain whose bights swung between them, rhythmically clanking.

> ... The outraged law, like the bursting shells, had come to them, an insoluble mystery from the sea.

> He was devoted to his books which were in apple-pie order. Everything else in the station was in a muddle – heads, things, buildings.

'The criminality of inefficiency and pure selfishness.' But of course there is more than that.

> I've seen the devil of violence, and the devil of greed, and the devil of hot desire; but, by all the stars! These were strong, lusty, red-eyed devils, that swayed and drove men – men, I tell you. But as I stood on this hillside, I foresaw that in the blinding sunshine of that land I would become acquainted with a flabby, pretending, weak-eyed devil of a rapacious and pitiless folly. How insidious he could be, too, I was only to find out several months later and a thousand miles farther.

This transition is critical: the recognition of a new kind of devil.

35

Joseph Conrad

And it is then astonishing that a whole school of criticism has succeeded in emptying *The Heart of Darkness* of its social and historical content, about which Conrad leaves us in no possible doubt. My quarrel with a whole tradition of criticism of fiction is about just this kind of endless reduction of deliberately created realities to analogues, symbolic circumstances, abstract situations. The Congo of Leopold follows the sea that Dombey and Son traded across, follows it into an endless substitution in which no object is itself, no social experience direct, but everything is translated into what can be called a metaphysical language – the river is Evil; the sea is Love or Death. Yet only called metaphysical, because there is not even that much guts in it. No profound and ordinary belief, only a perpetual and sophisticated evasion of these deliberately created, deliberately named, places and people, situations and experiences. It is an evasion masked by an imposed rhetoric – that playing with concepts of 'fiction' as alternatives to imaginatively written reality; concepts supported by discussions of technique which with all substance reduced or endlessly substituted can stand on their own as a detached methodology. It is then an abstract technique, playing with a series of abstract ideas; in the end a critic's fiction in which there is only method because the imaginative substance, the shaped reality of novels, is not available, is too much to conceive or to bear.

But of course you know the defence. The immediate situation, the local instance, is the Congo, but then what is developed is a 'larger' reality. And since all good novels depend on this kind of extension, so that they are more than the truth about only that man, that place, that time, this way of putting it can appear convincing. But there is all the difference in the world between discovering a general truth in a particular situation and making an abstract truth out of a contingent situation. It is the difference between creative seriousness and a now fashionable game.

[. . .]

2 English Reading*

FRANCIS MULHERN

The essay from which these passages are drawn is not primarily about Conrad, but is a critique of the work of the influential critic F. R. Leavis. However, since Leavis, in his book *The Great Tradition*, treats Conrad as an exemplary figure, Mulhern also examines Conrad's work in order to challenge Leavis's critical values and methods, and in so doing offers a highly suggestive, if brief, reading of Conrad's novella *Typhoon*. Leavis was opposed to literary theory, claiming instead to rely on 'concrete judgements' and the shared experience of reading. Mulhern compares this position to Conrad's statement that the purpose of his art was 'to make you *see*' (found in the Preface to *The Nigger of the 'Narcissus'*, a Preface which is generally taken as Conrad's most important account of his artistic objectives). Mulhern begins his essay with a version of the classic argument for the value of explicit literary theory (or a philosophy of criticism): that untheorised criticism, like untheorised reading of texts, contains unacknowledged assumptions; in this case assumptions about the national and cultural identity of the reader and critic. Here Mulhern evokes one of the principal debates of twentieth-century literary criticism. He criticises the 'governing values of Leavisian discourse', which he describes later in the essay as 'class-restrictive, (hetero)sexist and ethnocentric' (Mulhern, p. 259). Leavis had seen Conrad's novella *Typhoon* as a story of British 'discipline' and 'matter-of-factness' triumphing over nature and racial otherness. Mulhern draws on post-colonial theory, gay theory and psychoanalysis, re-reading *Typhoon* in terms of hybridity, homoeroticism and hysteria. Marxist and psychoanalytical terminology combine in the claim that Leavis's 'ideological relationship' to *Typhoon* leads him to endorse and repeat its repression of such challenges to masculinity, Englishness and empire.

---

* Reprinted from *Nation and Narration*, ed. Homi Bhabha (London: Routledge, 1990, rpt. 1993), pp. 250–2, 254–6.

Joseph Conrad

My task which I am trying to achieve is, by the power of the written word to make you hear, to make you feel – it is, before all else, to make you *see*. That – and no more, and it is everything.

(Joseph Conrad)

English ought to be kept up.

(John Keats)

What should we read, *how* should we read it, and *why*? Such questions are staple elements of any politics of reading. But they remain less than critical if they are put without consciousness of the unavowed answer they already insinuate. Issues of selection, procedure, and purpose are often settled in advance by the meanings assigned to the collective pronoun. So there is a further question: *as whom, as what* do 'we' read? Asked or not, this question is always answered, and on this occasion it may be worthwhile to consider the 'answer' given in an especially forceful practice of reading: the English literary criticism chiefly represented by F. R. and Q. D. Leavis.

I

Pressed for a philosophical defence of his criticism, F. R. Leavis offered a narrative:

The cogency I hoped to achieve was to be for other readers of poetry – readers of poetry as such. I hoped, by putting in front of them, in a criticism that should keep as close to the concrete as possible, my own developed 'coherence of response', to get them to agree (with, no doubt, critical qualifications) that the map, the essential order, of English poetry seen as a whole did, when they interrogated their experience, look like that to them also. . . . My whole effort was to work in terms of concrete judgements and particular analyses: 'This – doesn't it? – bears such a relation to that; this kind of thing – don't you find it so? – wears better than that', etc.[1]

In this way, Leavis sought to elude the very terms of René Wellek's demand. There would be no 'explicit' and 'systematic' account of principles, no 'abstract' evaluation of 'choices': only reading, and dialogue with other readers.

The upshot was paradoxical. Apparently unforthcoming, Leavis's counter-move was perhaps more revealing than a more compliant response would have been. The founding assumption of Leavisian

English Reading

criticism, it turned out, was a rigorous humanism: the experiential merging of critic and poem, and of both with the experience of 'other readers', was scarcely thinkable without the 'philosophical' guarantee of a human essence – something constant, universal, and, like the Arnoldian 'best self', potentially decisive.[2] However, there is a logical strain in the notion of an essence whose efficacy is contingent, and this is evident in Leavis's narrative of 'the common pursuit'. The imagined scene is ideal: critic and interlocutor in informal, even intimate exchange. But the very informality of the critic-narrator's questions betrays the imposture of openness: negatively phrased, they presume assent – or what is imagined at another moment as corroborative self-'interrogation'. The interlocutor, meanwhile, is silent; the expected 'critical qualifications', never uttered, remain parenthetical concessions in the discourse of the critic. Lacking this interlocutor, the situation and its justifying event are jeopardized, and Leavis seems almost resigned to the loss: 'I hoped . . . I hoped . . . my whole effort was . . .', he writes, as if telling a story of what might have been.

Leavis's half-realized character – present, presumably assenting, yet silent – embodies a compromise between two incommensurable entities: the ideal interlocutor whose active, confirming presence is the necessary ground of Leavisian criticism, and an actual, contingent readership that is neither present to the author nor predictable in the range and substance of its 'qualifications'. This, abstractly speaking, is a logical dilemma: Leavisian criticism is a long-drawn-out fallacy, endlessly bent on establishing what it already assumes to exist. But practically, it is a problem of suasion. 'My task', wrote Conrad, in a declaration uncannily close to Leavis's, 'is, before all else, to make you *see*. That – and no more, and it is everything'.[3] If so little is 'everything', it is because there is indeed something 'more'. The preferred reading of the passage is clearly signalled in its syntax and typography: the goal is shared vision. But these indications of emphasis are crossed by the counter-emphasis of repetition: the task is 'to make you . . . to make you . . . to make you . . .'. In a characteristic movement of disavowal, Conrad's words admit the moment of dictation in all writing. To represent the object is, measure for measure, to position the subject, the clarity of the one depending on the stability of the other. To 'make' is at once to compel and to compose: to compel the actual reader by composing an ideal one, to *pre-scribe* the subjective conditions of 'seeing'. No less than of Conrad's fiction, this is the rhetorical task of Leavisian criticism.

Leavis's task is to determine the object ('the map, the essential order') and, as a necessary part of this, to position the subject. His

39

Joseph Conrad

critical writing must work to reduce the discrepancy between its ideal interlocutor and real readers, to compose the *normal* subject of Leavisian reading–writing. In other words, the writing must complete the half-sketched second character in the exemplary narrative of criticism. And it really will be a 'character', not an ontological cypher. The sponsors of humanism are, dependably, rather more than generically 'human', and so equally are the normative images of their writing. As Perry Anderson observed nearly twenty years ago, the real solidarities of Leavisian humanism are quite specific in time and place.[4] The 'character' whose features emerge in Leavisian criticism is a fully historical being, and 'normal' in every way.

II

[...]

Of Leavis's three chosen novelists, only one (George Eliot) was English. James was Anglophone but American; the language of Conrad's novels was his third; and both learned significantly from other literatures. A key purpose of *The Great Tradition* was to reduce these complexities of formation to biographical accident and to 'naturalize' James and Conrad as exponents of a transcendent language that must be understood as adequate, and finally as necessary, to the novelistic exploration of 'essential human values'. The story of the book is the victory of an English tradition over the circumstances of origin and, crucially, over the latterday Renaissance, French realism. Thus, James may be located in 'a distinctively American' line, but this is as it were a ruse of tradition: Hawthorne emancipated James from the influence of Thackeray and from Flaubert, making possible an authentic, enabling connection with Eliot.[5] Conrad did indeed learn from 'the French masters': the stylism and exoticism of his weaker writing is derived from Chateaubriand, and *Nostromo* recalls Flaubert.[6] Yet Conrad's work, with its 'robust vigour of melodrama', is also 'Dickensian', 'Elizabethan' even.[7] And if he evinces that 'racy strength' it is because, his origins notwithstanding, his 'themes and interests' actually called for the English language rather than any other. He is 'unquestionably a constitutive part of the tradition, belonging in the full sense'.[8]

A second major theme of *The Great Tradition* is the novel as such. It was in the course of writing this book that Leavis substantiated his conception of the novel as linguistic art. 'The differences between a lyric, a Shakespeare play, and a novel, for some purposes essential,

English Reading

are not in danger of being forgotten; what needs insisting on is the community', he wrote in the early 1930s, and the criticism that ensued was to be interested not in 'character' and 'incident' but in the 'pattern of moral significances' that novelistic art might yield, in 'the novel as dramatic poem'.[9] Much of the meaning of this conception, and the polemical force with which Leavis promoted it, must be sought in the history of academic and lay literary criticism. Leavis, like others around him, was determined to redeem the novel from its common status as a cultivated (or narcotic) diversion and to establish its parity with the canonical arts of language. But his manner of doing so bears an interesting relation to his critical practice generally. His terminology disrupts the received classification of verbal art and redefines the novel (epic) as a combination of the two types from which it was classically distinguished, the lyric and the dramatic. The effect of this development – which reinforced an already well-established emphasis on the 'poetic' essence of verse drama – was to reorder the field of critical perception at the expense of *narrative*. All wider differences set aside, it can still be said that the greatest weakness of Leavisian criticism lay just here; and part of the sense of that weakness may be glimpsed in Leavis's reading of *Typhoon*.

The 'elemental frenzy' (Leavis's phrase) that occupies most of Conrad's story is a literal event: a British merchant ship is exposed to a devastating tropical storm and only narrowly escapes destruction. But from the outset it is metaphorized as a psychic and political ordeal. The ship's captain, MacWhirr, is an obsessional. Locks and charts are the emblems of his life; his letters to his wife are phatic* observances, without value as registrations of feeling or incident; his speech, which he enforces as a shipboard norm, is laconic, literal, and untouched by the smallest acquaintance with pidgin. However, the circumstances of this voyage are not wholly routine. The ship has been transferred from the British to the Siamese flag; and the 'cargo' on this occasion is human – 200 Chinese coolies returning from periods of labour in various colonies. Sailing under 'queer' colours, its crew outnumbered by their freight of alien bodies, the *Nan-Shan* heads into 'dirty' weather. The storm attacks every established social relationship of the vessel. Masculinity is abandoned for hysteria; linguistic order fails, as speech turns figural or obscene, is blocked by superstition or swept away by the gale. MacWhirr and his first mate, Jukes, reach for each other in encounters that mingle duty and desire, resolution and bewilderment; while in the hold the Chinese have apparently gone berserk. The lowering of the British ensign brings on a storm that unfixes identity ('He started shouting aimlessly to the man he could

41

Joseph Conrad

feel near him in that fiendish blackness, "Is it you, sir? Is it you, sir?" till his temples seemed ready to burst. And he heard in answer a voice, as if crying far away, as if screaming to him fretfully from a very great distance, the one word "Yes!".'), and *Homo Britannicus* is abandoned to a chaos of effeminacy, homoeroticism, and gibberish – the terrifying counter-order of the Chinese labourers below. The ship survives. But the restoration of order is understood as a furtive improvization, the hurried winding-up of an incident better forgotten. It is related not by the main narrator but in a chattily complacent letter from Jukes, who, in his uncertain sexual orientation (his regular correspondent is male) and openness to linguistic transgression (metaphor, pidgin), is socially perverse. Worse, the protagonist himself is fatally ambiguous: MacWhirr, as we have learned from an early narrative recollection, is not British but Irish. The chief officers of the *Nan-Shan*, ultimate guarantors of imperial order, bear the typhoon within themselves.

Leavis's account discloses virtually nothing of this. Where he quotes passages whose manifest sense discourages any other reading, he confines himself to dubious technical observations on 'a novelist's art', and his wider commentary on *Typhoon* strikes a directly contrary emphasis. It is the 'ordinariness' and 'matter-of-factness' of the ship's captain and crew that hold his attention, 'the qualities which, in a triumph of discipline – a triumph of the spirit – have enabled a handful of ordinary men to impose sanity on a frantic mob'.[10] Leavis's language reveals his ideological relationship to *Typhoon* and, at the same time, the strategy of his reading. Identifying himself with the norms of the text, he sets out to rewrite its ending and to *un*write the greater part of the narrative. *Typhoon* works through a fearsome 'return of the repressed'; Leavis's reading functions to assist repression, indeed to perfect it, simply silencing the anxieties that generated the story in the first instance.

Leavis's encounter with *Typhoon* may serve as a hyperbolic illustration of his critical relationship with narrative generally. Narratives vary, it need hardly be said; but the work of narrativity is always an opening and closing, a loosening and rebinding of sense. All but the most sedate or the most forensic narratives are in some degree unsettling – and *Typhoon* is neither. It may be ventured, then, that a criticism bent on affirming an essential human identity will be inhibited in the face of narrative, and will 'revise' its object-texts (as the ego is said to revise dreams and memories) in that interest. And it is apt that Leavis, confronted with a fictional dispersal of that identity, in a text of his own choosing by one of his canonical authors, should read with an averted eye.

[. . .]

42

English Reading

Notes

1. 'Literary Criticism and Philosophy', a reply to René Wellek's communication of the same title, *Scrutiny*, vol. 5, no. 4 (March 1936), reprinted in *The Common Pursuit* (Harmondsworth: Penguin, 1972), pp. 214, 215.

2. My critical use of the term 'humanist' bears only on this kind of essentialism. As a Marxist, I believe simple 'anti-humanism' to be theoretically shallow and morally evasive. Here and elsewhere I have summarized material from my *The Moment of 'Scrutiny'* (London: NLB, 1979) – to which this essay is in some other respects a corrective. I am grateful to Michèle Barrett, Clara Connolly, and especially Homi Bhabha, for their encouragement and critical advice.

3. Preface, *The Nigger of the 'Narcissus', Typhoon, Falk and Other Stories* (London, 1950), p. x.

4. 'Components of the National Culture', in Robin Blackburn and Alexander Cockburn (eds.), *Student Power* (Harmondsworth: Penguin, 1969), p. 271.

5. *The Great Tradition* (Harmondsworth: Penguin, 1972), pp. 148, 151.

6. Ibid., pp. 217, 218, 219.

7. Ibid., pp. 241, 225, 227.

8. Ibid., pp. 27, 29.

9. *Towards Standards of Criticism* (1933; London: Lawrence & Wishart, 1976), pp. 19–20.

10. *The Great Tradition*, p. 214.

Part Two

Narrative, textuality and interpretation

3 Joseph Conrad: The Revenge of the Unknown*

TERENCE CAVE

Terence Cave's wide-ranging book sets out to rehabilitate 'recognition' (*anagnôrisis*), which he sees as 'the least respectable term in Aristotelian poetics', often associated with scandal and triviality (Cave, p. 1). Defining recognition as 'the moment at which characters understand their predicament fully for the first time, the moment that resolves a sequence of unexplained and often implausible occurrences' (Cave, p. 1), Cave argues that it points to 'the capacity of fictions to astonish us, upset us, change our perceptions' (Cave, p. 2). He traces the history of recognition 'as both formal device and vehicle for themes of knowledge' (Cave, p. 4), looking at both poetics (the theory of literature) and at literary texts themselves. His chapter on *Under Western Eyes* serves as a reminder that literary theory is an ancient art and shows that post-structuralism and classical Greek literary theory can be combined productively in a reading of the narrative complexities and philosophical ambiguities of modernist fiction. As well as using the Aristotelian categories of *anagnôrisis* and *hamartia** (error), Cave draws on the work of Roland Barthes in his allusions to narrative desire. Deconstructive influences are also evident in his analysis of undecidable narrative cruxes, in his suggestion of a truth which eludes narration and in his description of Razumov as a void to which an arbitrary chain of signifiers attaches itself. His subtle and perceptive reading of *Under Western Eyes* elucidates Conrad's use of layers of narrative to thematise issues of truth and falsehood, knowledge and the unknowable, surface and depth, desire and death. Cave goes on to offer a symbolic and allegorical reading. This leads him to the radical claim that Conrad's narrative modes work against the moral assumptions which seem to anchor the fiction, so that his fiction offers us, not closure, but an unending pursuit of knowledge.

---

* Reprinted from *Recognitions: A Study in Poetics* (Oxford: Clarendon Press, 1988), pp. 464–88.

Joseph Conrad

An early reviewer of *Under Western Eyes* suggested that Conrad's shift to a more austere, less exotic narrative style (a shift deplored by the reviewer) might have owed something to the influence of Henry James.[1] There are certainly some Jamesian touches in the 'Author's Note', but that was written several years later.[2] As for the novel itself, the closest analogy would no doubt be with *The Ambassadors*. Both narratives are presented from the point of view of an ageing bachelor who is witness to a deceit; both culminate in the unmasking of that deceit. Like Strether, Conrad's old language-teacher gropes in a world he only half understands, a world whose co-ordinates are alien to him; coming from a 'respectable' society with its moral and political compromises firmly established, he finds himself caught up in a melodramatic fiction where violence and horror are always on the point of erupting from beneath the bland surface. Like Strether, too, he is drawn into this foreign story by an erotic attraction. Not so far in: the desire is distinctly one-sided, and his walks in the gardens of Les Bastions are hardly a substitute for the omelette and the straw-coloured Chablis. But then he is also different from Strether in that his imagination has been amputated, from the first sentence, by the author; he admits that he is blind to 'those subtle differences that are beyond the ken of mere professors'.[3] This insensitivity – a failure of interpretative skill – is the first premiss in the interplay of ignorance and knowledge that constitutes the plot: Strether's errors are largely due to over-interpretation, the language-teacher's to under-interpretation.

It is also evident that, in Conrad, cultural difference is exacerbated to the point of becoming virtually a hyperbole. The desire for narrative originates for him in the sailor's tale, the 'spinning of a yarn' in order to fill the void of a voyage and give shape to endlessly erratic wanderings. The romance voyage, limited to the Mediterranean basin, expands into areas still scarcely charted; the Thames estuary opens on to a route that may lead to the heart of darkness. In Marlow's attempt to recover the story of Kurtz, the sailor's yarn is transmuted into enigma as it comes up against the ultimately unknowable, an abyss in which Western values are swallowed up;[4] the tale of *Lord Jim*, beginning where Jim loses touch with the comfortable morality of his father's last letter, ends with extinction amid an alien race at the uttermost edge of the world. As Conrad's characters pursue their adventures, the codes by which they define themselves seem increasingly arbitrary and absurd. Only in science fiction fantasies (and not even there, in many cases) will romance heroes travel further. And unlike Odysseus' or Captain Kirk's, most of Conrad's voyages turn out to be irreversible. There is no homecoming – not even a moral one – for Kurtz and Jim:

Joseph Conrad: The Revenge of the Unknown

only their story comes home, a story without a verifiable meaning, or a story which can only safely be retold as a lie.[5]

In *Under Western Eyes*, there are no oceans, no jungles, no primitive tribes practising unspeakable rites. There is only Russia, as seen by a prim Englishman from the safety of insipid Geneva. Yet Russia is presented as immeasurably more impenetrable than Strether's Paris. Conrad uses once again the imagery of the 'heart of darkness' – the image of a great encroaching shadow – as a figure of its impenetrability. The darkness is both that of the Russian soul, which is governed by a kind of moral excess, and of the Russian political scene, where the conflict of entrenched autocracy and revolutionary idealism undermines any stable frame of reference by means of which an individual might be defined. The story that emerges out of this double – and reciprocal – darkness is presented by the narrator as alien and rather absurd: not as Kurtz's story is alien, but because it seems to belong to the realm of sensational fiction: 'To us Europeans of the West, all ideas of political plots and conspiracies seem childish, crude inventions for the theatre or a novel.'[6] The spy story is itself generically a story of anomy,* where the protagonist may be traitor or hero according to a decision made in advance about the rightness of the regimes in question: in the 'naïve' spy story, the hero's lies and subterfuges are the legitimate procedures of a 'good' regime seeking to defend itself against an 'evil' one; elsewhere decisions about the legitimacy of the procedures may be less easy, with the result that the spy may find himself caught in the moral cross-fire and may indeed be forced to refer to, or even construct, his own internal criterion. The court scene – a kind of recognition scene – in Le Carré's *The Spy Who Came in from the Cold* stages a particularly dramatic switching of the points, showing the protagonist's and the reader's inferences to have been based on too naïve a decision with regard to the good and the evil.

Conrad's narrator's patronizing attitude to the spy story may seem dated from the vantage point of the late twentieth century; it can also be seen as a narrative device designed to make the action appear plausible precisely by discounting in advance its 'sensational' aspect. But the risk of naïvety isn't great, since the autocratic regime and the wrong-headed revolutionaries are both seen in a consistently negative light. The Western view – the view from Geneva – is one of strict neutrality. This raises questions which will need to be considered later, but it is immediately clear that it has the effect of preventing the protagonist Razumov from belonging wholly to any defining frame of reference. His initial 'conversion' to faith in the status quo is presented as a *post hoc* rationalization of

Joseph Conrad

his desire to eliminate Haldin from his life; and in the last segment of his diary, he is careful to specify that he has not been converted to the revolutionary cause.[7] As Tony Tanner suggests, Razumov's is a classic Durkheimian case of anomy leading to a form of suicide.[8]

The point is considerably sharpened by the narrative decision to make Razumov illegitimate. The language-teacher returns again and again, both through his own discourse and through Razumov's, to this severance from all forms of kin. It is presented as an 'excuse' for Razumov's treachery (he is lonely and has no one to turn to; hence, too, his recourse to Prince K—, his real but unacknowledged father); and it also contributes to the motivation of the confession, both through the vision of the bereaved mother and, again, because of a total lack of human contact.[9] That illegitimacy should become in this way a motivation for the protagonist's acts marks an enormous difference from the ethos of romance, where the hero's severance from genealogical ties allows him to prove himself 'objectively' as it were before being reintegrated into the consecrated order.[10] Razumov is closer to the protagonists of nineteenth-century novels of social ambition: like Julien Sorel, for example, he is intelligent enough to adopt a hypocritical persona and make his way through a world which he despises; like Julien, too, he finally abandons his persona and finds a kind of authenticity in 'suicide'.[11]

Yet the anxiety of illegitimacy and isolation is far greater in *Under Western Eyes*: Razumov becomes almost a personification of Russian anomy; where the conflict of autocracy and revolution crushes and maims family relations. His name is an empty label, his patronymic a fiction;[12] nor can his repeated claim to be at least a Russian have any purchase since 'Russia' is itself in these circumstances only the label for an amorphous shadow.[13] According to Conrad's prefatory formula, the clash of factions makes naming a purely arbitrary gesture at the national level too: 'These people are unable to see that all they can effect is merely a change of names'.[14]

The true confession

It is a total severance, then, which creates the conditions for Razumov's error[15] and for the movement of the plot towards a scene of recognition. In the last pages, an analeptic* summary and exegesis of the plot is provided through the character of Sophia Antonovna:

> There are evil moments in every life. A false suggestion enters one's brain, and then fear is born – fear of oneself, fear for oneself. Or else a false courage – who knows? Well, call it what

Joseph Conrad: The Revenge of the Unknown

you like; but tell me, how many of them would deliver themselves up deliberately to perdition (as he himself says in that book) rather than go on living, secretly debased in their own eyes? How many? . . . And please mark this – he was safe when he did it. It was just when he believed himself safe and more – infinitely more – when the possibility of being loved by that admirable girl first dawned upon him, that he discovered that his bitterest railings, the worst wickedness, the devil work of his hate and pride, could never cover up the ignomy of the existence before him. There's character in such a discovery.[16]

The narrator accepts her conclusion in silence, providing a cue for the reader; Razumov's story may be understood within a reassuring moral framework as a progression through evil to something like salvation; or perhaps as an instance of hamartia (a moral error mitigated by its quasi-accidental character and by an appeal to common experience) followed by a recognition or discovery at the level of *êthos*.* But the articulation of the plot and of the possible interpretations to which it gives rise clearly exceeds this summary, which in some ways resembles those slightly patronizing editorial prefaces to narratives of confession that take the line 'who are we, after all, to condemn this man?' Since the character of the recognition and what it entails depends on the complex layering of the narrative, it will be necessary at this point to look in some detail at the plotting of the story.

The language-teacher is a first-person narrator whose discourse – the novel as it stands – is written in retrospect, from a position of full knowledge and saturated interpretation. Within that discourse, he appears as a participator in the action, ignorant of Razumov's imposture until the last moment. Even after the confession, it is still necessary for him to read Razumov's diary, which provides the 'correct' version of the story in detail, and to hear from Sophia Antonovna the episode of Razumov's confession to the conspirators, the loss of his hearing, and the road accident, together with the epilogue in Russia which exhausts his life-history.

However, the story is not presented in the order of the narrator's progression from ignorance to knowledge. The narrative begins with a reconstruction from the diary of the 'true' story of Haldin's betrayal, the story which will be suppressed for the greater part of the novel, giving rise to the question (for Natalia and her mother and for the conspirators) 'why did Haldin not escape?' The reader knows the answer from the outset, and is able in consequence to follow the ambivalence of all the ensuing dialogues in which Razumov takes part. The only part of the story which is deferred

Joseph Conrad

is the scene in which Razumov is induced by Mikulin to become a spy: as the narrator points out, the reader will probably have inferred it anyway,[17] and it is somehow embarrassing to have to put it into words – believing in spies, for the language-teacher, is a bit like believing in ghosts. The deferment nevertheless prevents the label 'spy' from being applied too crudely to Razumov during the crucial dialogues of Part Third, where what must be visible above all is the tension between the two versions of the narrative, the 'true' and the 'false'.

Elsewhere, the narrator interweaves his later knowledge with his ignorance as participator, either to point up moments where Razumov's behaviour seems particularly sinister or incomprehensible, or to supply explanations, motivations, justifications. All this organizing activity on the part of the language-teacher could be seen simply as the construction of a novel in such a way as to sustain the reader's interest and draw his attention to significant points and possible interpretations.[18] Yet the language-teacher is also, it would seem, a deficient narrator, both because he presents himself as unskilled in the narrative art, lacking in imagination, and because his responses often seem inadequate or over-conventional. He frequently refers to his embarrassment and constraint in narrating this strange story, and it is hard not to see the blazer and the old college tie in his immediate reaction to the confession itself:

> Incredulity, struggling with astonishment, anger, and disgust, deprived me for a time of the power of speech. Then I turned on him, whispering from very rage –
> 'This is monstrous. What are you staying for? Don't let her catch sight of you again. Go away!...' He did not budge. 'Don't you understand that your presence is intolerable – even to me? If there's any sense of shame in you...'[19]

In this light, the reader is likely to pay particular attention to the traces of Razumov's narrative. It is Razumov, after all, who has presumably written the 'authentic' version of his story: like Rousseau (whose image is part of the Genevan landscape of the novel), he begins by attempting a prize essay and ends up writing a confessional narrative as a kind of supplement to and palliative of his isolation.[20] Like Rousseau, he wants to 'become someone' by writing; he will eventually send the book of his life to Natalia as a substitute for the living self he has destroyed. For all these reasons, the reader is encouraged to ascribe authenticity to *his* first-person narrative rather than to the language-teacher's truncated and palely translated version.

Joseph Conrad: The Revenge of the Unknown

Yet the irony is that the 'authentic' first-person text is embedded irretrievably in the 'inauthentic' first-person text – the whole story is commanded and deployed by a narrator who tells us that 'because of the imperfection of language there is always something ungracious (and even disgraceful) in the exhibition of the naked truth'.[21] We can only give a special status to 'Razumov's' version by reading against the bias of the narrative. And it is essential to add at this point that it would be wrong to take the language-teacher's self-caricature absolutely at face value, as if he were just a rather silly and irritating 'character'. In his 'Author's Note', Conrad ascribes to himself qualities almost the opposite of those of his surrogate narrator, speaking of 'the clearness of [his] vision and the correctness of [his] judgement' and claiming that in writing the novel he 'had no other object in view than to express imaginatively the general truth which underlies its action'.[22] The amputation of the narrator's imagination thus appears as a deliberate strategy, a kind of self-irony: despite all disclaimers, the language-teacher observes and records with extreme skill and (of course) with considerable linguistic resources, so that he is not so different from Strether after all. The 'imperfection of language' becomes through his intervention an essential theme of the novel, exhibiting at a reflective level the problems that are implied by the narrative structure.

The 'confessional' story, then, the paradigm of the first-person mode, is set within and against another first-person voice which is alien to it; astringent, even antiseptic, the primary narrative is a means of constraining its tendency to excess.[23] Inversely, one could also say that the conflict between the two levels serves to bring out and even legitimize the lurid view of the story. Because we read against the bias, we compensate for the language-teacher's decorum and squeamishness and give credit to what might have seemed merely the apparatus of a sensational novel. The mode of narration is in this sense a bluff designed to make a potentially spurious plot *vraisemblable** by pre-empting any protestation a conventional reader might be inclined to make: the decorum of Racine's language works differently, but to similar effect (one can imagine what the language-teacher would have said about *Bajazet*), and there are close parallels in eighteenth-century narrative technique.

This account is still not quite adequate, however, because it doesn't allow for the language-teacher's complicity in the action that he narrates. One might better say that his discourse acts as a medium of transference for Razumov's almost unspeakable fears and desires, becoming itself contaminated by those fears and desires. His rather prudish and self-conscious references to his awareness of the 'sovereign power of [Natalia's] person',[24] his willingness

53

Joseph Conrad

– despite the sceptical filter – to tangle with the phantoms and
devils of Razumov's imagination, allow the horror of the story
to surface in a form which both makes it manageable and opens
it to further reaches of the imagination (the 'amputation' of
imagination operating thus as a relay between the author's
imaginative investment and the reader's). The narrator's imperfect
censorship leaves blanks we are bound to fill, which means we
in our turn are contaminated by the narrator's epistemophilia*
and thence by what one might call the 'uncontrollable' elements
of the plot.

One might yet wonder whether the word 'contamination'
is justified. The decisive evidence lies in a narrative possibility
expressed at the very last moment in the only verbatim extract
from the diary (hence the only unmediated fragment of Razumov's
discourse) and not otherwise referred to: the last word, as it were,
in the almost unspeakable. Razumov confesses that he had planned
to 'steal Natalia's soul' by marrying her:

> Listen – now comes the true confession. The other was nothing.
> To save me, your trustful eyes had to entice my thought to the
> very edge of the blackest treachery. [. . .] Victor Haldin had stolen
> the truth of my life from me, who had nothing else in the world,
> and he boasted of living on through you on this earth where I
> had no place to lay my head. She will marry some day, he had
> said – and your eyes were trustful. And do you know what I
> said to myself? I shall steal his sister's soul from her. [. . .] If you
> could have looked then into my heart, you would have cried out
> aloud with terror and disgust.[25]

In this new version of the story, which obliges one to go back and
fill in a crucial and unperceived blank in the whole central part of
the novel, the language-teacher, ironically enough, plays the part of
the devil: he eggs Razumov on by speaking of Natalia's loneliness
and defencelessness. It is easy enough to read this between the lines
of the narrator's earlier version, given that he depicts Natalia as a
woman ripe for seduction and clearly regards Razumov as a likely
candidate; his own sexual interest in Natalia endows him with the
prurience necessary for him to act as a kind of pander. In this sense
the language-teacher as a character in his own story is already
contaminated; his narration doubly so, since *it* knows what the
language-teacher didn't then know, namely that Razumov has
betrayed Haldin. And because it knows, we know, so that if we
want Razumov to seduce Natalia, we side with treachery and moral
violation. This is where the lure of evil is most deeply ingrained in
the plot.

54

Joseph Conrad: The Revenge of the Unknown

The very fact that Razumov articulates this further confession (the 'true' one), and thus writes into the story a narrative future forestalled by the confession scene itself, sufficiently demonstrates that some such ultimate twist *is* the object of our narrative desire: if it were not, the novel would fail as narrative, seem implausible or excessive (as Razumov indicates it might). The imaginary rape, the violence that would have made Natalia '[cry] out aloud with terror and disgust', is the melodramatic scene that the narrative conjures up without having to take responsibility for it. Hence the disappointment of the language-teacher when the confession forestalls narrative desire: 'And, by the by, that old man sprang up from somewhere as I was speaking to you, and raged at me like a disappointed devil.'[26] We too perhaps rage like disappointed devils; but the disappointment is part of the game of fiction, locating with some precision the point of balance between prurience and moral censorship. As for Conrad himself, the manuscript version of the novel indicates that he had originally planned (plotted?) to consummate the marriage and produce a child whose resemblance to Haldin, in some recognition scene *extra fabulam*,* would lead to the death of both Razumov and Natalia.[27] The desire for this ending, although it is only retained as a narrative trace in Razumov's diary, may thus be said to inform the plot from the outset.

A comedy of errors

The multiplication of narrative layers, of versions of the plot, of 'ghost' stories (as well as ghost stories), has the effect of producing among other things an element of narrative uncertainty. Most of the 'facts' of Razumov's history are unquestioned: he did betray Haldin, he did agree to become a spy, he did fall in love with Natalia, he did confess to her and to the revolutionaries, and so on. But on one crucial issue certainty is lacking, namely the motivation of the confession. In the scene of confession, the narrator already furnishes insights into the feelings and reactions of Razumov which he can only have derived from the diary; later, he introduces the diary fragment itself as follows:

> After some passages which have been already made use of in the building up of this narrative [...] comes a page and a half of incoherent writing where his expression is baffled by the novelty and the mysteriousness of that side of our emotional life to which his solitary existence had been a stranger.[28]

Joseph Conrad

It would seem, then, that the diary fragment merely supplements the earlier account, and that its function is rather to illustrate Razumov's ignorance of love and the character of his mode of expression (its 'incoherence') than to elucidate his motives as such. Yet the effect is to provide for the reader two different if not wholly incompatible views of the confession narrative, and the difference arises principally from the suppression in the first version of Razumov's intention of sustaining the deception and gaining possession of Natalia.

The language-teacher's account dwells on the drama of Razumov's encounter with the mother:

> The fifteen minutes with Mrs Haldin were like the revenge of the unknown: that white face, that weak, distinct voice; that head, at first turned to him eagerly, then, after a while, bowed again and motionless [. . .] had troubled him like some strange discovery.[29]

He leaves her precipitately ('It was frankly a flight') only to find himself confronted with the sister: ' "Must I repeat that silly story now?" he asked himself, and felt a sinking sensation.'[30] The language-teacher also tells us 'He had never forgotten the sister, only he had not expected to see her then or ever any more, perhaps.' In the diary fragment, by contrast, the interview with the mother appears as a minor and temporary obstacle to the firmly established purpose not only of seeing Natalia again but of 'stealing her soul':

> I trembled when I went in; but your mother hardly listened to what I was saying to her, and, in a little while, seemed to have forgotten my very existence. I sat looking at her. There was no longer anything between you and me. You were defenceless – and soon, very soon, you would be alone . . .[31]

Whose phrases, then, are 'the revenge of the unknown', 'some strange discovery'? Does this melodrama of the psyche take shape in the sterile yet complicit language of the narrator or in Razumov's, simply transcribed or paraphrased here? The question seems undecidable. Again, the language-teacher implies that it is the sudden confrontation with Natalia's saintliness and seduction which prompts an unpremeditated confession. But Razumov's account seems to suggest that, even before this (perhaps in his last few moments alone with the mother), the memory of her appearance had 'saved' her: 'I felt that I must tell you that I had ended by

Joseph Conrad: The Revenge of the Unknown

loving you. And to tell you that I must first confess. Confess, go out – and perish.'[32] This is followed by 'Suddenly you stood before me! You alone in the world to whom I must confess.' So, when the language-teacher sees in Razumov's eyes as he leaves Mrs Haldin 'the shadow of something consciously evil',[33] this may retrospectively be construed as the intention to possess Natalia, but only at the expense of changing the chronology of Razumov's narrative.

The maladjustment might seem to be secondary: it would perhaps be possible, if one worked hard, to find a plausible frame of reference that would iron out the apparent inconsistencies. But perhaps, on the other hand, the point is that we can never know exactly what happens in Razumov's heart of darkness: his 'incoherent' narrative can never tell the whole truth because the whole truth is precisely not narratable, not a sequence of discrete psychological events. The language-teacher's version must *a fortiori* inevitably arrange and re-arrange the materials, add and subtract, in order to compose a plausible sequence. In this respect, the confession scene in *Under Western Eyes* is not unlike that in *La Princesse de Clèves*, where motivation is partly accidental and certainly not commensurate with intention. At all events, the darkness which surfaces from the centre of Razumov's story is only a projection of the engulfing darkness figured by the shadow of Russia: Razumov's personal motivation is always overdetermined, from the moment of Haldin's irruption into his room, by the warped manipulative power of autocracy. His error is to that extent as 'accidental' as the confession: Haldin's presence betrays him, as it were, into betrayal (because it instantly implicates him *vis-à-vis* the regime); Natalia's presence ultimately makes him 'betray [himself] back into truth and peace'.[34] The structure of betrayal in this sense is necessarily that of a surface accident which reveals a hidden depth: it is a failure of presuppositions, a lapse of logic.

The image of a hidden depth is present at the moment when the error that constitutes the plot as betrayal becomes irrevocable:

Razumov ran forward unsteadily, with parted, voiceless lips. The outer door stood open. Staggering out on the landing, he leaned far over the banister. Gazing down into the deep black shaft with a tiny glimmering flame at the bottom, he traced by ear the rapid spiral descent of somebody running down the stairs on tiptoe. It was a light, swift, pattering sound, which sank away from him into the depths: a fleeting shadow passed over the glimmer – a wink of the tiny flame. Then stillness.[35]

57

Joseph Conrad

This image of the stairwell repeatedly returns to haunt Razumov's imagination; it has the nightmarish quality of Jim's leap into the darkness of moral ignominy: '"There was no going back. It was as if I had jumped into a well – into an everlasting deep hole..." [...] Nothing could be more true: he had indeed jumped into an everlasting deep hole. He had tumbled from a height he could never scale again.'[36] The error of such characters is represented as the crossing of the shadow-line between the security of a recognizable code and a lawless place of darkness, horror, devils and ghosts: the creatures of hell transposed into creatures of the unconscious. The error may itself be dependent on trivial circumstances, on some material ignorance or lapse of judgement: the nightmare events of *The Shadow-Line* are attributable to a failure to check the medicine-cupboard properly; Jim makes the false assumption that the ship will sink (he also jumps in place of George, who has died, accidentally, of a heart-attack); Razumov rehearses to Haldin himself the role of the unexpected and the accidental in the predicament he finds himself in, the apparently trivial material details which determine his course of action.[37] There is a fundamental non-equivalence between the random surface effects of everyday life and the consequences they may entail. Yet the hiatus may also seem to point towards a hidden 'truth'; the marginal sign is the one which betrays and delivers up to judgement. In the passage just referred to, Razumov speaks of the secret side of life – secrets of birth, secret motives of conduct. The plunge down the stairwell is a figure of the fall from the reassuring plane of outward existence into the abyss of secrecy.[38]

The relationship between the accidental surface and the secret depths is a paralogical* one in the sense that the second cannot with certainty be inferred from the first. This principle informs the whole of the plot, and indeed gives it its structure as a 'recognition' plot as well as a plot of betrayal. The details Razumov refers to in his last dialogue with Haldin (already a confession scene, misread by Haldin) are trivial, marginal, random, but they nevertheless function as signs. The grey whiskers of a passer-by are read as a synecdoche for the missing father, and thus prompt Razumov's recourse to the legitimizing framework of autocratic paternal authority; they betray him into choosing a false logic, in which he will thereafter become fatally enmeshed, the paralogism of imposture. Maintaining the appropriate configuration of signs – the configuration which always represses the deviant truth – is the appalling burden he labours under in all his dialogues, whether with representatives of the regime, with the revolutionaries, or with the language-teacher and the Haldin ladies. He is in constant danger

58

Joseph Conrad: The Revenge of the Unknown

of falling prey to the accidents of discourse, to the seemingly random details of phrasing which will be read as signs of the hidden depths and thus betray him; inversely, he is himself inclined to read chance phrasings of his interlocutors as signs that they know perilously more than they admit. The language-teacher is particularly prone to remarks that 'strike home' in this way;[39] but the problem recurs, for example, in the dialogue with Sophia Antonovna.[40]

This exacerbation of significance to which Razumov is prey becomes a kind of alienation, deforming both his language and his physiological responses. He is acutely aware that he may be betrayed by an absurdity, and absurdities cannot be mastered by his intelligence.[41] Under the strain, his mind sometimes drifts, noting with great precision physical details such as the flow of water under a bridge:[42] such moments of distraction derive no doubt from the malady of over-reading, over-attention, but they may also risk betraying him by allowing his suppressed consciousness to show through. Thus, too, the language-teacher notes in great detail the physical symptoms of his constraint, but is unable to interpret them: since he doesn't really believe in spies, he is hardly likely to suspect Razumov of being one. But in fact, from the outset, Razumov's character had been misread because of his silences, his reluctance to indulge in the flow of words.[43] He is read as an austere, dedicated 'idealist': the silence betokens a hidden depth of moral quality. This is why Haldin chooses him as an accomplice, and sends his sister a letter in which Razumov is characterized as one of the 'unstained, lofty, and solitary existences':[44] from this moment the misreading of Razumov is established, the misreading that both forces the imposture on him and makes it easy for him – despite the constant risk of a lapse – to maintain it. In this sense, Razumov's 'personality' is a void to which an arbitrary chain of signifiers* attaches itself, creating a fiction of such power that it absorbs every new detail that comes to light.

The key example is the culminating misinterpretation of the story of Ziemianitch. This is the story that threatens Razumov at every stage because he has suppressed it: it is the clue to the right reading, the clue that Mikulin would interpret as a sign that Razumov at first attempted to help Haldin, and that the revolutionaries would interpret as a sign that he betrayed him.[45] It is successfully suppressed because the view of Razumov as an unstained and lofty soul makes it impossible even for the acute and experienced Sophia Antonovna to identify him with the figure who beat Ziemianitch: such sadistic behaviour can only be plausibly assigned to a brutal police agent, disappointed that the trail has gone cold.

Joseph Conrad

The theme (as well as the enactment) of secrecy and of the reading of plausible signs runs through the novel as a whole,[46] but it is nowhere more distinctively present than at the point where Razumov is thus 'made safe' by a series of probable but mistaken inferences:

> Such were the last words of the woman revolutionist in this conversation, keeping so close to the truth, departing from it so far in the verisimilitude of thoughts and conclusions as to give one the notion of the invincible nature of human error, a glimpse into the utmost depths of self-deception. [. . .] This was a comedy of errors. It was as if the devil himself were playing a game with all of them in turn.[47]

The phrase 'comedy of errors', which also occurs earlier,[48] provides an intertextual echo demonstrating the affinity of *Under Western Eyes* with the fictions of mistaken identity, and preparing the reversal in which the misreadings will collapse. But the character of Conrad's plot might also lead one to evoke, yet again, the case of Martin Guerre: Arnaud du Tilh was, it seems, a better and a less anguished impostor than Razumov (and got more for his money), but his story too ended in the 'truth and peace' of confession.[49]

The story . . . the story!

> The paper, bearing a very faint design, was all but white. The light of an electric bulb high up under the ceiling searched that clear square box into its four bare corners, crudely, without shadows – a strange stage for an obscure drama.
> [. . . . .]
> 'The story, Kirylo Sidorovitch, the story!'
> 'There is no more to tell! [. . .] It ends here – on this very spot.' He pressed a denunciatory finger to his breast with force, and became perfectly still.[50]

It is perhaps an inevitable result of the intertextual pressure exerted by the tradition of recognition plots that, after all the deferments and misreadings, the proffering of the missing segment that corrects the story as a whole should be staged as a *scene*, a dramatic dialogue. The confession will only later take the form of a discourse, a narrative of authenticity like Rousseau's *Confessions*. Here, the truth emerges in exactly the same way as it had been suppressed, by allusions which are still open to paralogistic reading:

60

Joseph Conrad: The Revenge of the Unknown

Utterly misled by her own enthusiastic interpretation of two lines in the letter of a visionary, under the spell of her own dread of lonely days, in their overshadowed world of angry strife, she was unable to see the truth struggling on his lips.[51]

The reversal is brought about by a single deictic* gesture ('It ends here') which inserts the shifty subject into an apparently neutral, uncommitted narrative and thus changes the orientation of all the signs.

The gesture is melodramatic, emerging as it does from an obscure conflict of good and evil, and performed in a glaring white light. For the language-teacher, it prolongs his second glimpse behind the scenes, into the depths: the first was his view of the revolutionaries poring over a brightly illuminated map of Russia – the spurious and the sensational brought to life; the second, the vision of Mrs Haldin in the pose of the *pietà*.[52] Once again, it is his view which, in its would-be austerity, impartiality and high-mindedness, constitutes the scene as a lurid drama of the consciousness, in which a wounded psyche struggles to heal itself[53] and, in doing so, inflicts a violence akin to rape on an innocent soul. The language-teacher is once more forced to accept melodrama as life rather than as a marginal fiction.

Throughout, Razumov has continually felt the impulse to articulate the true story: again and again, he says more than he ought. But his interlocutors, following the decoys of the paralogistic reading, miss the signs by means of which their power could be asserted; nor do they figure for him as neutral recipients of confession, as Marlow does for Jim. The repetition of his error thus always occurs in a covert form until Razumov finds himself engaged in a dialogue of desire. The force of desire, mediated by the saintly image of grieving mother and trusting daughter, evades the inhibition and allows the repressed version of the story to grope its way out of the ambiguous shadow into full illumination; breaking the vicious circle, it supplies an ending that goes beyond desire towards death.

This process is seen to originate in the carefully staged initial recognition by Razumov of Natalia,[54] and is presumably advanced by the series of meetings at Les Bastions which the narrative omits to represent.[55] That it motivates the confession is what all the readings of the episode – the language-teacher's, Razumov's own, and Sophia Antonovna's – allow one to infer; and it is endorsed, even consecrated, by the metaphor of the veil. In a rather special sense, Natalia's veil operates in this scene in the manner of a recognition token. The play that Conrad makes with it is certainly

61

Joseph Conrad

not motivated by the demands of realist fiction: it may be plausible that she should wear a veil and remove it on coming indoors, but when she drops it, when Razumov picks it up and carries it off – to the marked dismay of the language-teacher – and when he subsequently sends her his diary wrapped up in it, we know, and the text knows we know, that it is placed as a significant detail for us to interpret.

Or rather, in the first place it is a significant detail for Razumov to interpret. The unveiling of her beauty is a recognition scene at one interpretative remove: he recognizes Natalia not as an individual but as the symbol of a transcendent value, although one that is only accessible through the workings of desire. Desire for her person is transposed metonymically* into desire for the truth, the removal of the last obstacle to full utterance:

> While speaking she raised her hands above her head to untie her veil, and that movement displayed for an instant the seductive grace of her youthful figure, clad in the simplest of mourning. In the transparent shadow the hat rim threw on her face her grey eyes had an enticing lustre. [...] I perceived that with his downcast eyes he had the air of a man who is listening to a strain of music rather than to articulated speech.[56]

It is striking that it is here the language-teacher who remarks on the 'seductive grace' and the 'enticing lustre': Razumov, eyes downcast, is *listening*, listening as it were for the inner meaning. Later, in the confessional narrative, he will imagine her as a symbolic statue:

> I remembered the shadow of your eyelashes over your grey trustful eyes. And your pure forehead! It is low like the forehead of statues – calm, unstained. It was as if your pure brow bore a light which fell on me, searched my heart and saved me from ignominy, from ultimate undoing.[57]

In *Lord Jim*, Conrad arranges things so that the ring that represents good faith rolls to Jim's feet at the moment where he redeems himself by taking responsibility for the death of Dain Waris. Such articles, proving their symbolic function by the inadequacy of any other motivation, are a well-worn device of quasi-allegorical narratives. Yet the veil goes one better than the ring, since unveiling (*alêtheia*) is the figure of allegory itself, the truth pointed to by a mediate object. The narrative and metaphorical loading of this scene insistently promotes the sense of a recovery of the truth, a steady, purifying gaze into the hidden depths. Natalia

Joseph Conrad: The Revenge of the Unknown

Haldin acts unwittingly as a psychopomp* and mystagogue,*
leading Razumov out of the cave of shadows, the prison-house
of lies.[58]

The allegorical reading, then, is strictly unavoidable, making this a
recognition scene in a plot of the psyche. In both senses: Razumov's
story could be retold – *mutatis mutandis* – as Proclus tells the story
of Odysseus' homecoming or Freud the story of Gradiva. Razumov
recognizes by anamnesis,* the recovery of a repressed or forgotten
level of his own consciousness; the narrative is in this sense *always*
a displaced first-person narrative, however much it may be comple-
mented by the 'factual' third-person recognitions of Natalia and the
language-teacher ('what *really* happened was that Razumov betrayed
Victor Haldin'). As it works itself out in the diary fragment and
the succeeding images of resignation, if not peace and forgiveness,
it seems to prove the healing power of stories that unveil.

Yet allegories have a nasty habit of being reversible. The sexual
implications consistently brought out by the language-teacher – as
if he were a kind of Pandarus – oblige one *also* to read the scene as
one of moral rape. The metaphor of unveiling hides and reveals a
desire for physical contact, possession and penetration: if Natalia is
an unwitting psychopomp, she is also an unwitting Salome. Her cry
'The story [. . .] the story!' is a cry of desire, desire for the secret,
almost unspeakable narrative that will taint her innocence for ever.
The collusion between Razumov and Natalia earlier in the scene is
eminently visible to the language-teacher, who draws the inevitable
conclusion from it that 'next time they met [he] would not be there,
either remembered or forgotten'.[59] And although that private scene
will not be enacted, its enticing possibility is demonstrated by the
second confession, which comes back wrapped in the black veil, like
some would-be erotic fiction. Does the melodrama, then, enact the
victory of virtue and truth over evil and lies? Is the disappointed
devil really exorcized? Or does the reader here witness something
darker and the more sinister for being veiled in the chaste figure
of an allegory? Can one really have it both ways?

Perhaps not simultaneously: the duck and the rabbit both
compose and eliminate one another. But it might indeed be that
this is how the novel operates, taken in its entirety. As is usual
with Conrad, a fundamental moral assumption has to be made
which seems to anchor the fiction: betrayal is evil, lies corrupt,
moral conscience is common to all mankind, regardless of what
may seem overwhelming differences of national culture (even Kurtz,
even Jim's natives bear witness to this). Razumov's recognition,
confession and 'cure' assert this value. Yet the mode of narration

Joseph Conrad

in this novel, as in *Heart of Darkness* and *Lord Jim*, works against the acceptance of it as the 'meaning' of what is narrated. In *Lord Jim*, for example, it is not the narrator who insists on the absolute value of the code of honour, but rather the French officer who successfully brings the crippled ship into port; Marlow prefers to adopt, at the key moment, a slightly scathing view of Jim as a 'small boy in trouble'.[60]

The balance is rather different in *Under Western Eyes*, but the effect is similar. While advertising his 'punctilious fairness' towards Razumov at the beginning of Part Fourth, the language-teacher claims that he is 'Unidentified with anyone in this narrative where the aspects of honour and shame are remote from the ideas of the Western world'.[61] As an actor in the drama, the language-teacher doesn't hesitate to judge Razumov by his own (English) ideas of honour and shame; as omniscient narrator, he recognizes an alternative code which is all but impenetrable to Western eyes. In consequence, 'honour and shame' appear as exacerbated personal modes of apprehension rather than as a public morality. Expressed as a moral value, the code by which Conrad's characters judge and punish themselves, often with ferocious severity, may seem chimerical; their lapses are much more a vertiginous *inward* fall into anomy, leading to a kind of paranoia as they ascribe to an indifferent world the relentless desire to exclude and depreciate them.

'How can you tell truth from lies?' Razumov asks the language-teacher: the margin might indeed seem narrow when, for example, the question arises of inventing what might easily be a 'pious fraud' to tranquillize Mrs Haldin.[62] Later, when Sophia Antonovna concludes her misreading of the Ziemianitch episode, the narrator speaks of 'the invincible nature of human error'.[63] Error is endemic, and it is only Razumov's Russian imagination, together with the magnifying effect of the Russian situation itself, that creates a melodrama of good and evil out of the accidents and false assumptions to which even the wisest or the cleverest are prone.

Struggling at the beginning of his narrative to pose the moral problem, the narrator had already discerned the difficulty of rendering

the moral conditions ruling over a large portion of this earth's surface [i.e. in Russia]; conditions not easily to be understood, much less discovered in the limits of a story, till some key-word is found; a word that could stand at the back of all the words covering the pages, a word which, if not truth itself, may

Joseph Conrad: The Revenge of the Unknown

perchance hold truth enough to help the moral discovery which should be the object of every tale.[64]

The product of this exercise, which retrospectively reviews the whole story, is the word 'cynicism': banal and reductive, it only serves to indicate the extent to which the narrator ultimately renounces moral discrimination. Like Razumov's name, it is an empty label for an unknown quantity. The reader doesn't need to accept this half-hearted attempt at a 'moral discovery' in order to perceive that the story goes beyond the limits of moral meaning, that the depth of anomy at which Razumov acts out his drama of confession makes the words good and evil, saint and devil, mere counters in a sombre psychomachy.*

From that angle, the notion of a 'cure' looks at best precarious (all cures being necessarily transient), at worst nostalgic and sentimental. The drama of confession becomes destructive, while the half-truths of paralogism might begin to seem almost reassuring, if they could only be released from the intolerable demands of epistemophilia. But of course paralogism is constituted as such by the desire for knowledge, and narrative is a paradigm of that desire and its consequences. The cure and the disease are inseparable; fictions have the power both to heal and to destroy; the 'story', told and retold until its powers are exhausted, is everything.[65] The only truth it may afford is a brief apprehension of the abyss beyond the shadow-line.

When visiting Prince K—, Razumov notices that he is worried lest the secret of his paternity should be uncovered:

> Probably he was afraid of scenes with his wife. She was said to be proud and violent.
> It seemed to him bizarre that secrecy should play such a large part in the comfort and safety of lives.[66]

'Secrecy' is the means by which ordinary life proceeds and sustains itself: to live on the level of surface signs, not wanting to probe, is in normal circumstances the only tolerable solution. The special world of espionage and counter-espionage provides the model of a desire for *absolute* knowledge, a desire like that of the jealous lover, the psychoanalyst and his patient, the novelist and his reader. All these risk the ultimate transgression, the removal of the veil.

The irony, in *Under Western Eyes*, is that when the veil is removed a residue of secrecy still remains: the horror which is the 'effect'

Joseph Conrad

rather than the allegorical meaning of the story[67] is the sense of being delivered up to the last unrecoverable reach of the secret, where the incessant flow of words ceases and men appear as mere puppets, or soundless obsessed phantoms. When Razumov is brutally deafened and the world is stripped of its interpretative echoes, he reverts to the silence from which he had originally emerged and which had betrayed him into the articulation of invincible human error.[68] His surdity, a physical version of the absurdities his intelligence had been unable to master, corresponds to the blinding of Oedipus, but in another mode: the mode of the novel that has passed beyond recognition.

It may appear as a final comment on the insatiability of narrative desire that, after finishing *Under Western Eyes*, Conrad underwent a prolonged period of breakdown during which he continued imaginary dialogues with the characters.[69] For him, the repetition continues, with its ineffaceable residue of horror: not, of course, for the 'real' Conrad, now more dead than Kurtz, but for posthumous readers like ourselves who can't let the story alone. In that sense, the sense of the phrase 'beyond recognition' as used here, life and fiction have switched places, as they always do when the desire and the horror are seen to spread across the boundaries of the narrative itself.

As for Razumov, he is out of the story now, restored at last to the comfort of secrecy. By which I mean that his *particular* story, like Oedipus' or Phèdre's, is closed; and that the image it gives us of a character receding, fading out, after his monstrous secret has been unveiled, is in itself an image of consolation.[70] Could not our secrets, then, equally be laid to rest? Ironically, the power of the fiction is that it deprives us of that comfort, calling in question both our secrets and our recognitions. All we can do, as the beast waits in the jungle for its moment to spring, is to continue the pursuit in a world that remarkably resembles the novel.

Notes

1. RICHARD CURLE, in the *Manchester Guardian*, October 1911, quoted in *Conrad: 'Heart of Darkness', 'Nostromo' and 'Under Western Eyes'*, ed. C. B. Cox (London: Macmillan, 1981), p. 43.

2. In 1920. Conrad's well-known tribute to James ('the historian of fine consciences') was written in 1904, not long after the publication of *The Ambassadors*; for this and earlier tributes, see JOSEPH CONRAD, *Selected Literary Criticism and 'The Shadow-Line'*, ed. Allan Ingram (London: Methuen, 1986), pp. 31–2, 48–9, 63–6.

Joseph Conrad: The Revenge of the Unknown

3. *Under Western Eyes*, ed. Jeremy Hawthorn (Oxford: Oxford University Press, 1983), p. 4. The narrator's avowed deficiency is not, however, necessarily to be taken at face value: the emphasis of the opening pages may well seem an over-emphasis, creating an ironic perspective essential to the confrontation of different cultural presuppositions in the novel and to its composite narrative structure (this question will be discussed further below; see also HAWTHORN, introduction to *Under Western Eyes*, pp. xiv–xviii).

4. The narrator in *Heart of Darkness* describes Marlow's stories as enigmatic, never following the pattern of the typical sailor's yarn. See *Youth, Heart of Darkness, the End of the Tether*, ed. Robert Kimbrough (Oxford: Oxford University Press, 1984), p. 48. None the less, the conventions of the yarn provide an intertextual point of departure for the transformation. For an analysis of 'story-telling' in *Heart of Darkness*, see PETER BROOKS, *Reading for the Plot: Design and Intention in Narrative* (New York: Knopf; Oxford: Clarendon Press, 1984), ch. 9; see also JEAN-YVES TADIÉ, *Le Roman d'aventures* (Paris: Presses Universitaires de France, 1982), pp. 149ff. (chapter on Conrad).

5. See for example the concluding scene of *Heart of Darkness*, where Marlow tells Kurtz's Intended a much bleaker lie than the one Pip tells Magwitch on his death-bed. Such consoling fictions might be regarded as exhibiting the extent to which 'full' recognition is precisely a lie or a consoling fiction; the recovery of knowledge is always accompanied by the shadow of ignorance, of knowledge lost or too painful to bear.

6. *Under Western Eyes*, p. 109 (Part II, chapter 1); see also 'Author's Note', p. xxxii.

7. Ibid., pp. 361–2 (IV. 4).

8. TONY TANNER, 'Nightmare and Complacency: Razumov and the Western Eye', *Critical Quarterly*, 4 (1962), pp. 197–214 (pp. 201–2).

9. See *Under Western Eyes*, pp. 341, 353–4 (IV. 3), 360 (IV. 4).

10. As in Chrétien de Troyes's *Yvain*, or Corneille's *Don Sanche*.

11. See BROOKS, *Reading for the Plot*, ch. 3.

12. See *Under Western Eyes*, pp. 10–11 (I. 1).

13. Cf. Balzac's *Le Colonel Chabert*, where Chabert's claim to be 'a Frenchman' is equally inadequate to provide a defining frame for his individuality.

14. *Under Western Eyes*, 'Author's Note', p. xxxii.

15. The word is used here in a strong sense and with some latitude (as one might use it in the case of Oedipus).

16. *Under Western Eyes*, pp. 379–80 (IV. 5); Conrad's *points de suspension*. Since Conrad used these quite frequently, my omission marks are signalled in this chapter by the use of square brackets.

17. Ibid., p. 293 (IV. 1).

18. For example, the narator's intervention at the beginning of the 'Mikulin' episode, where he speaks of 'throw[ing] a light on the general meaning of this individual case' (ibid., p. 293), is occasioned by the narrative shift itself.

19. Ibid., pp. 354–5 (IV. 3). See also p. 356: '"That miserable wretch has carried off your veil!" I cried, in the scared, deadened voice of an awful discovery.' The etiolated tone of moral indignation here is at variance with the force of the metaphor of unveiling, and indeed with the notion of a 'discovery' which, at this particular point, necessarily carries the whole burden of

Joseph Conrad

the narrative movement from ignorance to knowledge. The reader will instinctively believe that what *he* has seen or discovered goes deeper than any discovery of the language-teacher's. See TANNER, 'Nightmare and Complacency', pp. 199–201.

20. See the narrator's inconclusive (and no doubt strategically inadequate) conjectures as to his motivation in writing the diary (*Under Western Eyes*, p. 5; also pp. 214, 308–9, 339, 357). On the association of Rousseau with writing, see pp. 290–2 (III. 4), 316 (IV. 2) (though what Razumov writes in this episode is only spy-letters, not the confession; perhaps the difference makes its own ironic point).

21. Ibid., p. 293 (IV. 1).

22. Ibid., p. xxx.

23. One possible way of accounting for this balancing act (unprovable though the hypothesis may be) would be to posit an unresolved tension between the text of *Under Western Eyes* and its Dostoevskyan subtext. The unmistakable similarities between Conrad's novel and *Crime and Punishment* were never acknowledged by Conrad, who made a point of denigrating Dostoevsky and his work (see HAWTHORN, introduction, p. x). Dostoevsky would thus represent the 'excess' of the Russian perspective, a narrative contamination which Conrad cannot resist but against which he sets a suitably obtuse and obstinately *moderate* narrator.

24. *Under Western Eyes*, p. 358 (IV. 4); this particular phrase is apparently culled by the language-teacher verbally from Razumov's diary, but precisely at a point where Razumov's own lack of experience with women and his consequent awkwardness in expressing himself are highlighted. It strikingly echoes the phrase James uses of the Prince in *The Golden Bowl*, 'his sovereign personal power'. *The Golden Bowl*, ed. Virginia Llewellyn Smith (Oxford: Oxford University Press, 1983), p. 401 (II. 32).

25. *Under Western Eyes*, p. 359 (IV. 4). 'Disgust' is also the response of the language-teacher, as it was too of Strether in his prevision of disaster.

26. Ibid., p. 361 (IV. 4).

27. See G. JEAN-AUBRY, *Joseph Conrad: Life and Letters*, 2 vols. (London: Heinemann, 1927), ii. 65. In the published version, Conrad also substantially reduced the extent of the language-teacher's erotic attraction for Natalia (see HAWTHORN, introduction, p. xviii).

28. *Under Western Eyes*, pp. 357–8.

29. Ibid., p. 340 (IV. 3).

30. Ibid., p. 341.

31. Ibid., pp. 360–1 (IV. 4).

32. Ibid., p. 361.

33. Ibid., p. 337 (IV. 3).

34. Ibid., p. 358 (IV. 4).

35. Ibid., p. 63 (I. 2). Cf. p. 362 (IV. 4), where Razumov, after completing his diary, runs down the stairs at midnight to confess to the conspirators (the correspondence is marked in the text). The stairwell as a terrifying abyss, or as an exit from security, figures in other narrative fictions, notably *Great Expectations* and *Crime and Punishment*.

Joseph Conrad: The Revenge of the Unknown

36. *Lord Jim*, ed. John Batchelor (Oxford: Oxford University Press, 1983), pp. 111–12 (chs. 9–10). Cf. *Under Western Eyes*, pp. 257 (III. 3), 349 (IV. 3, the confession scene): 'He was like a man defying his own dizziness in high places and tottering suddenly on the very edge of the precipice'; also *Crime and Punishment*, trans. David Magarshack (Harmondsworth: Penguin, 1971), p. 133 (II. 2): 'His past seemed to be lying at the bottom of some fathomless chasm, deep, deep down, where he could only just discern it dimly.'

37. *Under Western Eyes*, pp. 59–60 (I. 2) (with reference also to p. 40).

38. This theme is central also to *The Secret Sharer*, which was written during the composition of *Under Western Eyes*. In this short story, secrecy is virtually personified in the figure of the young captain's double.

39. *Under Western Eyes*, pp. 183, 185, 186, 193 (II. 5).

40. Ibid., pp. 241, 248, 254–5, 260, 270 ff. (III. 3–4).

41. Ibid., p. 198 (III. 1). His state of mind in this respect is akin to Raskolnikov's.

42. Ibid. (See also the end of the previous chapter, II. 5.)

43. See pp. 15 (I. 1), 173 (II. 4).

44. Ibid., pp. 135 (II. 3), 169 (II. 4).

45. Both interpretations are in fact true, so that this element in the narrative becomes the crossing-over point, the moment which represents a fundamental indeterminacy in Razumov's position.

46. See for example pp. 39–40, 52, 53–4, 59–60 (I. 2), 107 (II. 1), 187, 197 (II. 5), 214 (III. 1).

47. Ibid., pp. 282, 284 (III. 4).

48. Ibid., p. 99 (I. 3).

49. See the phrase 'some formula of peace' (referring to the diary), p. 5; and especially Razumov's claim that Natalia was appointed to make him betray himself back 'into truth and peace' (p. 358, IV. 4).

50. Ibid., pp. 342, 354 (IV. 3).

51. Ibid., p. 354.

52. Ibid., p. 339, repeated p. 355 (IV. 3).

53. See pp. 350–1: 'It was as if he had stabbed himself outside and come in there to show it: and more than that – as though he were turning the knife in the wound and watching the effect.'

54. Ibid., pp. 158 ff. (II. 4). This occurs in a narrative by Natalia to the language-teacher of her visit to the Château Borel; indirection is therefore an essential aspect of the way the recognition is presented. It is spun out over several pages, with various deferments. Razumov's point of view is indicated briefly by the language-teacher as retrospective narrator (p. 167), and it is here that the vocabulary of recognition is most explicit ('he did not recognize her at once'; 'It was only her outstretched hand which brought about the recognition'). The presence of the language-teacher as the recipient of Natalia's account allows Conrad in addition to bring out the sense in which the meeting is also a *coup de foudre** (the language-teacher being privately jealous: see pp. 170–1).

55. See pp. 201 (III. 1), 322 (IV. 2).

Joseph Conrad

56. Ibid., pp. 347–8 (IV. 3).

57. Ibid., p. 361 (IV. 4).

58. See for example p. 359 (IV. 4): 'To save me, your trustful eyes had to entice my thought to the very edge of the blackest treachery.'

59. Ibid., p. 347 (IV. 3).

60. *Lord Jim*, p. 111 (ch. 9); for the French officer's verdict, see p. 148 (ch. 13).

61. *Under Western Eyes*, p. 293 (IV. 1).

62. Ibid., p. 118 (II. 5); for the 'pious fraud', see pp. 138 (II. 3), 190–1 (II. 5).

63. Ibid., p. 282 (III. 4).

64. Ibid., p. 67 (I. 3).

65. It is no doubt relevant that, even after the 'truth' has been fully – doubly – unveiled in the confession scene and the diary fragment, Razumov proceeds to repeat his story (the corrected version) once more to the revolutionaries. This repetition of the story mirrors earlier repetitions of the suppressed or 'incorrect' version of that same story; the secret of *Under Western Eyes* is a story, its story that of a secret.

66. Ibid., p. 52 (I. 2). This theme is also prominent in *The Secret Agent*; see HAWTHORN, introduction, pp. viii ff.

67. See also Kurtz's last words in *Heart of Darkness* (and BROOKS, *Reading for the Plot*, ch. 9).

68. That Razumov has unusually sharp hearing is more than once indicated in the story: see in particular p. 363 (IV. 4), on the threshold of Razumov's visit to the revolutionaries ('[he] listened attentively to the delicate tinkling of the doorbell somewhere within the house').

69. See Jessie Conrad's letter of 6 Feb. 1910, reproduced in part in *Conrad*, ed. Cox, p. 40.

70. Razumov begins as a character without a secret (p. 7); but his solitude *attracts* the contagion of secrecy, as it were, after which there is no comfort except in some form of secrecy (see p. 39, II. 2, on solitude as a hidden state which may be perceived momentarily when 'a fatal conjunction of events [lifts] the veil for an instant'). On Lord Jim and Oedipus, see DOROTHY VAN GHENT, *The English Novel: Form and Function* (New York: Holt, Rinehart and Winston, 1953), pp. 229–30.

4 Seeing and Believing: Represented Thought and Speech in Conrad's Fiction*

JEREMY HAWTHORN

Jeremy Hawthorn's principal critical tool here is narratology: the systematic analysis of the modes and techniques of narration which has developed since the 1960s under the influence of structuralism. Certain 'pure' versions of structuralism and narratology focused only on *how* meaning is created, and eschewed value judgements. However, as the title of his book suggests, Hawthorn is explicitly concerned to reconnect narratology with issues of moral and political judgement and authorial intention. The first chapter, from which these excerpts are drawn, is about the way in which Conrad manipulates the representation of the speech and thoughts of his characters in relation to his own authorial perspective. In his Introduction Hawthorn argues that such 'technical decisions' have moral and ideological implications, and that the artistic success or failure of Conrad's work often depends on whether his narratives are based on clear underlying values or not. Elsewhere in this chapter he argues that, in works such as *The Nigger of the 'Narcissus'* and *Chance*, Conrad lacks a clear view on certain issues of moral value, and that this results in an unproductive confusion as to which perspectives belong to the author and which to characters. In *Nostromo*, however, ambiguities are usually productive, since the basic values of the narrative are clear.

Introductory: what is represented speech and thought?

Tracing the development of Conrad's use of a particular narrative technique through his most productive years as a writer of fiction may seem a somewhat dull technical exercise. But a study of this particular narrative technique is unusually revealing. For in choosing how to represent the speech, thought, consciousness of his

---

* Reprinted from *Joseph Conrad: Narrative Technique and Ideological Commitment* (London: Edward Arnold, 1990), pp. 1–4, 14–16, 30–40.

71

Joseph Conrad

or her characters, a novelist simultaneously makes crucial choices regarding the attitude that the narrative takes to them. And at the same time, the novelist reveals something of his or her attitudes to the story told, something of his or her own values and commitments. All such choices, like the choices a film director makes concerning camera placing and angle, allow a novelist to include some things and to exclude others; they have a determining effect upon the mood and tone of the story in question, and they *situate* the reader in a particular way, not just with regard to technical perspective, but also with regard to moral and human viewpoint. A novelist's decision concerning what the reader knows and how he or she knows it inevitably has a bearing on a range of issues: the relationship between narrative and story,[1] the relationship between writer and reader, the relationship between writer and work, and the relationship between the writer and the world which inspires and receives his or her creative work.

But the technique I have referred to as represented speech and thought – more economically, Free Indirect Discourse[2] – is especially revelatory of an author's choices and commitments. It provides the writer of fiction with enormous narrative flexibility and mobility. With its help the narrative can not only move freely *to* any point of action or experience, but also *from* any one point in the work's implied value-system to another. Gérard Genette has familiarized us with the important distinction between perspective and voice, between 'who sees' and 'who speaks'. The distinction is not identical to that between technical and ideological perspective, but it has strong points of similarity. So that a study of an author's use of Free Indirect Discourse (henceforth FID) not only helps us to recognize what he or she is interested in revealing, but also from what standpoint – technical and evaluative – he or she wishes the reader to experience this revelation.

FID is found neither in drama nor in non-narrative poetry. Conrad could have learned its use from any one of a whole range of novelists he is known to have read, but given the technique's apparently independent appearance in a number of different literatures no direct influence needs to be posited; it seems that it is one which emerges naturally in prose narrative. Conrad's use of the technique varies in range and extent very considerably from work to work. *Heart of Darkness* has hardly any examples of its use, while *The End of the Tether* has repeated and extensive ones. But although examples can be found throughout Conrad's writing career, one can observe Conrad developing and perfecting his use of the technique as he matures as a writer.

Seeing and Believing

Let us start with the following passage:

> 'Kaspar! Makan!'
> The well-known shrill voice startled Almayer from his dream of splendid future into the unpleasant realities of the present hour. An unpleasant voice too. He had heard it for many years, and with every year he liked it less. No matter; there would be an end to all this soon.
>
> (*Almayer's Folly*, p. 3)[3]

The initial few lines of *Almayer's Folly*, Conrad's first published work, also represent the first published example in his fiction of FID. We can note that the opening lines of the novel move from Direct Speech, through what is clearly a statement from an extra-mimetic[4] narrative perspective, to sentences which give us Almayer's own thought processes, but in a rather special form. 'An unpleasant voice too. He had heard it for many years, and with every year he liked it less'. These two sentences *could* be read as continuing the detached statements of an extra-mimetic (or even omniscient) narrator. But the final sentence quoted above exhibits the classic features of FID, and reacts back on the two sentences preceding it, making it clear that they too belong to this characteristic form of narrative.

'No matter; there would be an end to all this soon'. Dorrit Cohn, in her book *Transparent Minds*, suggests that FID 'may be most succinctly defined as the technique for rendering a character's thought in their own idiom while maintaining the third-person reference and the basic tense of narration'.[5] We know that the above sentence does not come from the narrator – at least, we can be quite sure of this upon rereading the novel – because the narrator knows very well that there will *not* be an end to 'all this' soon; it is Almayer's mistaken assumption that this is the case. But even upon initial reading of the novel most readers will respond to certain signs that tell them that they are reading FID. What are these signs? Firstly, the truncated form of the sentence such as 'An unpleasant voice too', which we take as typical of spoken English and thus – by implication – of a character's mode of thinking. Such truncation is not normally associated with the expression of a narrator's opinion in extra-mimetic or omniscient narration. Secondly, the use of colloquialisms not normally utilized in Reported Speech without an explanatory comment assigning them to an originator, especially exclamations or ejaculations ('No matter' in the above extract, for example). Thirdly, FID gives the impression,

73

Joseph Conrad

as Shlomith Rimmon-Kenan has it in her book *Narrative Fiction*, of combining Direct Discourse with Indirect Discourse. Rimmon-Kenan sums up the differences between Direct Discourse [DD – what I call Direct Speech], Indirect Discourse [ID – what I call Reported Speech], and FID in the following example:

DD: He said, 'I love her'.
ID: He said that he loved her.
FID: He loved her.[6]

We see that in FID we have a characteristic deletion of the reporting verb and of the conjunction 'that' associated with Reported Speech – thus introducing a similarity with Direct Speech – along with a use of the verb form associated with Reported Speech. The transposition of tenses in FID involves, as Rimmon-Kenan points out, the same characteristic 'shift-back' of tenses to be found in Reported Speech. From the opening sentences of *Almayer's Folly*, therefore, we can reconstruct a hypothetical Direct Speech original for Almayer's thoughts: 'I have heard it for many years and with every year I like it less. No matter; there will be an end to all this soon'. Furthermore, FID normally retains deictics* used in Direct Speech but amended in Reported Speech. We can suggest the following illustrative table again:

Direct Speech: 'There will be an end to all this soon'.
Reported Speech: 'He said that there would be an end to all that shortly (or before long)'.
FID: 'There would be an end to all this soon'.

Thus both the word 'soon' and also the use of 'this' rather than 'that' indicate that Conrad's sentence is FID rather than Direct or Reported Speech. Finally, as I have suggested, on a rereading the presence of FID is betrayed by the actual content of the utterance: we know that the narrator would not make this statement, and we know that Almayer could. Very often content is the only firm clue that we are dealing with FID.

Brian McHale has suggested that grammatical approaches to the definition of FID have their limitations. He sees it as typical of 'derivational' approaches to FID (that is, approaches which work from a presumed 'original' Direct Speech utterance through to Reported Speech and FID versions) that they account for FID strictly grammatically. He suggests an alternative approach derived from the work of Paul Hernadi, based upon the traditional Platonic typology of modes of poetic discourse.

Seeing and Believing

Hernadi's innovation is to posit a third category midway between authorial presentation (diegesis) and *re*presentation/impersonation (mimesis), namely 'substitutionary narration.'[7]

As McHale notes, one advantage of this approach is that 'one is now free to take his three types as points on a continuum along which other types of representation may be located'.[8] For literary-critical purposes this has clear advantages, for it matches one's intuitive sense of the continuum-like nature of the phenomenon one is investigating (especially in Conrad's works, where we find an exceptional flexibility and mobility in the manipulation of narrative perspective), and obviates the need for a string of 'exceptions' to certain rigid grammatical rules defining three (or more) fixed grammatical categories.

The presence of FID so early in Conrad's work suggests that it formed a natural part of his armoury of narrative techniques (it is also to be found in the short story 'The Black Mate', for those inclined to believe Conrad's protestation that this was his first attempt at writing fiction). Much of Conrad's fiction relies very heavily on FID; we might even say that many characteristic Conradian features would have been impossible without it. A failure to be alert to Conrad's use of FID can lead to serious misreadings: typically, an attribution of statements and sentiments to Conrad's authorial narrator[9] instead of to the character whose consciousness the FID is actually presenting for the reader.

But something needs to be added to these technical comments. In the example I have quoted from *Almayer's Folly* it is clear, surely, that Conrad's use of FID contributes, crucially, to *the perspective on Almayer we are given*; it involves a decision as to how the reader is encouraged to see *and to judge* Almayer. Without its use, the way we perceive and respond to Almayer would be different from what it is. A study of the rôle of FID in Conrad's fiction leads us straight into the moral complexities of these works.
[. . .]

The 'dual voice' controversy

One general issue can be broached at this point. Perhaps the key dispute dividing recent studies of FID has been that between 'dual voice' and the 'single voice' theories. The title of Roy Pascal's book *The Dual Voice* makes his position on this issue clear. Pascal suggests that 'the simplest description' of what he prefers to term Free Indirect Speech, 'would be that the narrator, though preserving the

Joseph Conrad

authorial mode throughout and evading the "dramatic" form of speech and dialogue, yet places himself, when reporting the words or thoughts of a character, directly into the experiential field of the character, and adopts the latter's perspective in regard to both time and place'.[10] He argues, further:

> Critics have ... often maintained that the use of free indirect speech permits the reader to experience fully and exclusively in terms of, and from the perspective of, the character, the subject. But this is not the case. Mimicry itself, as Leo Spitzer wrote, implies a mimic as well as a person mimicked; and the effect (and the fun) of mimicry depends on our awareness of the difference between the imitation and the real thing, as well as the likeness. That is, the narrator is always effectively present in free indirect speech, even if only through the syntax of the passage, the shape and relationship of sentences, and the structure and design of a story ...[11]

However, Ann Banfield does not accept that FID involves 'mimicking':

> Represented speech and thought [for a note on problems of terminology, see note 2] is neither an interpretation of the reported speech or thought which implies an evaluating speaker, nor a direct imitation or presentation of the quoted speaker's voice. Instead, the speech or thought of the SELF represented retains all its expressivity without suggesting that its grammatical form was that uttered by an original speaker, whether aloud or silently.[12]

Banfield therefore argues against the 'dual voice' theory. Her arguments are extremely detailed, and cannot be cited in full here, but she makes it clear that in her view represented *speech* (but not represented thought) can sever the relation of SPEAKER and SELF such that in represented speech, 'there is still only one SELF, who is however the represented speaker, and not the SPEAKER of the E[xpression]'.[13] This distinction between speaker and self allows Banfield to argue that represented speech can represent but one self.

This would seem to fly in the face of my previous argument that FID can be used for ironic purpose, but Banfield contests this. She counters that a sentence of FID may be intended to be *read* ironically, but that 'the evidence for such a reading must come from elsewhere in the text', or even from extra-textual factors such as the reader's knowledge that the author of a novel is female.

Stated thus, the views of Banfield and of Pascal do not seem so much at variance as may first have seemed the case. We can posit

Seeing and Believing

that a sentence of FID represents but one *self*, but that the use of
FID may be such as to encourage the reader to set the expression
of this self in a certain context – an ironic one, for example. We can
agree with Pascal (and Spitzer) that mimicking involves a mimicker,
but not necessarily as a presence within the mimicking, more as
signs around the mimicking.
[. . .]

Nostromo

[. . .]
FID is a crucial and indispensable element in what is perhaps
Conrad's greatest novel. We may in retrospect remember *Nostromo*
as a novel characterized by its omniscient narrative perspective, a
work distinguished by the distance – ironic, contemptuous, and at
times even pitying – between narrator and characters or events.
But when we turn to a closer consideration of the narrative of this
work we find that it is, rather, characterized by extreme flexibility
of perspective, indeed by continual subtle shifts of voice and
perspective. In my opinion FID is by far the most important means
whereby this flexibility is attained. The narrative is not so much
God-like as ghost-like, less a detached and all-seeing perspective
looking down on characters and events, and more a wandering
presence drifting in and out of characters, backwards and forwards
in time, altering in identity from personified to non-personified
narrator. And it is by means of FID that this ghost-like penetration
of barriers, this continued shift of perspective, is achieved.

I want later to comment upon this contrast between the reader's
memory of the narrative of *Nostromo* as simple and consistent, and
its actual extreme flexibility and mobility. But first let me provide
a few illustrations.

> Then the tension of old Giorgio's attitude relaxed, and a smile
> of contemptuous relief came upon his lips of an old fighter
> with a leonine face. These were not a people striving for justice,
> but thieves. Even to defend his life against them was a sort of
> degradation for a man who had been one of Garibaldi's immortal
> thousand in the conquest of Sicily. He had an immense scorn for
> this outbreak of scoundrels and leperos, who did not know the
> meaning of the word 'liberty.'
> He grounded his old gun, and, turning his head, glanced at the
> coloured lithograph of Garibaldi in a black frame on the white
> wall; a thread of strong sunshine cut it perpendicularly. His eyes,

Joseph Conrad

accustomed to the luminous twilight, made out the high colouring of the face, the red of the shirt, the outlines of the square shoulders, the black patch of the Bersagliere hat with cock's feathers curling over the crown. An immortal hero! This was your liberty; it gave you not only life, but immortality as well!

For that one man his fanaticism had suffered no diminution.

(*Nostromo*, pp. 20–21)

The passage reads easily, and surely presents the average reader with no problems. And yet complicated things are going on here. In the first sentence the perspective is an external one: Viola is seen from the outside: it is not he who thinks that he is contemptuously relieved or that his face is leonine, but the narrator. But with the next sentence we move, I think, into Viola's consciousness by means of represented (verbal) thought: it is not the narrator who feels that it is a sort of degradation for Viola to defend his life against these 'thieves', this is what he himself is thinking and these are the words which constitute his thoughts. In the last sentence of the first paragraph quoted we may feel that the words 'He had an immense scorn' usher in a narrative comment on Viola, but the content of the second half of the sentence, with Viola's characteristic and habitual modes of thought and terminology, again make it clear that it is Viola's own consciousness to which we are being made privy.

With the beginning of the second paragraph quoted we are back with an external perspective, but in the last two sentences of this paragraph we appear to rejoin Viola's consciousness. I say 'appear' because there is a slight possibility of ambiguity here; these last two sentences could be read as the ironic commentary of a detached narrator, although I doubt that this is either what Conrad intended or how most readers read them. But with the start of the third quoted paragraph, we are unambiguously back outside of Viola's consciousness, for we know that Viola would not use a term such as 'fanaticism' about himself. (And although we may accept the argument that the words used in represented thought need not necessarily represent words utilized in the thought of the character concerned, we must I think recognize that even the concept of fanaticism is foreign to Viola's view of his political ideals and commitments. There is an important theoretical point which should not be allowed to escape here: sometimes one can only have a particular thought by means of a particular word. In such cases, a passage of represented thought can confirm that a particular word must have had an enabling function in a character's thought.)

I have said that FID is central to the narrative of *Nostromo*, but I should add that its use does vary according to narrative

Seeing and Believing

circumstance and from character to character. Perhaps not surprisingly it does not figure in Decoud's letter to his sister. For perhaps less immediately obvious reasons, although the speech or thought of Captain Mitchell is sometimes given to us by means of FID, it is more typically revealed by means of Direct or Reported Speech. With a character such as Viola, by contrast, FID is used far more frequently, almost every time that he appears. It is not hard to suggest explanations of why such variations in the use of FID should be found in *Nostromo*.

The absence of FID in Decoud's letter can be attributed to a number of factors. Firstly, such an absence makes a clear stylistic distinction between Decoud's letter and the rest of the narrative of *Nostromo*. Secondly, we may perhaps assume that Decoud's sister does not know the people about whom Decoud is writing well enough to be able easily to detect the use of FID by reference to the content of Decoud's pronouncements. Thirdly, Decoud's letter is more about larger political forces and events than individual characters. And, finally, Decoud's egocentricity makes it more difficult for him to slip out of his own persona and to assume the identity of another person.

If we ask why some characters should call forth the use of FID in the narrative far more than others, there are again various possible reasons. Viola's monomania, his imprisonment within the world of Garibaldi's struggle, makes it very easy to put the mark of his character on FID; there is seldom any significant ambiguity in the use of FID which is connected to Viola. Here is what seems to me to be a rare example.

Old Giorgio contemplated his children thoughtfully. There was two years difference between them. They had been born to him late, years after the boy had died. Had he lived he would have been nearly as old as Gian' Battista – he whom the English called Nostromo; but as to his daughters, the severity of his temper, his advancing age, his absorption in his memories, had prevented his taking much notice of them. He loved his children, but girls belong more to the mother, and much of his affection had been expended in the worship and service of liberty.

(*Nostromo*, pp. 28–9)

There is a relatively unimportant ambiguity in the second quoted sentence – it is not clear whether the narrator is telling us that there is two years difference between Viola's daughters' ages, or whether Viola is thinking this, although it is probably the former. A similar, unimportant ambiguity can be found in the next sentence, although

79

Joseph Conrad

it is likely that this is represented thought as the subsequent
sentence carries on from it and this sentence is unambiguously
represented thought: the use of the name 'Gian' Battista' makes
it clear that we are within Viola's consciousness. (There is a
certain clumsiness in the formulation, 'he whom the English called
Nostromo'; surely Viola would never *think* this, although he might
well *say* it. Such comments seem almost like musical motifs to
introduce a particular character, and it may be that this is how they
are read. The thought is made 'Viola-like' without its being intended
to represent the precise verbal form of Viola's thought.)

Following this the comment about Viola's being prevented from
taking much notice of his daughters by his absorption in his
memories must be authorial – the very point being made is that
Viola himself is not conscious of something, so he cannot be
thinking this himself. It is the final sentence which seems to me to
be more interestingly ambiguous: is it Viola, or the narrator, who
believes that 'girls belong more to the mother'? It seems to me that
the sentence can convincingly be read in both ways; 'service of
liberty' is a phrase that Viola himself would use, but it may be
being quoted ironically by the narrator, who is surely more likely
than Viola himself to talk of Viola's *worship* of liberty. Would Viola
himself believe that, 'much of his affection had been expended in
the worship and service of liberty'? I am not sure. We should notice
that this minor ambiguity can be attributed to our uncertainty about
the narrator's opinions: we know that Viola himself would probably
believe that girls belong more to the mother, but we are (or, at least
I am) less sure whether this would be likely to be the opinion of the
narrator.

This is a trivial example, but the point is a substantive one:
there is a clear relationship between the reader's sense of a
particular set of beliefs which are underwritten by the narrative,
and the avoidance of unproductive ambiguity with regard to the
use of FID.

Consider too the following example:

> Old Viola had risen. He followed with his eyes in the dark the
> sounds made by Nostromo. The light disclosed him standing
> without support, as if the mere presence of that man who was
> loyal, brave, incorruptible, who was all his son would have been,
> were enough for the support of his decaying strength.
>
> (*Nostromo*, p. 468)

Once again this seems very straightforward, but is actually
extremely complex. Much of this must be authorial comment.

80

Seeing and Believing

We have an external description of Viola, such as no character
– including Viola himself – would have given. The words 'as if'
clearly signal an authorial perspective: it is the narrator, and not
Viola, who suggests that it is as if (but not actually because)
Nostromo's qualities support him, that Viola can stand without
support. But in the same sentence, 'who was all his son would have
been' is equally clearly to be interpreted as a statement from Viola's
perspective rather than from that of the authorial narrator. And it
is Viola, of course, and not the authorial narrator who considers
Nostromo to be incorruptible. Such a statement from the narrator
would be inescapably ironic. But we should not necessarily assume
that Viola is actually *thinking* these thoughts at this moment, and
that is why I have used the term 'FID' rather than 'represented
thought'. What they represent is, perhaps, what Viola would have
thought had he been thinking about Nostromo, and how this man's
presence enabled him to stand without support. The words thus
represent an attitude which is potential rather than actual in Viola, a
set of beliefs of which he is not at this moment fully conscious, but
which can serve to characterize his behaviour and his personality.
What this short passage demonstrates to perfection is the supreme
flexibility that FID gives Conrad in *Nostromo*, such that in one
sentence we can glide from an authorial narrative perspective
into represented thought and back again – without the reader
being made conscious of the transitions at all (although of course
responding to them). The passage also shows how Conrad seems
almost incapable of avoiding FID when dealing with Viola: this
character's presence seems invariably to call out the technique.

With Captain Mitchell, Conrad seems concerned to indicate a
different sort of mental limitation from that illustrated in the case of
Viola. We are told of Mitchell that he had, 'a strange ignorance of
the real forces around him' (p. 136), that he 'did some hard but not
very extensive thinking' (p. 338), and that he was 'too pompously
and innocently aware of his own existence to observe that of
others' (p. 338). His thoughts are neither very interesting nor are
they significantly different from what he actually says, and so his
represented thought cannot give the reader all that much of value.
On occasions, we have to be told what he is not thinking, what he
is incapable of thinking – as in the passage in which we learn of
his lack of fear for his personal safety:

> He did some hard but not very extensive thinking. It was not of
> a gloomy cast. The old sailor, with all his small weaknesses and
> absurdities, was constitutionally incapable of entertaining for any
> length of time a fear of his personal safety. It was not so much

Joseph Conrad

firmness of soul as the lack of a certain kind of imagination – the kind whose undue development caused intense suffering to Señor Hirsch; that sort of imagination which adds the blind terror of bodily suffering and of death, envisaged as an accident to the body alone, strictly – to all the other apprehensions on which the sense of one's existence is based. Unfortunately Captain Mitchell had not much penetration of any kind; characteristic, illuminating trifles of expression, action, or movement, escaped him completely. He was too pompously and innocently aware of his own existence to observe that of others.

(*Nostromo*, p. 338)

Note how in the following passage we are informed that Mitchell's thoughts are not really coherent enough to be verbalized:

Captain Mitchell's heart was so heavy that he would have preferred for the time being a complete solitude to the best of company. But any company would have been preferable to the doctor's, at whom he had always looked askance as a sort of beachcomber of superior intelligence partly reclaimed from his abased state. That feeling led him to ask. . . .

(*Nostromo*, p. 346)

Note the word 'feeling'; we are not to suppose that Captain Mitchell thought, 'I have always looked askance at that man as a sort of beachcomber &c &c'. This is the verbal form into which the narrative translates Mitchell's *feeling*, a feeling he himself lacks the intelligence or self-awareness to bring to verbal specificity. In such a situation it is the narrative which has to *provide* words which crystallize the feeling into a thought. The use of represented thought would run the risk here of making Mitchell seem too self-aware, more intelligent, and more articulate about his mental processes. (I should admit that the passage could be read as represented thought, that it represents in words thoughts of Mitchell's which did not have this verbal form. But I think that this is unlikely, and that while the narrator is *telling* us that Mitchell had always considered Dr Monygham a sort of beachcomber of superior intelligence, we are not here to assume that at this moment Mitchell is *thinking* that he has always considered Monygham in this way.)

So far as Mitchell's speech is concerned, Conrad seems so concerned to indicate the extent to which this misses the point, that his narrative purposes are better served by techniques which reveal more accurately the actual words used by Mitchell: Direct or Reported Speech. For even where Conrad does use Reported Speech

Seeing and Believing

to convey Captain Mitchell's speech, it is often very close to Direct Speech. And even when dealing with Mitchell's iterative* narrative (it is characteristic of Mitchell that he delivers 'set speeches'), Conrad soon moves into Direct Speech. It is as if the ironic presentation of an absurd character such as Mitchell almost requires the use of a technique that draws attention to the actual words he uses.

> Then he would begin by describing the getting away of the silver, and his natural anxiety lest 'his fellow' in charge of the lighter should make some mistake. Apart from the loss of so much precious metal, the life of Señor Martin Decoud, an agreeable, wealthy, and well-informed young gentleman, would have been jeopardized through his falling into the hands of his political enemies. Captain Mitchell also admitted that in his solitary vigil on the wharf he had felt a measure of concern for the future of the whole country.
> 'A feeling, sir,' he explained. . . .
>
> (*Nostromo*, p. 324)

We can note how Conrad first signals his ironic use of Mitchell's own term by placing 'his fellow' in inverted commas; this is either the narrator mocking Mitchell's term 'my fellow'; or a represented speech transformation of 'my fellow' with the addition of inverted commas to indicate narrator irony. Whichever is the case, the reader is sensitized to the possibility of Mitchell's own speech being related, and is able easily to detect this speech in the represented speech of the following sentence. This movement allows for a heavy concentration of authorial irony in the sentence which starts, 'Captain Mitchell also . . .'.[14] It is in such sentences as this that the dual voice theory of FID seems to me to receive strongest support, although one needs to stress that these two voices are 'either–or' rather than simultaneous, and that they belong to entirely different narrative levels. In this sentence we are conscious both of Mitchell's utterance (and, indeed, of some of the words he probably used when making his point), and also of the narrator's distanced irony. From this point Conrad can move on into Direct Speech and can reap maximum effect from the contrast between what Mitchell says (and how he says it), and what the reader knows the situation actually to be.

The effects produced by such constant and subtle shifts of narrative perspective are central to the power and richness of *Nostromo*, its extraordinarily three-dimensional appearance to the reader. Characters and events are constantly seen from a variety of perspectives,

83

Joseph Conrad

perspectives which are set against and illuminate one another. Some of the shifts of perspective are extremely fleeting – but not the less effective for this. In the middle of a passage describing in Reported Speech Mrs Gould's thoughts after watching the troops depart, we find the following sentence: 'Something like a slight faintness came over her, and she looked blankly at Antonia's still face, wondering what would happen to Charley if that absurd man failed' (p. 166). The use of 'Charley' rather than 'Charles Gould' or 'Gould' precipitates us unambiguously into Mrs Gould's consciousness, from whence it is that Barrios appears an 'absurd man'. But in the next sentence we are back in Reported Speech, having been given an emotional jolt by means of this rapid shift into and out of the mind of Mrs Gould.

Such shifts can often be difficult to establish for certain. Take the following comment from an essay on *Nostromo* by Kiernan Ryan:

> Thus, although the text reveals only too clearly why the Sulacan people suffer, and will continue to suffer, under the *'imperium in imperio'* of Gould and the whole social order he represents, Conrad can nevertheless conclude from the scene in which Gould observes a woman kneeling by the side of a dying *cargador*, mortally wounded while defending the interests of the mine: 'The cruel futility of things stood unveiled in the levity and sufferings of that incorrigible people; the cruel futility of lives and [of] deaths thrown away in the vain endeavour to attain an enduring solution of the problem'.
>
> (The quotation is from *Nostromo*, p. 364. The word in square brackets is omitted in Ryan's quotation.)[15]

Let us look at the passage concerned. After an authorial description of Gould's witnessing of the dying *cargador*, it reads as follows.

> The cruel futility of things stood unveiled in the levity and sufferings of that incorrigible people; the cruel futility of lives and of deaths thrown away in the vain endeavour to attain an enduring solution of the problem. Unlike Decoud, Charles Gould could not play lightly a part in a tragic farce. It was tragic enough for him in all conscience, but he could see no farcical element. He suffered too much under a conviction of irremediable folly. He was too severely practical and too idealistic to look upon its terrible humours with amusement, as Martin Decoud, the imaginative materialist, was able to do in the dry light of his scepticism. To him, as to all of us, the compromises with his conscience appeared uglier than ever in the light of failure. His

84

Seeing and Believing

taciturnity, assumed with a purpose, had prevented him from
tampering openly with his thoughts; but the Gould Concession
had insidiously corrupted his judgment. He might have known,
he said to himself, leaning over the balustrade of the corridor,
that Ribierism could never come to anything. The mine had
corrupted his judgment by making him sick of bribing and
intriguing merely to have his work left alone from day to day.
Like his father, he did not like to be robbed. It exasperated him.
He had persuaded himself that, apart from higher considerations,
the backing up of Don José's hopes of reform was good business.
He had gone forth into the senseless fray as his poor uncle,
whose sword hung on the wall of his study, had gone forth – in
the defence of the commonest decencies of organized society.

(*Nostromo*, pp. 364–5)

Now it is indeed possible that the words quoted from *Nostromo* by
Ryan can properly be attributed to an authorial narrator (which is
not quite the same as saying that they can be attributed to Conrad
himself). But there are clues here which may lead us to believe that
rather than being a passage of authorial narrative, what we have
is actually represented thought, and that the sentiments contained
therein are more properly attributed to Charles Gould. Certainly
some parts of this long passage are unambiguously Gould's represented thought. The phrase 'his poor uncle' emanates, surely, from
Gould's rather than an authorial consciousness. And this suggests
that all that follows after the sentence which begins, 'He might
have known, he said to himself', is represented thought. But if so
one of the sentences in this sequence echoes part of one prior to it:
'The mine had corrupted his judgment'; 'the Gould Concession had
insidiously corrupted his judgment'. Thus it seems possible that a
large amount of the first part of this paragraph, including the words
quoted by Ryan, could be the represented thought of Charles Gould.

Certainly the words 'that incorrigible people' seem more likely to
be Gould's than the authorial narrator's here,[16] and attributing them
to Gould allows the reader to savour the irony of the fact that
Gould's own wife, later on in the novel, picks up Dr Monygham's
use of the word 'incorrigible' and applies this same word to her
husband.

Incorrigible in his devotion to the great silver mine was the Señor
Administrador! Incorrigible in his hard, determined service of the
material interests to which he had pinned his faith in the triumph
of order and justice. Poor boy!

(*Nostromo*, p. 521)

Joseph Conrad

With this reading, the irony is that Gould thinks the 'people' incorrigible from the assumed vantage point of *knowing* how to 'attain an enduring solution of the problem', but his wife sees him as just as incorrigible, just as entrapped in a 'vain endeavour' to attain this 'lasting solution'. And, compounding the irony, whereas Gould thinks of his 'poor uncle', his wife thinks of Gould himself as a 'poor boy!'.

On occasions one may suspect that Conrad uses represented speech in order to provide a less abrupt transition between authorial narrative and Direct Speech. Consider the following passage, in which Mrs Gould informs Viola that his house has been spared from demolition as a result of her intercession (Viola has, ironically, to leave the house later as a result of Nostromo's machinations to protect the silver).

> She talked to him in Italian, of course, and he thanked her with calm dignity. An old Garibaldino was grateful to her from the bottom of his heart for keeping the roof over the heads of his wife and children. He was too old to wander any more.
> 'And is it for ever, signora?' he asked.
>
> (*Nostromo*, p. 124)

There seems no obvious reason why Viola's response to Mrs Gould is given half in represented speech and half in Direct Speech other than to provide a bridge between authorial narrative and Direct Speech, unless Conrad wishes to maintain a distance from Viola's presence up to the point when his direct question can be introduced with maximal dramatic effect. In general Conrad seems to use Direct Speech when he wishes to push our consciousness of the narrator into the background and to stress the dramatic nature of particular scenes.

> Don Martin's soft hands suffered cruelly, tugging at the thick handle of the enormous oar. He stuck to it manfully, setting his teeth. He, too, was in the toils of an imaginative existence, and that strange work of pulling a lighter seemed to belong naturally to the inception of a new state, acquired an ideal meaning from his love for Antonia. For all their efforts, the heavily laden lighter hardly moved. Nostromo could be heard swearing to himself between the regular splashes of the sweeps. 'We are making a crooked path,' he muttered to himself. 'I wish I could see the islands.'
>
> (*Nostromo*, pp. 265–6)

86

Seeing and Believing

It seems likely here that so far as Decoud is concerned Conrad is more interested in his mental processes, and so uses (I think) represented thought in the third sentence quoted[17] to describe what is going on in his head, while with regard to Nostromo Conrad is more interested in what is happening, and so switches to Direct Speech. One could cite as a parallel the shift from represented thought to Direct Speech in the scene where Hirsch leaves the gathering at which he has had his unsuccessful meeting with Charles Gould (pp. 204–5). Hirsch's thoughts are given to us in represented thought up to the point at which he is suddenly struck by the oddness of what Gould has said about the dynamite – and at this crucial point a switch to Direct Speech arrests the reader and increases the dramatic effect of Hirsch's questions.[18]

If we turn to consider Conrad's use of represented thought in *Nostromo*, we find fewer examples than of represented speech, and most of these examples involve what is clearly verbal thought. I can cite no example of represented thought in which the thought represented is unambiguously non-verbal. I have already referred to an ambiguous passage involving Captain Mitchell; here is a paragraph involving Nostromo, at the point at which he is refusing to get a priest for Viola's wife:

> He was feeling uneasy at the impiety of this refusal. The Padrona believed in priests, and confessed herself to them. But all women did that. It could not be of much consequence. And yet his heart felt oppressed for a moment – at the thought what absolution would mean to her if she believed in it only ever so little. No matter. It was quite true that he had given her already the very last moment he could spare.
>
> (*Nostromo*, p. 255)

What strikes me here is that when Nostromo experiences non-verbal mental processes we move out of represented thought into Reported Speech ('He was feeling uneasy', 'And yet his heart felt oppressed for a moment'). We will see the same sort of shift in *Under Western Eyes*. Note too that the final sentence quoted above is ambiguous in a different way: it could be represented thought, giving us the words Nostromo reassures himself with – or it could be an inter-polated authorial narrative statement.

Let me return, now, to the issue I raised at the beginning of this section. Why is it that our memory of the narrative perspective of *Nostromo* is of a regularity and consistency that is at odds with its actual fluidity and mobility? The answer, it seems to me, is that

Joseph Conrad

there is a consistency of *ideological perspective* in this novel that encourages the reader to remember its *technical perspective* as much less varied than actually it is. In *Nostromo* we move from consciousness to consciousness, from vantage point to vantage point, but the narrative's ideological, moral, and political perspective on people and events – on *history* – remains constant in all its complexities. The narrative assessment of characters in this novel is always clear and always constant.

[. . .]

Notes

1. I say 'narrative' rather than 'narrator', as it is frequently misleading to suggest that a work of fiction has a narrator, even if it is narrated. Nevertheless, all works of narrative give the reader a more or less coherent sense of a determining force regulating the telling, and this sense of a determining force (which is not *mechanically* to be associated with the real-life author) inevitably leads the reader to associate the telling with a set of values, a view of the world.

2. Problems of terminology abound in this field in English. In French and German the terms *style indirect libre* and *erlebte Rede* are relatively straightforward. In English a bewildering range of terms can be found to apply to the same phenomenon: Free Indirect Speech (or Discourse); Represented Speech and Thought, Narrated Speech and Thought, and narrated monologue. After years of doggedly sticking to the term Free Indirect Speech on the grounds that it fits in well with the cognate terms Direct Speech and Reported (or Indirect) Speech, I have now to admit that represented speech and represented thought are terms which are more precise, which identify the technique with narrative, and which make an important distinction between the representation of speech and that of thought. In the interests of brevity, however, I shall often refer generally to Free Indirect Discourse when I do not wish to distinguish between the representation of speech and thought, and represented speech or represented thought when I do. It should be noted that not all Free Indirect Discourse represents either speech or thought; it can represent unexpressed attitudes, ideological assumptions, and so on. In accordance with current conventions I shall not capitalize the latter terms, but will continue to capitalize Free Indirect Discourse (FID), Direct Speech, and Reported Speech.

3. All quotations from Conrad's works are from the Dent Collected Edition (London and Toronto: J. M. Dent & Sons Ltd, 1923–28).

4. Extra-mimetic – outside the created world of the fictional text. The narrative voice in *Almayer's Folly* comes from a different level of reality from that in which the characters live – something that is not true of all novels, or of all novels written by Conrad. (It is often not true of those novels with a personified narrator.)

5. DORRIT COHN, *Transparent Minds: Narrating Modes for Presenting Consciousness in Fiction* (Princeton: Princeton UP, 1978), p. 100.

Seeing and Believing

6. SHLOMITH RIMMON-KENAN, *Narrative Fiction: Contemporary Poetics* (London: Methuen, 1983), p. 111.

7. BRIAN McHALE, 'FID: A Survey of Recent Accounts', *Poetics and Theory of Literature* 3 (1978), pp. 257–8.

8. McHALE, p. 258.

9. The term 'authorial narrator' should not be taken to imply that Conrad is speaking in his own voice, merely that the point of view is that of a narrator who has an existence 'outside the story being told'.

10. ROY PASCAL, *The Dual Voice: Free Indirect Speech and its Functioning in the Nineteenth-Century European Novel* (Manchester: Manchester UP, 1977), p. 9.

11. PASCAL, p. 137.

12. ANN BANFIELD, *Unspeakable Sentences: Narration and Representation in the Language of Fiction* (London: Routledge, 1982), p. 108. Banfield's approach is distinguished by its reliance upon a transformational-generative (TG) theoretical foundation, which is not uncontroversial. See McHale's criticism of an earlier article of Banfield's in his already-cited article. Where Banfield uses 'neither' and 'nor', I would prefer to use 'not necessarily . . . nor'.

13. BANFIELD, p. 123.

14. Josiane Paccaud has pointed out to me that this sentence could either be represented speech, with a Direct Speech original of Mitchell's something like 'I admit that . . .', or it could be Reported Speech, the content of which follows 'admitted that'.

15. KIERNAN RYAN, 'Revelation and Repression in Conrad's *Nostromo*'. In Douglas Jefferson and Graham Martin (eds.), *The Uses of Fiction: Essays on the Modern Novel in Honour of Arnold Kettle* (Milton Keynes: Open University Press, 1982), pp. 80–1. I should add that Ryan raises some very challenging and important problems concerning *Nostromo* in his article.

16. My argument here should acknowledge the fact that the word 'incorrigible' is applied to other characters in *Nostromo*. Decoud is described as 'incorrigible in his scepticism' by the authorial narrator (*Nostromo*, p. 300); Pedrito Montero is, this narrator tells us, 'incorrigibly lazy and slovenly' (*Nostromo*, p. 387), and Dr Monygham, referring to Father Corbelàn and Antonia, ejaculates 'Incorrigible!' to Mrs Gould (*Nostromo*, p. 510). It need not necessarily, therefore, be Charles Gould who considers the Costaguanians to be incorrigible; it might well be the authorial narrator. My feeling is, however, that on balance the former seems to be the more likely of these alternatives in this instance. It is perhaps worth noting that Stein, in *Lord Jim*, is also associated with this same word:

    'Stein was the man who knew more about Patusan than anybody else. More than was known in the government circles I suspect. I have no doubt he had been there, either in his butterfly-hunting days or later on, when he tried in his incorrigible way to season with a pinch of romance the fattening dishes of his commercial kitchen.'

    (p. 219)

17. It could be authorial comment.

18. Compare Charles Jones's detailed analysis of the presentation of the speech of Verloc and Winnie in *The Secret Agent*. Before the death of Stevie,

89

Joseph Conrad

Winnie's speech is presented almost entirely in Direct Speech, and where Reported Statements are made they 'have all strong hints of the *direct* throughout'. Verloc's speech at this time is, in contrast, 'revealed mainly by means of the *indirect* or the narrated'. With the death of Stevie these characteristics are reversed. Finally, subsequent to the murder of Verloc, 'no less than 95% of Winnie's speech is represented by type (iv) *direct*'. (That is, speech enclosed in inverted commas without the inclusion of Subject or Predicate.) (CHARLES JONES, 'Varieties of Speech Presentation in Conrad's *The Secret Agent*', *Lingua* 20, 1968, pp. 174–5.)

5 Skeptic Comedy and the Coercion of Character*

MARK WOLLAEGER

Mark Wollaeger sees Conrad as a philosophical novelist and seeks to place his work 'in a tradition of philosophical skepticism that extends from Descartes to the present' (Wollaeger, pp. xiii–xiv). Like Erdinast-Vulcan, he presents a divided Conrad, resistant to his own scepticism. Both critics employ Bakhtin's idea of the dialogic to explain how Conrad's conflicting impulses (towards scepticism on the one hand and transcendence on the other) interact in his fiction. However, whereas Erdinast-Vulcan associates scepticism with moral relativism and presents it in a negative light, Wollaeger sees it more positively, as a 'sustained interrogation' (Wollaeger, p. xvii) of the categories of reason. For Wollaeger Conrad's refusal of metaphysics and theology is a sign of integrity, whereas for Erdinast-Vulcan it is a sign of failure. Wollaeger uses this conception of Conrad to explore the themes of coercion, isolation and betrayal in his work in terms of the relations between author, narrator and characters. In this excerpt he draws on Foucault's idea of the body as a site for the inscription of power, in order to argue that the narrator of *The Secret Agent* adopts a coercive attitude to the characters of the novel. In this novel, Wollaeger suggests, Conrad abandons the dialogic in favour of 'authoritative discourse' (p. 96), reducing characters to mechanical figures, although the characters may resist.

Much more so than in *Nostromo*, characters in *The Secret Agent* often seem ruthlessly subjected to the author's will, and the coerciveness of that will must be separated into the events of the narrative and the manner of their narration. Setting aside for the moment the discourse of the narrator, I will turn first to the narrative logic of Winnie's suicide, which has been cited as an analogue of the

---

* Reprinted from *Joseph Conrad and the Fictions of Skepticism* (Stanford: Stanford University Press, 1990), pp. 142–55, with minor corrections and emendations kindly provided by the author.

Joseph Conrad

gratuitous dispatching of Decoud.[1] The severe irony governing narrative development in *The Secret Agent*, like the ironic perspective of the narrator, derives from a moral skepticism that transforms black comedy into what can be called the comedy of skepticism.

As in 'Heart of Darkness,' the narrative of *The Secret Agent* constitutes a gradual revelation of the intolerable within the benign. Here cannibalism, often suspected as Kurtz's 'unspeakable rites,' becomes a more explicit metaphor for the horror concealed behind perceptions conditioned by convention. Karl Yundt, one of the anarchists in Adolf Verloc's circle, condemns capitalism within earshot of Stevie, Winnie Verloc's retarded younger brother: 'Do you know how I would call the nature of the present economic conditions? I would call it cannibalistic. That's what it is! They are nourishing their greed on the quivering flesh and the warm blood of the people – nothing else'.[2] Late that night, when Verloc comes upon Stevie 'gesticulating and murmuring in the kitchen,' he heads upstairs to alert his wife, and for the first time he thinks about Stevie and his wife's mother, who also lives in the house, as two more bodies 'to provide for' (*SA*, p. 55). Verloc has just returned from his interview with Mr. Vladimir, whose insistent demand for a series of outrages must be met if Verloc is to keep his job as an agent provocateur. It is in part this economic pressure that induces Verloc to send Stevie on his ill-fated mission to blow up Greenwich Observatory, where the Professor's bomb reduces him to 'what might have been an accumulation of raw material for a cannibal feast' (*SA*, p. 86). A few pages later, as Inspector Heat examines Stevie's remains, Conrad pushes the grotesquerie further: 'the Chief Inspector went on peering at the table with a calm face and the slightly anxious attention of an indigent customer bending over what may be called the by-products of a butcher's shop with a view to an inexpensive Sunday dinner.'

In my summary the story takes on the aspect of a belabored and macabre joke. But in Conrad's handling cannibalism takes on the status of what Frank Kermode has called a narrative secret, a hidden story or pattern whose significance emerges only when the story is retold in order to draw together and reorder details whose connection might otherwise pass unnoticed.[3] Winnie's gradual recognition that it was Stevie who died in the explosion mirrors the reader's, for Conrad's manipulation of narrative chronology withholds the full meaning of 'the thing' first mentioned in Chapter Four until Chapter Nine, where Winnie, 'carving knife and fork in hand,' is told by her husband, 'you know you can trust me' (*SA*, pp. 192–3). We learn at the end of Chapter Two that Winnie almost married a young butcher, but, as we discover still later, there

92

Skeptic Comedy and the Coercion of Character

was not enough 'room' in his 'boat' for Stevie. For the security of her mother and brother she eventually married Verloc, whose 'barque seemed a roomy craft' (*SA*, p. 243). In a grim suggestion of malignant fatality, Verloc, who happened to be rooming in their boarding house, turns out to be more like her first suitor than she ever could have imagined. As the word 'butcher' slides from a benign designation of livelihood to a gruesomely sardonic perspective on Stevie's death, the 'clearly providential' nature of Verloc's availability recalls and amplifies the irony latent in Monygham's perception of providence in Nostromo's unexpected appearance in the Custom House.

Winnie's discovery of Verloc's failed plot is a shock that shatters her complacent assumption that her husband would at least be a good provider, and it confirms her suspicion that 'things do not stand much looking into' (*SA*, p. 177). The closer one looks 'into' things in *The Secret Agent* (just as Heat looks closely into Stevie's remains), the more one finds that 'inside' the shell of social, political, and familial conventions lurks one horror after another. Though in 'Heart of Darkness' the 'hidden' remains more mysterious – the 'unspeakable' remains just that, available to the reader only in the ambiguity of Kurtz's last words – the narrative logic in both texts depends on the opposition of inside and outside, surface and depth. But in *The Secret Agent* the narrative does not build toward moments of Schopenhauerian vision. No longer charged with the mysterious promise of total knowledge, the inside is less a sanctum than an emptiness guarded by repression, a kind of fold or pocket in the social fabric.

In this logic we see Conrad at his most Swiftian. One thinks of the more distinctly satiric use of cannibalism in 'A Modest Proposal,' but *A Tale of a Tub* suggests a clearer parallel. 'Happiness,' writes the Grub Street Hack, 'is a perpetual possession of being well deceived.'[4] The world is peopled by fools, those who remain secure in their delusions, and knaves, those who insist on 'unmasking' the underlying horror. The hack writer seems at first to prefer the fool's existence: 'so far preferable is that wisdom, which converses about the surface, to that pretended philosophy which enters into the depth of things, and then comes gravely back with informations and discoveries, that in the inside they are good for nothing.' Insight requires violence: if surfaces do not satisfy, 'then comes reason officiously with tools for cutting, and opening, and mangling, and piercing, offering to demonstrate, that they are not of the same consistence quite through.' The ambivalence is apparent already; neither choice will suffice. But Swift gives the argument a few more turns. Lest the reader rest easy with what

93

Joseph Conrad

came to be the Romantic commonplace that 'we murder to dissect,' the hack condemns analysis of the inside as 'the last degree of perverting nature,' only to assert in a sudden rhetorical pirouette that 'reason is certainly in the right, and that in most corporeal beings, which have fallen under my cognizance, the outside hath been infinitely preferable to the in.' The movement of the sentence forces one to experience the impossibility of choosing.[5] We expect that if reason is right, the inside should be preferred, but in the famous anatomizing of the 'carcass of a beau' (an ancestor of Stevie?), reason is again literalized as a form of murderous dissection. The categories of fool and knave are irreconcilable, irreducible, and inclusive.

Winnie Verloc, whose 'philosophy consisted in not taking notice of the inside of facts' (*SA*, p. 154), is, as Swift would have it, in 'the serene peaceful state of being a fool among knaves' until Stevie's death unmasks her husband. The logic of Conrad's narrative offers no other place for her: 'She did not see any alternative between screaming and silence, and instinctively she chose the silence' (*SA*, p. 246). Once Ossipon's betrayal harshly renews the lesson of the world's knavishness, she can escape from the governing categories of fool and knave only through suicide. Formerly a fool, Ossipon the knave is, at book's end, left paralyzed by passage from one state to the other.

What drops out of this summary is the overbearing presence of the narrator, whose harsh ironies at the characters' expense generally exceed those in *Nostromo*. The ironic treatment of character in *The Secret Agent* has drawn considerable critical attention.[6] Conrad wrote to Marguerite Poradowska that he was fond of *The Secret Agent* 'because I think that in it I managed to treat what is after all a melodramatic subject by the method of irony.'[7] This irony is usually well controlled, as in the description of Verloc's walk to the embassy that begins Chapter Two: 'It was unusually early for him; his whole person exhaled the charm of almost dewy freshness; he wore his blue cloth overcoat unbuttoned; his boots were shiny; his cheeks, freshly shaven, had a sort of gloss, and even his heavy-lidded eyes, refreshed by a night of peaceful slumber, sent out glances of comparative alertness' (*SA*, p. 11). The light humor of the sentence is of a piece with the rest of the long passage from which it is excerpted. But in other places, as in the description of Karl Yundt, irony verges on vituperation and revulsion: 'His worn-out passion, resembling in its impotent fierceness the excitement of a senile sensualist, was badly served by a dried throat and toothless gums which seemed to catch the tip of his tongue' (*SA*, p. 43). Irving Howe was the first to argue that in the absence of anyone

94

Skeptic Comedy and the Coercion of Character

to admire in the sordid world of *The Secret Agent*, the novel lacks 'a moral positive to serve literary ends.'[8] Clearly the sustained ironic treatment implies a range of unstated moral criteria that are necessary to make sense of the ironies, but Howe and others would like to see this moral awareness located in the characters. The technical virtuosity of Conrad's ironic method parts company with the moral imagination as embodied in character.[9]

I confess that I am one of those readers ready to find redeeming value in the technical brilliance and intellectual rigor of *The Secret Agent*, even as I am inclined to recoil from the tensely controlled fury and indignation that informs it at every point. The text holds, one could say, the 'fascination of the abomination' (*Heart of Darkness*, p. 50). The comic control of *Typhoon* becomes in *The Secret Agent* a rage for order that finds explicit thematic expression when Vladimir bullies Verloc into the Greenwich Observatory bombing in order to induce a police crackdown on anarchist activity. The order remains a comic one, but it is far blacker than in *Typhoon*.

Characters in *The Secret Agent* resist the imposition of an oppressive order only in the resentment and indignation that dominate their emotional lives. Verloc's delayed response to Vladimir when speaking with Winnie brings out the violence latent in these tensions: 'If I hadn't thought of you I would have taken the bullying brute by the throat and rammed his head into the fireplace' (*SA*, p. 239). Vladimir himself descends 'from generations victimized by the instruments of an arbitrary power' (*SA*, p. 224). But the Assistant Commissioner, whose consciousness is more comprehensive than any other in the novel, brings out the nature of the dynamic most distinctly: ' "Here I am stuck in a litter of paper," he reflected, with unreasonable resentment, "supposed to hold all the threads in my hands, and yet I can but hold what is put in my hand, and nothing else. And they can fasten the other ends of the threads where they please" ' (*SA*, p. 115). Not quite a puppet, the Assistant Commissioner nevertheless resents not having the power to be the puppeteer. The 'unreasonableness' of the resentment locates the moment as a mode in the text's crosscurrents of rebellious energy: no character in *The Secret Agent* is ever allowed to hold all the strings. Inspector Heat, though initially more in the know than the Assistant Commissioner and consequently less frustrated, shares 'the dislike of being compelled by events.' An encounter with the Professor, whom Heat knows is wired as a human bomb, irritates him because it did not leave him with that 'satisfactory sense of superiority the members of the police force get from the unofficial but intimate side of their intercourse with the criminal classes, by which the vanity of power is soothed, and the

Joseph Conrad

vulgar love of domination over our fellow-creatures is flattered as worthily as it deserves' (*SA*, p. 122). Whereas characters in *Nostromo* struggle to preserve their autonomy by resisting the tendency to become dominated by a monological order, the author of *The Secret Agent* remains unconcerned with his apparent implication in 'the vulgar love of domination.'

In consequence, his discourse approaches – from the point of view of the characters, primarily, but from our own as well – what Bakhtin has called authoritative discourse, a language that 'demands that we acknowledge it, that we make it our own; it binds us, quite independent of any power it might have to persuade us internally.' Bakhtin's love of terminology induces him to oppose the 'internally persuasive' to the authoritative, yet we can recognize the familiar distinction between the monologic and the fundamentally dialogic, in which every word is 'half-ours and half-someone else's.' Translated into the relationship between author and character, an orientation toward internally persuasive discourse requires that 'the author's discourse about a character [be] organized about *someone actually present*, someone who hears him (the author) and is *capable of answering him*.' Characters in Conrad frequently lack the capacity to respond directly to one another, let alone to the author. Nostromo, like Jim, is very often, as Bakhtin would have it, 'the mute, voiceless object' of another's words, but in both novels a dialogic tension remains, whether in Marlow's acknowledgment of Jim's essential otherness or in the confessional and rebellious dimensions I have mapped out in *Nostromo*.[10] Characters talk past one another more dramatically in *The Secret Agent* (consider Winnie's last scene with Verloc, or her ensuing conversation with Ossipon), and the sense of inevitably crossed purposes is compounded in the implied domination of character by author.

For the skeptic voice of *The Secret Agent* establishes an authoritative perspective on characters as wind-up toys capable of expressing only the thoughts programmed into them by the author. Although the London they inhabit is one of dissolving boundaries and disturbing metamorphoses,[11] the exchanges between narrator and character form, as it were, a one-way street. Near the middle of the text an appropriation of the characters' language by the narrator underlines the sense in which the author may listen, but characters are denied the capacity to respond. After Sir Ethelred mentions to the Assistant Commissioner his 'Bill for the Nationalization of Fisheries,' the Assistant Commissioner is described as 'a queer foreign fish' and the city streets as 'a slimy aquarium from which the water had been run off' (*SA*, pp. 145, 147). The foreignness of the Assistant Commissioner's appearance receives more attention

Skeptic Comedy and the Coercion of Character

a few pages later when he enters an Italian restaurant and surveys the bland homogeneity of its patrons:

> These people were as denationalized as the dishes set before them with every circumstance of unstamped respectability. Neither was their personality stamped in any way, professionally, socially, or racially. They seemed created for the Italian restaurant, unless the Italian restaurant had been perchance created for them. But that last hypothesis was unthinkable, since one could not place them anywhere outside those special establishments.
>
> (*SA*, p. 149)

England and its representative Sir Ethelred seem to conspire 'to nationalize' or assimilate fish, food, and people alike into a tightly controlled and lifeless order.[12] Even the cooking is 'fraudulent.' The Assistant Commissioner's foreign difference momentarily sets him apart from the others in the restaurant, yet the fish imagery, which recurs in later pages, tends to reassert control over him and pull him into the 'unconscious stream of people on the pavements' (*SA*, p. 63). The fact that the Assistant Commissioner experiences a sense of 'evil freedom' (*SA*, p. 148) after leaving his desk work to pursue Verloc only heightens the discrepancy between the characters' lack of self-awareness and the more comprehensive, authoritative perspective established by the narrative voice.[13] As verbal patterning draws our attention to the whir of narrative machinery operating beyond the characters' awareness, our understanding of the characters may become analogous to the Assistant Commissioner's attitude toward those in the restaurant: we see them as created for the story, unless the story has been created perchance for the characters, though one could not place them anywhere outside those special establishments.

Only Stevie actively resists the complacency of the established order in *The Secret Agent*. When Winnie and Stevie take their mother to a retirement home as if in 'the Cab of Death itself,' Winnie's cynical account of the police as oppressors of the poor upsets Stevie because 'he had formed for himself an ideal conception of the metropolitan police as a sort of benevolent institution for the suppression of evil' (*SA*, p. 172). He refuses at first to ride in the cab out of compassion for the emaciated horse, and after the cabman has forced on him a sense of the 'close association' of 'human and equine misery,' Stevie utters the sad truth that it is a 'bad world for poor people' (*SA*, p. 171). But Conrad deals harshly with Stevie's compassion. Although the narrative provides lines of crossed purposes to account for the destruction of Stevie, the

Joseph Conrad

verbal patterning of the text also suggests that his dismemberment literalizes the 'magnanimous indignation [that] swelled his chest to bursting' (*SA*, p. 169). Stevie's death also literalizes the moral disintegration found in Verloc's disregard for Stevie's safety and in his subsequent response to the accident: 'Stevie had stumbled within five minutes of being left to himself. And Mr. Verloc was shaken morally to pieces' (*SA*, p. 230). What may be called a violence of thematization – the sense that the author violently processes characters into expressions of theme – recurs in Verloc's death when, after Winnie stabs him, his dripping blood, ticking 'fast and furious like the pulse of an insane clock,' is cruelly transmuted into an expression of the text's recurrent concern with time (*SA*, p. 265).[14] Winnie's grotesque vision of Stevie's death, moreover, reads both as a confused recollection of his misadventures in a staircase with some catherine wheels and as a transformation of Stevie into an emblem of his characteristic response to 'tales of injustice and oppression' (*SA*, p. 9): she sees 'smashed branches, torn leaves, gravel, bits of brotherly flesh and bone, all spouting up together in the manner of a firework. . . . where after a rainlike fall of mangled limbs the decapitated head of Stevie lingered suspended alone . . . like the last star of a pyrotechnic display' (*SA*, p. 260). Since Stevie suffers the most gruesome of the three deaths in the novel, we may surmise that it was unwise of him to rebel against the morally suspect institutions the author constructed around him.[15]

Challenging the autonomy of character, the attack on the body in *The Secret Agent* may also represent a perverse expression of Conrad's longing for a form of rationality that does not (as Decoud's does) consume its own order in skeptical dissolution. Skeptic discourse requires the myth of the body as separating in order to account for the fact of our separation, even though it is not the body that shields one mind from another but consciousness itself.[16] Thus an impatience with the process of inference from empirical evidence produces Sterne's fantasy in *Tristram Shandy* of the body with a window to its inner workings. The desire for a *purely* rational world, one in which buildings do not seem to wander from their proper addresses or words (like Marlow's 'wretched cur') do not stick to the wrong object, must inevitably do greater damage to the body. (Compare the inscription of the law directly onto the body in [Franz Kafka's] *The Penal Colony* or the suffering human figures within the rigorously mapped Aristotelian structure of Dante's hell.) Violence against the body in *The Secret Agent* may be related to the proliferation of seemingly inexplicable geometric details associated with Verloc, whose code name appears in the text as a triangle, and Stevie, who obsessively scrawls

Skeptic Comedy and the Coercion of Character

'circles, circles, circles; innumerable circles, concentric, eccentric; a coruscating whirl of circles' (*SA*, p. 45). Such details often surface in descriptions of the London scene too: Winnie's cry that Verloc 'was a devil' seems 'lost as if in a triangular well of asphalt and bricks, of blind houses and unfeeling stones' (*SA*, p. 276). Given Conrad's fascination with anarchy, it is perhaps inevitable that geometric precision is also persistently shadowed by the impossibility of rational order, just as the 'repeated curves, uniformity of form, and confusion of intersecting lines' mapped by Stevie's circles suggest 'a rendering of cosmic chaos.' The play between geometry and chaos recalls Nietzsche's remark that 'among philosophers as well as artists, one finds a passionate and exaggerated worship of "pure forms": let no one doubt that he who *needs* the cult of surfaces to that extent has at some time or other made a calamitous attempt to get *beneath* them'.[17] Stevie and Verloc look beneath the familiar only near the end of their lives, but Winnie's widely shared inclination not to look too deeply into things must be read against Conrad's insistent suggestion that he himself has.

As it does violence to the body, Conrad's desire for order in *The Secret Agent* also transforms the status of character. Although the narrator often dips into a character's mind to discuss his or her motivation, verbal patterning, along with the abstract commentary of the narrator, comes to supplant the kind of characterization found in the traditional novel. If we pursue character analysis, the apparent arbitrariness of Winnie's collapse into fear after murdering Verloc may be understood as a version of the monomania rampant in Conrad's fiction. Winnie's fixed idea is the sheltering of Stevie; and when the deaths of Stevie and Verloc free her for the first time in her life, rather than becoming an independent agent, she fills her inner void with fears of retribution. When Ossipon comes on the scene, she simply clings to him as her new object of devotion and begins to consider the possibility of escape. One might argue further that such behavior makes sense as the typical response of an unexpectedly widowed or divorced woman who has never been independent.

But the text does not really solicit a naturalistic motivation for Winnie's behavior. She has been presented from the start as a somnambulist, and the most important act of her life, the murder of her husband, is described in utterly nonnaturalistic terms: 'Mr. Verloc heard the creaky plank in the floor, and was content. He waited. Mrs. Verloc was coming. As if the homeless soul of Stevie had flown for shelter straight to the breast of his sister, guardian, and protector, the resemblance of her face with that of her brother grew at every step, even to the droop of the lower lip, even to the

Joseph Conrad

slight divergence of the eyes' (*SA*, p. 262). The passage inscribes Winnie into the pattern of explosive overreaction exemplified in Stevie, for whom 'the anguish of immoderate compassion was succeeded by the pain of an innocent but pitiless rage' (*SA*, p. 169); Stevie's response has become Winnie's. If metempsychosis* is difficult to accept as a motive, we could read this as a parody of a certain kind of sentimental writing.[18] Or, given that Ossipon later (*after* discovering Winnie has murdered Verloc) meditates on 'the fact of that resemblance' (*SA*, p. 298), perhaps we should simply read the passage as the expression of emotional affinities between brother and sister that later heighten Ossipon's sensitivity to overlooked physical similarities. But rather than trying to preserve the authority of an earlier fictional paradigm, we should focus on the interesting way in which the passage hovers between naturalistic illusion and the purely textual. Responding to Winnie's elliptical allusion to her murder of Verloc, Ossipon figures the response of the reader: 'There were suggestions of triumph, relief, gratitude in the indefinable tone of these words. It engrossed the whole attention of Ossipon to the detriment of mere literal sense' (*SA*, p. 277).

Winnie's mind has always been dominated by a single concern – whether Stevie, Ossipon, or, when she looks into 'the very bottom of this thing,' 'the gallows' (*SA*, p. 267) – and so the entry of Stevie's soul into her body suggests, like Monygham's manipulation of Nostromo, the filling of an empty vessel. Resonating with the language of disembodied souls elsewhere in *The Secret Agent*, the trope of possession establishes a network of narrative secrets that points, I suggest, toward the absent presence of the author who supervises the kind of Conradian transmigrations that also figure prominently in *Nostromo*. First, more examples from *The Secret Agent*.

The only true author in *The Secret Agent* (aside from Ossipon, who is only a pamphleteer) is Michaelis, who spends night and day writing his 'Autobiography of a Prisoner.' Michaelis pours himself into the project because it allows him 'the liberation of his inner life, the letting out of his soul into the wide world' (*SA*, p. 120). The trope describing Michaelis's self-expression picks up the language of disembodied souls and can be read as reflexive commentary on the idea of authorship implicit in the text.[19] Indeed, his self-engrossment resembles the narrator's monologic indifference to the fate of the characters: 'Michaelis pursued his idea. . . . He talked to himself, indifferent to the sympathy or hostility of his hearers, indifferent indeed to their presence' (*SA*, p. 44). In the Author's Note to *The Secret Agent* Conrad defends the book by claiming that 'there was no perverse intention, no secret scorn for the natural sensibilities of mankind at the bottom of my impulses' (*SA*, p. viii). A reader of the

100

Skeptic Comedy and the Coercion of Character

resulting text may well quarrel with Conrad's reconstruction of his intentions; their realization, in any case, is quite often perverse in the sense of being deeply misanthropic. Judging from the recurrent concerns of the Note, Conrad too, when rereading *The Secret Agent* after thirteen years, may have had misgivings: 'I confess that it makes a grisly skeleton. But still I will submit that . . . I have not intended to commit a gratuitous outrage on the feelings of mankind' (*SA*, p. xv). When Winnie wishes to set right an ill-considered outburst against Verloc, the narrator attributes her threat to 'the demon of perverse inspiration' (*SA*, p. 196). Although 'perverse' here primarily means 'contrary,' the expression also picks up the language of the Author's Note and anticipates the translation of Stevie's soul into Winnie when the inspiration to murder Verloc fully possesses her.

Conrad often described his own creation of a fictional world in language that closely resembles the account of Michaelis's authorship. As implied in 'Karain' and *Lord Jim*, the trope of incarnation is basic to Conrad's understanding of artistic realization: 'I write very little, but inspiration comes to me in looking at the paper. Then there are soaring flights; my thought goes wandering through vast spaces filled with shadowy forms. All is yet chaos, but, slowly, the apparitions change into living flesh, the shimmering mists take shape, and – who knows? – something may be born of the clash of nebulous ideas'.[20] From vapor to living flesh, the idea clothes itself as a living character, and a fictional world is set in motion. Although it is impossible to offer conclusive substantiation for issues extending beyond the fictional frame,[21] I believe that Conrad's writing as a whole legitimates my claim that the imagery of disembodied souls in *The Secret Agent* and *Nostromo* traces the circulation of authorial intentions. In this argument, Conrad's presence in the text – Bakhtin's secondary author – is not limited to incarnated figures for the writer.

In *The Secret Agent* wandering souls are hard-pressed to find a human body to enter, and from the mechanical quality of the characters Conrad derives a good deal of Bergsonian comedy. When Winnie, in shock from the revelation of Stevie's gruesome death, suddenly stands up 'as if raised by a spring,' her husband remarks uneasily, 'you're looking more like yourself' (*SA*, p. 251). The arbitrary and mechanical in Winnie's behavior is more explicit in Verloc when, just after his return from the botched bombing, Winnie asks him to answer the door: 'Mr. Verloc obeyed woodenly, stony-eyed, like an automaton whose face had been painted red. And this resemblance to a mechanical figure went so far that he had an automaton's absurd air of being aware of the machinery inside of

101

Joseph Conrad

him' (*SA*, p. 197). Most of the characters in *The Secret Agent* are more or less self-conscious robots, ghosts in machines, and the cruel edge of the comedy sometimes draws a smile that may as quickly become a grimace. During the prolonged conversation preceding Verloc's stabbing, the narrator resolutely ignores the emotional charge of the scene as Verloc tries ineptly to console his wife. Rendered from a perspective unflinchingly removed from human emotions, the couple's nervous movements around the room become comic spectacle: 'It all had the appearance of a struggle for the possession of a chair, because Mr. Verloc instantly took his wife's place in it' (*SA*, pp. 234–5). The sentence resonates nicely with the implication in the first chapter that Verloc, who 'took over' Winnie's mother 'with the furniture,' is the type of man who, in the absence of a chair, might absentmindedly sit on his mother-in-law.

Reducing the human to the mechanical, the comedy of moral skepticism can be understood in its place both as a classic issue of skepticism and as an expression of Conrad's cultural moment. One form that the philosophical discussion of other minds often takes is the problem of articulating how one could distinguish a self-conscious automaton from a human being.[22] As early as the mid-eighteenth century La Mettrie, inspired by Descartes's hypothesis of the animal as machine, championed the idea of the man-machine. Though it was inevitable that 'what Descartes said of animals would one day be said of man,'[23] during the early nineteenth century the idea's heretical appeal to Enlightenment rationalism was eclipsed by the ascendancy of philosophical idealism and the Romantic valorization of introspection and the organic. The problem of other minds, which now may seem a purely academic discussion (of the 'who cares?' variety), began to take on urgency later in the nineteenth century in the wake of the redefinitions of consciousness sparked by physiological psychology, Darwinian biology, and renewed interest in philosophical materialism.[24] By 1894 T. H. Huxley could write of three proto-Darwinian essays he first published thirty-two years earlier: 'most of the conclusions . . . are now to be met with among other well-established and, indeed, elementary truths, in the text-books.'[25] And in 1874 Huxley voiced a thought to which *The Secret Agent* may now seem a monument: 'We are conscious automata.'[26] As the twentieth century draws to a close we can expect to see Huxley's slogan recirculated in debates about computer simulations of human consciousness or 'artificial intelligence.'

With the boundaries between men, machines, and animals eroding, the concept of the soul becomes increasingly important to those invested in preserving man's privileged position in the

Skeptic Comedy and the Coercion of Character

world.[27] In this context Conrad's language of disembodied souls registers as a response to the prominence of the mechanical in the second machine age and as a shadow of resistance to the effacement of the newly dubious category of 'the human.'[28] (Even the description of the writing process Conrad sent to H. G. Wells, 'the conversion of nervous force into phrases,' presents the human under the aspect of mechanical physics.) Ironically, what may be called the soul of authorial intentions in *The Secret Agent* has the effect of dehumanizing the human by turning the ghost in the machine into the specter of the mechanical.[29]

In *Nostromo*, as in *The Secret Agent*, tropes* of embodiment and disembodiment come to the foreground in moments of crucial decision. In *Nostromo*, however, characters are less inclined to acquiesce easily to the manipulations of the author whose intentions 'take possession' of them.

[. . .]

Notes

1. See, for instance, KINGSLEY WIDMER, 'Conrad's Pyrrhonistic Conservativism: Ideological Melodrama Around "Simple Ideas"', *Novel* 7 (1974), pp. 137–42; MARTIN PRICE, *Forms of Life: Character and Moral Imagination in the Novel* (New Haven, CT: Yale University Press, 1983), pp. 358–9 n. 30.

2. JOSEPH CONRAD, *The Secret Agent*, p. 51. References are to *Joseph Conrad: Complete Works* (Garden City, NY: Doubleday, Page, 1924) and will be given in the text as *SA*.

3. FRANK KERMODE, 'Secrets and Narrative Sequence', *Critical Inquiry* 7 (1980), pp. 83–101. The essay, which interprets some of the puzzling imagery in *Under Western Eyes*, is reprinted in Kermode's *The Art of Telling*.

4. JONATHAN SWIFT, *Gulliver's Travels and Other Writings*, ed. Louis Landa (Boston: Houghton Mifflin, 1960), p. 332. Succeeding quotations are from pp. 332–3.

5. For a review of this crux in Swift, see JOHN R. CLARK, *Form and Frenzy in Swift's Tale of a Tub* (Ithaca, NY: Cornell University Press, 1970), pp. 3–35.

6. See, in addition to those critics cited in the notes that follow, R. A. GEKOSKI, *The Moral World of the Novelist* (London: Paul Elek, 1978), p. 142: *The Secret Agent* 'creates a group of unworthy and contemptible characters – and then brilliantly castigates them for their unworthiness and contemptibility'. And see IAN P. WATT (ed.), Conrad: *The Secret Agent: A Casebook*, pp. 77–80, who finds that 'the tension between what is seen and how it is presented betokens an admirable elasticity of spirit'.

7. 20 June, 1912, in JOHN A. GEE and PAUL J. STURM (trans. and eds.), *Letters of Joseph Conrad to Marguerite Poradowska, 1890–1920* (New Haven, CT: Yale University Press, 1940), p. 116.

8. IRVING HOWE, *Politics and the Novel* (1957; reprinted New York: Discus-Avon, 1970), p. 96.

Joseph Conrad

9. See MARTIN PRICE, 'Conrad: Satire and Fiction', *Yearbook of English Studies* 14 (1984), pp. 226–42, who surveys the relevant commentaries and shows that critical response makes clear 'the way in which the irony seems to effect a moral levelling of all the characters and the way in which the aloofness or comic distance of the novelist makes us associate our feelings more with his virtuosity than with the minds of his characters' (p. 234). The book, Price concludes, succeeds neither as satire nor as fiction: 'We are not allowed the full detachment which might allow us to scorn the shams and bunglers alike. Nor are we allowed to entertain very long or far the sympathy which the more complex characters awaken' (p. 242).

10. MIKHAIL BAKHTIN, *The Dialogic Imagination*, trans. Caryl Emerson and Michael Holquist (Austin: University of Texas Press, 1981), pp. 342, 345; BAKHTIN, *Problems of Dostoevsky's Poetics*, ed. and trans. Caryl Emerson (Minneapolis: University of Minnesota Press, 1984), p. 63. For Ford's claim that he and Conrad agreed that characters should *never* respond to each other, see FORD MADOX FORD, *Joseph Conrad, A Personal Remembrance* (London: Duckworth, 1924), p. 188. For my discussion of character and authorial coercion in *Nostromo*, see *Joseph Conrad and the Fictions of Skepticism* (Stanford: Stanford University Press, 1990), pp. 120–42.

11. See J. HILLIS MILLER'S reading in *Poets of Reality: Six Twentieth-Century Writers* (Cambridge: Harvard University Press, 1965) for an excellent account of this dimension of the text.

12. Compare MARK CONROY, *Modernism and Authority: Strategies of Legitimation in Flaubert and Conrad* (Baltimore, MD: Johns Hopkins University Press, 1985), p. 150, who analyzes this scene in the course of a fine discussion of Foucault's 'panopticism'* and 'the imprisonment of the characters' in *The Secret Agent*.

13. The association between the 'evil freedom' of the foreign-looking Assistant Commissioner and the denationalizing effect of the restaurant may also derive from Conrad's ambivalent desire to assimilate. Defensively disdainful of the English audience, Conrad nevertheless worried that his Polishness kept him from being more popular. The evil would lie in denying the claims of his Polish ancestry. Writing to Galsworthy (at the time a *very* popular novelist) about the commercial failure of *The Secret Agent*, Conrad lamented: 'I suppose there is something in me that is unsympathetic to the general public, – because the novels of Hardy, for instance, are generally tragic enough and gloomily written too, – and yet they have sold in their time and are selling to the present day'. At this point in the letter we can imagine Conrad pausing to reflect further on what distinguished him from Galsworthy and Hardy before going on to write a one-sentence paragraph: 'Foreignness, I suppose'. 6 January, 1908, in *Joseph Conrad: Life and Letters*, ed. G. Jean-Aubry, 2 vols. (Garden City, NY: Doubleday, Page, 1927), II: 65. For the pathos of Conrad's self-division, see 'Amy Foster', where foreignness becomes fatal.

14. The attempt to destroy the observatory, the seat of Greenwich Mean Time, is only the most obvious expression of the theme. The classic analysis is ROBERT W. STALLMAN, 'Time and *The Secret Agent*', in Robert W. Stallman (ed.), *The Art of Joseph Conrad: A Critical Symposium* (East Lansing: Michigan State University Press, 1960), pp. 234–54.

15. It is also unwise to try to escape from them. Clearly Winnie commits suicide because Ossipon betrays her, yet her death by drowning in the English Channel also coincides with her aborted attempt to escape from the 'insular nature of Great Britain', which had 'obtruded itself upon [Ossipon's] notice in an odious form' as he planned their flight (*SA*, p. 282).

104

Skeptic Comedy and the Coercion of Character

16. See STANLEY CAVELL, *The Claim of Reason: Wittgenstein, Skepticism, Morality, and Tragedy* (Oxford: Oxford University Press, 1979), p. 369.

17. FRIEDRICH NIETZSCHE, *Beyond Good and Evil: Prelude to a Philosophy of the Future*, trans. R. J. Hollingdale (Harmondsworth: Penguin, 1973), p. 66.

18. Likewise with the motivation borrowed from 'Heart of Darkness', which could be taken as the half-mocking ironic evocation of primeval feelings and archaic energies: 'Into that plunging blow . . . Mrs Verloc had put all the inheritance of her immemorial and obscure descent, the simple ferocity of the age of caverns, and the unbalanced nervous fury of the age of bar-rooms' (*SA*, p. 263).

19. The connection survives Conrad's professed loathing for this kind of romantic self-indulgence and for the kind of Rousseau-like self-justification Michaelis would write. Conrad's excessive denunciations of Rousseau, like his condemnation of Dostoevsky, represent refusals to acknowledge the confessional dimension of his own fiction, as well as the project of self-justification undertaken in *A Personal Record*. It has been widely recognized, moreover, that *Under Western Eyes* is indebted to *Crime and Punishment*.

20. To Poradowska, 29 March or 5 April, 1894, in GEE and STURM (eds.), *Letters to Poradowska*, p. 64.

21. On the other hand, life (as we read of it in a short pamphlet by Jessie Conrad) imitated Conrad's art on this score. Several years after Conrad's death, Jessie decided to lay to rest various rumors that he had returned from the dead to chat with Stephen Crane (also a spirit, which makes the trip seem rather unnecessary), Lord Northcliffe, and Arthur Conan Doyle, who wrote to the bereaved widow informing her that during a séance conducted by a Mrs Dean, Conrad had returned to imprint his face on a plate. Jessie suspects forgery and is relieved to report that she has found a photograph of her husband that looks remarkably like the plate. See MRS. JOSEPH CONRAD [Jessie George], *Did Joseph Conrad Return as a Spirit?* (Webster Groves, MO: International Mark Twain Society, 1932).

22. CAVELL, *The Claim of Reason*, meditates on the question in response to Hilary Putnam's classic articulation of the issue in 'Robots: Machines or Artificially Created Life?', *Journal of Philosophy* 61 (1964), pp. 668–91.

23. KEITH THOMAS, *Man and the Natural World: A History of the Modern Sensibility* (New York: Pantheon, 1983), p. 33.

24. See ARAM VARTANIAN, 'Man-Machine from the Greeks to the Computer', in *Dictionary of the History of Ideas*, ed. Philip P. Weiner, III (New York: Scribner's, 1973–74), as well as my discussion of Cavell on other minds in Chapter 3 of *Joseph Conrad and the Fictions of Skepticism*.

25. THOMAS H. HUXLEY, *Man's Place in Nature: and Other Anthropological Essays* (London: Macmillan, 1894), p. v.

26. THOMAS H. HUXLEY, 'On the Hypothesis that Animals Are Automata', in *Methods and Results: Essays* (New York: Appleton, 1894), p. 244.

27. THOMAS, *Man and the Natural World*, pp. 30–6, 122–3.

28. Cross-cultural psychology offers yet another perspective on Conrad's overdetermined language of wandering souls. RICHARD SHWEDER, 'Menstrual Pollution, Soul Loss, and the Comparative Study of Emotions' in *Culture and Depression: Studies in the Anthropology and Cross-Cultural Psychiatry of Affect and Disorder*, ed. Arthur Kleinman and Byron Good (Berkeley: University of California Press, 1985), describes the

Joseph Conrad

phenomenology of depression: 'When you feel depressed you feel as though your soul has left your body. What you feel is empty, and a body emptied of its soul loses interest in things, except perhaps its own physical malfunctioning as a thing. The phenomenon of soul wandering is widely acknowledged among the world's cultures, and the phenomenology of soul loss has, for millennia, been a topic of theoretical and practical concern' (p. 193). One thinks of Winnie after Stevie's death, and of Nostromo on discovering Decoud's death. Conrad himself suffered from numerous depressive episodes, and his correspondence provides a great deal of support for Shweder's claims: 'Under the stress of physical suffering the mind sees falsely, the heart errs, the soul unguided wanders in an abyss'. To Poradowska, 23 March, 1890, in GEE and STURM (eds.), *Letters to Poradowska*, 8. For Conrad's depressed self-image as a malfunctioning thing – a broken doll – see the letter to Poradowska, 16 October, 1891, in ibid., p. 38. See also the biographies by Meyer and Najder for discussion of Conrad's depression: BERNARD C. MEYER, *Joseph Conrad: A Psychoanalytic Biography* (Princeton: Princeton University Press, 1967); ZDZISŁAW NAJDER, *Joseph Conrad: A Chronicle* (New Brunswick, NJ: Rutgers University Press, 1983).

Turning to another depressive, we can compare Woolf on the melancholia of Lily Briscoe's experience of the artistic process: 'before she exchanged the fluidity of life for the concentration of painting she had a few moments of nakedness when she seemed like an unborn soul, a soul reft of body, hesitating on some windy pinnacle and exposed without protection to all the blasts of doubt'. VIRGINIA WOOLF, *To the Lighthouse* (1927; reprinted New York: Harcourt, Brace & World, 1955), p. 237.

29. For provocative meditations on the mechanical in modernist aesthetics, see HUGH KENNER's anecdotal approach in *The Mechanic Muse* (New York: Oxford University Press, 1987).

Part Three

Imperialism

6 An Image of Africa: Racism in Conrad's *Heart of Darkness**

CHINUA ACHEBE

Chinua Achebe's article began life as a lecture and retains some of the immediacy of address of that form. It has probably provoked more discussion, and fiercer arguments, than any other single piece of Conrad criticism because it describes Conrad, who has routinely been accorded the status of 'great' modern writer, as a 'thorough-going racist'. Like Nina Pelikan Straus's article, which claims that *Heart of Darkness* is 'brutally sexist' in its conventions (p. 173), Achebe's piece strikes an overtly personal note and is written in anger. It would be a mistake to take this as indicative of a 'naive' or untheoretical approach. Rather it reflects the emphasis, in post-colonial theory, on the politics of representation (including questions of who is speaking and who is represented), and resistance to a Eurocentric perspective masked by a spurious detachment and universalism. Elsewhere Achebe has attacked the use of 'universal' as 'a synonym for the narrow self-serving parochialism of Europe' (*Morning Yet on Creation Day* (London, Ibadan, Nairobi, Lusaka: Heinemann, 1975), p. 9), and this issue is integral to his argument in the Conrad essay. What is at stake is not simply Conrad's favourable or unfavourable representation of African people, but the assumption that Africa and its people are available for discursive appropriation by the European writer. *Heart of Darkness* is sometimes defended as a symbolic examination of the European mind and experience, not a realist representation of Africa. This, however, misses the point that the reduction of African society to a symbol dehumanises and devalues its people and their multiple and complex pre-colonial societies. Achebe's account of the ideological structure of *Heart of Darkness* is clearly susceptible of modification (see Introduction, p. 9), but the politics and ethics of

---

* This is an amended version of the second Chancellor's Lecture at the University of Massachusetts, Amherst, February 1975; later published in the *Massachusetts Review*, vol. 18, no. 4, Winter 1977, Amherst. Reprinted from *Hopes and Impediments: Selected Essays 1965–1987* (London: Heinemann, 1988), pp. 1–13.

Joseph Conrad

retaining as an enormously popular set text and a classic of modernism a work that contains racist assumptions remain problematic. One consequence of the debate has been to encourage 'teaching the conflicts': debating rather than ignoring the question of racism when teaching *Heart of Darkness*.

In the fall of 1974 I was walking one day from the English Department at the University of Massachusetts to a parking lot. It was a fine autumn morning such as encouraged friendliness to passing strangers. Brisk youngsters were hurrying in all directions, many of them obviously freshmen in their first flush of enthusiasm. An older man going the same way as I turned and remarked to me how very young they came these days. I agreed. Then he asked me if I was a student too. I said no, I was a teacher. What did I teach? African literature. Now that was funny, he said, because he knew a fellow who taught the same thing, or perhaps it was African *history*, in a certain community college not far from here. It always surprised him, he went on to say, because he never had thought of Africa as having that kind of stuff, you know. By this time I was walking much faster. 'Oh well,' I heard him say finally, behind me: 'I guess I have to take your course to find out.'

A few weeks later I received two very touching letters from high-school children in Yonkers, New York, who – bless their teacher – had just read *Things Fall Apart*. One of them was particularly happy to learn about the customs and superstitions of an African tribe.

I propose to draw from these rather trivial encounters rather heavy conclusions which at first sight might seem somewhat out of proportion to them. But only, I hope, at first sight.

The young fellow from Yonkers, perhaps partly on account of his age but I believe also for much deeper and more serious reasons, is obviously unaware that the life of his own tribesmen in Yonkers, New York, is full of odd customs and superstitions and, like everybody else in his culture, imagines that he needs a trip to Africa to encounter those things.

The other person being fully my own age could not be excused on the grounds of his years. Ignorance might be a more likely reason; but here again I believe that something more wilful than a mere lack of information was at work. For did not that erudite British historian and Regius Professor at Oxford, Hugh Trevor-Roper, also pronounce that African history did not exist?

If there is something in these utterances more than youthful inexperience, more than a lack of factual knowledge, what is it? Quite simply it is the desire – one might indeed say the need – in

110

An Image of Africa: Racism in Conrad's Heart of Darkness

Western psychology to set Africa up as a foil to Europe, as a place of negations at once remote and vaguely familiar, in comparison with which Europe's own state of spiritual grace will be manifest.

This need is not new; which should relieve us all of considerable responsibility and perhaps make us even willing to look at this phenomenon dispassionately. I have neither the wish nor the competence to embark on the exercise with the tools of the social and biological sciences but do so more simply in the manner of a novelist responding to one famous book of European fiction: Joseph Conrad's *Heart of Darkness*, which better than any other work that I know displays that Western desire and need which I have just referred to. Of course there are whole libraries of books devoted to the same purpose but most of them are so obvious and so crude that few people worry about them today. Conrad, on the other hand, is undoubtedly one of the great stylists of modern fiction and a good story-teller into the bargain. His contribution therefore falls automatically into a different class – permanent literature – read and taught and constantly evaluated by serious academics. *Heart of Darkness* is indeed so secure today that a leading Conrad scholar has numbered it 'among the half-dozen greatest short novels in the English language'.[1] I will return to this critical opinion in due course because it may seriously modify my earlier suppositions about who may or may not be guilty in some of the matters I will now raise.

Heart of Darkness projects the image of Africa as 'the other world,' the antithesis of Europe and therefore of civilization, a place where man's vaunted intelligence and refinement are finally mocked by triumphant bestiality. The book opens on the River Thames, tranquil, resting peacefully 'at the decline of day after ages of good service done to the race that peopled its banks.'[2] But the actual story will take place on the River Congo, the very antithesis of the Thames. The River Congo is quite decidedly not a River Emeritus. It has rendered no service and enjoys no old-age pension. We are told that 'going up that river was like travelling back to the earliest beginning of the world.'

Is Conrad saying then that these two rivers are very different, one good, the other bad? Yes, but that is not the real point. It is not the differentness that worries Conrad but the lurking hint of kinship, of common ancestry. For the Thames too 'has been one of the dark places of the earth.' It conquered its darkness, of course, and is now in daylight and at peace. But if it were to visit its primordial relative, the Congo, it would run the terrible risk of hearing grotesque echoes of its own forgotten darkness, and falling victim to an avenging recrudescence of the mindless frenzy of the first beginnings.

Joseph Conrad

These suggestive echoes comprise Conrad's famed evocation of the African atmosphere in *Heart of Darkness*. In the final consideration his method amounts to no more than a steady, ponderous, fake-ritualistic repetition of two antithetical sentences, one about silence and the other about frenzy. We can inspect samples of this on pages 103 and 105 of the New American Library edition: (a) 'It was the stillness of an implacable force brooding over an inscrutable intention' and (b) 'The steamer toiled along slowly on the edge of a black and incomprehensible frenzy.' Of course there is a judicious change of adjective from time to time, so that instead of 'inscrutable,' for example, you might have 'unspeakable,' even plain 'mysterious,' etc., etc.

The eagle-eyed English critic F. R. Leavis[3] drew attention long ago to Conrad's 'adjectival insistence upon inexpressible and incomprehensible mystery.' That insistence must not be dismissed lightly, as many Conrad critics have tended to do, as a mere stylistic flaw; for it raises serious questions of artistic good faith. When a writer while pretending to record scenes, incidents and their impact is in reality engaged in inducing hypnotic stupor in his readers through a bombardment of emotive words and other forms of trickery, much more has to be at stake than stylistic felicity. Generally normal readers are well armed to detect and resist such underhand activity. But Conrad chose his subject well – one which was guaranteed not to put him in conflict with the psychological predisposition of his readers or raise the need for him to contend with their resistance. He chose the role of purveyor of comforting myths.

The most interesting and revealing passages in *Heart of Darkness* are, however, about people. I must crave the indulgence of my reader to quote almost a whole page from about the middle of the story when representatives of Europe in a steamer going down the Congo encounter the denizens of Africa:

We were wanderers on a prehistoric earth, on an earth that wore the aspect of an unknown planet. We could have fancied ourselves the first of men taking possession of an accursed inheritance, to be subdued at the cost of profound anguish and of excessive toil. But suddenly, as we struggled round a bend, there would be a glimpse of rush walls, of peaked grass-roofs, a burst of yells, a whirl of black limbs, a mass of hands clapping, of feet stamping, of bodies swaying, of eyes rolling, under the droop of heavy and motionless foliage. The steamer toiled along slowly on the edge of the black and incomprehensible frenzy. The prehistoric man was cursing us, praying to us, welcoming us

112

An Image of Africa: Racism in Conrad's Heart of Darkness

– who could tell? We were cut off from the comprehension of our surroundings; we glided past like phantoms, wondering and secretly appalled, as sane men would be before an enthusiastic outbreak in a madhouse. We could not understand because we were too far and could not remember because we were travelling in the night of first ages, of those ages that are gone, leaving hardly a sign – and no memories.

The earth seemed unearthly. We are accustomed to look upon the shackled form of a conquered monster, but there – there you could look at a thing monstrous and free. It was unearthly, and the men were – No, they were not inhuman. Well, you know, that was the worst of it – this suspicion of their not being inhuman. It would come slowly to one. They howled and leaped, and spun, and made horrid faces; but what thrilled you was just the thought of their humanity – like yours – the thought of your remote kinship with this wild and passionate uproar. Ugly. Yes, it was ugly enough; but if you were man enough you would admit to yourself that there was in you just the faintest trace of a response to the terrible frankness of that noise, a dim suspicion of there being a meaning in it which you – you so remote from the night of first ages – could comprehend.[4]

Herein lies the meaning of *Heart of Darkness* and the fascination it holds over the Western mind: 'What thrilled you was just the thought of their humanity – like yours . . . Ugly.'

Having shown us Africa in the mass, Conrad then zeros in, half a page later, on a specific example, giving us one of his rare descriptions of an African who is not just limbs or rolling eyes:

And between whiles I had to look after the savage who was fireman. He was an improved specimen; he could fire up a vertical boiler. He was there below me, and, upon my word, to look at him was as edifying as seeing a dog in a parody of breeches and a feather hat, walking on his hind legs. A few months of training had done for that really fine chap. He squinted at the steam gauge and at the water gauge with an evident effort of intrepidity – and he had filed his teeth, too, the poor devil, and the wool of his pate shaved into queer patterns, and three ornamental scars on each of his cheeks. He ought to have been clapping his hands and stamping his feet on the bank, instead of which he was hard at work, a thrall to strange witchcraft, full of improving knowledge.[5]

As everybody knows, Conrad is a romantic on the side. He might not exactly admire savages clapping their hands and stamping their

113

Joseph Conrad

feet but they have at least the merit of being in their place, unlike this dog in a parody of breeches. For Conrad things being in their place is of the utmost importance.

'Fine fellows – cannibals – in their place,' he tells us pointedly. Tragedy begins when things leave their accustomed place, like Europe leaving its safe stronghold between the policeman and the baker to take a peep into the heart of darkness.

Before the story takes us into the Congo basin proper we are given this nice little vignette as an example of things in their place:

> Now and then a boat from the shore gave one a momentary contact with reality. It was paddled by black fellows. You could see from afar the white of their eyeballs glistening. They shouted, sang; their bodies streamed with perspiration; they had faces like grotesque masks – these chaps; but they had bone, muscle, a wild vitality, an intense energy of movement, that was as natural and true as the surf along their coast. They wanted no excuse for being there. They were a great comfort to look at.[6]

Towards the end of the story Conrad lavishes a whole page quite unexpectedly on an African woman who has obviously been some kind of mistress to Mr Kurtz and now presides (if I may be permitted a little liberty) like a formidable mystery over the inexorable imminence of his departure:

> She was savage and superb, wild-eyed and magnificent . . . She stood looking at us without a stir and like the wilderness itself, with an air of brooding over an inscrutable purpose.

This Amazon is drawn in considerable detail, albeit of a predictable nature, for two reasons. First, she is in her place and so can win Conrad's special brand of approval; and second, she fulfils a structural requirement of the story: a savage counterpart to the refined, European woman who will step forth to end the story:

> She came forward, all in black with a pale head, floating toward me in the dusk. She was in mourning . . . She took both my hands in hers and murmured, 'I had heard you were coming' . . . She had a mature capacity for fidelity, for belief, for suffering.[7]

The difference in the attitude of the novelist to these two women is conveyed in too many direct and subtle ways to need elaboration. But perhaps the most significant difference is the one implied in the author's bestowal of human expression to the one and the

An Image of Africa: Racism in Conrad's Heart of Darkness

withholding of it from the other. It is clearly not part of Conrad's purpose to confer language on the 'rudimentary souls' of Africa. In place of speech they made 'a violent babble of uncouth sounds. They 'exchanged short grunting phrases' even among themselves. But most of the time they were too busy with their frenzy. There are two occasions in the book, however, when Conrad departs somewhat from his practice and confers speech, even English speech, on the savages. The first occurs when cannibalism gets the better of them:

> 'Catch 'im,' he snapped, with a bloodshot widening of his eyes and a flash of sharp white teeth – 'catch 'im. Give 'im to us.' 'To you, eh?' I asked; 'what would you do with them?' 'Eat 'im!' he said curtly.[8]

The other occasion was the famous announcement: 'Mistah Kurtz – he dead.'[9]

At first sight these instances might be mistaken for unexpected acts of generosity from Conrad. In reality they constitute some of his best assaults. In the case of the cannibals the incomprehensible grunts that had thus far served them for speech suddenly proved inadequate for Conrad's purpose of letting the European glimpse the unspeakable craving in their hearts. Weighing the necessity for consistency in the portrayal of the dumb brutes against the sensational advantages of securing their conviction by clear, unambiguous evidence issuing out of their own mouth Conrad chose the latter. As for the announcement of Mr Kurtz's death by the 'insolent black head in the doorway,' what better or more appropriate *finis* could be written to the horror story of that wayward child of civilization who wilfully had given his soul to the powers of darkness and 'taken a high seat amongst the devils of the land' than the proclamation of his physical death by the forces he had joined?

It might be contended, of course, that the attitude to the African in *Heart of Darkness* is not Conrad's but that of his fictional narrator, Marlow, and that far from endorsing it Conrad might indeed be holding it up to irony and criticism. Certainly Conrad appears to go to considerable pains to set up layers of insulation between himself and the moral universe of his story. He has, for example, a narrator behind a narrator. The primary narrator is Marlow but his account is given to us through the filter of a second, shadowy person. But if Conrad's intention is to draw a cordon sanitaire between himself and the moral and psychological *malaise* of his narrator his care seems to me totally wasted because he neglects to hint, clearly and

115

Joseph Conrad

adequately, at an alternative frame of reference by which we may judge the actions and opinions of his characters. It would not have been beyond Conrad's power to make that provision if he had thought it necessary. Conrad seems to me to approve of Marlow, with only minor reservations – a fact reinforced by the similarities between their two careers.

Marlow comes through to us not only as a witness of truth, but one holding those advanced and humane views appropriate to the English liberal tradition which required all Englishmen of decency to be deeply shocked by atrocities in Bulgaria or the Congo of King Leopold of the Belgians or wherever.

Thus Marlow is able to toss out such bleeding-heart sentiments as these:

> They were all dying slowly – it was very clear. They were not enemies, they were not criminals, they were nothing earthly now – nothing but black shadows of disease and starvation, lying confusedly in the greenish gloom. Brought from all the recesses of the coast in all the legality of time contracts, lost in uncongenial surroundings, fed on unfamiliar food, they sickened, became inefficient, and were then allowed to crawl away and rest.[10]

The kind of liberalism espoused here by Marlow/Conrad touched all the best minds of the age in England, Europe and America. It took different forms in the minds of different people but almost always managed to sidestep the ultimate question of equality between white people and black people. That extraordinary missionary, Albert Schweitzer, who sacrificed brilliant careers in music and theology in Europe for a life of service to Africans in much the same area as Conrad writes about, epitomizes the ambivalence. In a comment which has often been quoted Schweitzer says: 'The African is indeed my brother but my junior brother.' And so he proceeded to build a hospital appropriate to the needs of junior brothers with standards of hygiene reminiscent of medical practice in the days before the germ theory of disease came into being. Naturally he became a sensation in Europe and America. Pilgrims flocked, and I believe still flock even after he has passed on, to witness the prodigious miracle in Lamberene, on the edge of the primeval forest.

Conrad's liberalism would not take him quite as far as Schweitzer's, though. He would not use the word 'brother' however qualified; the farthest he would go was 'kinship.' When Marlow's African helmsman falls down with a spear in his heart he gives his white master one final disquieting look:

An Image of Africa: Racism in Conrad's Heart of Darkness

And the intimate profundity of that look he gave me when he received his hurt remains to this day in my memory – like a claim of distant kinship affirmed in a supreme moment.[11]

It is important to note that Conrad, careful as ever with his words, is concerned not so much about 'distant kinship' as about someone *laying a claim* on it. The black man lays a claim on the white man which is well-nigh intolerable. It is the laying of this claim which frightens and at the same time fascinates Conrad, 'the thought of their humanity – like yours ... Ugly.'

The point of my observations should be quite clear by now, namely that Joseph Conrad was a thoroughgoing racist. That this simple truth is glossed over in criticisms of his work is due to the fact that white racism against Africa is such a normal way of thinking that its manifestations go completely unremarked. Students of *Heart of Darkness* will often tell you that Conrad is concerned not so much with Africa as with the deterioration of one European mind caused by solitude and sickness. They will point out to you that Conrad is, if anything, less charitable to the Europeans in the story than he is to the natives, that the point of the story is to ridicule Europe's civilizing mission in Africa. A Conrad student informed me in Scotland that Africa is merely a setting for the disintegration of the mind of Mr Kurtz.

Which is partly the point. Africa as setting and backdrop which eliminates the African as human factor. Africa as a metaphysical battlefield devoid of all recognizable humanity, into which the wandering European enters at his peril. Can nobody see the preposterous and perverse arrogance in thus reducing Africa to the role of props for the break-up of one petty European mind? But that is not even the point. The real question is the dehumanization of Africa and Africans which this age-long attitude has fostered and continues to foster in the world. And the question is whether a novel which celebrates this dehumanization, which depersonalizes a portion of the human race, can be called a great work of art. My answer is: No, it cannot. I do not doubt Conrad's great talents. Even *Heart of Darkness* has its memorably good passages and moments:

The reaches opened before us and closed behind, as if the forest had stepped leisurely across the water to bar the way for our return.

Its exploration of the minds of the European characters is often penetrating and full of insight. But all that has been more than fully discussed in the last fifty years. His obvious racism has, however, not been addressed. And it is high time it was!

Joseph Conrad

Conrad was born in 1857, the very year in which the first Anglican missionaries were arriving among my own people in Nigeria. It was certainly not his fault that he lived his life at a time when the reputation of the black man was at a particularly low level. But even after due allowances have been made for all the influences of contemporary prejudice on his sensibility there remains still in Conrad's attitude a residue of antipathy to black people which his peculiar psychology alone can explain. His own account of his first encounter with a black man is very revealing:

> A certain enormous buck nigger encountered in Haiti fixed my conception of blind, furious, unreasoning rage, as manifested in the human animal to the end of my days. Of the nigger I used to dream for years afterwards.[12]

Certainly Conrad had a problem with niggers. His inordinate love of that word itself should be of interest to psychoanalysts. Sometimes his fixation on blackness is equally interesting as when he gives us this brief description: 'A black figure stood up, strode on long black legs, waving long black arms'[13] – as though we might expect a black figure striding along on black legs to wave white arms! But so unrelenting is Conrad's obsession.

As a matter of interest Conrad gives us in *A Personal Record* what amounts to a companion piece to the buck nigger of Haiti. At the age of sixteen Conrad encountered his first Englishman in Europe. He calls him 'my unforgettable Englishman' and describes him in the following manner:

> [his] calves exposed to the public gaze ... dazzled the beholder by the splendour of their marble-like condition and their rich tone of young ivory ... The light of a headlong, exalted satisfaction with the world of men ... illumined his face ... and triumphant eyes. In passing he cast a glance of kindly curiosity and a friendly gleam of big, sound, shiny teeth ... his white calves twinkled sturdily.[14]

Irrational love and irrational hate jostling together in the heart of that talented, tormented man. But whereas irrational love may at worst engender foolish acts of indiscretion, irrational hate can endanger the life of the community. Naturally Conrad is a dream for psychoanalytic critics. Perhaps the most detailed study of him in this direction is by Bernard C. Meyer, MD. In his lengthy book Dr Meyer follows every conceivable lead (and sometimes inconceivable ones) to explain Conrad. As an example he gives

118

An Image of Africa: Racism in Conrad's Heart of Darkness

us long disquisitions on the significance of hair and hair-cutting in Conrad. And yet not even one word is spared for his attitude to black people. Not even the discussion of Conrad's antisemitism was enough to spark off in Dr Meyer's mind those other dark and explosive thoughts. Which only leads one to surmise that Western psychoanalysts must regard the kind of racism displayed by Conrad as absolutely normal despite the profoundly important work done by Frantz Fanon in the psychiatric hospitals of French Algeria.

Whatever Conrad's problems were, you might say he is now safely dead. Quite true. Unfortunately his heart of darkness plagues us still. Which is why an offensive and deplorable book can be described by a serious scholar as 'among the half-dozen greatest short novels in the English language.' And why it is today perhaps the most commonly prescribed novel in twentieth-century literature courses in English departments of American universities.

There are two probable grounds on which what I have said so far may be contested. The first is that it is no concern of fiction to please people about whom it is written. I will go along with that. But I am not talking about pleasing people. I am talking about a book which parades in the most vulgar fashion prejudices and insults from which a section of mankind has suffered untold agonies and atrocities in the past and continues to do so in many ways and many places today. I am talking about a story in which the very humanity of black people is called in question.

Secondly, I may be challenged on the grounds of actuality. Conrad, after all, did sail down the Congo in 1890 when my own father was still a babe in arms. How could I stand up more than fifty years after his death and purport to contradict him? My answer is that as a sensible man I will not accept just any traveller's tales solely on the grounds that I have not made the journey myself. I will not trust the evidence even of a man's very eyes when I suspect them to be as jaundiced as Conrad's. And we also happen to know that Conrad was, in the words of his biographer, Bernard C. Meyer, 'notoriously inaccurate in the rendering of his own history.'[15]

But more important by far is the abundant testimony about Conrad's savages which we could gather if we were so inclined from other sources and which might lead us to think that these people must have had other occupations besides merging into the evil forest or materializing out of it simply to plague Marlow and his dispirited band. For as it happened, soon after Conrad had written his book an event of far greater consequence was taking place in the art world of Europe. This is how Frank Willett, a British art historian, describes it:

119

Joseph Conrad

Gauguin had gone to Tahiti, the most extravagant individual act of turning to a non-European culture in the decades immediately before and after 1900, when European artists were avid for new artistic experiences, but it was only about 1904–5 that African art began to make its distinctive impact. One piece is still identifiable; it is a mask that had been given to Maurice Vlaminck in 1905. He records that Derain was 'speechless' and 'stunned' when he saw it, bought it from Vlaminck and in turn showed it to Picasso and Matisse, who were also greatly affected by it. Ambroise Vollard then borrowed it and had it cast in bronze ... The revolution of twentieth century art was under way![16]

The mask in question was made by other savages living just north of Conrad's River Congo. They have a name too: the Fang people, and are without a doubt among the world's greatest masters of the sculptured form. The event Frank Willett is referring to marked the beginning of cubism and the infusion of new life into European art that had run completely out of strength.

The point of all this is to suggest that Conrad's picture of the peoples of the Congo seems grossly inadequate even at the height of their subjection to the ravages of King Leopold's International Association for the Civilization of Central Africa.

Travellers with closed minds can tell us little except about themselves. But even those not blinkered, like Conrad with xenophobia, can be astonishingly blind. Let me digress a little here. One of the greatest and most intrepid travellers of all time, Marco Polo, journeyed to the Far East from the Mediterranean in the thirteenth century and spent twenty years in the court of Kublai Khan in China. On his return to Venice he set down in his book entitled *Description of the World* his impressions of the peoples and places and customs he had seen. But there were at least two extraordinary omissions in his account. He said nothing about the art of printing, unknown as yet in Europe but in full flower in China. He either did not notice it at all or, if he did, failed to see what use Europe could possibly have for it. Whatever the reason, Europe had to wait another hundred years for Gutenberg. But even more spectacular was Marco Polo's omission of any reference to the Great Wall of China, nearly four thousand miles long and already more than one thousand years old at the time of his visit. Again, he may not have seen it; but the Great Wall of China is the only structure built by man which is visible from the moon![17] Indeed travellers can be blind.

As I said earlier Conrad did not originate the image of Africa which we find in his book. It was and is the dominant image of

An Image of Africa: Racism in Conrad's Heart of Darkness

Africa in the Western imagination and Conrad merely brought the peculiar gifts of his own mind to bear on it. For reasons which can certainly use close psychological inquiry the West seems to suffer deep anxieties about the precariousness of its civilization and to have a need for constant reassurance by comparison with Africa. If Europe, advancing in civilization, could cast a backward glance periodically at Africa trapped in primordial barbarity it could say with faith and feeling: There go I but for the grace of God. Africa is to Europe as the picture is to Dorian Gray – a carrier on to whom the master unloads his physical and moral deformities so that he may go forward, erect and immaculate. Consequently Africa is something to be avoided just as the picture has to be hidden away to safeguard the man's jeopardous integrity. Keep away from Africa, or else! Mr Kurtz of *Heart of Darkness* should have heeded that warning and the prowling horror in his heart would have kept its place, chained to its lair. But he foolishly exposed himself to the wild irresistible allure of the jungle and lo! the darkness found him out.

In my original conception of this essay I had thought to conclude it nicely on an appropriately positive note in which I would suggest from my privileged position in African and Western cultures some advantages the West might derive from Africa once it rid its mind of old prejudices and began to look at Africa not through a haze of distortions and cheap mystifications but quite simply as a continent of people – not angels, but not rudimentary souls either – just people, often highly gifted people and often strikingly successful in their enterprise with life and society. But as I thought more about the stereotype image, about its grip and pervasiveness, about the wilful tenacity with which the West holds it to its heart; when I thought of the West's television and cinema and newspapers, about books read in its schools and out of school, of churches preaching to empty pews about the need to send help to the heathen in Africa, I realized that no easy optimism was possible. And there was in any case something totally wrong in offering bribes to the West in return for its good opinion of Africa. Ultimately the abandonment of unwholesome thoughts must be its own and only reward. Although I have used the word 'wilful' a few times here to characterize the West's view of Africa it may well be that what is happening at this stage is more akin to reflex action than calculated malice. Which does not make the situation more but less hopeful.

The *Christian Science Monitor*, a paper more enlightened than most, once carried an interesting article written by its Education Editor on the serious psychological and learning problems faced by little children who speak one language at home and then go to school

121

Joseph Conrad

where something else is spoken. It was a wide-ranging article taking in Spanish-speaking children in America, the children of migrant Italian workers in Germany, the quadrilingual phenomenon in Malaysia and so on. And all this while the article speaks unequivocally about language. But then out of the blue sky comes this:

> In London there is an enormous immigration of children who speak Indian or Nigerian dialects, or some other native language.[18]

I believe that the introduction of 'dialects,' which is technically erroneous in the context, is almost a reflex action caused by an instinctive desire of the writer to downgrade the discussion to the level of Africa and India. And this is quite comparable to Conrad's withholding of language from his rudimentary souls. Language is too grand for these chaps; let's give them dialects!

In all this business a lot of violence is inevitably done not only to the image of despised peoples but even to words, the very tools of possible redress. Look at the phrase 'native language' in the *Science Monitor* excerpt. Surely the only *native* language possible in London is Cockney English. But our writer means something else – something appropriate to the sounds Indians and Africans make!

Although the work of redressing which needs to be done may appear too daunting, I believe it is not one day too soon to begin. Conrad saw and condemned the evil of imperial exploitation but was strangely unaware of the racism on which it sharpened its iron tooth. But the victims of racist slander who for centuries have had to live with the inhumanity it makes them heir to have always known better than any casual visitor, even when he comes loaded with the gifts of a Conrad.

Notes

1. ALBERT J. GUERARD, introduction to *Heart of Darkness* (New York: New American Library, 1950), p. 9.

2 JOSEPH CONRAD, *Heart of Darkness and The Secret Sharer* (New York: New American Library, 1950), p. 66.

3. F. R. LEAVIS, *The Great Tradition* (London: Chatto and Windus, 1948; second impression 1950), p. 177.

4. CONRAD, *Heart of Darkness*, pp. 105–6.

5. Ibid., p. 106.

6. Ibid., p. 78.

7. Ibid.

An Image of Africa: Racism in Conrad's Heart of Darkness

8. Ibid., p. 148.

9. Ibid., p. 153.

10. Ibid., p. 82.

11. Ibid., p. 124.

12. Conrad, quoted in JONAH RASKIN, *The Mythology of Imperialism* (New York: Random House, 1971), p. 143.

13. CONRAD, *Heart of Darkness*, p. 142.

14. Conrad, quoted in BERNARD C. MEYER, MD, *Joseph Conrad: A Psychoanalytic Biography* (Princeton University Press, 1967), p. 30.

15. Ibid., p. 30.

16. FRANK WILLETT, *African Art* (New York: Praeger, 1971), pp. 35–6.

17. About the omission of the Great Wall of China I am indebted to 'The Journey of Marco Polo' as recreated by artist Michael Foreman, published by *Pegasus* magazine, New York, 1974.

18. *Christian Science Monitor*, Boston, 25 November 1974, p. 11.

7   A Man of the Last Hour*

CHRIS BONGIE

Chris Bongie's book is a study, not of colonialist literature in general, but of an important element within both colonialist ideology and critiques of colonialism, the 'literary and existential practice' (p. 125) called exoticism. Exoticism, as Bongie describes it, is 'intent on recovering "elsewhere" values "lost" with the modernization of European society' (Bongie, p. 5). His use of quotation marks here signals his sense of the strong element of fantasy in such an intention. Exoticism has an ambivalent relationship to colonialism, because the impulse to seek out a place beyond or before modernity can fuel the exploration and conquest that builds an empire, but can also prompt a lament over the loss of difference and separation which conquest and control produce. So Bongie distinguishes two forms of exoticism: 'imperialist exoticism', which assumes 'the superiority of civilization over savagery' and 'exoticizing exoticism' which privileges 'savagery' over 'civilization' and is dominated by desire for the Other (p. 134). His other key distinction is between an Old Imperialism of adventure, exploration and discovery and a New Imperialism which takes the form of a race to control and exploit lands already mapped out. Bongie sees Conrad as one of the late-nineteenth-century writers who, faced with the reality of the New Imperialism, could not sustain their belief (evident in Conrad's early work) in the reality of exotic places, peoples and values, supposedly untouched by mass communications and global capitalism.

Bongie's account of Conrad's response to this dilemma draws on the postmodernist theory of the Italian philosopher Gianni Vattimo, in particular his concept of 'weak thought'. This phrase denotes a way of living with and within the traces of categories which we can no longer strongly assert. So Conrad, according to Bongie, does not wholly abandon the 'empty project' (Bongie, p. 20) of the

---

* Reprinted from *Exotic Memories: Literature, Colonialism and the Fin de Siècle* (Stanford: Stanford University Press, 1991), pp. 4–5, 15, 17–18, 20, 22, 148–72.

A Man of the Last Hour

exotic: he abandons it as ideology but conserves it rhetorically, reinscribing himself in it while knowing it to be a dream. Bongie asserts his own belief in the ethical value of such a 'weak' or decadent response, avoiding as it does the imposition of new strong beliefs. Bongie's book exemplifies the willingness of postmodernist criticism to draw on a wide range of literary theory, including structuralism, new historicism, psychoanalysis, deconstruction, post-colonial theory and Foucauldian discourse analysis. He also links modernity and the loss of the exotic to a decline in the 'sovereign individual', thus partaking of literary theory's deconstruction and historicisation of subjectivity.

[. . .]

For the purposes of this study, exoticism is defined as a nineteenth-century literary and existential practice that posited another space, the space of an Other, outside or beyond the confines of a 'civiliza-tion' (and I will henceforth, as much as possible, spare the reader the quotation marks that ought to be placed around this and other such loaded words) that, by virtue of its *modernity*, was perceived by many writers as being incompatible with certain essential values – or, indeed, the realm of value itself. What modernity is in the process of obliterating 'here' might still prove a present possibility in this alternative geopolitical space: such is the primary credo of the exoticist project. The initial optimism of this project, however, gives way in the second half of the century to a deep pessimism stemming from the rapid spread of colonial and technological power. How can one recuperate 'elsewhere' what civilization is in the process of eliminating if this same process has already taken on global proportions?

[. . .]

As a project, exoticism necessarily presumes that, at some point in the future, what has been lost will be attained 'elsewhere,' in a realm of ad-venture that bypasses the sort of contemporary present that a symbolic form such as the bildungsroman,* by contrast, prepares us for. But if exoticism partakes of modernity and its promise, what the future promises – and here, of course, is the central irony of this particular project – is a recovery of the past and of all that a triumphant modernity has effaced. Indeed, the very emergence of this project is unthinkable without such a triumph. Because of this vicious circle that draws the future and the past together, the exoticist project is, from its very beginnings, short-circuited: it can never keep its promise. And therein, I will eventually suggest, lies the promise that it holds out to us.

[. . .]

Joseph Conrad

Whereas imperialist exoticism affirms the hegemony of modern civilization over less developed, savage territories, exoticizing exoticism privileges those very territories and their peoples, figuring them as a possible refuge from an overbearing modernity. What needs underlining here, however, is that they are both grounded in a common belief: namely, that there still exist places on this earth that are Other than those in which modernity has come to hold sway. The autonomy of alternative cultures and territories, their fundamental difference from what we might call 'the realm of the Same,' is the one requisite condition of exoticism: only given this difference can the individual hope to exercise – be it for imperialist or exoticizing ends – that heroic sovereignty denied him in post-revolutionary Europe.

[...]

The initial optimism of the exoticist project gives way, in the last decades of the century, to a pessimistic vision in which the exotic comes to seem less a space of possibility than one of impossibility. This critical transformation of the exotic imaginary, which we begin to see at work in writers like [Jules] Verne and [Pierre] Loti, is conterminous with the phase of acute geopolitical expansion initiated by the European nation-states during the last decades of the nineteenth century and commonly referred to as the New Imperialism. Most frequently associated with the Scramble for Africa, this unprecedented period of expansion marks the moment when nineteenth-century colonialism, and with it the immeasurable problematic of modernity, first asserts itself as a *global* phenomenon – one that inevitably, and irreparably, puts into question the Other's autonomy, absorbing this Other into the body of the Same and thereby effacing the very ground of exoticism.

What were the central features of this New Imperialism? Annexation of land was pursued with a new sense of urgency, and the State came to play a much more important role in organizing this geopolitical takeover: 'The Scramble involved the *rapid* acquisition of large peripheral areas to be ruled on a *formal* basis.'[1] By 1880 the age of exploration was largely over: the globe had been mapped to such an extent that little or no territory was beyond the pale of Euro-American knowledge and techniques of control and communication. This new awareness of the world's finitude in turn partially accounts for the intensity of what, in New Imperialist parlance, had become a territorial steeplechase. Those lands not yet under the control of a Great Power had nonetheless been identified and transformed into objects of a colonial desire.

[...]

A Man of the Last Hour

In responding to the finite world of the New Imperialism, Conrad will only say of himself, in his best fin de siècle French: 'Moi je regarde l'avenir du fond d'un passé très noir et je trouve que rien ne m'est permis hormis la fidélité à une cause absolument perdue, à une idée sans avenir' ('For myself, I look at the future from the depths of a very dark past, and I find I am allowed nothing but fidelity to an absolutely lost cause, to an idea without a future').[2] Where, I will ask, does this sort of negative thinking lead, and what, if anything, does this 'idea without a future' promise? Is this decision to inhabit the scene of decadence, to renounce the future for a present that is conditioned by an absolutely lost cause, merely a nihilistic gesture? I will eventually argue that something more than a sterile nostalgia is at stake in this attachment to a cause that has once and for all been lost.
[...]
In the age of the New Imperialism, the exotic necessarily becomes, for those who persist in search of it, the sign of an aporia – of a constitutional absence at the heart of what had been projected as a possible alternative to modernity. All the writers studied here give voice to this sign (be it inadvertently or strategically); they register the exotic as a space of absence, a dream already given over to the past. This is one half of the decadentist intuition that provides so much of fin de siècle writing with its largely unheard resonance; that such dreams can be followed up on, and traced back, albeit posthumously, is the second half of this intuition, one whose literary and political consequences I will be emphasizing.
[...]
Unwilling, in his confrontation with modernity and mass society, to remain in the tragic state of tension that characterizes the great works of his middle period, late Conrad will come to uphold the integrity of values such as 'individuality' and 'genius' that a work like *Heart of Darkness* had already effectively hollowed out. This unproblematical return to his former beliefs is evident, for instance, in the brief preface that Conrad wrote in 1922 for a book of travels by his friend Richard Curle. Collected in his *Last Essays* (pp. 84–92), this seldom-mentioned piece is worth looking at here since it is his most concentrated and theoretical account of what it means to write about exotic locales in an age when 'our very curiosities have changed, growing more subtle amongst the vanishing mysteries of the earth.'

In his reading of Curle's *Into the East*, Conrad sketches a deeply pessimistic analysis of the 'spirit of modern travel' that he feels the book embodies. Nowadays, he notes, 'many people encompass the

127

Joseph Conrad

globe'; they go rushing through the world with blank notebooks and even blanker minds, incapable of realizing what such 'infinitely curious and profoundly inspired men' as Hugh Clapperton and Mungo Park experienced in their journeys through darkest Africa (p. 89).[3] The time for voyages, and books, like those of Marco Polo 'is past': little or nothing remains to be done in the way of traveling 'on this earth girt about with cables, with an atmosphere made restless by the waves of ether, lighted by that sun of the twentieth century under which there is nothing new left now, and but very little of what may still be called obscure' (p. 88).

Conrad insistently assures his reader that the days of 'heroic travel' are gone, 'unless, of course, in the newspaper sense, in which heroism like everything else in the world becomes as common if not as nourishing as our daily bread.' Formerly exotic settings have long since been despoiled of 'their old black soul of mystery'; soon they 'will be bristling with police posts, colleges, tramway poles.' Curle would seem to be perfectly suited to the task of chronicling this 'marvellously piebald' world: 'He is very modern, for he is fashioned by the conditions of an explored earth in which the latitudes and longitudes having been recorded once for all have become things of no importance, in the sense that they can no longer appeal to the spirit of adventure, inflame no imagination, lead no one up to the very gates of mortal danger' (p. 90). Appealing to the 'spirit of adventure,' inflaming the imagination, leading one's reader up to 'the very gates of mortal danger': such are the possibilities still open to those writers not yet fashioned by 'the conditions of an explored earth.'

But where, we might well ask, does the author of these lines stand in relation to this ongoing process of decline? Conrad's slightly condescending tone toward the younger Curle would certainly lead us to believe that he considers himself to be something rather less than 'very modern.' No doubt. And yet I would suggest that this preface gains its full resonance only if we consider this portrait of Curle as first and foremost a piece of displaced autobiography. Shunted off onto the generation of writers that follows in his tracks is a problem that, from the beginning, fashions Conrad's own work as a writer: the problem of a truly global modernity. Everywhere and in everything, this modernity cancels out whatever might once have differed from it, reducing both the earth and those who inhabit it to a single common denominator. As David Simpson has argued, convincingly to my mind, Conrad writes from within an undifferentiated world: 'Conrad has reduced all the potentially dialectical elements in the antitheses of primitive and civilized societies, whereby each

A Man of the Last Hour

might function as an image of what the other is not, to a state of monotonous, undifferentiated oneness. . . . The fetishized world of the colonial nations has imposed itself upon the far-flung corners of the earth, creating a commerce in the images of its own alienation.'[4] Within the global space of this 'monotonous, undifferentiated oneness,' goods take the form of commodities, fetishized, mechanically reproduceable, and we ourselves come to seem no more than the interchangeable parts of a mass society whose fate is inseparable from the impersonalized machinations of the bureaucratic State.

In Conrad, then, the dialectical encounter between primitive and civilized worlds, between an outside and an inside, that was at the heart of nineteenth-century exoticism is determinedly absent. The New Imperialist crisis that I have been chronicling in this book is Conrad's point of departure as a writer, and for this very reason, as Simpson goes on to say, he 'does not tend to show us the genesis of this process of [colonial] exportation; to do so would be to introduce the energetic antithesis of innocence and corruption which he clearly means to avoid.' To write from within an undifferentiated world means forgoing the sort of 'energetic' ideological oppositions that were at the heart of the exoticist project. The difference between innocence and corruption, or between savagery and civilization, is from this perspective no difference at all; it is entirely unreal.

But Simpson's claim needs to be nuanced in at least two ways, both of which I hope to expand upon in this chapter through a discussion of Conrad's evolution as a writer from 1895 to 1900. First, there are indeed many signs of such 'energetic antitheses' in his first novels, although Conrad is unable to join them into a coherent whole. The failure of his early works to achieve this heroic coherence is a symptom of that undifferentiated perspective which is already his, from the time he first takes pen to paper, but with which he will only come to grips in *Heart of Darkness* and *Lord Jim*. In these works, the matter of guilt and innocence is no longer at issue; it can never again be a real issue for one who takes a worldwide modernity as his point of departure. But, and here is the second (and all-important) nuance that must be attached to Simpson's claim, the passage from exotic difference to colonial indifferentiation is nonetheless not forgotten in these more properly Conradian works. The 'energetic antitheses' of exoticism continue to haunt the world of Conrad's novels, in spite of his by-now complete awareness of their inadequacy to the present. Conrad de-energizes these oppositions, hollowing them out and yet nonetheless conserving them in this weakened form; they inhabit the text as absence, as what has been canceled out of an indifferent world girt round by

Joseph Conrad

wires and enlightened by the sun of disenchantment. The creation
of this absence will occupy us in the following pages: the tragic
absence of that 'hour before last' without which, I have been
suggesting, the 'last hour' of our modernity cannot (begin to)
be thought.

The crowds of the anxious earth: (rewriting) the individual in decline, 1895–1900

'What's good for it?' He lifted up a long forefinger. 'There is only
one remedy! One thing alone can us from being ourselves cure!'
The finger came down on the desk with a smart rap. The case
which he had made to look so simple before became if possible
still simpler – and altogether hopeless. There was a pause. 'Yes,'
said I, 'strictly speaking, the question is not how to get cured, but
how to live.'

(J. Conrad, *Lord Jim*)

Conrad's early novels, which we, along with the vast majority
of Conradians, may think of as the products of his 'artistic
immaturity,'[5] subscribe – albeit uneasily – to the traditional vision
that generated nineteenth-century exoticism. Gauguin's 'native of
old' is assuredly present in *Almayer's Folly* (1895) and *Outcast of
the Islands* (1896): indigenous females, mysterious and potentially
salvational objects of desire; sovereign figures who conjure up the
image of what Conrad would much later refer to (in the preface for
Into the East) as those 'real chieftain[s] in the books of a hundred
years ago.' After briefly examining these novels, I will go on to
show, paying special attention to his shifting representation of
individuals and crowds, how this already vacillating belief in the
exotic collapses in the *Tales of Unrest* (1898) that follow upon his
first two novels. Conrad's attempts at finding a discursive resolution
to this situation lead him, on the one hand, to the historicist vision
of 'solidarity' that shapes the *Nigger of the 'Narcissus'* (1897) and, on
the other, to the memorialistic strategy that he adopts in *Heart of
Darkness* (1899) and, most notably, in *Lord Jim* (1900). The story of
Conrad's evolution as an exotic writer does not, obviously, end
with the two Marlow novels, but the literary and political matrix
of subsequent works like *Nostromo* (1904), *The Secret Agent* (1907),
or *Victory* (1915) ought, I believe, to be traced back to the tragic
insight that he develops there. In different, though intimately

A Man of the Last Hour

related ways, they testify to the same cultural malaise that the author of *Lord Jim* had diagnosed as incurable – a diagnosis that seems to leave Conrad with no room to operate but which in fact proves the precondition of his essentially posthumous enterprise.

Gareth Jenkins has argued that in Conrad's early novels 'natives are natives – colourful, exotic, essentially "different" – and European life and language, which encapsulate and place this exoticism, are assumed to be superior.'[6] Jenkins is, I think, at least partially correct. The omniscient narrator of Conrad's first novel, *Almayer's Folly*, is indeed committed to the representation of 'savagery' in all its difference from the world of 'civilization' – an autonomy assured by, among other things, the fact that colonialism in the Malayan peninsula is as yet a relatively limited phenomenon (Dutch control over the state of Sambir is said to be only 'nominal'; the interior of 'unknown Borneo' is consistently invoked as one of the remaining dark places of the earth). But the assumed 'superiority' of European life and language is quite another matter. If it is fair to say that the Conradian narrator would like to valorize this civilization, it is nonetheless obvious, as any reader of *Almayer's Folly* (and *An Outcast of the Islands*) knows, that he more often than not ends up exposing it – or at least a particular version of it – to the light of a corrosive irony. This irony is in great part defused, however, by the narrator's positive emphasis on savagery: paradoxically, the unsullied existence of savagery ensures the continued possibility of that truly 'superior' civilization in which the narrator still places, if only with the greatest of difficulty, his Old Imperialist faith.

What must be avoided at all costs in the manichean world of Conrad's Malayan novels is an indifferent mingling of these two distinct spheres. It is just such a confusion that initially characterizes the half-caste Nina Almayer: brought up in the colonial world of Singapore and then 'thrown back again into the hopeless quagmire of barbarism,' she had, we are told, 'lost the power to discriminate.' The two worlds appear all too similar to her:

> Whether they plotted for their own ends under the protection of laws and according to the rules of Christian conduct, or whether they sought the gratification of their desires with the savage cunning and the unrestrained fierceness of natures as innocent of culture as their own immense and gloomy forests, Nina saw only the same manifestations of love and hate and of sordid greed chasing the uncertain dollar in all its multifarious and vanishing shapes.

(p. 43)

131

Joseph Conrad

David Simpson cites this passage as evidence of the lack of differentiation that the 'configured structure of imaginative commerce' has exported to the far-flung reaches of the globe.[7] As I have argued, this 'lack of differentiation' will soon come to dominate Conrad's experience of the exotic; here, though, the case is not quite so desperate. If at this early point in the novel Nina has indeed lost the power to differentiate savagery and civilization, the same cannot be said of the narrator: that Europeans and Malayans pursue many similar ends merely proves that, as he says elsewhere, 'there are some situations where the barbarian and the, so-called, civilized man meet upon the same ground' (p. 67). The original division that is constitutive of exoticism still holds true, even if one of its terms, the 'so-called civilized,' has been covered over with the shroud of irony and rendered, for the moment, inoperable.

The 'savage cunning' of Nina's Malay kinsmen is no illusion: it is a quality that makes a difference, as Nina herself comes to see. Their 'savage and uncompromising sincerity of purpose' will appear preferable to the 'virtuous pretences of such white people as she had had the misfortune to come in contact with' (p. 43). Given the opportunity, the half-caste chooses the side of her 'savage' mother over that of 'a feeble and traditionless father,' Almayer. That Nina is still capable of making such a choice is the novel's exotic presupposition – one effectuated by the arrival on the scene of a heroic native male, 'the ideal Malay chief of her mother's tradition' (p. 64). A quintessentially romantic figure, whose father, significantly enough, is the *independent* Rajah of Bali, Dain Maroola wins Nina over with 'the rude eloquence of a savage nature giving itself up without restraint to an overmastering passion' (p. 69). At the end of the novel, having escaped Sambir, the Dutch, and the enraged but powerless Almayer, the two will produce an heir for the Rajah – a son whose birth signals an extension of the Other's line into the indefinite future.

The difference that separates the world of the Malay from that of the European becomes especially clear if we consider one of the novel's central thematic motifs: vision. In *Almayer's Folly* Conrad opposes Dain's way of seeing to Almayer's in a manner that might well be characterized as Wordsworthian. In Book Twelve of *The Prelude*, Wordsworth speaks of a time when he was under the 'absolute dominion' of 'the bodily eye, in every stage of life / The most despotic of our senses.'[8] It is this 'despotism' that characterizes Dain's exotic world: concerning his initial encounter with Nina we are told, for instance, that 'from the very first moment when his eyes beheld this – to him – perfection of loveliness he felt in his inmost heart the conviction that she would be his; he felt the subtle

132

A Man of the Last Hour

breath of mutual understanding passing between their two savage natures' (p. 63). Almayer's vision, on the other hand, is a badly flawed version of what Wordsworth (in 'I Wandered Lonely as a Cloud,' among other places) called the 'inward eye' – that internalized vision by which the Wordsworthian subject is rescued from and redeems the power of the first, despotic eye. Rather than enlightening the exotic realm of the senses, however, Almayer merely projects upon it his own murky desire for material possessions. Entirely given over to 'the commercial imagination,' he can envision nothing more 'in his mind's eye' than 'the rich prize in his grasp' (p. 65); an adventurer like Lingard can only become 'a hero in Almayer's eyes' because of 'the boldness and enormous profits of his ventures' (p. 8).

Because of the failure of Almayer's vision, Conrad cannot, in a Wordsworthian manner, pursue a dialectical reconciliation of this opposition in favor of the 'inward eye' of civilization. Rather, he must preserve the integrity of Dain's savage vision until such time as the two ways of seeing can effectively be brought together. In point of fact, though, one character in the novel is already capable of seeing with both an inward and a bodily eye: the half-caste Nina, whose face is early on described as being 'turned towards the outer darkness, through which her dreamy eyes seemed to see some entrancing picture' (p. 16). But the reconciliation of inside and outside that Nina thus figures is not one Conrad can embrace, because her double vision is for him only another symptom of a hybrid condition that can no longer see any real difference between the worlds of savagery and civilization. It is a product of her *métissage*,* and as such a sign of the disappearance of the truly exotic – a sign that must, ultimately, be erased if the original project of exoticism is to remain possible.

In order for the story to reach its exotic conclusion, Nina must forget the ambivalent, indifferentiating vision to which she is at first subject. She must give herself entirely over to the 'outer darkness.' In this respect, it is no doubt significant that Conrad transformed the original model for Almayer, Olmeijer, from a half-caste into a man of pure European stock; as Ian Watt points out, 'this has the effect of dramatising the conflict in Nina's loyalties between her European father and her Malayan mother.'[9] Figuring Nina's *métissage* as primary, rather than secondary, facilitates what for Conrad is the necessary task of erasing the (modern) condition of hybridity that she embodies; by virtue of her genetic proximity to the purely exotic, she can the more easily be thought of as effecting the dramatic return to savagery that her status as a half-caste would seem to have precluded.

133

Joseph Conrad

Despite the air of exotic primitivism in *Almayer's Folly*, which the end of the novel would appear to consecrate, Conrad's sympathies are, ultimately, on the side of what I have termed imperialist exoticism, which assumes, as Jenkins puts it, the superiority of civilization over savagery and affirms the desirability of drawing the bodily eye up into the realm of mind. But, as the narrator's frequent outbursts of irony bear witness, this distinction was becoming increasingly difficult for Conrad to maintain. Imperialist exoticism posits a form of contact between the worlds of Same and Other that does not end with the victory of Flaubertian *bêtise** and the effacement of cultural difference in the name of a gregarious colonial bureaucracy; it depends upon the idea of a heroic individual capable of effecting the genial reconciliation of savagery and civilization that an older paternal figure like Tom Lingard is said to have achieved. To have attempted directly to represent this positive experience would have led Conrad to question the viability of his Old Imperialist beliefs in the age of the New Imperialism – and this, of course, will be the rock upon which his novel about Lingard, 'The Rescuer' (begun in 1896 and abandoned three years later), runs aground. Instead, Conrad chooses to sidestep the issue and engage in a narrative that derives most of its strength from the exoticizing mode of exoticism. In privileging savagery at the expense of a civilization about which he was becoming increasingly cynical, Conrad succeeds, at least provisionally, in securing a field of action where a truly imperial subject might still, at some point in the future, exercise the heroic sovereignty expected of him.

Because he can hold out this possibility of a properly imperialist vision, Conrad is able to present Almayer's own flawed way of seeing as an anomaly: rather than being typical of a new colonial state of affairs, Almayer's 'commercial imagination' is a quirk. The half-finished building that he has constructed in anticipation of the British Borneo Company's takeover of that part of the island – in anticipation, that is, of the coming of the New Imperialism to Sambir – proves no more than a folly in an (Old Imperialist) world where colonialism has its limits. If, at the end of the novel, this building becomes Almayer's dwelling place, it is his alone – a madhouse that is more an emblem of his own decadence than a sign of the imminent, and eminently reprehensible, colonial ascendancy his murky vision anticipates. Conrad must sacrifice Almayer, mark him off as a pathological case, an anti-hero, if he is to maintain the possibility of a heroic successor to the imperialist tradition that an adventurer like Lingard embodies. And yet no worthy successor to Lingard will emerge in Conrad's next novel,

A Man of the Last Hour

An Outcast of the Islands – a fact that no doubt strengthened the author's sense that his original exoticist project was misguided.

Looking back on the *Outcast* in his 'Author's Note' (1919) to the novel, Conrad remarks that 'it brought me the qualification of "exotic writer"': 'For the life of me I don't see that there is the slightest exotic spirit in the conception or style of that novel. It is certainly the most *tropical* of my eastern tales' (p. xiii). In fact, tropical scenery is about all that is left of an 'exotic spirit' that can barely find a place in the novel: the world of savagery has been reduced to a state of nature, more or less emptied of its cultural content. Exotic nature – brooding, menacing, sublime – survives, in the midst of a narrative that even more so than *Almayer's Folly* fails to live up to its exoticist presuppositions.

Since the problems the *Outcast* raises and attempts to deflect are the same as those that troubled Conrad's first effort, we need not linger over it here. Worth pointing out, though, is the fact that its protagonist, Willems, assumes a role diametrically opposite to that of Almayer. Whereas the latter, his 'inward eye' corrupted by visions of lucre, obviously fails to match the imperatives of a properly imperialist exoticism, Willems, in his tortured attachment to and repulsion from the 'primitive woman' Aïssa, is a man who cannot live up to those of exoticizing exoticism; he cannot abandon his own inwardness and take up residence in the despotic realm of the senses. Although he briefly glimpses the outside world into which Dain and Nina escaped, Willems proves incapable of following through on his transgressive vision, mostly because of his 'clear conviction of the impossibility for him to live with her people' (p. 152). Willems's self-deluding racism is the pathological flaw that disables him as the subject of an exoticizing exoticism; it prevents him from giving himself over to the Other, despite his desire for it in the person of Aïssa.

Presumably, a better man than Willems would have succeeded in detaching himself from his prejudices, or not have held them in the first place: this is one conclusion that the reader can draw from Conrad's often desultory account of the outcast's downfall. But the narrator lays down the foundation for a different interpretation, one based upon what I will be terming a *historicist* vision that willfully situates the exotic in the past, cutting it off from the degradation of the present. This historicist vision figures the past as free from the malaise that governs a present in which mediocrities like Almayer or Willems are typical rather than anomalous. With the building of the Suez Canal, we are told early on in the novel, the mystery of the sea was destroyed: 'Like all mysteries, it lived only in the hearts

Joseph Conrad

of its worshippers. The hearts changed; the men changed. The once loving and devoted servants went out armed with fire and iron, and conquering the fear of their own hearts became a calculating crowd of cold and exacting masters' (pp. 12–13). There is no trace of this historicism in *Almayer's Folly*, and very little in *An Outcast of the Islands*: its presence, though, signals the possibility of the impossibility of continuing on as if a recourse to the exotic were still a present option in an age when hearts had changed and men had become part of a 'calculating crowd.' In the following examination of his *Tales of Unrest* and *The Nigger of the 'Narcissus,'* I will take a closer look at the dissolution of the exotic in Conrad's work and the simpleminded historicism – as simpleminded, in its own way, as Willems's racism, although perhaps more agreeable to the modern ear – with which he at first tried to combat this collapse. That Conrad found a way of putting this vision to a more complex, and politically more interesting, use in his 'elegiac romances' *Heart of Darkness* and *Lord Jim* is the argument of this chapter's concluding section.[10]

The Malayan peninsula of his youth, Conrad asserts in his late essay 'Geography and Some Explorers,' made up part of 'the old Pacific mystery, a region which even in my time remained very imperfectly charted and still remote from the knowledge of men' (p. 18). His first novels, although set in the past, remain committed to extending this 'time' into our own day and age; the exotic 'mystery' they invoke apparently remains unsolved. Almayer's folly and Nina's *métissage*, to be sure, point to a very different situation, but their fallen world is one that can still be wished, and written, away through a recourse to a form of narrative closure similar to that we find in a writer like Captain Marryat – whose novels, as Conrad himself noted in the 1898 essay 'Tales of the Sea,' invariably end in inheritance and marriage. The inadequacy of this resolution, which is already pretty well absent from the *Outcast*, soon impresses itself upon Conrad: his 'time,' and the uncharted world it once contained, has been displaced by a modernity that has no time for such mysteries. What he once lived can now only be remembered; perhaps, indeed, it was never anything more than the memory that it has become. Between 1896 and 1899, Conrad begins to probe both this hiatus that separates a desired but no longer possible exotic past from a repugnant but unavoidable colonial present and the nature of that bridge which his memory (de)constructs between them.

As Frederick Karl has noted, during the period immediately following the publication of *Outcast of the Islands* in 1896, Conrad

136

A Man of the Last Hour

was 'caught at the conjunction of several literary styles':[11] he would experiment with at least three styles, each of which entailed a different approach to the figure of the individual, whose decline Conrad could no longer overlook. In 'The Rescuer,' he attempted to pursue the exotic vein of the early novels; the notorious difficulties he had in finishing this manuscript (abandoned in 1899, it would get taken up again some fifteen years later and eventually be published as *The Rescue* in 1920) derive in great part from his wish to portray Tom Lingard, a 'simple, masterful, imaginative adventurer,'[12] as a viable alternative to the inadequate proto-colonial subjects who had taken center stage in his first two novels. 'The Return,' on the other hand, is characterized by an archly cosmopolitan prose that attempts to match its, for Conrad, unusual subject matter; his account of Alvan Hervey's marital problems hesitantly opens up onto the world-weary perspective of fin de siècle decadentism. In seemingly direct contrast to this story, *The Nigger of the 'Narcissus'* puts into play, as Karl says, 'a more "natural" style, though without the irony that would become characteristic of his middle career' (p. 401). The lack of irony signals the *Nigger* as Conrad's most positive fictional portrayal of the individual, whose modern decline, it is insinuated, can be arrested through an allegiance to and dependence upon a traditional community, the ship's crew; but the often-remarked 'polyphonies' in this text deprive it of the ideological certitude that Conrad there aspires after.[13] The problem of the individual will, he discovers, require a quite different sort of (lack of) resolution.

Conrad was certainly aware of this shift in his work after the first two novels. In his 'Author's Note' (1919) to the *Tales of Unrest*, he speaks of the brief story 'The Lagoon' as marking 'in a manner of speaking, the end of my first phase, the Malayan phase with its special subject and its verbal suggestions.' For the moment, the exotic alternative disappears from Conrad's horizon – to be replaced by the explicitly colonial scene of 'An Outpost of Progress,' the refined atmosphere of 'The Return,' and the shipboard setting of the *Nigger*. The exotic disappears; or, rather, it makes one last appearance, in a register of loss that anticipates its treatment in *Heart of Darkness* and *Lord Jim*. If, Conrad remarks, 'anybody can see that between the last paragraph of An Outcast and the first of The Lagoon there has been no change of pen, figuratively speaking' (p. v), it is equally obvious that something quite different is at stake in 'Karain: A Memory': 'I had not gone back to the Archipelago, I had only turned for another look at it' (p. vii). The Malayan peninsula can no longer be returned to; it can be apprehended only across a distance that is not spatial but temporal – recorded by a look that, in its

Joseph Conrad

secondariness (*another* look), must inevitably betray what was seen before. The 'memory' of the man who narrates this story cannot reach its object, the exotic world of the native prince Karain. The space marked in the story's title by a colon, while it joins their two worlds together, also separates them definitively.

Karain, in reality no more than 'a petty chief of a conveniently isolated corner of Mindanao,' once offered the story's narrator the comprehensive vision of cultural alternatives that nineteenth-century exoticism thrived on. He stands for an entire way of life distinct from 'ours': 'He seemed too effective, too necessary there, too much of an essential condition for the existence of his land and his people, to be destroyed by anything short of an earthquake. He summed up his race, his country, the elemental force of ardent life, of tropical nature. He had its luxuriant strength, its fascination; and like it, he carried the seed of peril within' (p. 7). With its anaphoral* insistence, this passage captures the sort of sovereign vision, or vision of a sovereign, that a writer like Loti craved. Filling the stage 'with barbarous dignity' (p. 8), Karain embodies his culture and represents his people – 'that crowd, brilliant, festive, and martial' who help make up the 'gorgeous spectacle' of exoticism to which the narrator and his fellow adventurers bear witness (pp. 4, 7). 'An adventurer of the sea, an outcast, a ruler,' Karain retains the power 'to awaken an absurd expectation of something heroic going to take place' (pp. 8, 6).

What does take place, of course, is something rather less heroic than might have been expected; Karain produces not deeds but words – a story within a story, a memory within a memory. He tells his shipboard audience about the life-sapping spell he finds himself under: he has come to be haunted by the unrestful shade of a dead friend whom he once betrayed. The tale at an end, one of his English listeners, Hollis, breaks the spell, returning Karain to his former self by giving him a 'charm' made out of a Jubilee sixpence bearing 'the image of the Great Queen' (p. 49). That this episode reveals (on the part, one suspects, of both Hollis *and* Conrad) a condescending attitude toward native superstition is an obvious and banal point; more interesting is the fact that the renewal of Karain's exotic power coincides with his (unwitting) inclusion in the world of money/information – a world in which the figure of the sovereign is no more than an image subordinated to the purposes of commerce. It is at precisely this moment of ambiguous renewal that the narrator loses track of Karain; what becomes of him is left up in the air (although we are led to believe that quite possibly he is 'making it hot for the caballeros' who rule the Eastern Archipelago). But the capacity for action that has here been given back to Karain

138

A Man of the Last Hour

prepares the ground for a similarly counterfeit sovereignty that, as we will see, Conrad's *Lord Jim* explores in depth. Although his fatal leap from the *Patna* has forever put in doubt 'the sovereign power enthroned in a fixed standard of conduct' (p. 50), Jim nonetheless goes on to reassert that power in the tropical solitude of Patusan.[14]

This, however, is to anticipate matters. It is not so much Karain's tale, and its problematical resolution, that need concern us here as the last pages of the story, where the narrator's evocation of an exotic past is explicitly situated in the degraded present of writing ('now'). Some years after parting company with Karain, the narrator meets one of his fellow adventurers, Jackson, in the Strand: 'His head was high above the crowd . . . he had just come home – had landed that very day! Our meeting caused an eddy in the current of humanity. Hurried people would run against us, then walk round us, and turn back to look at that giant' (p. 53). Jackson stands out from the urban crowd by virtue of his recent contact with a world outside it. He appeals to the narrator, whose exotic tale about Karain will be inspired by this meeting with Jackson, in the same way that Lingard appealed to the omniscient narrator of *Outcast of the Islands*: 'The breath of his words, of the very words he spoke, fanned the spark of divine folly in his breast, the spark that made him – the hard-headed, heavy-handed adventurer – stand out from the crowd, from the sordid, from the joyous, unscrupulous, and noisy crowd of men that were so much like himself' (p. 273). Lingard, though, is a man among men: the 'crowd' in which he plays a significant part is, if unscrupulous and sordid, also joyous, and compatible with his heroic individualism. The narrator of 'Karain,' by contrast, finds himself in a very different sort of crowd, one that (as the last lines of the story make clear) puts into question the present reality of his and Jackson's shared experience of the past.

In this anonymous 'current of humanity,' from which only the gigantic Jackson still stands out, or seems to, we have one of the first appearances in Conrad of what will become perhaps his preferred metonym for the global indifferentiation of modernity: the crowd, a 'bad' crowd entirely lacking in any of the positive qualities that characterized other, traditional, group formations of men (Lingard's joyous and unscrupulous crowd of adventurers; Karain's brilliant, festive, and exotic crowd). For Conrad, as he makes clear in 'An Outpost of Progress' (written after *Outcast of the Islands* and before 'The Lagoon'), the herd mentality of this modern, essentially urban crowd is identical to that governing the new colonial subject.

With its biting and omniscient narratorial voice, a voice not yet marked by the nostalgia pervading *Heart of Darkness*, 'An Outpost of Progress' represents Conrad's most direct literary attack against

Joseph Conrad

the New Imperialism and the impoverished minds that serve it. The colonial traders Kayerts and Carlier, both 'incapable of independent thought,' are exemplary of the individual's rapid decline in an age of mass society:

> They were two perfectly insignificant and incapable individuals, whose existence is only rendered possible through the high organization of civilized crowds. Few men realize that their life, the very essence of their character, their capabilities and their audacities, are only the expression of their belief in the safety of their surroundings. The courage, the composure, the confidence; the emotions and principles; every great and every insignificant thought belongs not to the individual but to the crowd: to the crowd that believes blindly in the irresistible force of its institutions and of its morals, in the power of its police and of its opinion. But the contact with pure unmitigated savagery, with primitive nature and primitive man, brings sudden and profound trouble into the heart.[15]

(p. 89)

Conrad puts forward a double thesis in this passage. First, the 'civilized' individual is not an independent being but, rather, the epiphenomenon* of an obtuse collectivity. Conrad's thinking here shows a marked resemblance to that of Gustave Le Bon, who a few years before, in his study *The Crowd* (1895), had loudly proclaimed the new predominance of *la voix des foules*: 'The destinies of nations are elaborated at present in the heart of the masses, and no longer in the councils of princes'.[15]

If this collective voice had drowned out every other, then our situation would indeed be dismal. Fortunately, and here is where Conrad's second thesis comes in, this is not (at least not yet) the case. Mass society has an outside: 'pure unmitigated savagery' exists and is capable of disaggregating the herd, bringing 'sudden and profound trouble' into its heart; indeed, this outside is, presumably, the point from which Conrad-as-narrator is able to launch his direct critique of mass society. But should this 'savagery' disappear (and the presence of Makola, the 'civilized nigger,' signals this as an imminent possibility), then all likelihood of that absolutely necessary contact with a troubling outside would cease. In such a closed and enclosing society, there would be no more openings for a truly individual action – or even, as in the case of Kayerts and Carlier, reaction.

This is the dramatic sense of closure that comes to dominate much of fin de siècle literature, and to which Conrad too will, in his own way, accede. The problem these writers confronted was that of

A Man of the Last Hour

preserving a degree of autonomy for the individual in a world from which the possibility of such autonomy seemed absent. In *A rebours*, for instance, Huysmans has his hero, des Esseintes, try living out Baudelaire's idea of the artist – solitary, childless, but nonetheless 'his king, his priest, and his God' – in an out-of-the-way place to the south of Paris, where 'the uproar of foul crowds' ('le brouhaha des immondes foules') has not penetrated.[16] And yet this convalescent retreat from mass society results in nothing more than an *immobilité* that, ultimately, provides neither cure nor satisfaction. Far from resolving the problem of decadence and the individual's looming disintegration 'in the century's vile and servile throng' ('dans la turpide et servile cohue du siècle'; p. 335), des Esseintes's retreat merely ends up confirming the (impossible) necessity of *mouvement* – as we see in the ending, with its dilation back out into the fallen world of the metropolis.

Conrad, clearly, does not valorize this futile retreat into the self, and yet his work is in large part determined by the same sense of closure that so predominates in an author like Huysmans. The dilemma is clear: if his second thesis proves untenable, then all that remains for him is to chronicle, à la Flaubert, the *bêtise* of a 'civilized' world – the sort of world introduced in his most ostensibly fin de siècle piece of writing, 'The Return.' Yet it is precisely in the midst of this *bêtise*, where the inadequacy of the 'civilized' individual becomes most apparent, that we catch a glimpse of another approach to the dilemma – one that matches the problematical turn to memory we witnessed in 'Karain' and that draws out the essentially *hypocritical* nature of this turn.

Alvan Hervey, self-righteously appalled by his wife's aborted attempt at leaving him and their unsatisfactory but socially respectable marriage, engages her in a long, and imminently shallow, argument meant to sway her from the paths of scandal. Arguing for the status quo, he has occasion at one point to recall their past:

'Now, a scandal amongst people of our position is disastrous for the morality – a fatal influence – don't you see – upon the general tone of the class – very important – the most important, I verily believe, in – in the community. I feel this – profoundly. This is the broad view. In time you'll give me . . . when you become again the woman I loved – and trusted . . .'
He stopped short, as though unexpectedly suffocated, then in a completely changed voice said, 'For I did love and trust you' – and again was silent for a moment. She put her handkerchief to her eyes.

(p. 164; ellipses in original)

Joseph Conrad

This change of voice, to my mind, is the central event of the story. Here, memory has reworked the past (whether or not Hervey actually did at some point love and trust his wife is beside the point) and intruded upon the atrocious insincerity of the present. This is not to say that the change marks a return to sincerity, but merely that it registers another moment that is both different from the first, ongoing moment of hypocrisy and yet inseparable from it. Hervey's change of voice is, thus, doubly hypocritical: his initial hypocrisy is not displaced but merely supplemented. Although it disturbs the present, this memory-induced change of voice remains complicitous with the degraded strategies of persuasion that it at once reveals and participates in. Hervey's change of voice, in other words, anticipates the Conradian problem of the lie in which, as Marlow says in *Heart of Darkness*, resides 'a taint of death, a flavour of mortality' (p. 82). For Conrad it is this mortal hypocrisy that must be grasped if anything is to come out of the sense of 'one's own mediocrity and the world's corruption and degradation' that, as Edward Said has rightly argued, characterizes the vast bulk of late-nineteenth-century British and Continental literature.[17]

'Pure uncomplicated savagery' can never(more) be disengaged from the colonial context that disables it as a present reality. If savagery and the sovereign individual resurface in Conrad, they will do so only in such a way that their hollowness remains in evidence. Marlow, for instance, is attracted to what he calls the 'original' Kurtz, and his first, proleptic* vision of the man seems to conform to his idea of Kurtz as an exemplary individual, removed from the degradations of the Central Station: 'As to me, I seemed to see Kurtz for the first time. It was a distinct glimpse: the dugout, four paddling savages, and the lone white man turning his back suddenly on the headquarters, on relief, on thoughts of home' (p. 90). This original exotic vision of Kurtz cannot, however, be realized: what Marlow eventually finds at the Inner Station is, as we have seen, the 'atrocious phantom' of a sovereign individual and indigenous peoples who offer not the relief of 'pure, uncomplicated savagery' (p. 132) but the subtle horror of a 'crowd of savages' (p. 134). In the heart of difference rises up the gregarious figure of the Same – a 'wild mob' (p. 146) that resembles what it is supposed to be most different from. With this resemblance Marlow's superimposition of an untimely exotic vision onto the colonial scene becomes glaringly visible; the figure of indifferentiation haunts every invocation of difference. This disclosure of Marlow's hypocrisy is the revelation of Conrad's own, and it is in the giving voice, a changed voice, to this duplicitous vision that his distinction as a writer, and his potential as a thinker of our modernity, resides.

142

A Man of the Last Hour

What Conrad discovers in writing the *Tales of Unrest*, then, is that any invocation of the difference that was originally to have constituted the exotic can, from the perspective of one who is firmly situated within the confines of mass society, be grounded only in a revocation of that difference. The 'murmuring stir' of Karain's 'ornamented and barbarous crowd' (p. 4), which seemed at the beginning to hold out the promise of real difference, proves in the end – an end that precedes the beginning of the story, an end that is the precondition of its telling – no more than a literary (re)construction. Amid the 'sombre and ceaseless stir' of the urban crowd in which the narrator of 'Karain' finds himself immersed (p. 54), the (re)constructed nature of the exotic, and of the individual who was to have realized himself by crossing over into it, becomes apparent. Their reality is retroactively erased in the face of a global indifferentiation that forms, as Simpson has argued, the point of departure for much, if not all, of Conrad's writing. And yet this moment of memorialization by which Conrad returns to the scene of cultural difference troubles, although it cannot displace, the indifferent world in which he must write.

This initial erasure and subsequent re-vision of the past will generate the 'elegiac romances.' Characteristic of what I have termed Conrad's historicism, by contrast, is a view of the past as that which has been, alas, eclipsed but whose objective reality is not thereby put into question. It is this historicist faith that engages Conrad in *The Nigger of the 'Narcissus'*; this work appeals to historical (temporal) difference in the same unproblematical way that the first novels invoke geographical (spatial) difference.

I have already pointed out a preliminary instance in *Outcast of the Islands* of Conrad's historicism: there, although the mystery of the sea was said to be a thing of the past in our own cold and calculating age, we were nonetheless led to believe that it could be remembered as it was. Present degradation does not, by this account, affect past glory: Conrad's historicist strategy valorizes the past – a past that has been effectively disengaged from the present in all its corruption. This valorization serves a tacitly dialectical purpose. The past becomes the preserve of positive values that, at some point in the future, we may hope to recover. As Giuseppe Sertoli puts it, in an account of Conrad's historicism to which I am much indebted here: 'The past, rescued, shows up again, in the future, as that which must be re-established in order to leave decadence behind and avoid the end.'[18] If steam, to cite one of Conrad's favorite historicist dichotomies, has replaced sail, by virtue of sail's difference from steam (the difference between a heroic craft and a degraded technology) the essence of sail can someday be

143

Joseph Conrad

restored, even though in all likelihood its superficial form shall have been substantially altered. The insight of 'Karain,' on the other hand, is that the past cannot be remembered without its very essence being put into question. It is the past's complicity with, rather than its difference from, the modern world that Conrad must come to terms with before he can write *Heart of Darkness* and *Lord Jim* – although, to be sure, the memorialistic strategy he adopts in these novels would be unthinkable without traces of the simpleminded historicism that guides a work like *The Nigger of the 'Narcissus.'*

If in his fiction Conrad quickly gives up on the unproblematical valorization of the past that he promotes in the *Nigger*, this historicist outlook will nonetheless continue to dominate, though with an increasing sense of futility, much of his nonfictional prose. One such instance, taken from 'Autocracy and War,' is worth citing here because it provides a vivid idea of how the historicist model is meant to work in the *Nigger*. Conrad there affirms of the French Revolution that it was 'except for its destructive force . . . in essentials a mediocre phenomenon' (p. 86). The Revolution, which, as Jonathan Arac has remarked, was 'the historical experience that imprinted the urban crowd on all modern sensibilities,'[19] functions in this essay as the inaugural event of a destructive modernity radically different from the constructive tradition it has replaced but not sullied. Separating off a constructive past from a destructive present allows Conrad to offer the admittedly slim hope of a real return to this past and its values: at the end of the revolutionary tunnel could be glimpsed, he affirms, 'the idea of a Europe united in the solidarity of her dynasties which for a moment seemed to dawn on the horizon of the Vienna Congress through the subsiding dust of Napoleonic alarums and excursions' (p. 103). However, this renewal of a venerable idea, Conrad laments, was rapidly extinguished; the dynastic unity of nations gave way to the abstract unity of modern States led by political chiefs who, unlike the sovereigns of old Europe, would remain 'fatherless, heirless.' The optimistic moment of Conrad's analysis, which asserts that we had a chance to leave the revolutionary present behind and return to a more organic way of life, is thus, in the end, overcome by a dark pessimism that foresees no further chance for any such historicist recuperation of the past.

Conrad here aligns himself with a long list of conservative thinkers who, faced with the undeniable but (they hoped) merely provisional displacement of traditional society, would in the interim choose to valorize the figure of the individual as a bulwark against

144

A Man of the Last Hour

modernity. Romantic individualism evolves as a form of compensation for the destruction (the *hypothetical* destruction) of organic community and its replacement by what critics of the Revolution condemned as a society of and for the masses. As Arac has argued with reference to Conrad, 'The pressures of mass society demand in response a strongly assertive constitution of individuality which may permit a later reconstitution of community' (p. 78). For some nineteenth-century writers, this 'strong individuality' becomes an end in itself; [Viktor] Segalen clearly falls into this category. For others, such as Conrad, it remains only a means of conserving – with an eye to its future recuperation at the level of community – a realm of values they saw as having been lost with the Revolution.

In *The Nigger of the 'Narcissus,'* Conrad attempts to think this means entirely in terms of the end that it serves; the narratological matrix shifts from the geographical to the historical, and from the isolated individual to the once and future collective. Significantly described in its preface as 'an unrestful episode in the obscure lives of a few individuals out of all the disregarded multitude of the bewildered, the simple and the voiceless' (p. xvi), the *Nigger* is Conrad's most concerted effort at thinking beyond, or before, the figure of the individual – at inserting, or re-inserting, him within a community organized in accord with values that held sway in the past. Once his fate has again been attached to that of the traditional community, the individual can no longer hope to avoid the fate of that community: if the individual on his own can stay clear of the present and its degradation (that, at least, is what nineteenth-century exoticism posits), once reinserted into a traditional community he too must be subjected to its inevitable breakup. The risk to which Conrad here puts the individual by linking his fate to a community whose time has passed is justified by his historicist faith that this community will be capable of reconstituting itself in a 'new/old' future, having passed through the alienation of the present. The tale of loss and restoration that the *Nigger* enacts doubles the historicist meta-narrative* that provides the novel with its ideological ground. The narrative, in other words, does what history has not yet done, and yet must do: it effects the return to a past order after that order has been shattered; it does away with the present disorder, revealing it as nothing more than an interregnum.

I will now briefly show this historicist narrative at work by charting the progress of one of the novel's central images: the 'crowd' – a crowd that crops up obsessively in the *Nigger*, notwithstanding the author's own famous description of the

145

Joseph Conrad

circumstances under which it was written ('writing in a solitude almost as great as that of the ship at sea the great living crowd outside is somehow forgotten'[20]).

At the beginning of the novel, the crew of the *Narcissus* is referred to as a good 'crowd,' one that can be 'mustered,' brought to order. Two men, the Captain and old Singleton, represent this order – the one politically, the other in a more overtly symbolic way. The Captain is 'the ruler of that minute world,' a sovereign figure embodying the central authority that for Conrad binds the traditional community together. Singleton's relation to the Captain parallels Michel Strogoff's to the Czar. His unquestioning fidelity to the figure of authority establishes his own authority and makes of him an individual distinct from and yet, in this distinction, representative of the rest of the crew: 'Taciturn and unsmiling, he breathed amongst us – in that alone resembling the rest of the crowd' (p. 41). However, if in Verne's novel historical process was necessarily occluded, here it proves essential to the unfolding of the plot. Singleton's heroic distinction is marked off as a thing of the past: he is 'a lonely relic of a devoured and forgotten generation' (p. 24). If the novel is to progress toward a future in which the values embodied by Singleton can be regenerated, it must confront a world without value, one in which 'the grown-up children of a discontented earth' (p. 25) have usurped the place of an in some ways infantile and primitive father (Singleton, we are told, 'resembled a learned and savage patriarch'; p. 6). Strogoff's displacement in space, which takes him into the realm of the Other in order that the realm of the Same might be further consolidated, here turns into an essentially temporal displacement: a voyage out of the past and into the alienation of the present, which is to result in a future recovery of this past.

What must be dialectically restored is the story's point of departure: the 'good' crowd that 'mustered in' the novel. What must be passed through is the 'bad' crowd, in which collective action gives way to collective reaction, legitimate authority to the demagoguery of a usurper. As Ian Watt has pointed out, 'Conrad's treatment of the psychology of the crew of the *Narcissus* is ... similar to ... Gustave Le Bon's *La Psychologie des Foules*.'[21] In its journey through the present, the crew of the *Narcissus* loses touch with the order that originally constituted it and takes on the sort of negative features that Le Bon saw as typifying all mass formations. With the appearance of this 'bad' crowd, the individual disappears from sight: 'In the collective mind [*âme*] the intellectual aptitudes of the individuals, and in consequence their individuality, are weakened. The heterogeneous is swamped by the homogeneous,

146

A Man of the Last Hour

and the unconscious qualities obtain the upper hand' (p. 29). This 'unconscious' crowd is, Le Bon asserts, capable of both heroism and violence; however, in either case, its predominance results in the fall from conscious action to blind reaction, the sacrifice of the individual's autonomy to a collective 'soul' and, simultaneously, the emergence of a leader (*le meneur*), who fascinates the crowd, of which he is himself only an epiphenomenon, by miming the very individuality that each of its members has lost.

Thus, Le Bon – and thus Conrad, with one important difference. Conrad's organicist ideology (whose essential contradictions I pointed out in Chapter 2) allows him to posit the existence of a traditional collective whose 'psychology' would be qualitatively different from the one that motivates Le Bon's crowds: a positive community dependent upon the exemplary conduct of each of its members and ordered according to a hierarchy that finds its supreme embodiment in a single figure of authority. By virtue of his belief in this community, Conrad can, in the *Nigger* at least, assume a dialectical perspective that is markedly absent from Le Bon – one that foresees a restoration of the 'good' crowd and an end to the dominion of the masses that both he and Le Bon pessimistically identified as the central characteristic of their own age.[22]

Le Bon's negative analysis of the crowd certainly applies, though, to the crew of the *Narcissus* once its original order begins to erode. Its behavior becomes increasingly hysterical and the influence of the Captain and Singleton – those exemplary figures of the past – gives way during the present crisis, the crisis of the present, to that of their decadent doubles, Donkin and Wait. By-product of the crowd, the 'fascinating Donkin' ends up representing it: 'independent offspring of the ignoble freedom of the slums full of disdain and hate for the austere servitude of the sea,' he knows how to conquer 'the naïve instincts of that crowd' (pp. 11, 12). From Conrad's traditionalist perspective, Donkin is the individual – or, rather, the facsimile of an individual – who must be made to bear the guilt for the crew's fall into the present; the task of historicism is rendered all that much easier if some one person can be held responsible for the degeneration of the clean, white forecastle into a 'black cluster of human forms' bent on destruction. Just as Donkin mimes, and undermines, the legitimate authority of the Captain, Wait provides a symbolic counterpoint to the primitive Singleton. He 'fascinated us,' the narrator notes (p. 46); his heavy eyes sweep over them, 'a glance domineering and pained, like a sick tyrant overawing a crowd of abject but untrustworthy slaves' (p. 35). But if Wait's domination helps draw the crew into a decadent present – 'through him we were becoming highly humanised, tender,

147

Joseph Conrad

complex, excessively decadent' (p. 139) – his character is nonetheless profusely ambivalent. Unlike the clear-cut opposition that holds between Donkin and the Captain, the difference separating Wait from Singleton is hardly, as it were, one of black and white; indeed, he will come to assume many of the same almost metaphysical qualities ascribed to that 'lonely relic.'

The proximity of these two characters, who should be opposed as black to white, as present to past, signals the existence of a blind spot in Conrad's historicist strategy, one that produces many of the often-remarked and by-now glaring 'polyphonies' in the novel. Interesting as these may be, a discussion of them would not be to the point here. Rather, we need only keep to the novel's most basic narrative line and remark how neatly the strategy appears to dispose, at least when it comes to Donkin, of the social disorder that it cannot help but confront. The process set in motion by Donkin eventually leads to a brief uprising in which the ever more agitated crew comes into its own as an 'unconscious' force, a body of men whose every vestige of individuality has been momentarily lost: 'the crowd took a short run aft in a body' (p. 123), directing its fury toward the Captain and his mates. Their run, of course, will not be a long one: the Captain soon reasserts his authority, shaking a finger at the crowd and thereby initiating the first phase of its coming (back) to order. The onrushing group of men becomes 'the impressed and retreating crowd' (p. 137), and the threat posed by Donkin's angry masses is definitively put to rest; the crisis of the present is over, at least on this explicitly political front. The victory over Wait's troublingly metaphysical illness is, of course, a rather more uneasy one, and the reader of the *Nigger* is left to ponder whether Wait's excessive decadence has indeed been swallowed up once and for all by the sea or has taken on even more cosmic proportions – like those stars, which, remote in the eternal calm, glitter 'hard and cold above the uproar of the earth . . . more pitiless than the eyes of a triumphant mob, and as unapproachable as the hearts of men' (p. 77).

Notwithstanding these doubts, by the end of the novel, the narrator can return to the *Nigger*'s point of departure – asserting, as if the crisis had never occurred (and, indeed, from the perspective of a redeemed future, modernity must seem no more than a blink in the eye of history): 'You were a good crowd. As good a crowd as ever fisted with wild cries the beating canvas of a heavy foresail; or tossing aloft, invisible in the night, gave back yell for yell to a westerly gale' (p. 173). The cost of this encomiastic* return to the 'good' crowd, though, is the narrator's separation from the once-again-orderly crew of which he was a part: as many critics have

A Man of the Last Hour

pointed out,[23] after the *Narcissus* enters port, the 'I' is obtrusively divorced from the perspective of an 'us.' Contemporaneous with the appearance of this isolated individual is the *re*-appearance of a problem that seemed to have been left behind for good and that now presents itself in a different and more ominously modern form: 'Tall factory chimneys appeared in insolent bands and watched her [the *Narcissus*] go by, like a straggling crowd of slim giants, swaggering and upright under the black plummets of smoke, cavalierly aslant' (p. 163). This is the real future that opens out before the narrator, now cut adrift from a pre-industrial community that only his memory can restore ('you *were* a good crowd'): the historicist narrative enacted in *The Nigger of the 'Narcissus'* is, in these last pages, itself historicized, placed in the context of a modernity that disrupts the novel's reassertion of traditional community. The voyage of the *Narcissus* toward a restored future only leads back, and thus forward, into the continued degradation of the present.

In his excellent article on the *Nigger*, Sertoli shows at great length how the historicist strategy that Conrad there attempts to put into effect is itself continually undermined by what he calls the 'text.' Conrad's positive affirmation of (bourgeois) social values – of a past salvaged and proposed as a restorative, a means of overcoming the decadence of modernity – can, Sertoli argues, be achieved only through a repression of historical contradictions; we witness the return of the repressed at the (unconscious) level of the 'text,' where apparently black and white distinctions – for instance, those between Nature and Culture, or between Singleton and Wait – break down and turn in upon themselves. Sertoli's deconstruction of Conrad is certainly convincing. I suggest, however, that in the final pages of the novel Conrad performs a more or less identical operation upon himself and his beliefs. In disengaging his narrator from the 'good crowd,' he undoes what the historicist strategy had purported to do; the singled-out narrator can only remember the community he would valorize, in a place that denies such memories the objective weight they must possess if they are to achieve their dialectical end. The guiding light of *The Nigger of the 'Narcissus'* – that decadence can be overcome by a restoration of the past – here fails. If the textual ambiguities brought out by Sertoli make this point against Conrad's own intentions, the final turn to memory bears witness to Conrad's own capacity for that 'self-critical lucidity' Sertoli attributes to the 'text' alone.

Both the inadequacy of the historicist strategy that was to have allowed him to think a way outside of mass society and the purely commemorative nature of his enterprise have become apparent to

Joseph Conrad

Conrad. *Lord Jim*, in line with this 'self-critical lucidity,' abandons the historicist vision – or, rather, situates it, and the past it upholds, firmly within the bounds of the present that both gives rise to and delegitimizes it as a strategy. *To the destructive element submit yourself*: the values put forward in *The Nigger of the 'Narcissus'* are those in which Conrad placed his faith, and yet in order to conserve them he will now have to reveal their complete inadequacy to his own time, or to any other. The existence of the past he valorizes is of no matter in the present that denies it, 'except, perhaps, to the few of those who believed the truth, confessed the faith – or loved the men' (p. 25). That this 'truth' is a fiction, utterable only amid 'the undying murmur of folly, regret, and hope exhaled by the crowds of the anxious earth' (p. 164), is the sole insight by which it can (never) be regained. The distinction between innocence and corruption that provided the ground for Conrad's historicism gives way to the vision of a world in which such distinctions have no force: Conrad abandons narratives of ideological resolution, adopting instead an engaged form of nostalgia that continues to put into question a modernity to which it can no longer put an end. [. . .]

Notes

1. MICHAEL W. DOYLE, *Empires* (Ithaca, NY, 1986), p. 345.

2. JOSEPH CONRAD, *The Collected Letters of Joseph Conrad*, ed. Fredrick R. Karl and Laurence Davies, 5 vols. (Cambridge: Cambridge University Press, 1983–96), 2: 159–60, and 161 for the translation (letter of 8 February 1899).

3. All references to the works of Conrad are to *Collected Works*, Medallion edition, 22 vols. (London, 1925–28).

4. DAVID SIMPSON, *Fetishism and Imagination: Dickens, Melville, Conrad* (Baltimore, 1982), p. 119.

5. D. C. R. A. GOONETILLEKE, *Developing Countries in British Fiction* (Totowa, NJ, 1977), p. 93.

6. GARETH JENKINS, 'Conrad's *Nostromo* and History,' *Literature and History* 6 (1977), pp. 138–78 (p. 138).

7. SIMPSON, p. 99.

8. WILLIAM WORDSWORTH, *The Fourteen-Book 'Prelude'*, ed. W. J. B. Owen (Ithaca, NY, 1985), p. 236 (ll. 128–9).

9. IAN WATT, *Conrad in the Nineteenth Century* (Berkeley, CA, 1979), p. 37.

10. The term is the guiding motif of KENNETH A. BRUFFEE's *Elegiac Romance: Cultural Change and Loss of the Hero in Modern Fiction* (Ithaca, NY, 1983); in its general outlines, his account of the development of Conradian narrative in the early novels and stories is similar to the one put forward here, although to very different ends (see pp. 73–95). For another interesting

A Man of the Last Hour

argument about a shift in Conrad's thinking at the time of *Heart of Darkness* and *Lord Jim*, see ALLAN HUNTER, *Joseph Conrad and the Ethics of Darwinism* (London, 1983), pp. 108–20.

11. FREDERICK R. KARL, *Joseph Conrad: The Three Lives* (New York, 1979), p. 401.

12. CONRAD, *Collected Letters*, 1: 381 (letter of 6 September 1897).

13. See, e.g., BENITA PARRY's excellent account in *Conrad and Imperialism: Ideological Boundaries and Visionary Frontiers* (London, 1983), pp. 60–75.

14. For an interesting interpretation of this passage from *Lord Jim*, see J. H. MILLER, *Fiction and Repetition: Seven English Novels* (Cambridge, MA, 1982), pp. 26–30; for a good discussion of the early short stories as a whole and their links to the longer fiction, see GAIL FRASER, *Interweaving Patterns in the Works of Joseph Conrad* (Ann Arbor, MI, 1988).

15. GUSTAVE LE BON, *The Crowd: A Study of the Popular Mind*, ed. Robert K. Merton (New York, 1960), p. 15.

16. JORIS-KARL HUYSMANS, *Œuvres complètes*, vol. 7, *A rebours* (Geneva, 1972), p. 37.

17. EDWARD SAID, 'Kim, the Pleasures of Imperialism', *Raritan* 7.2 (1987), pp. 27–64 (p. 61). Said's account of 'The Return' in his *Joseph Conrad and the Fiction of Autobiography* (Cambridge, MA, 1966, pp. 104–11) remains one of the most thoughtful discussions of this story.

18. GIUSEPPE SERTOLI, 'Una negazione testuale: Frammento di lettura da *The Nigger of the "Narcissus"* di Joseph Conrad', *Nuova Corrente* 61–62 (1973), pp. 382–412 (p. 407).

19. JONATHAN ARAC, 'Romanticism, the Self and the City: *The Secret Agent* in Literary History', *Boundary 2* 9.1 (1980), pp. 75–90 (p. 84).

20. CONRAD, *Collected Letters*, 1: 430 (letter of 23 December 1897).

21. WATT, p. 115. Although Watt has stated (pers. comm.) that he doubts Conrad ever read Le Bon, Zdzisław Najder suggests that the origin of Conrad's fear of 'anarchistic destructive rabble' can probably be traced 'not only to the historical and sociological books he had read (Taine, Gustave Le Bon) or to conservative political propaganda, but also to his own experiences with the urban and port mobs he later described with contempt in *The Nigger of the "Narcissus"* '. *Joseph Conrad: A Chronicle* (New Brunswick, NJ, 1983), pp. 88–89.

22. Le Bon's pessimism, on the other hand, is palliated by a belief that 'the genius [*âme*] of the race exerts a paramount influence upon the dispositions of a crowd' (p. 158). Whereas 'the substitution of the unconscious action of crowds for the conscious activity of individuals is one of the principal characteristics of the present age' (p. 3), the distinction between 'primitive, inferior, middling, and superior races' serves as a more or less efficacious counter to this homogenizing process. On this point, see especially his *Lois psychologiques de l'évolution des peuples* (1894).

23. See, e.g., BRUFFEE, pp. 79–80.

Part Four

Gender and sexuality

8 'Ghosts of the Gothic': Spectral Women and Colonized Spaces in *Lord Jim**

PADMINI MONGIA

This essay, one of the most recent collected here, shows the way in which the integrated use of a variety of theoretical perspectives can generate a radically new reading of a novel. Mongia begins with a classic feminist project, that of bringing to light marginalised women (in this case within a fictional text), attending to their story, and at the same time analysing why masculine discourse requires both the presence and the marginality of such women. To follow through these aims, she draws on the theory of literary genres (looking at elements of Gothic, adventure and romance), on psychoanalytical theory (specifically the processes of identity-formation in women) and on cultural geography as applied to the discourses of imperialism (the way in which colonial fantasies map ideas of gender onto constructions of space and place). These theories are synthesised so that, for example, a feminist psychoanalytical view of the Gothic, as concerned with mother–daughter relations, allows Mongia to read the village of Patusan, in Conrad's *Lord Jim*, as a region of feminised enclosure and insecure identity boundaries. Both Jim and Jewel, she suggests, inhabit this space for a time; one of Mongia's most original conclusions is that Jim plays the role of Gothic heroine at certain stages. However, Jewel remains stuck in this space of non-separation from the mother, which Jim escapes only by taking a leap out of the Gothic narrative of enclosure into an adventure narrative of masculine resolve. So Mongia sees the generic ambivalence of *Lord Jim* as indicative of the gender anxieties of the *fin de siècle*.

This paper begins with an irritant, a persistent nub that demands attention in my reading of *Lord Jim*. Tucked away in Patusan, but haunting the entire story, is the ghost of a woman that will not be laid to rest. Jewel's mother, long dead before the tale we are told

---

* Reprinted from *Conrad and Gender*, ed. Andrew Michael Roberts (Amsterdam and Atlanta: Rodopi, 1993), pp. 1–16.

Joseph Conrad

in the novel begins, is alive in the daily veneration granted her by Jewel and Jim. Attaching itself to this spectral presence is the figure of Jewel, the daughter who repeats her mother's history so completely that, at the end of the story, she becomes another spectre, half-alive, wafting on Stein's arm through his garden. What I want to question is the tale's necessity for these spectral figures, the need for repetition in the history of mother and daughter, and the connection between these ghostly women and the colonized spaces they represent.

By blurring the boundaries between mother and daughter, Conrad's novel highlights the threat of engulfment posed by the feminine, a threat embodied geographically as well in the rendition of Patusan as a feminized region. The Patusan section of *Lord Jim* relies on a subtext of the Gothic, transmuted in various ways from the 'classic' Gothic of the eighteenth century. Helpless women in need of rescue, threatening masculine figures, a dead-undead mother, and the terrors associated with enclosing spaces are all features common to the Gothic and to the second half of *Lord Jim*. While Jewel and her mother form the primary focus of my interest, Jim too plays a special role in the Gothic narrative. Conrad invests in Jim not just the heroic stuff of adventure and romance – virile agency that finds its fulfilment in masculine action – but also the features of the colonized, helpless 'feminine.' Jim is as much the figure in white – virginal, helpless, in need of rescue by the master story-teller Marlow – as he is the masculine god who orders the chaos of Patusan. Recognizing the 'feminization' of Jim allows for an understanding of a tension between the Gothic and adventure narratives in *Lord Jim*; the Gothic, primarily concerned with a 'feminine' domain, is eventually subsumed by the adventure narrative in which Jim plays out the possibilities of 'masculine' resolve. Masculinity, then, is clearly developed differently from femininity within the novel. Jim, I show, leaves the Gothic realm with its threat of engulfment to participate instead in an adventure story where he can be a 'hero.' In the process of exploring the traces of the Gothic in *Lord Jim*, I suggest the novel engages with the construction of gendered identities, an engagement built upon numerous negotiations of gender and genre which offer a glimpse into the tensions resulting from colonial and gender anxieties in the *fin de siècle*.

The nature and presence of the Gothic

It is by now a critical commonplace to suggest that Conrad's allegiances to high modernism are interrupted by what Jameson has called the 'degraded' forms of popular culture like romance

'Ghosts of the Gothic'

and adventure.[1] Several critics have studied these popular culture elements; Jameson himself is most interested in the traces of romance in a text such as *Lord Jim*, whereas Chris Bongie and Martin Green draw attention to Conrad's nostalgic evocation of adventure.[2] However, there is no clear distinction between romance and adventure. Romance, with its link to chivalric possibility, hovers behind the more 'prosaic' adventure model Conrad uses.[3] The Gothic, too, shares numerous elements in common with adventure and romance; the most obvious might be that all three genres rely on a simple manichæan world of good and evil, light and dark. The similarities between the three genres can perhaps best be understood by emphasizing the development of adventure and Gothic from the romance.

The Gothic has been the least studied form in the area of Conrad studies. The critical work that is available centres, for the most part, on Conrad's use of grotesques and so does not address what we might call 'classic' Gothic elements.[4] Joan Steiner's unpublished dissertation, 'Joseph Conrad and the Tradition of the Gothic Romance,' deals with the points of connection between Conrad's works and the classic Gothic but emphasizes his existential crises vis-à-vis 'man's' position in the world.[5] In *Rule of Darkness*, Patrick Brantlinger calls the genre that interlaces elements of adventure with Gothic and flourished at the *fin de siècle*, 'Imperial Gothic.' Brantlinger points out that for writers such as H. Rider Haggard, H. G. Wells, and Conrad, imperial Gothic allows the expression of 'anxiety about the waning of opportunities for heroic adventure'.[6] Imperial Gothic, though, is forcefully informed by atavism and occultism. For Brantlinger, imperial Gothic leaves its traces in Conrad's work, although his *œuvre* is not the best example of the form. While Conrad's work does not wholeheartedly participate in the usual excesses of late-Victorian fantasy literature, traces of superstitions and extra-rational fears appear in his fictions.[7]

Retaining aspects of Brantlinger's description of imperial Gothic, I want now to introduce another dimension of the Gothic, but one which is informed by a very different perspective. I want to ask what happens to the Gothic in Conrad when viewed from a feminist psychoanalytic perspective such as the one suggested by Claire Kahane in her 'Gothic Mirrors and Feminine Identity.' In this interesting and moving essay, Kahane sees in the Gothic formula not the overt Œdipal drama of threatened incest with 'a helpless daughter confronting the erotic power of a father or brother,' but instead, a repressed family drama in which a heroine must search for her origins by addressing her identification with, and separation from, the various mothers who inhabit Gothic tales.[8]

157

Joseph Conrad

Kahane suggests that the scenario of threatened incest which forms the surface plot of traditional Gothic is merely a convention; for her the Gothic fear is generated by the maternal which the daughter must address in order to know her own origins.[9] The secret interior of the Gothic is thus a bedchamber in which a woman has died, a space which represents the 'spectral presence of a dead-undead mother, archaic and all-encompassing, a ghost signifying the problematics of female identity formation which the heroine must confront' (p. 48). Kahane's description is informed by the work of theorists such as Nancy Chodorow and Dorothy Dinnerstein, who see the issue of female identity formation as inextricably linked to the critical pre-Œdipal period of human development. They suggest that whereas the male infant arrives at a sense of his identity by knowing his separation from the all-powerful mother of infancy, for the female child, identity is much more tenuous since she must know herself as both different from and similar to the mother.[10] Kahane describes the situation as follows: 'Not only does the girl's gender identification with her mother make it difficult for her to grasp firmly her separateness, but her mother frequently impedes that process by seeing in her daughter a duplication of herself, and reflecting that confusion' (p. 48). This fundamental confusion, woven into the identity of both mothers and daughters, can be seen as a chief interest of the Gothic.

Strewn across the pages of Gothic fictions are numerous mother–daughter scenarios. In Ann Radcliffe's *The Mysteries of Udolpho*, for instance, Emily must confront several surrogate mother figures, women at once suggesting the maternal but also the mirrored reflection of Emily's possibilities of selfhood. In M. G. Lewis's *The Monk*, the child-mother Agnes clutches the corpse of her decaying child within the womb/catacomb of a convent where she has been imprisoned by the mother-superior. Agnes has already had to negotiate her identity with another mother surrogate: Donna Rodolpha, her aunt, impedes Agnes's union with her lover Raymond, because the aunt herself vies for his attention. Even in *Northanger Abbey*, Austen includes in her parody the bed-chamber in which a mother has died, a space which the wandering Gothic heroine Catherine must intrude upon before understanding the Tilney family. Nor is this confusion a feature only of Gothic novels written by women, although it might be a partial explanation for why the Gothic as a form appealed, and continues to appeal, mostly to women writers and readers.

From such a perspective, we can view the Gothic fear as the fear of the beckoning womb-like spaces that demand a struggle over

'Ghosts of the Gothic'

identity. One might also say, then, that the Gothic form concerns itself with the feminine.[11] The overt plot is a male fantasy of power, but beneath this structure lie the more disturbing spaces of enclosure, the catacombs and dungeons into which Gothic heroines are repeatedly locked. Not just this secret centre, but the larger enclosing space of the Gothic is crucial for the articulation of the formula. Remote mansions and castles, burdened with ages of unsavory history, operate as metaphors for the maternal body which threatens complete engulfment. Not accidentally, given England's nation-building enterprise of the eighteenth century, these structures are usually located in a region constructed as 'barbaric,' often in an Italy or Germany represented as crude and rapacious. In the late nineteenth century, by the time Conrad is writing, the colonial context allows for the presentation of remote and alien regions created as spaces of excess, spaces which threaten engulfment and a loss of demarcating boundaries.

Anne McClintock has argued, in a reading of H. Rider Haggard's *King Solomon's Mines*, that the colonial adventure map, such as the one printed in Haggard's novel (and resembling an inverted female body), might be read as a 'document of pathology'.[12] Specifically, she offers the provocative suggestion that the pathology it reveals 'might be called paranoia, for it is only in the discourse of paranoia that one finds simultaneously and in such condensed form both delusions of grandeur and delusions of engulfment' (p. 151). The colonial adventure tale, even when not directly relying upon a map as Haggard's novel does, renders a geography which is often feminized; the story the adventure tale offers can be read as the valorization of the white male adventurer as he dominates the colonized female body. One might well wonder if the adventure novel, defined as it is by a flight from the feminine, does not articulate the thread of engulfment posed by the feminine as well as the containment of this threat through the control exerted by the penetrating adventurer. Haggard's novel might be an extreme example of this structure. However, even a cursory glance at Conrad's 'revised' colonial adventures reveals his reliance on tropes that conflate the colonized region with the female body; the threat posed by the Africa of *Heart of Darkness* or the Patusan of *Lord Jim* suggests a fear of engulfment similar to that which marks the culmination of the adventure in *King Solomon's Mines*.[13]

Patusan is overlaid with images of engulfing forests and gloom that threaten the loss of the features and values which define the metropolitan region left behind. It is first introduced in the novel by Marlow as a region of another planet: 'I don't suppose any of you had ever heard of Patusan? . . . It does not matter; there's many

159

Joseph Conrad

a heavenly body in the lot crowding upon us of a night that mankind had never heard of, it being outside the sphere of its activities and of no earthly importance to anybody' (*Lord Jim*, p. 218). Reminiscent of aspects of imperial Gothic, Conrad's Patusan reminds us of the appeal of regions beyond earthly boundaries, an appeal that stemmed from the sense that the world had become too small to allow for 'genuine' adventure any longer. As a fantasy world, Patusan enables the text to create a space for ghouls and terrors, a region both haunted and haunting, engulfed in green gloom and 'circumscribed by lofty impassable mountains' (p. 228). Even Gentleman Brown describes the effect of Patusan on him and his crew as 'weird' so that 'every individual man of them felt as though he were adrift alone in a boat, haunted by an almost imperceptible suspicion of sighing, muttering ghosts' (p. 399).

Enclosure is Patusan's dominant effect. From the mountains split by a fissure to the ribbon of the river, it is a space carefully bordered, a space that captures. Jewel's situation in Patusan is one of entrapment. Jim describes Jewel when he first arrives in Patusan as 'somebody drowning in a lonely dark place' (p. 304), whereas Marlow repeatedly stresses Jewel's ignorance of anything but the reality of Patusan. He says: 'She had grown up there; she had seen nothing, she had known nothing, she had no conception of anything. I ask myself whether she were sure that anything else existed. What notions she may have formed of the outside world is to me inconceivable' (p. 307). Marlow, in addition, imagines the solitude of the lives of Jewel and her mother as crippling, and cannot help but imagine their lives as made up of 'the awful sameness and the swift passage of time, the barrier of forest, the solitude and the turmoil' (p. 277), imaginings that place the two women into a virtual live burial.[14]

For Marlow, too, Patusan is a region of enclosure. His departure from Patusan is described as an emergence from constraint: 'I let my eyes roam through space, like a man released from bonds who stretches his cramped limbs, runs, leaps, responds to the inspiring elation of freedom' (pp. 331–2). The journey to this area of openness is made up of sweltering in the 'stagnant superheated air' where the 'primeval smell of fecund earth, seemed to sting' (p. 331). Patusan is a space repeatedly figured in terms of the feminine. As Marianna Torgovnick puts it in *Gone Primitive*:

> when Jim shows Patusan to Marlow, he points out with proprietal pleasure a moonrise between 'the summits of two steep hills very close together, and separated by what looks like a deep fissure, the cleavage of some mighty stroke' [p. 220]. Like landmarks such

160

'Ghosts of the Gothic'

as 'Sheba's breasts' in Rider Haggard's *King Solomon's Mines*, and like the use of the African woman in *Heart of Darkness*, the passage proceeds from an axiomatic identification of 'primitive' landscape with the female body.[15]

As a metaphor for the female body, Patusan can be seen as a space of womb-like enclosure, the maternal darkness which produces so much of the fear and terror in the Gothic.

In an essay entitled 'Gothic Possibilities,' Norman Holland and Leona Sherman suggest that the Gothic allows for an interpretation of 'body by means of castle and castle by means of body'.[16] The castle evokes the earliest stage in human development 'when the boundaries between inner and outer, me and not-me, are still not sharply drawn, and self cannot distinguish itself from the mother who is the outside world' (p. 283).[17] Clearly, Patusan cannot be read as a simple equivalent of the castle in the Gothic novel. But this point of connection allows us to interpret the engulfing enclosure of Patusan as a region that demands from the daughter the consideration of, and struggle for, an identity separate from her mother's. That this is impossible for Jewel is clear from the beginning, despite attempts to subvert the pattern already set for her via her constantly vigilant attitude towards Jim. Whatever else Jewel does not know and understand, her fear that her experience with Jim will repeat the trajectory of her mother's life is never in doubt.

Marlow, of course, sees Jewel as a replica of her mother. Describing the love of women such as these two, he says: 'But I am sure that the mother was as much of a woman as the daughter seemed to be' (*Lord Jim*, p. 277). For Cornelius, too, the two are virtually inseparable; he says of Jewel: 'Like her mother – she is like her deceitful mother. Exactly. In her face, too. In her face. The devil!' (p. 329). Both women exist merely to traumatize his life. Jewel herself recognizes the horrible similarity in her life, her mother's, and her mother before. She says, distrusting Jim's pledge to remain with her, 'Other men had sworn the same thing. . . . My father did. . . . Her father, too' (p. 314). Each woman has a white lover and each lover abandons the woman. The shadow of the grave that haunts the relationship between Jim and Jewel is thus not merely a throw-back to the world of La Vallée in *The Mysteries of Udolpho* – which ends with the dubiously joyous picture of the newly-weds visiting Emily's mother's grave daily – but a grim recognition of the inseparability of mother and daughter.

Cornelius's offer, to look after Jewel for a paltry sum of money once Jim leaves, reflects the reality of the relationships between

161

Joseph Conrad

white men and native women. Rather than a sordid deal offered by the 'vile' Cornelius, as Marlow reads this gesture, Cornelius's statement, 'every gentleman made a provision when the time came to go home' (p. 328) alludes specifically to the role he has played for Stein. By marrying Jewel's mother, he became Stein's agent in Patusan. The deal Cornelius offers is an instance of the 'traffic in women' Gayle Rubin describes as inherent in patriarchal structures.[18] Power is exchanged between men, but women, like Jewel and her mother, become the medium of exchange. Though no deal is struck with Cornelius for Jewel's maintenance, Stein steps in at the end of the novel in the role of surrogate patriarch to look after Jewel.

Chodorow suggests that the anxiety which attends the daughter's separation from the mother is a feature of all familial structures in which mothers are primary care-givers and fathers essentially absent.[19] This patriarchal family structure has also been read as containing within it the threat of violence. An examination of Jewel's life, which we know more fully than her mother's, reveals the abuse she undergoes from Cornelius as a result of her position as 'daughter.' Although Cornelius is not cast as an overtly powerful patriarch, his role as surrogate father to Jewel and husband of Jewel's mother allows him to exert his power in ways which can only be read as violent. To begin with, he insists that Jewel call him father, 'and with respect, too – with respect' (p. 288). Marlow says: 'It appears Cornelius led her [Jewel] an awful life, stopping only short of actual ill-usage' (p. 288). When Jim first meets Jewel, she is subjected to ugly harangues by Cornelius that leave her 'agitated, speechless, clutching her bosom now and then with a stony, desperate face' (p. 289). At other times, she demonstrates a scorn towards Cornelius born of her superior mind that is reminiscent of Emily in *The Mysteries of Udolpho*. This scorn allows her to confront Cornelius 'in silence, her face sombre and contracted, and only now and then uttering a word or two that would make the other jump and writhe with the sting' (p. 288).

Jewel's memory of her mother's death underscores the disruptive power of Cornelius. Marlow tells us of Jewel's recollection of this death: 'She went on explaining that, during the last moments, being alone with her mother, she had to leave the side of the couch to go and set her back against the door, in order to keep Cornelius out. He desired to get in, and kept on drumming with both fists, only desisting now and again to shout huskily, "Let me in! Let me in!"' (p. 312). Although Cornelius is also cast as a 'repulsive beetle' (p. 285), aspects of a dominating Montoni figure linger in his characterization; while he does not exert the kind of pervasive threat usually unleashed against the Gothic heroine, his role as father and

162

'Ghosts of the Gothic'

husband does grant him the power to brutalize psychologically and perhaps physically. But for Jewel, beneath this more overt Gothic structure of violence threatened by a father lies the issue of her inseparability from the maternal. The secret centre of her drama is again the confusion between mothers and daughters, a bed-chamber in which a woman has died, and the daughter's struggle to create for herself an identity separate from her mother's.

If the dead mother haunts the space of Patusan, limiting by her life and death the extent of possibility available to Jewel, Jewel is already a haunting shade long before she dies. Jewel is repeatedly described as disembodied; when she awakens Jim to save him from a plot on his life, she appears as 'the head of some apparition, some unearthly being, all in white' (p. 296). For Marlow, her 'ghostly figure swayed like a slender tree in the wind' (p. 308); her eyes suggest to him the depths of a deep well, and make him ask whether what moves there is 'a blind monster or only a lost gleam from the universe' (p. 307). Although Conrad avoids the overt creation of crudely powerful women with the capacity to haunt, such as Haggard's Ayesha, Jewel and her mother can be seen as paler versions of women who emasculate men, women who threaten men's power and contain their possibilities.[20] Jewel, in her refusal to forgive Jim, for instance, denies his memory a safe haven in the heroic world of romance that the novel evokes at the end. 'He shall have no tears from me. Never, never. Not one tear' (p. 349), she says and remains unmoved by Marlow's and Stein's pleas on Jim's behalf. When Marlow first meets her after Jim's death, this is the description he offers: 'Her white figure seemed shaped in snow; the pendent crystals of a great chandelier clicked above her head like glittering icicles. . . . I was chilled as if these vast apartments had been the cold abode of despair.' He is 'glad to escape' from her presence. According to Marlow, 'All the heat of life seemed withdrawn within some inaccessible spot in her breast' (p. 348). The shock of Jim's death had 'turned her passion into stone' (p. 351).

By the end of the novel, then, Jewel is buried alive in Stein's house as in a 'scrubbed cave underground' (p. 347). Within this more complete space of enclosure, of a live burial granted not just by the imaginings of Jim and Marlow but by experience itself, Jewel ekes out her days walking listlessly on Stein's arm. With this ending, Jewel is denied all possibility of marking out an identity for herself different from her mother's. By the end of the novel, she knows that her fears regarding Jim were correct: 'He has left me . . . you always leave us – for your own ends' (p. 348), she says, echoing the truth of her mother's experience. Condemned, then, by

163

Joseph Conrad

Jim's actions to repeat her mother's history, Jewel takes her place in a generational drama which allows the colonized woman no role other than abandonment by the colonizing white man.

Into this drama of repetition is woven one further twist. The world which includes Jewel and her mother offers them a single characterization they must share. While both women are represented as beings from another world – recall Marlow's famous description of the love of such women who rise 'above the trammels of earthly caution' and offer men an 'extra-terrestrial touch' (p. 277) – the maternal body's twin secrets of procreation and sexuality are signified only by Jewel's mother. The mother's life in Patusan is made necessary by some unknown but disruptive event in her past. When Stein first introduces Patusan in the novel, Marlow says, 'I can only guess that once before Patusan had been used as a grave for some sin, transgression, or misfortune' (p. 219). Jewel's mother is, thus, the obvious sign of sexual transgression and knowledge, whereas Jewel is an almost empty signifier. Jewel, despite bearing external signs of sexuality – the predictable flowing hair, for example, or Marlow's assertion of her passionate nature – remains curiously asexual. Marlow and Jim repeatedly describe her as a child. In fact, she is almost boyish, a child-soldier reminiscent of Stein's wife, the princess. The women seem to be placed, then, on a scale which associates sexuality with a dead woman, whereas Jewel, the ostensibly living embodiment of this energy, is only sexualized by external markers.[21]

In fact, Jewel can be read as an aspect of Jim, one more secret sharer amongst the many in the novel. Marlow describes the moonlit conversations between the two as 'a self-communion of one being carried on in two tones' (p. 284). They speak alike as well: her English has Jim's 'own clipping, boyish intonation' (p. 283). Indeed, for Marlow, 'she lived so completely in his contemplation that she had acquired something of his outward aspect, something that recalled him in her movements, in the way she stretched her arm, turned her head, directed her glances' (p. 283). More importantly, perhaps, Jim says of Jewel: 'You take a different view of your actions when you come to understand, when you are *made* to understand every day that your existence is necessary – you see, absolutely necessary – to another person' (p. 304). Echoing the many dependant yet split selves of nineteenth-century novels (Frankenstein and his creature, Jekyll and Hyde), Jim sees Jewel as dependent upon him for the very sustenance that creates life. He too, is dependent upon her: 'You've got his heart in your hand' (p. 317), Marlow tells her, although Jim's dependence is obviously of a different order, as the ending of the novel illustrates.

164

'Ghosts of the Gothic'

Jim as Gothic heroine

Jim too is placed on the scale of sexuality which includes Jewel
and her mother. The marks of sexuality are borne by the dead
mother. Vis-à-vis the mother, Jewel is a child; she is sexualized only
in terms of the external markers needed for her role as Jim's lover.
In addition, she is the helpless woman of Victorian literature and
art, a child-woman who glides 'without touching the earth' (p. 303),
a woman whose movements are described as 'flitting' (p. 278), a
woman with a 'little hand' (p. 283) and eyes that reveal 'childish
ignorance' (p. 307). Jim, too, is asexual and pure in a manner also
reminiscent of these women. As Jewel touches Marlow by 'her
youth, her ignorance, her pretty beauty, which had the simple
charm and the delicate vigour of a wild-flower' (p. 309), Jim evokes
a similar description; recall the picture offered by Marlow's friend
who first employs Jim after the *Patna* episode: 'one could have said
he was blooming – blooming modestly – like a violet' (p. 187).
Gentle, blooming flowers, Jewel and Jim wander in Patusan in
white, evoking all the purity and virginity suggested by this cultural
marker. In addition, just as Jewel stirs Jim to participate in her
rescue from Cornelius, Jim moves Marlow into an engagement
with his life that will allow Jim once again to become 'one of us.'
Marlow's tale-telling is the primary form of this rescue, but there
are also, of course, the numerous material rescues Marlow offers
Jim.[22]

Helpless, pure, gentle, Jim recalls a description of the Gothic
heroine. He is a child, 'the youngest human being now in existence'
(p. 219). Also, as the veiled unknown – a description to which
Marlow repeatedly resorts in order to explain Jim – he evokes the
many veils of Gothic novels, veils which hide gory secrets but also
feminine identities. Jim's 'opportunity,' we remember, is repeatedly
described by Marlow as a veiled Eastern bride, hovering by his side
from the moment he enters Patusan. Marlow explicitly describes
Jim's future as feminine; the bride 'opportunity' is at once Jim's
potential (and so part of his self) and a feminine temptation (and
so other). The potential held out by Patusan, by Jim's 'opportunity,'
would require a merger with the feminine, for only through a
merger could Jim realize his opportunity. Marlow's statement: 'For
it may very well be that in the short moment of his last proud and
unflinching glance, he had beheld the face of that opportunity
which, like an Eastern bride, had come veiled to his side' (p. 416)
suggests the fulfilment implicit in Jim's death.[23]

As Jim's 'opportunity' is veiled for him, so Jim is veiled for
Marlow.[24] His desire to unveil Jim cannot be separated from the

165

Joseph Conrad

adventurer's desire to un-cover or dis-cover new regions which forms so much of the colonial context of the adventure novel. The novel repeatedly associates physiognomy and geography to describe Jim; the most obvious example is the description of the privileged man's approach to the packet containing Jim's story as if he were approaching an 'undiscovered country.' Marlow also says: 'The views he let me have of himself were like those glimpses through the shifting rents in a thick fog – bits of vivid and vanishing detail, giving no connected idea of the general aspect of a country' (p. 76). Just as Jewel and her mother become associated with a geographical region, so too does Jim. Viewed as land, his unknowability offers an impetus to Marlow's unveiling fantasies. The text thus conflates geography, the feminine, and the colonial in a manner that makes of Jim the helpless female to Marlow's energetic, masculine, rescuing ability.

Enclosure, which threatens to engulf Gothic heroines, also affects Jim. Remember that his entry into Patusan is described as a burial – twenty feet underground. Although difficult to enter, once penetrated, Patusan closes around him just as it does for Jewel. 'The land, the people, the friendship, the love, were like the jealous guardians of his body' (p. 262), as Marlow tells us. Repeatedly Jim's location is described in similar ways; he is a 'captive' (p. 247) in Patusan, so that the forests and land 'possessed him and made him their own to the innermost thought, to the slightest stir of blood, to his last breath' (p. 248). Jim negotiates this territory, understanding its threats, its internal divisions, and creates for himself a literal and metaphoric space. The features, then, that suggest Gothic traces in *Lord Jim* are also associated with Jim who is thus figured as the 'colonized feminine,' even as he is defined by masculine, heroic energy when we follow another generic strain – that of the adventure – in the novel.

The adventure *vs.* the Gothic

As Jewel's experience in Patusan demands an engagement with identity formation, so too does Jim's. Once engulfed within this womb-like space, Jim too responds to the area as if it were a total environment, not demanding a separation between self and other. Although racially different from everyone around him, Jim nevertheless is made to seem as necessary to Patusan as it is to him. As Marlow tells us, 'Jim the leader was a captive in every sense' (p. 262). The maternal space of Patusan, the symbolic womb, protects Jim and allows him a new birth; like the enclosing castles

'Ghosts of the Gothic'

of Gothic novels, this space becomes evocative of the earliest moments of a child's identification with the mother, 'when the boundaries between inner and outer, me and not-me, are still not sharply drawn' (Holland, p. 283). Just as in *Heart of Darkness*, for example, the Congo is represented as a 'primitive' and feminine space of man's origins, so too Patusan in *Lord Jim* becomes the region of origins, demanding from both Jim and Jewel an engagement with their definitions of self.[25]

Significantly, though, the similarities between the two cease in the final answers the novel offers. Whereas Jewel is condemned to non-separation from the mother, to recognizing her inability to create a separate identity, Jim is able to leave Gothic engulfment behind and take his place in the trajectory offered by the adventure story. Although Jewel attempts to engulf him, 'devouring him with her eyes' (*Lord Jim*, p. 412) and claiming Jim as a possession, 'Thou art mine' (p. 413), Jim breaks free from her arms and moves away from the feminine. At the end of the novel, by choosing his death, Jim is able to make himself the hero of his dreams. The ability to transgress boundaries – the only active role allowed the traditional Gothic heroine – is denied to Jewel but granted to Jim. By stepping outside the enclosure, Jim, like the male infant described in the work of Chodorow and Dinnerstein, knows his identity by his ability to see the boundary from the maternal. In doing so, he leaves behind the terror and fear of the female Gothic and asserts the primacy of the adventure narrative that allows the adventurer a fantasy of active agency and engagement. In his Œdipal drama – with the surrogate patriarch Cornelius – he is able to dominate the father by leaving behind the entire realm of the battle.

The subtext of the Gothic in *Lord Jim* foregrounds the novel's interest in identity formation and its relation to a colonized geo-graphical region. The Gothic affords Jim a complete return to an archaic space within which he can cast himself in a completely new light. In Patusan, Jim creates a primal bond of oneness, a psychological 'pre-Œdipal' union with the maternal. However, since the 'feminine East' threatens complete engulfment, Jim must separate and define himself as a masculine participant in an adventure plot. The women who represent the colonized, maternal region, though, flounder in its all-encompassing quality. The novel's engagement with the construction of identity breaks down along predictable gender lines: Jewel is condemned to a live burial and Jim is granted virile agency in the adventure plot.

The end of the novel allows Jim a place in the romantic world of adventure ironized at the beginning of the text. *Lord Jim* is better

Joseph Conrad

understood as revealing Conrad's ambivalence towards adventure, rather than as an indictment of it. Also, though Patusan may be the region of fantasy, ambivalence defines the drama that unfolds here. In terms of characterization, Conrad shifts the ground constantly: Jim is both a masculine hero and a retiring, veiled woman; Jewel is at once boyish and a delicate child-woman; Cornelius is a vile, abject beetle but also a threatening patriarch. Not simply part of a 'pure' adventure world or of a pure Gothic one, Conrad's representations speak most directly of the anxiety generated both by changing gender roles in Britain and by the epistemological* uncertainties generated by the New Imperialism which marked the *fin de siècle*.[26] The anxiety and nostalgia that mark the end of *Lord Jim* speak of a profound ache of longing for a 'simpler' world, one which allowed for 'genuine' possibilities of adventure. The pleasures of masculinity the narrative finally offers Jim are difficult to arrive at, requiring an initial merger with the feminine followed by a leap into the masculine through death. The context of colonialism makes possible Jim's role as adventure 'hero' and reveals one method for reshaping masculinity in a besieged world.[27]

Notes

1. FREDRIC JAMESON's study of *Lord Jim* is, in part, built around an analysis of the Patusan section of the novel as it reveals the emergence 'not merely of what will be contemporary modernism ... but also ... of what will variously be called popular culture or mass culture'. *The Political Unconscious: Narrative as a Socially Symbolic Act* (Ithaca: Cornell University Press, 1981), p. 206.

2. CHRIS BONGIE shows Conrad's allegiance, particularly in his early works, to the 'Old Imperialism' which ostensibly allowed 'genuine' possibilities for heroism. See *Exotic Memories: Literature, Colonialism, and the Fin de Siècle* (Stanford: Stanford University Press, 1991). While Green too associates the realm of adventure with imperialism, Bongie's approach differs since it is always informed by the epistemological crises inherent in the advent of modernity.

3. See MARTIN GREEN's *Dreams of Adventure, Deeds of Empire* (New York: Basic Books, 1979) for an analysis of the dependence of the adventure form on the romance, especially pp. 8–36.

4. See, for example, WILLIAM A. COVINO, 'Lugubrious Drollery: Humor and Horror in Conrad's Fiction', *Modern Fiction Studies* 23 (1977), pp. 217–25; ELSA NETTELS, 'The Grotesque in Conrad's Fiction', *Nineteenth-Century Fiction* 29 (1974), pp. 144–63; ANNE LUYAT, 'Conrad's Feminine Grotesques', *The Conradian* 11 (1986), pp. 4–15.

5. JOAN ELIZABETH STEINER, 'Joseph Conrad and the Tradition of the Gothic Romance', dissertation, University of Michigan, 1971.

6. PATRICK BRANTLINGER, *Rule of Darkness* (Ithaca: Cornell University Press, 1988), p. 239.

'Ghosts of the Gothic'

7. Recall, for example, the 'amazing Jim-myth' that accompanies Marlow as he travels up the river to Patusan. See JOSEPH CONRAD, *Lord Jim* (London: Dent, 1946), p. 210. (All further references are to this edition of *Lord Jim*.) In the myth, Jewel is cast as a precious emerald, probably unlucky, but signifying the wealth of the white man since his rationality allows him to overcome superstition and, therefore, retain the 'gem'.

8. CLAIRE KAHANE, 'Gothic Mirrors and Feminine Identity', *Centennial Review* 24 (1980), pp. 43–64 (p. 47).

9. For Kahane, the maternal signifies the 'mysterious not-me world with its unknown forces, as well as the world of the flesh' (p. 48). To put it another way, the maternal body evokes at once both the reproductive and the sexual and, therefore, the mysterious and the material.

10. NANCY CHODOROW, *The Reproduction of Mothering* (Berkeley: University of California Press, 1978); DOROTHY DINNERSTEIN, *The Mermaid and the Minotaur: Sexual Arrangements and Human Malaise* (New York: Harper & Row, 1976). Chodorow argues that the pre-Œdipal mother–daughter relationship is more extended than the mother–son relationship. In the former case, there is a greater tendency 'toward boundary confusion and a lack of sense of separateness from the world' (pp. 109, 110).

11. From this angle, imperial Gothic, as defined by Brantlinger, undergoes a change. I do, however, want to retain for my analysis his emphasis on the anxiety generated by the sense of 'waning adventure' that gave rise to the peculiar manifestation of the gothic in the late nineteenth century.

12. ANNE McCLINTOCK, 'Maidens, Maps, and Mines: The Reinvention of Patriarchy in Colonial South Africa', *South Atlantic Quarterly* 87 (1988), pp. 147–92 (p. 151).

13. I explore Conrad's construction of feminized geographies more fully in my 'Empire, Narrative, and the Feminine in Conrad's *Lord Jim* and "Heart of Darkness" ', in *Contexts for Conrad*, ed. Keith Carabine, Owen Knowles, and Wieslaw Krajka (East European Monographs; Boulder: University of Colorado Press, 1993).

14. Live burial, of course, is a common feature of Gothic novels. Recall Agnes, for example, from *The Monk*, who spends several days entombed in the catacombs beneath a convent carrying around the putrefying corpse of her dead child.

15. MARIANNA TORGOVNICK, *Gone Primitive* (Chicago: University of Chicago Press, 1990), p. 156.

16. NORMAN HOLLAND and LEONA SHERMAN, 'Gothic Possibilities', *New Literary History* 8 (1976–77), pp. 279–94 (p. 282).

17. According to Holland and Sherman, the castle, the engulfing space of the Gothic, admits a variety of relationships: 'it becomes all the possibilities of a parent or a body. It can threaten, love, or confine, but in all these actions it stands as a total environment in a one-to-one relation with the victim, like the all-powerful mother of earliest childhood. The castle becomes the entire world of possible relationships for its prisoner' (p. 283).

18. GAYLE RUBIN, 'The Traffic in Women: Notes Toward a Political Economy of Sex', in *Toward an Anthropology of Women*, ed. Rayna Reiter (New York: Monthly Review Press, 1975), p. 210.

19. The object-relations theory that Chodorow and Dinnerstein use has been criticised for its inability to accommodate psychic dimensions to human development. While I agree with this critique insofar as it suggests the

Joseph Conrad

limitations of the theory, I nevertheless find much that is useful in it for understanding mother–daughter relations and for foregrounding issues of gender construction in a text.

20. Rebecca Stott offers a useful examination of Conrad's women in the context of the more popular discourses of race and gender in the *fin de siècle*. See REBECCA STOTT *The Fabrication of the Late Victorian Femme Fatale* (London: Macmillan, 1992), particularly pp. 126–62.

21. The most striking conflation of death and the feminine is the mother's grave. As if this monument did not make the connection clear enough, Marlow offers a sinister description to underscore the threatening aspects of female sexuality: 'The lumps of white coral shone round the dark mound like a chaplet of bleached skulls' (p. 322). Reminiscent of *Heart of Darkness*, this description evokes the devouring, engulfing, cannibalistic features so often associated with the feminine.

22. My essay 'Imperialism and Narrative Understanding in Conrad's *Lord Jim*' (*Studies in the Novel* 24 (1992), pp. 173–86) addresses more fully Marlow's need to 'rescue' Jim; there I focus more directly on the narrative's need to bring Jim back into the ranks of the British merchant marine.

23. Marianne DeKoven argues that Jim's journey East is inscribed as a movement towards the feminine and away from his 'Western (white, imperialist, patriarchal) patrimony'. MARIANNE DEKOVEN, *Rich and Strange: Gender, History, Modernism* (Princeton: Princeton University Press, 1991), p. 150. While I agree with much of DeKoven's argument, I see *Lord Jim* as finally subscribing to the very adventure code it had earlier critiqued (associated with an essentially masculine possibility for fulfilment); DeKoven, however, sees the ending as open. In my reading, Jim's merger with the feminine (opportunity) makes possible his entry into masculinity (adventure hero).

24. Nina Pelikan Straus's assertion that in '*Heart of Darkness* women are used to deny, distort, and censor men's passionate love for one another' can be applied just as well to *Lord Jim*. NINA PELIKAN STRAUS, 'The Exclusion of the Intended from Secret Sharing in *Heart of Darkness*', *Novel* 20 (1987), pp. 123–37 (p. 134). I develop some of the implications of this view in my 'Empire, Narrative, and the Feminine in *Lord Jim* and *Heart of Darkness*'.

25. Marianne DeKoven also argues for the understanding of Patusan as a maternal space which affords Jim a symbolic rebirth.

26. Rather than revisit territory that has been well described by other critics, let me here invoke those works which have contributed to my understanding of those race and gender tensions which culminated in the *fin de siècle*: ELAINE SHOWALTER's *Sexual Anarchy: Gender and Culture at the* Fin de Siècle (New York: Viking Penguin, 1990); EVE KOSOFSKY SEDGWICK's *Between Men: English Literature and Male Homosocial Desire* (New York: Columbia University Press, 1985); MARIANNA TORGOVNICK's *Gone Primitive*; ANNE McCLINTOCK's 'Maidens, Maps, and Mines'; MARTIN GREEN's *Dreams of Adventure, Deeds of Empire*.

27. This essay is part of an ongoing project on the interrelations among race, gender, and empire as they are constructed by Conrad. I thank Radhika Mongia and Andrew Michael Roberts for their responses to earlier versions of this essay; I benefited greatly from their comments.

9 The Exclusion of the Intended from Secret Sharing in Conrad's *Heart of Darkness**

NINA PELIKAN STRAUS

The strength of argument and rich suggestiveness of this analysis of *Heart of Darkness* have made it an inspiration and starting point for much recent work on gender and sexuality in Conrad's fiction. Straus seeks to demonstrate that a feminist reading of this classic modern text is 'central to the enterprise all readers share' (p. 186) because it reveals both the hidden agenda of the text and the hidden motives of a masculinist critical tradition. She uses concepts derived from reader-response criticism and from psychoanalysis, as well as elements of 'personal' or autobiographical criticism, to identify how the symbolic structure of the text and the conventions of mainstream criticism exclude women readers and satisfy the desire of male readers for heroic identification. At the same time she produces a striking new reading of *Heart of Darkness* as a text about 'art's relation to horror' (p. 184), about the guarding of secret knowledge and about the expression and repression of male narcissism, homoerotic desire and homocentric loyalty.

In a stirring but sketchy essay entitled 'Finding Feminist Readings: Dante-Yeats,' Gayatri Spivak writes that 'feminist alternative readings might well question the normative rigor of specialist mainstream scholarship through a dramatization of the autobiographical vulnerability of their provenance.' Such autobiographical dramatization, Spivak points out, has already begun in the work of Jacques Derrida and other male critics, but 'the privilege of autobiography to counter the rigor of theoretical sanctions is accessible to very few of the world's women' (p. 47).

The feminist reader's access to a text like Conrad's *Heart of Darkness* is especially problematic in the terms Spivak considers. Not only is the tale concerned with a kind of mainstream male experience associated with traditional Western high art (penetration into a female wilderness, confrontation with monstrosity, male rites

---

* Reprinted from *Novel: A Forum on Fiction* 20.2 (Winter 1987), pp. 123–7.

Joseph Conrad

of passage, life at the 'edge'), but those who write about it may be tempted to ally themselves with the heroic consciousness that Conrad presents. The feminist reader, in contrast, is apt to be more skeptical about and alienated from this masculinist tradition, and her access to Conrad's text may be so inhibited that her commentary is thrown off its most responsive and useful center. Her pleasure-in-the-text in Roland Barthes' sense may be rendered uneasy. Her understanding of Marlow or Kurtz may produce not psychic plenitude* but psychic penury. The question of the reader-participator's sense of self in imagined contexts obtrudes, and in reading *Heart of Darkness* she becomes aware of a particular kind of ambiguity. Even if the sexism of Marlow and Kurtz is part of the 'horror' that Conrad intends to disclose, the feminist reader cannot but consider that the text is structured so that this horror – though obviously revealed to male and female reader alike – is deliberately hidden from Kurtz's Intended. If *Heart of Darkness* is one of the Ur* texts of modernist high art by which our reading (and teaching) habits are tested, it is a text which makes us tend to distinguish between women *inside* texts and women outside texts, between women as fictive characters and women as living readers. Conrad's tale thus opens several difficult questions: must the woman reader neutralize awareness of her gender so that her reading becomes 'objective' (non-autobiographical) in the way that male readings supposedly are? Is this neutralization in any way a complicity with the sexism of 'mainstream commentary'? Might not the disclosure of her own autobiographical vulnerability throw light on *Heart of Darkness* as an example of how high art functions, or on the question of why, in Spivak's words, 'the traditions and conventions of art are so brutally sexist' (p. 60)?

Not only is the feminist reader traumatized by decades of nearly exclusive male commentary surrounding *Heart of Darkness*, but she may recognize that her own literary response is influenced by this traumatization. She may not be able to take the starting point of her own reading for granted; she may confess, as Spivak does in another context, to the necessity of self-scrutiny regarding the 'intractable starting points' of any literary investigation, to the inevitability of deconstructing her own reading, and to the fact that 'in disclosing complicities the critic-as-subject is herself complicit with the object of her criticism' ('Draupadi,' pp. 382–3). The deliberate installation of an autobiographical response in her own commentary can thus be posited as a way of investigating the repressed irritation that *Heart of Darkness* produces as a type of highly artistic intimidation. But it is not only Conrad as artist towards which this investigation is aimed; it is also aimed at the

172

The Exclusion of the Intended from Secret Sharing

mainstream critics whose own autobiographical resonances are hidden within supposedly objective commentary, and finally at those radical critics who insist on the infinitely regressing 'openness' of *Heart of Darkness*.

Although the woman reader may attempt to take as much pleasure in Conrad's art as does the male reader, this pleasure is aborted by the fact that Marlow presents a world distinctly split into male and female realms – the first harboring the possibility of 'truth' and the second dedicated to the maintenance of delusion. 'Truth,' then, is directed at and intended for men only. As Edward Said suggests, 'the Conradian encounter is not simply between a man and his destiny ... but ... it is the encounter between speaker and hearer. Marlow is Conrad's chief invention for this encounter, Marlow with his haunting knowledge that a man such as Kurtz or Jim "existed for me, and after all it is only through me that he exists for you." The chain of humanity – "we exist only in so far as we hang together" – is the transmission of actual speech' (p. 176). Marlow speaks in *Heart of Darkness* to other men, and although he speaks *about* women, there is no indication that women might be included among his hearers, nor that his existence depends upon his 'hanging together' with a 'humanity' that includes the second sex. The contextuality of Conrad's tale, the deliberate use of a frame to include readers as hearers, suggests the secret nature of what is being told, a secrecy in which Conrad seems to join Marlow. The peculiar density and inaccessibility of *Heart of Darkness* may be the result of its extremely masculine historical referentiality, its insistence on a male circle of readers. This *donnée** is not arbitrary: it determines what Hans Jauss calls the reader's reception, his 'horizon of expectation.' If the impact of a literary work can be described by referring to the 'frame of reference of the reader's expectation' which develops in 'the historical moment of its appearance and from a previous understanding of the genre, from the forms and themes of already familiar works' (pp. 11, 14); the degree to which the woman reader feels herself excluded from worlds familiar to men is the degree to which her reading will be 'pulled from the straight and made to alter its clear vision in deference to external authority' (Woolf, p. 77), or alternately, will be pulled towards the practice of feminist terrorism that mistakenly argues that sexist high art is not high art because it is sexist.

No doubt that the artistic conventions of *Heart of Darkness* are brutally sexist, but this is only the beginning of a larger recognition of the ways in which sexism has so profoundly conventionalized and obscured itself in literature and in literary commentary. An awareness of the different autobiographical vulnerabilities of male

Joseph Conrad

and female readers encountering *Heart of Darkness* is warranted by the fact that Marlow-Conrad discriminates between male and female views of the world, and by the fact that both mainstream and radical critics tend to agree that the novel involves 'irreconcilable points of view in sexually stereotyped characters' (Thompson, p. 461) and 'sets women, who are out of it, against men who can live with the facts' (Miller, p. 47). This is not to suggest that a woman reader cannot identify with Kurtz or Marlow any more than she can identify with the African woman or the Intended, but that her response to the Strong Poet* who is both Conrad and Marlow involves a self-defensiveness and self-consciousness that the male commentator probably does not experience. It is Conrad's text itself that stimulates the notion that the psychic penury of women is a necessary condition for the heroism of men, and whether or not *Heart of Darkness* is a critique of male heroism or is in complex complicity with it, gender dichotomy is an inescapable element of it.

Because 'truth' in *Heart of Darkness* is the possession of men and is hidden 'luckily' from the text's women, the male critic who apprehends this truth, no matter how abominable or ironic, may be enlarged by it. For him, Spivak's question – 'how is the figure of the woman used to achieve this psychotherapeutic plenitude in the practice of the poet's craft?' ('Dante-Yeats,' p. 48) – may be answered by referring to age-old literary and sexual conventions. Gordon Thompson argues, for example, that, for Marlow, woman is the spiritual potential in man's life (p. 451) and that Conrad is 'less interested in the truth or illusion of feminine vision than he is in the impact of that vision on a man seeking meaningful action' (p. 461). Not only are women readers kept in their places within the mainstream criticism to which Thompson makes his addition, but the more radical criticism offered, for example, in J. Hillis Miller's '*Heart of Darkness* Revisited' (1985) casts itself in a mode of skepticism towards Conrad's text whereby doubt is given a status that pays little attention to feminist perceptions. Describing Conrad's text as an apocalyptic parody, Miller argues that 'male practicality and idealism reverse, however. They turn into their opposites because they are hollow at the core. They are vulnerable to the horror. They *are* the horror' (p. 47). By reducing male heroism to the horror of emptiness, Miller seems to detonate the feminist critic's contention that male criticism is self-serving. Yet Miller, like Thompson, can be argued to have penetrated that circle of discourses which Said so astutely recognizes as the Conradian encounter. In complicity with the exemptions literary greatness may claim, the commentator inscribes traces of his (perhaps fantasized) autobiography by analyzing and attaching himself to the Strong

174

The Exclusion of the Intended from Secret Sharing

Poet whose disclosure of horror's meaning certifies the high art of his text. As Annette Kolodny suggests in a reference to the work of Harold Bloom, this inscribing of the critic's closeness to the author is a 'pleasure an (intended and mostly male) readership will take in the discovery that their own activity replicates the psychic adventure of The Poet, every critic's *figura** of heroism' (p. 48).

This kind of critical activity and the psychotherapeutic plenitude it achieves for the commentator is most apparent in the Norton Critical Edition of *Heart of Darkness* (1963). Though revised in 1971 – with addition of a single essay by a female commentator, and this dating back to 1955 – it remained the model. And it clearly suggests the extent to which criticism can be a form of covert autobiography, without the vulnerable consciousness of being so. Indeed, the degree to which the (all male) commentators understand Marlow or Kurtz is the degree to which they can identify the nature of their heroism. No matter how the meaning of *Heart of Darkness* is defined – as a quest within, as a journey to a mythic underworld, as apocalypse, as a critique of imperialism or of Western civilization – the standard commentary centers upon the secret sharings of male characters whose isolation from female language or experience evokes (if not sanctions) the dream of a homocentric universe.

The inhabitants of this universe are not confined to fictional characters or their authors; they include the commentator writing in the masculinist tradition – a tradition, as Geoffrey Hartman reminds us, that provides us with 'a definite term for the man who is so much greater than we are, not morally perhaps but in mode of being – Nietzsche would have said he stands beyond good and evil' and 'he is the hero' (p. 68). The pleasure of identifying oneself, no matter how humbly, with either the character's or the author's heroism is the pleasure of entering a circle of communications about high art to which the concerns of women or woman questions are subordinated. The mainstream critic thus replicates the pattern of the text he describes; his literary method is to stress the formal and aesthetic ingredients at the expense of its sexist resonances; to exclude the possibility of woman's intended views just as Marlow excludes the Intended from sharing in the views his tale discloses. Designed to camouflage the autobiographical origins of its commentary, the Norton essays sustain the masculinist myths they are said to analyze. Stewart Wilcox lyrically summarizes the standard analysis which transforms misogyny into heroism or rationalizes Conrad's aesthetic 'function' for women as morally necessary:

> As a foil to Kurtz's Intended, the native girl signifies his passionate involvement with Time and the Flesh. Adorned with the ivory

Joseph Conrad

of his unholy quest, 'She was savage and superb, wild-eyed and magnificent. . . . And in the hush that had fallen suddenly upon the whole sorrowful land, the immense wilderness, the colossal body of the fecund and mysterious life seemed to look at her, pensive, as though it had been looking at the image of its own tenebrous passionate soul.' . . . What is more to the present purpose, however, is the function of the Intended and the native girl in 'Heart of Darkness.' 'We must help them to stay in that beautiful world of their own, lest our world get worse.' The emphasis here is on moral contrast. . . . The Intended is 'one of those creatures that are not the playthings of Time.' The one is a partner in Kurtz's plunge into Satanic unspeakable rites; the other an examplar of the Fidelity to which man must cling for salvation. Because Kurtz could neither trust in nor be trusted by any other human being, he is forever lost to both women, lost to both the flesh and the spirit.

(p. 216)

Disregarding the contradictions in this passage (Kurtz is both passionately involved with the flesh and lost to it), it is clear that the facile opposition of the native girl's 'flesh' and the Intended's 'spirit' functions here to sustain the commentator's sense of plenitude. As long as the woman of light and the woman of darkness retain their significations as binary opposites, there will be (for male commentator as well as male character) Satanic pleasuring and danger on the one hand and a dutifully sanctioned Fidelity on the other. The answer to Spivak's question becomes possible here: woman is exploited as a signifier, fictively adjusted to conform to the commentator's need to identify himself with characters who have access to *both* light and darkness, whose exclusive incorporation of the dual limitations represented by Kurtz's women (indeed, beyond their good and evil) is the sign of heroism itself. This psychic dependence on the contrasting images of women is never acknowledged, however; and the use of women as one-dimensional objects is rationalized as necessary for 'moral contrast' and the aesthetic (high art) properties of the tale. If moral contrast is a necessary component of high art, it apparently does not strike the male commentator that this morality is immoral – that it justifies sexism and racism – nor that this contrast between soulless flesh and fleshless soul is a jarring note of psychologically reductive simplicity in a text which, when referring to male characters, is psychologically dense.

The tactics by which mainstream critics of *Heart of Darkness* sustain their masculinist brotherhoods do not necessarily depend on the

The Exclusion of the Intended from Secret Sharing

unquestioning misogyny illustrated in the Norton edition. Those who address the Woman Question more directly, who are aware of Conrad's gynophobia* (described so persuasively by Bernard Meyer), nevertheless approach this question in terms that evade the issue of why the high art of *Heart of Darkness* must be so 'brutally sexist.' While some mainstream critics discover rationalizations for excluding women from their consideration by describing female characters as embodying such allegories as Fidelity or Wilderness, others like Ian Watt treat the problem of Kurtz's Intended by referring to Conrad's critique of 'society' as though society were a neutral phenomenon in which sexism and patriarchal self-empowering were non-existent.

> It follows that merely by allotting women a leisure role, society has in effect secluded them from discovering reality; so it is not by chance or fault of hers that the Intended inhabits an unreal world.... Marlow's opinion of leisured women marks the negative example of the idea that work is the basis of the individual's sense of reality; but it also makes them positive examples of the complementary idea of the danger of relying on words.... [The Intended] is armoured by the invincible credulity produced by the unreality of public rhetoric.
>
> (pp. 244–5)

Watt's linkage of the Intended's exclusion from 'reality' with her susceptibility to 'public rhetoric' is persuasive here, but his autobiographical vulnerability is exposed in the phrase 'work is the basis of the individual's sense of reality.' Because the Intended does not work, the argument runs, she is doomed to a delusive innocence. Because Marlow (and Watt) do work, they are both, as Conrad's character and Conrad's critic, installed in a world from which the Intended and all leisurely women are excluded. 'Society' here is given no etiology, but the Intended's exclusion from Reality is. Whereas the cause of woman's inhabiting 'an unreal world' is clearly specified, the reason why 'society' allots her such a role does not appear to interest the commentator. Although Conrad's text suggests that men's society would be threatened if women were allowed access to the male-dominated realm of work where horrifying secrets are discovered, Watt's reading is based on deliberate and traditional omission of this possibility. The notion of 'work' as a heroic enterprise is taken for granted, just as the idea that 'society' is responsible for female unreality can be presented as unquestionable fact. The possibility that the 'psychological power compulsion of men' originated 'the primacy of sexual oppression

177

Joseph Conrad

over all other forms in society' (Mitchell, p. 178) does not complicate the smooth assertion of contrasts in Watt's analysis. The final payoff of this analysis is that the commentator can afford to be generous to the Intended and to leisured women in general, confirming that 'it is not by chance or fault of hers' that she is deluded and excluded.

The issues of sexism and racism have been discussed in recent studies of Conrad, particularly by Edward Said, Karen Klein, Sandra Gilbert, Susan Brodie, Ruth Nadelhaft, among others. However, it seems dubious to argue that Conrad knew well what he wrote in *Heart of Darkness*, and that women are excluded from the circle of readers not *by him*, but by the speaker Conrad seeks to expose. Nadelhaft argues that in *Almayer's Folly* and *An Outcast of the Islands* 'women, frequently half-breeds, represent the clearest means of challenging and revealing Western male insularity and domination' (pp. 242–3). Certainly Winnie Verloc in *The Secret Agent* and Miss Haldin of *Under Western Eyes* are evoked with a complexity quite different from the treatment of the Intended or the African woman in *Heart of Darkness*. But these texts are not about a Congo wilderness in which 'the stillness of an implacable force brood[s] over an inscrutable intention'; they do not insist that the 'savage' woman is 'like the wilderness itself, with an air of brooding over an inscrutable purpose.' They do not close in their last pages with the teller of the tale confronting one woman while thinking about the other, placing the dark figure over the light figure like a transparency as though this layering replicated the mysterious obscurity of the 'truth' itself:

> I will see this eloquent phantom as long as I live, and I shall see her too, a tragic and familiar Shade, resembling in this gesture another one, tragic also, and bedecked with powerless charms, stretching bare brown arms over the glitter of the infernal stream, the stream of darkness.

In *Heart of Darkness* Conrad's impressionistic metaphors work with a looseness of association that suggests the inscribing of unconscious or at least dream-like condensations regarding women. The savage woman, condensed into Wilderness, presides over the 'infernal' horror and mystery; and the Intended, emblem of society, is nothing less than another kind of horror – another inscrutable 'intention' that Marlow defends himself against through his specious complicity with her need to describe Kurtz as having a 'noble heart.' It is possible that the images of women in *Heart of Darkness* are thus immobilized in order to suggest a critique of Marlow's heroism – a

178

The Exclusion of the Intended from Secret Sharing

critique of his delusion that 'what saves us is efficiency' – which attaches Marlow to the destructive coil of the imperialist venture itself. Yet the narrator who tells us that 'Marlow was not typical,' that 'to him the meaning of an episode was not inside like a kernel but outside, enveloping the tale which brought it out only as a glow brings out a haze,' is also (as J. Hillis Miller suggests) describing his own literary method. That this method depends on the production of 'haze,' of deliberate ambiguity, makes the question of Conrad's intentions for his tale difficult to adjudicate. What can be analyzed, however, is the effect of Conrad's words on various readers; and it is the contention of this essay that these words are understood differently by feminist readers and by mainstream male commentators. In the possible paranoia that this text generates for certain women readers, the production of literary 'haze' seems to function not only to hide something from Marlow, but from Conrad himself. The 'horror' of the wilderness/society polarity suggests the difficulty Conrad, along with his surrogate spokesman, has in finding a clear place to stand in relation to them – a difficulty, moreover, which replicates the difficulty of the male's standing in relation to both 'wild' and civilized women. Whether Marlow is intended to be a parody of a wiseman or whether he is, as the last paragraph of the tale indicates, meant to preside as Conrad's 'meditating Buddha,' the Conradian encounter is between men and men, or at the most, between men and women who are willing to suspend their womanliness far enough to forever disassociate themselves from the women characters in *Heart of Darkness*.

As receiver, 'foil,' 'moral contrast,' or emblem of 'armoured unreality,' the Intended is reserved for the role of white lady in the tower, just as Marlow, among the other roles he plays, is reserved for the role of heroic deliverer of that lady. As in the *Romance of the Rose*, literary convention demands that Marlow as hero must penetrate the thorny thicket that surrounds the lady; in this case the 'sepulchral city' with its 'people hurrying through the streets to filch a little money . . . to dream their insignificant and silly dreams.' The form Marlow's heroism takes is that of rescuing the Intended from 'inner truth.' The lie Marlow offers her is understood to be a form of chivalric, albeit ironic, sacrifice, cryptically underscoring an ideology that defines a protective lie as a moral act. We are meant to see Marlow grit his teeth as he does it; he, like Prometheus, risks the wrath of the Gods. 'It seemed to me that . . . the heavens would fall upon my head.' Unlike Prometheus, however, Marlow brings truth to men by virtue of his bringing falsehood to women. Heroic maleness is defined precisely in adverse relation to delusional

179

Joseph Conrad

femininity. And Marlow's power to incorporate both the 'truth' of 'darkness' and the necessary illusions of 'light' is exactly what separates him from those deluded others incapable of grasping his psychic plenitude.

Psychotherapeutic plenitude is thus reserved for those who can identify with Marlow, and through Marlow, with Kurtz. For a woman reader to do so is to court self-degradation, and this is not a problem specific to *Heart of Darkness* but also to Yeats and Dante and to much of what constitutes the canon of high art. At the end of Conrad's tale Seymour Gross reminds us, 'the transformation has been complete; "the benign immensity of unstained light" has become "the heart of an immense darkness." Now [the narrator], like Marlow, will be set apart from all those who do not know the truth' (p. 202). And it is clear that for Seymour Gross, as well as Watt and the host of male critics who are able to identify the imaginative autobiography of their masculinity with Marlow's, this set-apartness, this full psychic cup engineered by transcending 'good and evil,' is what they expect from reading and analyzing *Heart of Darkness.*

A woman's experience of the text is quite different. Whether the woman 'armours' herself as Watt describes with the 'public rhetoric' of female purity and 'Fidelity,' and thus attempts to identify with the Intended; or whether the reader psychically enacts a 'flight from womanhood,' to use Karen Horney's words (p. 211) – a flight which an identification with Marlow or Kurtz might entail – the woman reader has no access to the sense of pleasure or plenitude which male critics display in their readings of *Heart of Darkness.* A third possibility for the woman reader is to identify with Kurtz's savage queen, that mirror of wilderness, that earth mother in bangles in whose body the white man seeks to bury his civilization's discontents. The queen's image, though visually full, is psychically void and nearly inhuman; for it is explicitly allied with that abominable darkness described by Marlow, essentialized in Kurtz's voice; and Conrad's text offers no woman's voice or variant female version of wilderness to the reader. In terms of the autobiographical impulse which we have argued here to be an unexpungeable element in criticism, the brown queen offers nothing to the feminist reader but the possible dream of regression.

Of the three alternatives, none is full; each suggests the degradation of the other; and high art seems nearly to be defined by its propensity to stimulate the woman reader to abandon her own concerns. Goethe's revolutionary question, 'What is it for *me?*' seems clearly answered in terms of women: it is *not* for you; it is not *intended* to be for you. Implied here is the curious semantic

180

The Exclusion of the Intended from Secret Sharing

puzzle that might also be one of the conventions of a language which tells lies to women about herself: You are the INTENDED. How can an INTENDED have INTENTIONS?

At this point, Spivak's third question: 'what, then, does a woman do with the reactionary sexual ideology of high art?' becomes inexorable. If such art is traditionally the occasion for the male critic to sustain archetypal autobiography through conventional language techniques that mask the subjective resonance of his commentary so that it appears to be 'objective,' then a radical feminist criticism of high art would remove the mask to disclose the particular delusions intrinsic to a particular literary work.

In one sense psychoanalysis has already done this, if we are to take Freud's rather mocking description of the hero in 'The Poet and Day-Dreaming' as the measure of modern de-mystification:

> There is one very marked characteristic in the productions of these writers which must strike us all: they all have a hero who is the centre of interest, for whom the author tries to win our sympathy by every possible means, and whom he places under the protection of a special providence. . . . The feeling of security with which I follow the hero through his dangerous adventures is the same as that with which a real hero throws himself into the water to save a drowning man, or exposes himself to the fire of the enemy while storming a battery. It is this very feeling of being a hero which one of our best authors has well expressed in the famous phrase, 'Nothing can happen to me!' [trans.] It seems to me, however, that the significant mark of invulnerability very clearly betrays – His Majesty the Ego, the hero of all day-dreams and novels.
>
> (pp. 50–1)

No doubt Freud is prone to literary reductiveness here, yet the passage foreshadows his later discussions of narcissism. For Freud was to discover in this heroic 'nothing can happen to me!' the roots of a narcissistic paranoia and melancholy. Although Marlow is often presented as one who, after Kurtz's death, comes back to Brussels heroically carrying the psychic load (if not dead body) of his secret sharer in order to somehow deliver its remains to the Intended, the thing the woman reader can 'do' is to note how contingent Marlow's mental state is upon the decision he makes to lie to the Intended, to decide that the truth about Kurtz is 'too dark' to reveal to her, and to harbor within himself a mystery he will reveal much later only to those 'man' enough to take it.

181

Joseph Conrad

Mourning for Kurtz, nearly driven 'mad' by his revelations in the Congo, Marlow's self-reproaches are oddly passionate and each one of them is connected to Kurtz:

> And then they nearly buried me.
> However, as you see, I did not go to join Kurtz then and there. I remained to dream the nightmare out to the end, and to show my loyalty to Kurtz once more. Destiny. My Destiny! Droll thing life is – that mysterious arrangement of merciless logic for a futile purpose. The most you can hope from it is some knowledge of yourself – that comes too late – a crop of inextinguishable regrets . . .

Speaking of his near death, Marlow tells his hearers that 'I was within a hair's breadth of the last opportunity for pronouncement, and I found with humiliation that probably I would have nothing to say. This is the reason why I affirm that Kurtz was a remarkable man. . . . He had summed up – he had judged. "The horror!" He was a remarkable man. . . . he had stepped over the edge, while I had been permitted to draw back my hesitating foot. . . . Better his cry. . . .'

Better than what? Marlow never tells. Better than Marlow's 'having nothing to say,' and obviously better than the Intended's hysterical 'I loved him – I loved him' and 'I want – something!' But the point is that Marlow's self-disgust colors all he sees: the 'intruders' in the 'sepulchral city' whose 'bearing, which was simply the bearing of commonplace individuals going about their business in the assurance of perfect safety, was offensive to me like the flautings of folly in the face of danger it is unable to comprehend.' Marlow 'totter[s]' about the streets, finds the official who comes for Kurtz's papers 'darkly menacing,' has a vision of Kurtz on the 'stretcher, opening his mouth voraciously, as if to devour all the earth with all its mankind.' And in these images of being devoured, in the sense that Marlow is set apart with Kurtz from the 'commonplace,' a glimpse of Marlow's narcissistic dream emerges. Censored and distorted by the language of romantic agony, Marlow's language is nonetheless immersed in what Freud calls 'narcissistic identification' where 'the object' (Kurtz) 'has been set up in the ego itself.'

> He lived then before me; he lived as much as he had ever lived – a shadow insatiable of splendid appearances, of frightful realities; a shadow darker than the shadow of the night, and draped nobly in the folds of a gorgeous eloquence. . . . The vision

The Exclusion of the Intended from Secret Sharing

seemed to enter the house with me – the stretcher, the phantom-bearers, the wild crowd of obedient worshippers, the gloom of the forests, the glitter of the reach between the murky bends, the beat of the drum, regularly and muffled like the beating of a heart – the heart of a conquering darkness. It was a triumph for the wilderness, an invading and vengeful rush which, it seemed to me, I would have to keep back alone for the salvation of another soul.

Freud argues that in narcissistic identification, which is closer to homosexual object-choice than to the heterosexual kind, the self-reproaches and regrets are in the service of 'repelling an undesirably strong homosexual impulse. . . . The subject . . . strikes with a single blow at his own ego and the loved and hated object' (*Introductory Lectures*, pp. 426–7).

Marlow's language, intertwining descriptions of Kurtz's 'abject pleadings' with his 'gorgeous eloquence' and with Marlow's own 'humiliation' and suspicion that 'perhaps . . . all truth, and all sincerity, are just compressed into that inappreciable moment of time in which we step over the threshold of the invisible' – suggests what Freud calls narcissistic 'ambivalence.' For it is clear that Marlow's identification with Kurtz is of a violently passionate kind; it leads to self-loathing, to the shadowing of self called depression, to an urge to escape from this state itself – an urge Marlow articulates in his 'there remained only his memory and his Intended – and I wanted to give that up, too.' There are glimpses in the text's imagery of Marlow's wish to be swallowed by Kurtz, to 'join' him in death, and finally to be 'rush[ed]' and invaded by the wilderness which Kurtz embodies. Finally, in the passage quoted above, a particular movement of psychic energy is dramatized: a vision of Kurtz appears to Marlow, intensifies ('enter[ed] the house with me') and blossoms into savage rites for a dying god. In images which compound terror with desire (sexual energy with violence, if you will), the climactic moment is described in terms of the 'beating of a heart.' It is at that climactic and visionary moment of excitement when Marlow's identification with Kurtz is most intense that Marlow decides to 'keep back' what he knows, the depth of what he feels, from the Intended.

Marlow's rationalization comes quickly, is perhaps hardly noticeable to the reader who accepts as heroic Marlow's decision to lie. The morality of 'salvation of another soul' is intrinsic to the conventions of high art from the story of Jesus through Joyce's *Ulysses*. But whom does such morality save here? Does not Marlow

183

Joseph Conrad

save himself, at this crucial moment of memory, hate and desire, from the disclosure of a knowledge that is 'too dark' for him to bear? 'Not the least of the ironies of *Heart of Darkness*,' suggests David Thorburn in his *Conrad's Romanticism*, 'is Marlow's blindness to the fact that his comments about Kurtz's harlequin exactly describe his own responses to Kurtz and to the task of telling about him. His evasive account, as Guerard has shown, approaches Kurtz only reluctantly, postponing the climactic encounter with obsessive ingenuity. Like the harlequin, Marlow, his life filled with Kurtz, is yet "jealous of sharing with any the peculiar blackness of that experience"' (p. 143). Having gone this far in explaining the nature of Marlow's relation to Kurtz, both Thorburn and Guerard stop. The connection between Marlow's 'blindness' and his final encounter with the Intended does not interest these critics, for the Intended is not considered as in any way part of the text's problem. Whether Marlow is trustworthy or blinded, he is understood to heroically deliver the Intended from 'darkness,' and his capacity to deliver insinuates his link to a more traditional heroism.

It is clear that Marlow prefers Kurtz's cry of 'the horror' to the Intended's cry of 'I loved him.' For 'horror' is the secret password in the brotherhood of men who 'know.' Frederick Karl comes very close to acknowledging that there is less a moral question involved than an aesthetic one, one that has to do with the conventions of art per se. 'Kurtz:death: ivory:art are intermingled. He *is* ivory' (p. 459 n.). To take this one step further towards the questions posed in this essay, the woman reader might notice that *Heart of Darkness* is *about* art's relation to horror – that the excitement and mystery of horror, the 'fascination of the abominable' is the revelation that Marlow offers to his brotherhood of 'hearers' who constitute both his mates inside the text and his mates outside of it. If for Conrad/Marlow, art is inextricably linked with a horror which only men can experience, it is finally this art-horror that Marlow must 'keep back alone' from the Intended who is woman.

If Marlow's sense of horror is unmasked to reveal his love for Kurtz, his love for Kurtz's 'cry' which is his art, then the woman reader comes closer to understanding the motive for Marlow's behavior with the Intended. So deeply impressed is Marlow with Kurtz's ability to 'cry' and 'say' something about the 'profound riddle of life' – that Marlow incorporates this riddle and these words of horror which embody it. He comes not only to possess these words but to jealously guard them; and finally, faced with the task of symbolically rendering Kurtz unto the Intended, Marlow cannot bear to share him with her.

184

The Exclusion of the Intended from Secret Sharing

To answer Spivak's question more directly: what the woman reader can 'do' is to recognize that in *Heart of Darkness* women are used to deny, distort, and censor men's passionate love for one another. Projecting his own love on to the form of the Intended, Marlow is able to conceal from himself the dark complexity of his own love – a love that strikes him with horror – for Kurtz. This is not to claim that the conventions of high art are homosexual, but rather to suggest that Marlow's relation to Kurtz as his commentator is a paradigm of the relation of the male critic's relation to the Strong Poet. That a homocentric loyalty exists (a loyalty to the sexist nightmare of one's choice) is not surprising, for it confirms the relations of love between men who are each other's 'narcissistic objects'; or to put it another way, whose enterprise as readers and critics (hearers-speakers) affirms the greatness of the one and the possessive attempt to appropriate that greatness by the other.

The 'psychotherapeutic plenitude' of which Spivak speaks may therefore be a result of gender identification. This suggests that high art is in some way a confirmation of the one gender's access to certain secrets (in this case the secret conjunction of art and horror) which would be both deconstructed and demystified if the Intended had access to it. Could Marlow's truth be dramatized without the Intended's contrasting delusion? Would such notions as romantic agony and secret experience of 'inner truth' be able to be named if there were not a nameless one who is 'allotted' (to use Watt's word) to a world of merely outer or 'public rhetoric'? The guarding of secret knowledge is thus the undisclosed theme of *Heart of Darkness* which a woman reader can discover. Marlow's protectiveness is no longer seen in the service of woman's deluded desires, but serves the therapeutic end of keeping the woman/intended mute. The male hearers of Marlow's tale never hear the Intended's name. She remains in the stereotypically convenient world of 'she.' She lacks that one distinguishing feature of the beloved, which is that she is absolutely individual to the one who loves her. The Intended is thus thrice voided or erased: her name is never spoken by Kurtz, by Marlow, or by Conrad; and it is determined that it will never be spoken by Conrad's commentators.

The erasure of the Intended represents a final stage in the development of the brutally sexist conventions of high art. Dante's Beatrice and Yeats' Maud have faces, voices, and names. But Conrad's Intended is no more than a 'pale head, floating towards me in the dusk.' What this figure achieves, as perhaps few other female characters in fiction do, is what could nicely be called negative capability* but which is psychologically symbolic of the

Joseph Conrad

male's need for an infinite receptivity and passivity. Male heroism and plenitude depend on female cowardice and emptiness. Dante creates truth and embodies it; when Maud shrieks from the lectern, Yeats is unmanned. Because the female figure's psychic penury is so valuable in asserting the heroism of the Strong Poet and the Strong Poet's character, the male commentator (who serves both) is filled with pleasure – a pleasure so therapeutic that it subverts his capacity to discover *on what terms* Marlow is a hero or a coward.

Because the woman reader is not so 'filled,' she is in the position to insist that Marlow's cowardice consists of his inability to face the dangerous self that is the form of his own masculinist vulnerability: his own complicity in the racist, sexist, imperialist, and finally libidinally satisfying world he has inhabited with Kurtz.

Lionel Trilling, in a discussion from *Sincerity and Authenticity*, makes this clear when he notes that 'Marlow accords to Kurtz an admiration and loyalty which amounts to homage, and not, it would seem, despite of his deeds but because of them' (p. 106). If this loyalty to Kurtz is constituted by Marlow's knowledge that the 'black shadows of disease and starvation,' the trophy fence of shrunken human heads, the 'rapacious folly' and fascinating 'abomination' are all Kurtz's creations, then Marlow's lie to the Intended is neither heroic nor protective so much as self-deluded. It serves not the Intended but Marlow's own subconscious intentions.

Although a woman cannot, since Henry James, distort the Strong Poet's *donnée* nor re-write his ending, as Samuel Johnson was impelled to do in the case of *King Lear*, she can register her radical protest against the continual romanticization of a work like *Heart of Darkness*, and against the ongoing critical insistence that this work is in some way moral. Art is not moral. High art may be especially immoral. Its province is pleasure, 'psychotherapeutic plenitude.' The question for the future is: whose pleasure does it serve? Does *Heart of Darkness* become less authentic, less finally recognizable as the truth of our times, when it is recognized that it is less the comprehensive human Id that is disclosed than a certain kind of male self-mystification whose time is passing if not past? The cultural context in which a woman character can be exploited in the ways Conrad's Intended is exploited, cannot be affirmed in a humanist criticism without embarrassment to both men and women. What this leads to is the degree to which feminist commentary on literature is central to the enterprise all readers share. One would hope that the exposure of male autobiographical vulnerability in the choosing of literary canons, in the perpetuating of certain myths about what constitutes morality, will contribute to the confidence that women commentators and women novelists are seeking. The

186

The Exclusion of the Intended from Secret Sharing

privilege of *conscious* autobiographical dramatization on a woman commentator's part must become less rare. Perhaps new artistic conventions will be created thereby, conventions which are able to serve both art *and* truth.

Works cited

All quotations from *Heart of Darkness* are taken from Joseph Conrad, Norton Critical Edition, *Heart of Darkness*, ed. Robert Kimbrough. New York: W. W. Norton, 1963.

Brodie, Susan Lundvall. 'Conrad's Feminine Perspective'. *Conradiana* 16 (1984), pp. 141–54.

Freud, Sigmund. *Introductory Lectures on Psychoanalysis*, ed. & trans. Lytton Strachey. New York: W. W. Norton, 1966.

—— 'The Relation of the Poet and Daydreaming'. *Creativity and the Unconscious: Papers on the Psychology of Art, Literature, Love, Religion*, ed. Benjamin Nelson. New York: Harper and Row, 1958, pp. 44–54.

Gilbert, Sandra. 'Rider Haggard's Heart of Darkness'. *Partisan Review* 50 (1983), pp. 444–53.

Gross, Seymour. 'A Further Note on the Function of the Frame in *Heart of Darkness*'. Joseph Conrad, Norton Critical Edition, *Heart of Darkness*, ed. Robert Kimbrough. New York: W. W. Norton, 1963.

Guerard, Albert. *Conrad the Novelist*. Cambridge MA: Harvard University Press, 1958.

Hartman, Geoffrey. *Beyond Formalism: Literary Essays*. New Haven: Yale University Press, 1970.

Horney, Karen. *Feminine Psychology*. New York: W. W. Norton, 1967.

Jauss, Hans Robert. 'Literary History as a Challenge to Literary Theory'. *New Literary History* 2 (1970), pp. 7–37.

Karl, Frederick. *Joseph Conrad: The Three Lives, A Biography*. New York: Farrar, Straus and Giroux, 1979.

Klein, Karen, 'The Feminist Predicament in Conrad's *Nostromo*'. *Brandeis Essays in Literature*, ed. John H. Smith. Waltham, MA: Dept. of English and American Literature, Brandeis University, 1983.

Kolodny, Annette. 'A Map of Rereading: Gender and the Interpretation of Literary Texts'. *The New Feminist Criticism: Essays on Women, Literature and Theory*, ed. Elaine Showalter. New York: Pantheon Books, 1985, pp. 46–62.

Meyer, Bernard. *Joseph Conrad: A Psychoanalytic Biography*. Princeton, NJ: Princeton University Press, 1967.

Miller, J. Hillis. '*Heart of Darkness* Revisited'. *Conrad Revisited*, ed. Ross C. Murfin. University: University of Alabama Press, 1985.

Mitchell, Juliet. *Woman's Estate*. New York: Pantheon Books, 1971.

Nadelhaft, Ruth. 'Women as Moral and Political Alternatives in Conrad's Early Novels'. *Theory and Practice of Feminist Literary Criticism*, ed. Gabriela Mora and Karen S. van Hooft. Ypsilanti, MI: Bilingual Press, 1982.

Said, Edward. 'The Text, the World, the Critic'. *Textual Strategies: Perspectives in Post-Structuralist Criticism*, ed. Josue V. Hararl. Ithaca, New York: Cornell University Press, 1979, pp. 161–88.

Spivak, Gayatri Chakrovorty. 'Draupadi' by Mahasveta Devi, trans. with a Foreword by Gayatri Spivak. *Critical Inquiry* 8 (1981), pp. 381–402.

—— 'Finding Feminist Readings: Dante-Yeats'. *American Criticism in the Post-Structuralist Age*, ed. Ira Konigsberg. Ann Arbor: University of Michigan Press, 1982.

Joseph Conrad

Thompson, Gordon. 'Conrad's Women'. *Nineteenth Century Fiction* 32 (1978), pp. 442–63.

Thorburn, David. *Conrad's Romanticism*. New Haven: Yale University Press, 1974.

Trilling, Lionel. *Sincerity and Authenticity*. Cambridge, MA: Harvard University Press, 1972.

Watt, Ian. *Conrad in the Nineteenth Century*. Berkeley: University of California Press, 1979.

Wilcox, Stewart C. 'Conrad's "Complicated Presentations" of Symbolic Imagery'. Joseph Conrad, Norton Critical Edition, *Heart of Darkness*, ed. Robert Kimbrough. New York: W. W. Norton, 1963.

Woolf, Virginia. *A Room of One's Own*. New York: Harcourt Brace and World, 1957.

10 Conrad's and Ford's Criminal Romance*

WAYNE KOESTENBAUM

This excerpt is an example of how gay criticism can re-read a canonical author, in this case combining biographical information with close attention to double meanings within the text. Koestenbaum focuses on *Romance*, a collaborative exercise in romantic fiction by Conrad and his fellow novelist Ford Madox Ford. This novel is rarely judged worthy of much critical attention, but interest in issues of gender and sexuality has tended to widen the range of Conrad texts (see Introduction, p. 3). Gay criticism has increasingly been concerned, not only to rediscover and revalue the work of avowedly or evidently homosexual writers, and texts about gay experience, but also to examine the construction of masculinity in other texts. Koestenbaum's aim is not to claim that Conrad was, in any decisive sense, homosexual, but to position Conrad's collaboration with Ford on the homosocial spectrum of bonds between men. Nevertheless, it is part of his argument that homoerotic energies and fantasies were involved in many male friendships which, at the time, disavowed them. Ford and Conrad, like other literary collaborators such as Ezra Pound and T. S. Eliot, 'collaborated in order to separate homoeroticism from the sanctioned male bonding that upholds patriarchy' (Koestenbaum, p. 3). Nevertheless, according to Koestenbaum, 'men who collaborate engage in a metaphorical sexual intercourse' (Koestenbaum, p. 3), with the text alternately given the role of child and of shared woman.

Although Conrad was 41 and Ford was 24 when they began in 1898 to write *Romance*, the most substantial of their three collaborative novels, neither writer was master. Ford later claimed that Conrad had sought him out because he was the most 'boomed' writer in England at the time, while partisans of Conrad considered that Ford was an interloper 'shamelessly laying eggs' in the other man's

---

* Reprinted from *Double Talk: The Erotics of Male Literary Collaboration* (New York and London: Routledge, 1989), pp. 166–73.

Joseph Conrad

nest; and yet *Romance*, an apprentice novel on which they lavished six years, hatched both men's careers.[1] Pound turned Yeats into a modernist; Conrad and Ford did the trick for each other. They described the gestation of their collaborative novels in terms of childbearing, even if they claimed the results were more manly than maternal.

When Conrad and Ford began writing *Romance*, each of their wives had recently delivered a first child. Their second collaborative novel, *The Inheritors* (whose title suggests its concern with issue and generation), was written while Elsie Hueffer, Ford's wife, was pregnant. Women's biology affected the men's pronouncements on collaboration. In the preface to their third and last joint novel, *The Nature of a Crime* (1909), Conrad described the work as a mystery born and then forgotten: 'the details of its birth ... remain for me completely forgotten.'[2] Ford continued the birth metaphor when describing the difficulties of urging his collaborator to write: Ford pushed him 'towards writing as the drake manoeuveres the sitting duck back to the nest when she has abandoned her eggs.'[3] They also turned to language of male reproductive sexuality: Conrad, commenting on their extravagant writing sessions, exclaimed, 'This is collaboration if you like! Joking aside the expenditure of nervous fluid was immense.'[4] Debt follows from excessive spending: Conrad owed Ford money, which remained unpaid as late as 1921, though they had quarreled in 1909 and parted ways.

Despite their investment in maternity, Conrad and Ford tried to keep their prose clear of women. They could remove women from their fiction because they never admitted women into their conversation – or so Ford claims, insisting that 'in all our extreme intimacy, lasting for many years, neither of us ever told what is called a smoking-room story. We never even discussed the relations of the sexes.'[5] The women who appeared in their collaborative novels were Ford's exclusive responsibility, and were so bothersome to Conrad that he once exclaimed, 'Damn Ford's women.'[6] Though he included women in their novels, Ford omitted Conrad's wife from his 200-odd page memoir, *Joseph Conrad: A Personal Remembrance*; she retaliated by denouncing Ford in a letter to the *Times Literary Supplement*. Ford's literary technique of 'impressionism' permitted him to sentimentalize the bygone days of the two men's friendship and to do away with all evidence that Conrad had a wife.

Pining for a past of pure form and beauty (much as Pater and the aesthetes yearned for a homosexual Renaissance), Conrad and Ford turned to [Robert Louis] Stevenson's name and works for succor. Though they consciously imitated that progenitor of the boy's book, Conrad professed surprise when W. E. Henley invoked the master

190

Conrad's and Ford's Criminal Romance

in connection with their paltry plans for *Romance*. Conrad humbly exclaimed that Stevenson and Dumas were 'big names and I assure You it had never occurred to me they could be pronounced in connection with my plan to work with Hueffer [Ford].'[7] Conrad, who assumed that Stevenson would never have stooped to collaborate, feared 'sneers at collaboration – sneers at those two men who took six years to write "this very ordinary tale" whereas R. L. S. single handed produced his masterpieces.'[8] Conrad implies that only weak men collaborate, and forgets that Stevenson's labors were not all singlehanded. Like many writers of their time, Conrad and Ford demanded that prose be manly. Ford considered his collaborator a 'he-man,' and envied his few but virile contributions to *The Inheritors*: whenever words of Conrad's appear, they 'crepitate from the emasculated prose like firecrackers amongst ladies' skirts.'[9] Ford assumes that prose is most masculine when it can shock and harm women.

Despite their hostility to women, and their reactionary conviction that 'the writing of novels is the only pursuit worth while for a proper man,'[10] they attempted a new kind of novel that might undermine masculinity by complicating it. Ford believed that narrative chronology, when shattered, would unmask the British man and reveal his secret neurasthenia. The problem with the British novel, according to Ford, was that 'it went straight forward'; however, when getting to know an 'English gentleman at your golf club,' you only discover his character gradually, and never 'go straight forward.' The man who originally seems 'beefy, full of health, the model of the boy from an English Public School of the finest type,' turns out to be 'hopelessly neurasthenic.' The only way to capture such a man in fiction is to 'work backwards and forwards over his past,' and to eschew chronological order.[11] Conrad and Ford avoided moving 'straight forward'; indulging in temporal weaving, they could present a man who was *not* straight. Ford used the very word 'queer' to describe his loathing for *The Inheritors*, 'a queer, thin book which the writer has always regarded with an intense dislike.' Only a 'psychopathic expert,' Ford claimed, could find the 'obscure nervous first cause' that motivated his 'hatred and dread.'[12] Ford associated queerness with an illogical hatred, and straightness with a traditional fiction that was, however, unable to register finer points of degenerate character.

Conrad, too, used the word 'queer' to demarcate a region of feeling he could not explain. In the veiled autobiography of *The Mirror of the Sea*, he described his 'queer symptoms' – 'inexplicable periods of powerlessness, sudden accesses of mysterious pain.'[13] For this hysteria, the captain ordered a silent rest cure. Ford, who

Joseph Conrad

played the doctor's part within the collaboration, remedied Conrad's writing block by applying hypnotic pressure: according to Conrad, his partner exerted that 'gentle but persistent pressure which extracted, from the depths of my then despondency, the stuff of the *Personal Record*.'[14] Pulling unformed 'stuff' from depths, an act of midwifery, places Ford in the analyst's position; and yet he, too, suffered hysteria, seeing a specialist who diagnosed nervous breakdown, prescribed sea voyage, and forbade work for six months.[15] Both Conrad and Ford suffered from a hysteria that collaboration could successfully treat.

Collaboration may have alleviated their hysteria, but it also inspired new anxieties. Writing with another man meant entering his prose's body: Wells, afraid that Ford would wreck Conrad's style, warned, 'It's as delicate as clockwork and you'll only ruin it by sticking your fingers in it.'[16] Wells, who narrowly avoided collaborating with James, describes double writing as a matter of fingers stuck where they do not belong. Conrad and Ford, however, enjoyed this sensation of transgression, and proudly labeled their work criminal. Conrad wrote, 'You cannot really suppose that there is anything between us except our mutual regard and our partnership – in crime'; and Ford remembered Conrad shuffling the manuscript pages of *Romance* 'distastefully as if they had been the evidence of a crime.'[17] Their collaboration was criminal because its ambitions were so revolutionary: they meant to alter the techniques that fiction used to represent masculinity. Working with Conrad on *Romance* at night, Ford recalls whispering 'in a conspiracy against the sleeping world.'[18] *Romance* provides evidence of other, more tangible crimes that double writing displaced.

Romance is caught between an allegiance to the 'boy's book' and to an enameled perfection that the collaborators associate with Flaubert. A primer in *le mot juste*, the novel also indicts literature as an effeminate pastime, and longs for the rough sea life. The boyish protagonist, John Kemp, flees England to rebel against the literary impotence of his father, a man 'powerless and lost in his search for rhymes,' who sits all day, 'happy in an ineffectual way,' 'inscribing "ideas" every now and then in a pocket-book.'[19] Kemp wistfully remarks, 'I think he was writing an epic poem' (p. 5). Anti-imperialist as Conrad's and Ford's politics might have been, the novel mistily renders this boy's desire for a patriarchal strength his father's poems could not attain; the novel broods on the chimerical vision of an 'England stable and undismayed, like a strong man who had kept his feet in the tottering of secular edifices shaken to their foundations' (p. 120). Although Conrad and Ford depict empire as morally murky, the ardor in the novel arises from scenes of men

Conrad's and Ford's Criminal Romance

exerting sexual power over each other, a charismatic influence that the novel cannot say is either good or evil. The novel's very artfulness makes it hard to tell the villains and the heroes apart; leaving the reader in the dark, the novel will not decide whether one man's sexual sway over another man is base or ecstatic.

Like Stevenson, Conrad and Ford declare this ambiguity through the word 'queer.' In *Romance*, everything is queer, from ships ('Queer-looking boats crawled between the shores') to the knowledge garnered from long voyage ('I was another man by that time, with much queer knowledge and other desires') (p. 34). Leaving England, Kemp is transformed into the very pirates he fears; indeed, he enters the outlaw's life under the grip of a hypnotic Carlos who looked him 'straight in the face with a still, penetrating glance of his big, romantic eyes,' and 'whispered seductively,' 'I like you, Jack Kemp' (pp. 37–8). Kemp, fascinated, noted that Carlos 'was all eyes in the dusk, standing in a languid pose' (p. 38). This seductive man, whose proposition, according to the recipient, rings 'so sweetly and persuasively that the suggestiveness of it caused a thrill in me' (p. 38), and whose hand-clasp 'thrilled me like a woman's' (p. 40), urges the narrator to enter a Romance; through this scene of homosexual seduction, Conrad and Ford describe the allure of a collaborative practice associated with Stevenson's genre. When Carlos leaves, he 'leaned over and kissed me lightly on the cheek, then climbed away. I felt that the light of Romance was going out of my life' (pp. 40–1). The 'Romance' that so sways Kemp and his authors is a homosexual love affair, a literary genre, and a nimbus of attractive degeneracy surrounding fantasies of English power.

The novel is so filled with near-naked men, in postures of threat and repose, that one searches, baffled, for the node in the narrator's voice from which these scenes emanate. Are Conrad and Ford indifferent to the flesh they depict? The scenes pass as realism and local color; they convey menace – for the naked ones are usually pirates who might easily murder the narrator or expose his identity. And yet the flesh exceeds its apparent purpose; Conrad and Ford interpret 'romance' to mean a man's life among men and wish sexual implications to go undetected. Hairy pirates populate the book; the more bloodthirsty they are, the less clothed. A ruffian 'paused, and undid his shirt, laying bare an incredibly hairy chest; then slowly kicked off his shoes. "One stifles here," he said. "Ah! in the old days – "' (p. 100). This pirate turns to Kemp 'with an air of indescribable interest, as if he were gloating over an obscene idea' (p. 100). Conventions of the Stevenson-forged 'romance' novel permit Conrad and Ford to depict, as objects of desire, men whose menace prevents the scenes from lapsing into sex. A man who

193

Joseph Conrad

almost murders Kemp on board a ship turns lovely a few pages
later: 'To this day I remember the beauty of that rugged, grizzled,
hairy seaman's eyelashes. They were long and thick, shadowing the
eyes softly like the lashes of a young girl' (p. 245). The pirate's life,
like the career of the fin de siècle homosexual, is circumscribed by
threat of blackmail and entrapment; secret signs help him recognize
possible sexual partners. Kemp spies a man who might be enemy or
friend: 'From a wine-shop . . . issued suddenly a brawny ruffian in
rags, wiping his thick beard with the back of a hairy paw' (p. 360).
In one inchoate instant, Kemp sees nakedness and the telltale
earring: 'I noticed the glitter of a gold earring in the lobe of his
huge ear. His cloak was frayed at the bottom into a perfect fringe
and, as he flung it about, he showed a good deal of naked skin
under it' (p. 360). But how is Kemp or the reader to sort this
information? If Kemp succumbs to the erotic invitation, he risks
discovery: he dares not say yes to a 'young smooth-faced mulatto'
who wore 'new straw slippers with blue silk rosettes over his
naked feet,' and who 'lounged cross-legged at the door.' Beckoning
the narrator, 'he held a big cigar tilted up between his teeth, and
ogled me, like a woman, out of the corners of his languishing
eyes' (p. 359). Because Kemp is a wanted man traveling incognito,
acquiescence to this straw-slippered flirt might mean arrest and
death.

Kemp's susceptibility to discovery and unveiling makes any
attack 'romantic'; the sensation of being ambushed taps the energies
of Stevenson's adventure fiction and of homosexual pornography.

> Something hairily coarse ran harshly down my face; I grew blind;
> my mouth, my eyes, my nostrils were filled with dust. . . . I had
> no time to resist. I kicked my legs convulsively. . . . Someone
> grunted under my weight. . . . My surprise, rage, and horror had
> been so great that, after the first stifled cry, I had made no sound.
> I heard the footsteps of several men going away.
>
> (pp. 74–5)

In another scene, Kemp feels six men fling 'their arms round me
from behind'; with a sudden 'exaggerated clearness of vision,' he
can see 'each brown dirty paw reach out to clutch some part of me.'
Night falls as they fight, and afterwards the narrator finds himself
'lying gasping on my back on the deck of the schooner; four or
five men were holding me down' (p. 94). The authors may have
dedicated *Romance* to their wives, but the novel centers on male
bodies fighting each other in a distant past that Conrad and Ford,
at the novel's end, call 'Romance': 'And, looking back, we see

Conrad's and Ford's Criminal Romance

Romance – that subtle thing that is mirage – that is life' (p. 428). Like 'queer,' 'romance' is a word meant to obscure.

Heterosexual love does occur in *Romance*, and yet the narrator confesses that he came to it rather late: before he met Seraphina, daughter of the patriarch Don Riego, he 'had never been tempted to look at a woman's face' (p. 126). She is lovely to the narrator because of her connection to two phallic emblems, the dagger and the lizard. Calling her 'an apparition of dreams – the girl with the lizard, the girl with the dagger' (p. 126), Kemp enjoys the knife-point of her touch: he thrills to the soft warmth of her hand because it is 'as if she had slipped into my palm a weapon of extraordinary and inspiring potency' (p. 204). As a purveyor of masculinity, she brings the narrator closer to Romance; however, she is not integrated into the novel, and was absent altogether from the first draft, which Ford composed himself. In the final version, she remains overshadowed by pirates, a 'band of brothers, each loving the other' (p. 383). One pirate makes it explicit that, in this world of Romance, male combat has more value than heterosexual play: threatening Kemp, this pirate says, 'Don't you dream of tricks. I've cut more throats than you've kissed gals in your little life' (p. 383). Another pirate draws out an 'immense pointed knife,' which he kisses 'rapturously,' exclaiming 'Aha!... bear this kiss into his ribs at the back' (p. 383). Although Conrad and Ford describe Seraphina's and Kemp's affair as a 'romance of persecuted lovers' (p. 84), the pirates – who kiss the knives they shove into each other's backs – are emblems of lovers more urgently persecuted in the England of 1898.

Appropriately, Conrad and Ford end their novel back in an English courtroom, where Kemp is on trial as a pirate. Romance, as a literary mode and as a sexual style, is being judged: to save his life, Kemp must tell it grippingly. In this situation of extremity, he discovers for himself the literary method Conrad and Ford have been using all along: Kemp realizes that if 'there were to be any possibility of saving my life, I had to tell what I had been through – and to tell it vividly – I had to narrate the story of my life.' But he must do so with a thrusting firmness: 'I rammed all that into my story.' Telling the story, he feels an odd separation from the 'I'; his voice splits between 'the one"I"' who is narrating, and a second 'I' who stays detached, conscious of 'raving in front of a lot of open-eyed idiots, three old judges, and a young girl.' His story consists in the counterpoint between two narrating 'I's: 'in a queer way, the thoughts of the one "I" floated through into the words of the other, that seemed to be waving its hands in its final struggle, a little way in front of me' (pp. 421–2). Though he finds this self-division

195

Joseph Conrad

'queer,' he makes good use of it: Kemp on the witness stand, trying to save his life, discovers the utility of double speaking.

Kemp tries to defend his romance against England's laws; in another courtroom scene, three years before Conrad and Ford began collaborating, Oscar Wilde had also been forced to defend his romance. But Kemp wears no green carnation. In fact, he pits his ramming Romance against the aesthete – embodied in a witness for the prosecution whom Kemp describes as a 'mincing swell': 'A tiny, fair man, with pale hair oiled and rather long for those days, and with green and red signet rings on fingers that he was forever running through that hair, came mincingly into the witness-box' (p. 414). Conrad's and Ford's *Romance*, despite its interest in naked pirates, ultimately does battle with the specter of Wilde. Because Kemp's final speech of vindication, which defines the homosexual witness as its enemy, didactically asserts itself as the entire work's microcosm and climax, Conrad's and Ford's *Romance* takes place in a courtroom where the writers stand trial for effeminate double writing, a charge they must refute by, paradoxically, composing a powerful Romance.

Conrad's and Ford's other two novels are soberer tales, rooted in England, without exotic touches; and yet, by dwelling on sensations of ambiguity or queerness, these works resume the themes of *Romance*. In *The Inheritors*, the narrator Etherington Granger (about whom a stranger asks, 'Is he queer?') collaborates with an important man of letters and considers it 'a tremendous – an incredibly tremendous – opportunity'.[20] But he denies that his desire for literary force is sexual. Reading an article by another man, he admiringly thinks that 'the touch was light, in places even gay,' and admits that the man's writing 'set me tingling with desire, with the desire that transcends the sexual; the desire for the fine phrase, for the right word – for all the other intangibles' (pp. 109–10). *The Inheritors*, which takes place in modern, post-Wilde England, felt pressured to deny the sexual nature of its narrator's desire for another man's gay linguistic touch. In Conrad's and Ford's last novel, *The Nature of a Crime*, wishing to naturalize the crime of collaboration, they use the novel's heterosexual plot as a mask for their own writerly marriage. The narrator notes, 'For the union with you that I seek is a queer sort of thing; hardly at all, I think, a union of the body, but a sort of consciousness of our thoughts proceeding onwards together' (p. 69). The union that the narrator seeks is queer indeed, for he observes, 'She is alarmed and possibly fascinated because she feels that I am not "straight" – that I might, in fact, be a woman or a poet' (pp. 47–8). The narrator further exposes himself as not straight when he describes the bundle of

196

Conrad's and Ford's Criminal Romance

letters he is writing as a faggot: he gives the 'little fagot' of letters to a sleepy girl, who will deliver the packet to his beloved. Conrad's and Ford's story, *The Nature of a Crime*, is a sequence of letters that its narrator brands a 'little fagot' (p. 86). It seems questionable to poise an entire book on male collaboration, soon to end, on a word like 'fagot' whose sense has notoriously shifted. Collaboration fertilizes a work with double meanings that can never be justified and that sustain a dreamy half-life, impossible to dismiss and impossible to prove.

[. . .]

Notes

1. FORD MADOX FORD, 'Working with Conrad', *The Yale Review*, Summer 1929; reprinted Autumn 1985, pp. 13–28. H. L. Mencken remembers Mrs Conrad denouncing Ford in these terms: see BERNARD C. MEYER, *Joseph Conrad: A Psychoanalytic Biography* (Princeton: Princeton University Press, 1967), p. 152n. For background on Conrad's and Ford's collaboration, see RAYMOND BREBACH, *Joseph Conrad, Ford Madox Ford, and the Making of 'Romance'* (Ann Arbor: UMI Research Press, 1985); NICHOLAS DELBANCO, *Group Portrait* (New York: William Morrow, 1982); FREDERICK KARL, *Joseph Conrad: The Three Lives* (New York: Farrar, Straus and Giroux, 1979); MEYER, *Joseph Conrad*; and ARTHUR MIZENER, *The Saddest Story: A Biography of Ford Madox Ford* (New York: World Publishing Co., 1971).

2. JOSEPH CONRAD and FORD MADOX FORD, *The Nature of a Crime* (Garden City, New York: Doubleday, Page, and Co., 1924), p. ix. Page numbers will appear in my text.

3. Quoted in MEYER, *Joseph Conrad*, p. 152.

4. Conrad to Edward Garnett, 26 March 1900, in *Letters from Joseph Conrad 1895–1924*, ed. Edward Garnett (Indianapolis: Bobbs-Merrill Co., 1928), p. 168.

5. FORD MADOX FORD, *Joseph Conrad: A Personal Remembrance* (London: Duckworth & Co., 1924), pp. 73–4.

6. FORD, *Joseph Conrad*, p. 135.

7. Conrad to Henley, 18 October 1898, in *The Collected Letters of Joseph Conrad*, vol. 2, ed. Frederick R. Karl and Laurence Davies (New York: Cambridge University Press, 1983), p. 107.

8. Quoted in KARL, *Joseph Conrad*, p. 549.

9. FORD, 'Working with Conrad', p. 23. FORD, *Joseph Conrad*, p. 134.

10. Quoted in MIZENER, *Saddest Story*, p. 49.

11. FORD, *Joseph Conrad*, pp. 129–30.

12. FORD, *Joseph Conrad*, p. 118.

13. JOSEPH CONRAD, *The Mirror of the Sea: Memories and Impressions* (London: Methuen and Co., 1907), p. 83. Quoted in MEYER, *Joseph Conrad*, p. 55.

14. FORD, 'Working with Conrad', p. 19.

Joseph Conrad

15. See THOMAS MOSER, *The Life in the Fiction of Ford Madox Ford* (Princeton: Princeton University Press, 1980), p. 56.

16. FORD, *Joseph Conrad*, p. 51.

17. Conrad's comment is quoted in KARL, *Joseph Conrad*, p. 521. Ford makes his observation in FORD, *Joseph Conrad*, p. 29.

18. FORD, *Joseph Conrad*, p. 38.

19. JOSEPH CONRAD and FORD MADOX FORD, *Romance* (1903; reprinted New York: Carroll and Graf Publishers, 1985), pp. 112, 5. Page numbers will appear in my text.

20. JOSEPH CONRAD and FORD MADOX FORD, *The Inheritors* (1901; reprinted New York: Carroll and Graf Publishers, 1985), pp. 195, 73. Page numbers will appear in my text.

Part Five

Class and ideology

11 Romance and Reification: Plot Construction and Ideological Closure in Joseph Conrad*

FREDRIC JAMESON

The work of Fredric Jameson exemplifies the eclectic sophistication of post-Althusserian Marxist criticism, in that it seeks to assimilate post-structuralism and psychoanalytical theory to a Marxist methodology. In *The Political Unconscious*, from which the excerpt is drawn, Jameson transforms the Freudian concept of the (individual) unconscious mind into a social and historical concept which he uses to detect the traces, in literary works, of fundamental but repressed historical realities: class struggle, productive labour and economic relations. Jameson is influenced by Louis Althusser's technique of 'symptomatic reading', which attends to gaps and blind spots in the text, and by Pierre Macherey's idea that literature 'produces' ideology (in the sense of making ideology manifest, rather than in the sense of creating it). This 'production' of ideology makes it available to critical analysis. Jameson's method in this book is what he terms 'metacommentary', in which the object of study is 'less the text itself than the interpretations through which we attempt to confront [it]' (Jameson, pp. 9–10). So, in this excerpt, he reads the differing modes of the two sections of Conrad's *Lord Jim* as symptomatic of shifts in the 'cultural spaces' where interpretation takes place (specifically, as symptomatic of the emergence of two spheres, of 'high' art and 'mass' culture). His interpretation of Conrad (and elsewhere in the book, of Balzac and Gissing) serves a wider political and philosophical project. He aims to trace in fiction the construction and disintegration of the bourgeois subject, to demonstrate that Marxism is the 'untranscendable horizon' (Jameson, p. 10) which subsumes without effacing other intepretative models and to make the process of narrative central to questions of history and ideology. These concerns generate rich readings of important aspects of Conrad's work including, here, the significance of the sea and the political ambivalence of the

---

* Reprinted from *The Political Unconscious: Narrative as a Socially Symbolic Act* (1981; London: Routledge, 1989), pp. 206–19.

Joseph Conrad

value which Conrad attaches to hard work and to ideas of duty and honour.

Nothing is more alien to the windless closure of high naturalism than the works of Joseph Conrad. Perhaps for that very reason, even after eighty years, his place is still unstable, undecidable, and his work unclassifiable, spilling out of high literature into light reading and romance, reclaiming great areas of diversion and distraction by the most demanding practice of style and *écriture**alike, floating uncertainly somewhere in between Proust and Robert Louis Stevenson. Conrad marks, indeed, a strategic fault line in the emergence of contemporary narrative, a place from which the structure of twentieth-century literary and cultural *institutions* becomes visible as it could not be in the heterogeneity of Balzacian registers, nor even in the discontinuities of the paradigms which furnish materials for what is an increasingly unified narrative apparatus in Gissing. In Conrad we can sense the emergence not merely of what will be contemporary modernism (itself now become a literary institution), but also, still tangibly juxtaposed with it, of what will variously be called popular culture or mass culture, the commercialized cultural discourse of what, in late capitalism, is often described as a media society. This emergence is most dramatically registered by what most readers have felt as a tangible 'break' in the narrative of *Lord Jim*,[1] a qualitative shift and diminution of narrative intensity as we pass from the story of the *Patna* and the intricate and prototextual search for the 'truth' of the scandal of the abandoned ship, to that more linear account of Jim's later career in Patusan, which, a virtual paradigm of romance as such, comes before us as the prototype of the various 'degraded' sub-genres into which mass culture will be articulated (adventure story, gothic, science fiction, bestseller, detective story, and the like). But this institutional heterogeneity – not merely a shift between two narrative paradigms, nor even a disparity between two types of narration or narrative organization, but a shift between two distinct cultural spaces, that of 'high' culture and that of mass culture – is not the only gap or discontinuity that *Lord Jim* symptomatically betrays. Indeed, we will have occasion to isolate the stylistic practice of this work as a virtually autonomous 'instance'* in its own right, standing in tension or contradiction with the book's various narrative instances or levels – just as we will insist on the repressed space of a world of work and history and of protopolitical conflict which may in this respect be seen as the trace and the remnant of the content of an older realism, now displaced and effectively marginalized by the emergent modernist discourse. The paradigm

Romance and Reification

of formal history which must now be presupposed is thus evidently more complex than the framework of a movement from Balzacian realism to high realism with which we have previously worked. Schematically, it may be described as a structural breakdown of the older realisms, from which emerges not modernism alone, but rather two literary and cultural structures, dialectically interrelated and necessarily presupposing each other for any adequate analysis: these now find themselves positioned in the distinct and generally incompatible spaces of the institutions of high literature and what the Frankfurt School conveniently termed the 'culture industry,' that is, the apparatuses for the production of 'popular' or mass culture.[2] That this last is a new term may be dramatically demonstrated by the situation of Balzac, a writer, if one likes, of 'best sellers,' but for whom this designation is anachronistic insofar as no contradiction is yet felt in his time between the production of best sellers and the production of what will later come to be thought of as 'high' literature.

The coexistence of all these distinct but as yet imperfectly differentiated cultural 'spaces' in Conrad marks his work as a unique occasion for the historical analysis of broadly cultural as well as more narrowly literary forms. It also offers a no less unique occasion for the type of investigation around which this book has been organized, namely the 'metacommentary,' or the historical and dialectical reevaluation of conflicting interpretive methods.[3] For the discontinuities objectively present in Conrad's narratives have, as with few other modern writers, projected a bewildering variety of competing and incommensurable interpretive options, which it will be our task to assess in what follows. We have already implicitly touched on two of these: the 'romance' or mass-cultural reading of Conrad as a writer of adventure tales, sea narratives, and 'popular' yarns; and the stylistic analysis of Conrad as a practitioner of what we will shortly term a properly 'impressionistic' will to style.[4] Alongside these, however, and not related to them in any immediately evident way, we can distinguish other influential kinds of readings: the myth-critical, for instance, in which *Nostromo* is seen as the articulation of the archetype of buried treasure;[5] the Freudian, in which the failure of Oedipal resolution is ratified by the grisly ritual execution of Conrad's two son-heroes (Jim and Nostromo) by their spiritual fathers;[6] the ethical, in which Conrad's texts are taken literally as books which raise the 'issues' of heroism and courage, of honor and cowardice;[7] the ego-psychological, in which the story of Jim is interpreted as the search for identity or psychic unity;[8] the existential, in which the omnipresent themes of the meaninglessness and absurdity of human existence are foregrounded as 'message'

203

Joseph Conrad

and as 'world-view';[9] and finally, more formidable than any of these, the Nietzschean reading of Conrad's political vision as a struggle against *ressentiment*,* and the structuralist-textual reading of Conrad's form as an immanent dramatization of the impossibility of narrative beginnings and as the increasing reflexivity and problematization of linear narrative itself.[10]

The competing claims and conflicts of these various interpretations constitute a network of leitmotifs within the reading of *Lord Jim* and *Nostromo* that will now, in the form of a kind of gradual reconstruction of formal levels, be presented. Here, as nowhere else in the present work, the double focus of the metacommentary must be apparent: we seek to construct a model of Conrad's text for its own sake, presupposing the intrinsic interest of this project; yet at the same time, this model, from another perspective, will serve as something like a pretext for a commentary on other critical methods. It is appropriate, however, that our reading draw on momentum already acquired, and that we should initially return to the problem of narrative totality and framing devices or strategies of containment developed in previous chapters, which may be expected to take on new and original forms in Conrad's work.

I

The privileged place of the strategy of containment in Conrad is the sea; yet the fact of the sea also allows us to weigh and appreciate the relative structural difference between the 'nascent modernism' that we will observe in these texts and the more fully achieved and institutionalized modernisms of the canon. For the sea is both a strategy of containment and a place of real business: it is a border and a decorative limit, but it is also a highway, out of the world and in it at once, the repression of work – on the order of the classic English novel of the country-house weekend, in which human relations can be presented in all their ideal formal purity precisely because concrete content is relegated to the rest of the week – as well as the absent work-place itself.

So the sea is the place from which Jim can contemplate that dreary prose of the world which is daily life in the universal factory called capitalism:

> His station was in the fore-top, and often from there he looked down, with the contempt of a man destined to shine in the midst of dangers, at the peaceful multitude of roofs cut in two by the brown tide of the stream, while scattered on the outskirts of the

Romance and Reification

surrounding plain the factory chimneys rose perpendicular against a grimy sky, each slender like a pencil, and belching out smoke like a volcano.

(p. 5)[11]

Jim's externality to this world, his absolute structural distance from it, can be measured by a process to which we will shortly return, namely the impulse of Conrad's sentences to transform such realities into impressions. These distant factory spires may be considered the equivalent for Jim and, in this novelistic project, for Conrad, of the great Proustian glimpses of the steeples of Martinville (with the one obvious qualification that the latter are already sheer impression and need neither aesthetic transformation, nor the Archimedean point of a structural externality, all the energy of Proustian style now being invested in the meditation on the object itself).

Two comments on this geographical strategy of containment need to be made before we do justice to its historical ambiguity. First of all, in a certain sense Jim tries to reverse one of Marx's classical ideological models (the repetition in pure thought of concrete social situations) and to reenact in reality what his father achieves symbolically, in speech and idea. His father's vocation, as ideologue in the characteristic British class system (he is an Anglican parson), is carefully underscored in the paragraph that precedes the one quoted above:

Jim's father possessed such certain knowledge of the Unknowable as made for the righteousness of people in cottages without disturbing the ease of mind of those whom an unerring Providence enables to live in mansions.

(p. 4)

From our point of view, and from the logic of its insertion in Conrad's text, this ideological function of religion is also to be grasped in terms of containment and totality; the geographical vision of cottage, mansion, and 'little church' (the place of the production of the ideology that harmonizes them) requires that neither class position be able to focus or indeed to see the other. Jim's method for living this geography, harmonized by ideological blindness, is an uncommon one: choosing a vocation such that he can step completely outside all three class terrains and see them all equally, from over a great distance, as so much picturesque landscape.

Yet if Jim's choice of the sea as space and as vocation is a kind of unconscious denunciation of ideology by way of its enactment

Joseph Conrad

and its reversal, it is no less dependent for its realization on a rather different level of ideological production, namely, that of the aesthetic. We must, indeed, carefully stress, as does Conrad in these preparatory pages, Jim's *bovarysme*,* the relationship between his work and the 'course of light holiday literature' that first suggests it to him:

> On the lower deck in the babel of two hundred voices he would forget himself, and beforehand live in his mind the sea-life of light literature. He saw himself saving people from sinking ships, cutting away masts in a hurricane, swimming through a surf with a line; or as a lonely castaway, barefooted and half-naked, walking on uncovered reefs in search of shell-fish to stave off starvation. He confronted savages on tropical shores, quelled mutinies on the high seas, and in a small boat upon the ocean kept up the hearts of despairing men – always an example of devotion to duty, and as unflinching as a hero in a book.
>
> (p. 5)

Nowhere in Conrad are the Flaubertian accents stronger than in such a passage, which reproduces at a lower level of verbal intensity the great cadences of the Flaubertian lyric illusion, as in Emma's youthful dreams of romance, or even Félicité's musings about the outside world. We must indeed take Conrad seriously when he tells us that the only thing that interested him in Flaubert was the latter's style.[12] Yet precisely here we have not only the transition from the naive naming of the outside world in realism to the presentation of the image, a transition to modernism and impressionism which is itself dependent on the very ideology of the image and sense perception and the whole positivist pseudo-scientific myth of the functioning of the mind and the senses; we also have a preselection of narrative material such that thought can be fully realized in images, that is to say, a rejection of the conceptual in favor of the two great naturalist psychic and narrative texts of daydreaming and hallucination. Where Conrad marks an 'advance,' if that is the right term to use about this historical process, is in his own mesmerization by such images and such daydreaming. *Madame Bovary* invented a register of impressionistic daydreaming in order then sharply to differentiate its own 'realistic' language from the other, to use the first register of language as the object to be demystified by the second, to create a decoding machinery which does not have its object external to itself but present within the system – and a presence which is no longer merely abstract, in the form of the 'illusions' and ideals of the

206

Romance and Reification

Balzacian or Stendhalian heroes, but stylistic and molecular, of a piece with the text and the life of the individual sentences. The force of Flaubert lies in the nonrealization of the image – and this most poignantly at those moments, the endings of *La Tentation de Saint Antoine* and the various tales of the *Trois Contes*, when a regression to religious ideology seems to permit us to posit a *parole pleine* or full mystical and visionary experience. But the point we wish to develop about *Lord Jim* is that in the second half of the novel Conrad goes on to write precisely the romance here caricatured both by himself and, implicitly, by way of stylistic pastiche, by his great predecessor.

Thus the non-place of the sea is also the space of the degraded language of romance and daydream, of narrative commodity and the sheer distraction of 'light literature.' This is, however, only half the story, one pole of an ambiguity to whose objective tension we must now do justice. For the sea is the empty space between the concrete places of work and life; but it is also, just as surely, itself a place of work and the very element by which an imperial capitalism draws its scattered beachheads and outposts together, through which it slowly realizes its sometimes violent, sometimes silent and corrosive, penetration of the outlying precapitalist zones of the globe. Nor is the sea merely a place of business; it is also a place of labor, and clearly we will say nothing of consequence about the author of *The Nigger of the 'Narcissus,' Typhoon*, and *The End of the Tether* if we overlook the 'realistic' presentation of working life at sea, of which all these narratives give a characteristic glimpse. Yet strategies of containment are not only modes of exclusion; they can also take the form of repression in some stricter Hegelian sense of the persistence of the older repressed content beneath the later formalized surface. Indeed, I have argued elsewhere that such vertical repression and layering or sedimentation is the dominant structure of the classical modernistic text.[13] In this respect, too, Conrad, as a merely emergent moment in such a strategy, has suggestive and emblematic things to show us, as witness the following supremely self-conscious art-sentence, whose Flaubertian triplication is a virtual allegory of manifest and latent levels in the text:

Above the mass of sleepers, a faint and patient sigh at times floated, the exhalation of a troubled dream; and short metallic clangs bursting out suddenly in the depths of the ship, the harsh scrape of a shovel, the violent slam of a furnace-door, exploded brutally, as if the men handling the mysterious things below had their breasts full of fierce anger: while the slim high hull of the

Joseph Conrad

steamer went on evenly ahead, without a sway of her bare masts, cleaving continuously the great calm of the waters under the inaccessible serenity of the sky.

(p. 12)

Ideology, production, style: on the one hand the manifest level of the content of *Lord Jim* – the moral problem of the 'sleepers' – which gives us to believe that the 'subject' of this book is courage and cowardice, and which we are meant to interpret in ethical and existentializing terms; on the other, the final consumable verbal commodity – the vision of the ship – the transformation of all these realities into style and the work of what we will call the impressionistic strategy of modernism whose function is to derealize the content and make it available for consumption on some purely aesthetic level; while in between these two, the brief clang from the boiler room that drives the ship marking the presence beneath ideology and appearance of that labor which produces and reproduces the world itself, and which, like the attention of God in Berkeleyan idealism, sustains the whole fabric of reality continuously in being, as Marx reminded Feuerbach in one of the most dramatic perorations of *The German Ideology*:

So it happens that in Manchester, for instance, Feuerbach sees only factories and machines, where a hundred years ago only spinning-wheels and weaving looms were to be seen, or in the Campagna di Roma he finds only pasture lands and swamps, where in the time of Augustus he would have found nothing but the vineyards and villas of Roman capitalists. Feuerbach speaks in particular of the perception of natural science; he mentions secrets which are disclosed only to the eye of the physicist and chemist; but where would natural science be without industry and commerce? Even this 'pure' natural science is provided with an aim, as with its material, only through trade and industry, through the sensuous activity of men. So much is this activity, this unceasing sensuous labor and creation, this production, the foundation of the whole sensuous world as it now exists that, were it interrupted only for a year, Feuerbach would not only find an enormous change in the natural world, he would very soon find that the whole world of men and his own perceptive faculty, nay his own existence, were missing.[14]

So this ground bass of material production continues underneath the new formal structures of the modernist text, as indeed it could not

Romance and Reification

but continue to do, yet conveniently muffled and intermittent, easy to ignore (or to rewrite in terms of the aesthetic, of sense perception, as here of the sounds and sonorous inscription of a reality you prefer not to conceptualize), its permanencies ultimately detectable only to the elaborate hermeneutic geiger counters of the political unconscious and the ideology of form.

This reality of production is, of course, at one with the intermittent vision of the sea's economic function, and with Conrad's unquestionable and acute sense of the nature and dynamics of imperialist penetration. We will shortly see how even awareness of this latter historical and economic type is 'managed' in the text itself. As for the productive relationship of human beings to nature, I will argue that Conrad's consciousness of this ultimate building block of social reality (as well as of its class content under capitalism – the 'fierce anger' of the muffled sounds) is systematically displaced in two different ways. The first is by a recoding of the human pole of the labor process in terms of the whole ideological myth of *ressentiment*. Indeed the narrative of *The Nigger of the 'Narcissus,'* with its driving power and ideological passion, may in this respect be characterized as one long tirade against *ressentiment*; the work concludes with the transformation of its villain, Donkin, the epitome of the *homme de ressentiment*, into a labor organizer (who 'no doubt earns his living by discussing with filthy eloquence upon the right of labour to live'.)[15] The other pole of the labor process, that nature which is its material object and substratum, is then strategically reorganized around one of the great conceptual containment strategies of the day, one which we have come to call existentialism, and becomes the pretext for the production of a new metaphysic – a new myth about the 'meaning' of life and the absurdity of human existence in the face of a malevolent Nature. These two strategies – *ressentiment* and existentializing metaphysics – allow Conrad to recontain his narrative and to rework it in melodramatic terms, in a subsystem of good and evil which now once again has villains and heroes. So it is no accident that Jim's first experience of the violence of the sea is at once coded for us in existential terms, the sea, the source of this mindless violence, becoming the great adversary of Man, in much the same way that Camus' vision of absurdity rewrites an essentially nonhuman nature into an anthropomorphic character, a vengeful God ('the first assassin, because he made us mortal'):

> Only once in all that time he had again the glimpse of the earnestness in the anger of the sea. That truth is not so often made apparent as people might think. There are many shades in the

Joseph Conrad

danger of adventures and gales, and it is only now and then that there appears on the face of facts a sinister violence of intention – that indefinable something which forces it upon the mind and the heart of a man, that this complication of accidents or these elemental furies are coming at him with a purpose of malice, with a strength beyond control, with an unbridled cruelty that means to tear out of him his hope and his fear, the pain of his fatigue and his longing for rest: which means to smash, to destroy, to annihilate all he has seen, known, loved, enjoyed, or hated; all that is priceless and necessary – the sunshine, the memories, the future, – which means to sweep the whole precious world utterly away from his sight by the simple and appalling act of taking his life.

(p. 7)

But if you believe this version of the text, this particular rewriting strategy by which Conrad means to seal off the textual process, then all the rest follows, and *Lord Jim* really becomes what it keeps telling us it is, namely a tale of courage and cowardice, a moral story, and an object-lesson in the difficulties of constructing an existential hero. I will argue that this ostensible or manifest 'theme' of the novel is no more to be taken at face value than is the dreamer's immediate waking sense of what the dream was about. Yet as this is a complex argument, which will ultimately be validated only by the rest of the present chapter, I will simply suggest, at this point, that our business as readers and critics of culture is to 'estrange' this overt theme in a Brechtian way, and to ask ourselves why we should be expected to assume, in the midst of capitalism, that the aesthetic rehearsal of the problematics of a social value from a quite different mode of production – the feudal ideology of honor – should need no justification and should be expected to be of interest to us. Such a theme must mean *something else*: and this even if we choose to interpret its survival as an 'uneven development,' a nonsynchronous overlap in Conrad's own values and experience (feudal Poland, capitalist England).

At any rate, with the problematic of existentialism and the heroic confrontation with the malignant absurdity of Nature, we are obviously very far from that productive process with which we began; the capacity of the new strategy to displace unwanted realities thereby becomes clear. We will return to the strategic function of the ideology of *ressentiment* later on; for the moment one reflection may be in order about the paradoxical relationship between labor and that non-space, those places of strategic narrative containment (such as the sea) which are so essential in what the

210

Romance and Reification

Frankfurt School called the 'degradation' of mass culture (that is, the transformation of formerly realistic materials into repetitive diversions which offer no particular danger or resistance to the dominant system). The paradox lies in the relationship between the peculiarly unpleasant narrative raw materials of the sea – not only that of sheer physical exertion and exposure to the elements, but also that of isolation, sexual privation, and the like – and the daydreaming fantasies of the mass public, for whom such 'diversions' are destined. Such paradoxes are not new in aesthetic theory (think, for instance, of the classic problem of the aesthetic pleasurability of tragedy, that is, of the starkest contemplation of death and of what crushes human life), but in consumer culture they take on a heightened significance. I think, for example, of that relatively late mass-cultural genre, the 'space opera'; we would understand a great deal about the mechanics of mass culture and the ideological operation of this particular narrative form, if we could grasp the dynamics of that purely imaginative excitement and sense of adventure which readers derive from the contemplation of one of the most physically restrictive situations into which human beings can be thrust – if we could sense the intimate relationship between the libidinally gratifying experience of the reading of such texts and the unimaginably barren sensory privation which is their content and the 'lived truth' of the experience of space flight. The intergalactic spaceship is, at any rate, an avatar of Conrad's merchant vessels, projected into a world that has long since been reorganized into a capitalist world system without empty places.

Analogous problems arise, therefore, wherever we choose to articulate the generic discontinuities in the text of *Lord Jim*: whether we understand its stylistic modernism as the repression of a more totalizing realism both expressed and recontained or managed within the narrative as a whole; or, on the contrary, register the emergence of something like the nascent mass-cultural discourse of a degraded romance from that quite different high-cultural or textual discourse of the *Patna* episode. The categories of periodization employed in such readings – troublesome indeed if we take them as exercises in linear diachrony where they seem to generate the usual unanswerable questions about the chronological establishment of this or that 'break,' this or that 'emergence' – are meaningful only on condition we understand that they draw on a linear fiction or diachronic* construct solely for the purpose of constructing a synchronic* model of coexistence, nonsynchronous development, temporal overlay, the simultaneous presence within a concrete textual structure of what Raymond Williams calls 'residual' and 'emergent' or anticipatory discourses.[16]

211

Joseph Conrad

Ultimately, however, the justification for this kind of deconstruction and reconstruction of the text of *Lord Jim* cannot be an immanent one, but derives from juxtaposition with the more fully achieved possibilities of *Nostromo* as a companion text: it is the new collective framework of this second novel, the explicitly socioeconomic terms of its narrative vision, and above all, the transformation of its strategies of containment from those still narrowly physical ones of the sea and its enclosed vessels to the later novel's national and political geography, which by contrast allow us, as we shall see, to formulate the structural limits of the earlier narrative experiment more concretely.

[. . .]

Notes

1. 'The presentment of Lord Jim in the first part of the book, the account of the inquiry and of the desertion of the *Patna*, the talk with the French lieutenant – these are good Conrad. But the romance that follows, though plausibly offered as a continued exhibition of Jim's case, has no inevitability as that; nor does it develop or enrich the central interest, which consequently, eked out to provide the substance of a novel, comes to seem decidedly thin'. F. R. LEAVIS, *The Great Tradition* (New York: New York University Press, 1969), p. 190.

2. T. W. ADORNO and MAX HORKHEIMER, 'The Culture Industry', in *Dialectic of Enlightenment*, trans. J. Cumming (New York: Herder & Herder, 1972), pp. 120–67. And see my 'Reification and Utopia in Mass Culture', *Social Text*, No. 1 (Winter, 1979), pp. 130–48.

3. See my 'Metacommentary', *PMLA*, 86 (1971), pp. 9–18.

4. See for example the remarks on 'qualities' in J. HILLIS MILLER, *Poets of Reality* (Cambridge: Harvard University Press, 1965), pp. 24–29, 46–51; and see also NORMAN HOLLAND, *The Dynamics of Literary Response* (New York: Oxford University Press, 1968), pp. 226–37. The 'impressionism' debate of course greatly transcends the work of Conrad; for a critical evaluation see IAN WATT, *Conrad in the Nineteenth Century* (Berkeley: University of California Press, 1980), pp. 169–200.

5. DOROTHY VAN GHENT, 'Introduction', to Joseph Conrad, *Nostromo* (New York: Holt, Rinehart, & Winston, 1961), pp. vii–xxv.

6. BERNARD MEYER'S *Joseph Conrad: A Psychoanalytic Biography* (Princeton: Princeton University Press, 1967) overstresses the maternal pole of Conrad's work; perhaps this is the place to suggest that the classical Freudian complex of familial relationships often functions as a free form of closure, emptied of its psychoanalytic content (see, for instance, EDWARD SAID, *Beginnings* [New York: Basic Books, 1975], pp. 137–152). The Freudian acts which close *Nostromo* and *Lord Jim* may thus be seen as arabesques which seal these two narrative discourses, rather than as genuine symptoms.

7. TONY TANNER, *Conrad: Lord Jim* (London: Arnold, 1963).

8. The canonical reading, symptomatically based on 'The Secret Sharer', is that of ALBERT J. GUERARD, *Conrad the Novelist* (Cambridge: Harvard University

Romance and Reification

Press, 1958); but see also DOROTHY VAN GHENT, *The English Novel* (New York: Rinehart, 1953), pp. 229–44: 'the story of Lord Jim is a spiritually fertilizing experience, enlightening the soul as to its own meaning in a time of disorganization and drought'. Van Ghent's elaborate parallels with Sophocles necessarily lean on the second part of the novel for their evidence.

9. See for example MURRAY KRIEGER, *The Tragic Vision* (New York: Holt, Rinehart, & Winston, 1960).

10. Indeed, Conrad's work has been the occasion for major statements in two significant and specifically American forms of post-structuralism: *Nostromo* for SAID's *Beginnings*, pp. 100–37; and *Lord Jim* for J. HILLIS MILLER's 'The Interpretation of *Lord Jim*', in MORTON W. BLOOMFIELD, *The Interpretation of Narrative* (Cambridge: Harvard University Press, 1970), pp. 211–28.

11. Page references are given in the text to the following editions: *Lord Jim*, ed. T. Moser (New York: Norton, 1968); and *Nostromo* (Harmondsworth: Penguin, 1963).

12. 'You say that I have been under the formative influence of *Madame Bovary*. In fact, I read it only after finishing *Almayer's Folly*, as I did all the other works of Flaubert, and anyhow, my Flaubert is the Flaubert of *St Antoine* and *Education sentimentale*, and that only from the point of view of the rendering of concrete things and visual impressions. I thought him marvelous in that respect. I don't think I learned anything from him. What he did for me was to open my eyes and arouse my emulation. One can learn from Balzac, but what could one learn from Flaubert? He compels admiration – about the greatest service one artist can render to another.' Letter to H. Walpole, 7 June 1918, in G. JEAN-AUBRY, *Joseph Conrad. Life and Letters* (New York: Doubleday, Page, 1927), II, 206.

13. 'Modernism and Its Repressed: Robbe-Grillet as Anti-Colonialist', *Diacritics*, vol. VI, no. 2 (Summer, 1976), pp. 7–14.

14. KARL MARX and FRIEDRICH ENGELS, *The German Ideology* (Moscow: Progress, 1976), p. 46.

15. JOSEPH CONRAD, *The Nigger of the 'Narcissus', Typhoon and Other Stories* (Harmondsworth: Penguin, 1963), p. 143.

16. RAYMOND WILLIAMS, *Marxism and Literature* (Oxford: Oxford University Press, 1977), pp. 121–7.

12 Stasis, Signs and Speculation: *Nostromo* and History*

JIM REILLY

Jim Reilly's book interprets the novels of Thomas Hardy, George Gissing and Conrad as stages in a process by which history came to seem increasingly impossible to represent in the modern world. His theoretical approach is Marxist insofar as he attributes this alienation from history to the development of capitalism, and draws on thinkers such as Walter Benjamin, Theodor Adorno and Michel Foucault. But Reilly's sense of history as a problematic category is based on a deconstructive account of meaning and representation, exemplified in his claim (made earlier in the book) that 'a sign simultaneously evokes the presence of the signified* it posits and acts as the evidence of its absence' (Reilly, p. 10). The word 'history', Reilly notes, presents this paradox in intense form, because it seems to unite event and representation: 'history' means both what happened (the events), and the narratives we construct *about* what happened (representations of events): it tries to present the past to us (to make it seem 'present' to our understanding) even while identifying it *as* the past (and therefore absent). In the work of the philosopher Hegel, a century and a half before deconstruction, Reilly finds the radical suggestion that event and discourse (or representation) are produced simultaneously (Reilly, p. 9). These ideas inform Reilly's account of *Nostromo*, which he sees as offering a critique of capitalism from inside. For Reilly the limitation of Conrad's novel lies in its fear of imagining political alternatives, while its strength lies in its honest self-awareness of its own implication in the values it critiques. This self-awareness prompts the recognition that global capitalism tends to erode any possibility of an external or 'disinterested' standpoint. Reilly's account elucidates Conrad's combination of explicitly conservative values with what seems a radical understanding of economic oppression. Reilly relates the sense of deadlock and stasis in *Nostromo* to Georg Lukács's view

---

* Reprinted from *Shadowtime: History and Representation in Hardy, Conrad and George Eliot* (London: Routledge, 1993), pp. 143–59.

Stasis, Signs and Speculation: Nostromo *and History*

that reifying description in nineteenth-century realism is indicative of subservience to an ideology. However, Reilly goes on to use Walter Benjamin's account of epic theatre to suggest that *Nostromo* conveys, not the stasis of reification, but the strain of unresolved contrary forces, in society, in history, and in its author.

[. . .]

Foul skies / heavy weather

Nostromo is not merely a self-conscious, but actually a self-critical text. It acknowledges a possibly debilitating paradox at the heart of its own project in that it attempts to analyse the historical development of capitalism and its correlative colonialism, while being itself a strand within the discourse of capitalism/colonialism and hence disposed to endorse its values. Characteristic of the novel is a sense of oppressive deadlock of which its epigraph – 'So foul a sky clears not without a storm' – is exactly expressive. This deadlock can be seen to derive from its combination of a frank analysis of its own implication within conservative positions, and a fearful reticence about imagining political alternatives. Typical of Conrad is a thoroughly fraught and unstable representation of his characters' ideas – and sometimes his own – when they appear to have a Marxist cast. In Conrad, an irrational loathing directed at Marxist characters is indicative of something plausible in their perspective which he is afraid to acknowledge – 'There are some things I *must* leave alone' (Conrad, 1983–90, vol. 4, p. 89). The novel is uncertain as to what it fears most; the 'foul sky' of current political formations, or the 'storm' that would remove them.

In the 'Author's Note' to *An Outcast of the Islands,* written in 1919 and hence the decade after *Nostromo,* there are a couple of instances where Conrad describes his experience of artistic impasse and eventual activity in terms which echo the characterisation of Charles Gould and suggest an affinity of concerns and mental states.

> [Mr Gould's] face was calm with that immobility of expression which betrays the intensity of inner struggle.
>
> (Conrad, 1986, p. 321)

> I was a victim of contrary stresses which produced a state of immobility.
>
> (Conrad, 1984, 'Author's Note', p. 7)

215

Joseph Conrad

> Charles Gould ... was the visible sign of the stability that could
> be achieved on the shifting ground of revolutions.
>
> (Conrad, 1986, p. 16)

> And thus a dead point in the revolution of my affairs was
> insidiously got over.
>
> (Conrad, 1984, 'Author's Note', p. 17)

I would suggest that Conrad is particularly prone to setting off
verbal echoes between his self-characterisation in non-fictional
writings and his fictional characterisations. These are admittedly
slight connections, but in line with Freud's conception of jokes
and slips-of-the-tongue can be seen as articulations from within
the unconscious of the text of affinities and relationships not
acknowledged on its surface. Famously, there is the term 'standing
jump' he used for his renunciation of all his family and class
affiliations in leaving Poland for a career at sea echoing Lord Jim's
'jump' which proves so crucial and ambiguous an act of desertion
or betrayal (Reilly, 1991, pp. 17–18). In *The Nigger of the 'Narcissus'*
(1897) there is a single moment of insight into the mind of the
despised and feared Jimmy Wait in a description of his delirious
dream of a ship discharging grain: 'and the wind whirled the dry
husks in spirals along the quay of the dock with no water in it. He
whirled along with the husks – very tired and light' (Conrad, 1983,
p. 97). The memorable husks image is reworked in the 'Author's
Note' to *The Secret Agent*, describing Conrad's mental exhaustion
on completing *Nostromo* which 'made me feel (the task once done)
as if I were left behind, aimless amongst mere husks of sensations'
(Conrad, 1980 (1), 'Author's Note', p. 8).

While these examples from *Lord Jim* and *The Nigger of the
'Narcissus'* show Conrad empathising at a perhaps unacknowledged
level with disgraced and despised figures who seem challengingly
disruptive or unconventional to those around them, in *Nostromo* the
telling verbal affinities are not with anyone equivalently positioned
within that novel but rather with the great Gould, 'King of Sulaco',
agent of Western material interests and hence the novel's pivot
of historical and economic power. That Conrad's affinity here is
particularly with the embodiment of capitalism suggests the degree
to which Conrad and the novel are enmeshed within conservative
positions and capitalist/colonialist assumptions and the degree to
which, if it is a critique of such positions, the novel simultaneously
acknowledges – in a possibly debilitating paradox – that such a
critique is articulated from *inside* such positions rather than from
outside. Indeed, an aspect of *Nostromo*'s honesty and profundity is

216

Stasis, Signs and Speculation: Nostromo *and History*

its insistence upon capitalism's ability to consume and digest all opposition, even that offered by *Nostromo* itself. In the novel the outside-ness of outsiders – variously manifested as their rebellious-ness, detachment or heroic independence – proves illusory as even figures as variously detached and independent as Viola, Decoud and Nostromo find themselves enmeshed within a capitalism so arrogantly monumental as to suffer the existence of no 'outside' and no 'outsiders'.

A play on words crystallises this issue. Antonia and Decoud have a crucial dialogue about the possibility of being 'disinterested'.

'Men must be used as they are. I suppose nobody is really disinterested, unless, perhaps, you, Don Martin.'
'God forbid! It's the last thing I should like you to believe of me.'
(Conrad, 1986, p. 439)

Antonia and Decoud are partly speaking at cross-purposes. Antonia means by 'disinterest' Decoud's apparent ironic detachment from the political commitments she holds so dear, while he is trying to bend her words into a personal and romantic meaning and so protests at the idea that he is emotionally 'disinterested' in her. But in a novel so obviously and centrally concerned with the immanence of 'material interests' the 'idle boulevardier's' admission that not even he is 'disinterested' is a telling indication of how spurious is the pose of detachment. The term is used again by Mrs Gould of Nostromo, 'I prefer to think him disinterested, and therefore trustworthy' (Conrad, 1986, p. 204), but the novel subsequently unpicks both Decoud's and Nostromo's belief in their own disinterest. No one in capitalist culture is 'disinterested' in 'material interests'. Part of the brilliance – and characteristic excruciating sense of heaviness, tension and deadlock – of *Nostromo* stems from its attempt to analyse 'material interests' in the light of a full recognition that there is no critical perspective or narrating position which can escape them. Capitalism in its world monopoly phase comes to erode a favoured dichotomy of eighteenth- and nineteenth-century discourse between detachment and participation. Conrad undertakes a scathing analysis of material interest where there can be no pretence of 'disinterest'. To cite Adorno,

The detached observer is as much entangled as the active participant; the only advantage of the former is insight into his entanglement, and the infinitesimal freedom that lies in knowledge as such. His own distance from business at large is a luxury which only that business confers.

(Adorno, 1974, p. 26)

217

Joseph Conrad

Thus the novel can be seen to be highly self-conscious about its own enclosure within the conditions capitalism demands. The novel's eponymous hero comes to feel he has 'silver welded into his veins' and silver is the novel's own alpha and omega – its first words, in the title of the first part, are 'The Silver of the Mine', its last sentence describes a cloud formation as 'like a mass of solid silver'. Gold and silver underpin capitalism, not merely in a vaguely metaphorical sense, but quite specifically in that they are the 'security' held in reserve by countries and their banks which guarantees the value of the bonds and paper money which are in immanent circulation. One aspect of the sense of debilitating stalemate the novel creates, paradoxically in contrast to its apparent welter of political drama, is the difficulty Conrad has in acknowledging any 'Other' to this capitalist hegemony. The representation of Communistic ideas exposes Conrad's deepest insecurities and draws from him quite unstable and contradictory formulations.

One aspect of Conrad's evidently very fraught attitude towards Communistic ideas is the absurd, spluttering invective he directs at the characters who voice them. He reserves for them a physical loathing never otherwise apparent in his characterisation, the virulency of which anticipates the grossest of twentieth-century anti-semitic or racial propagandist abuse where physical repulsion poses as moral criticism. Donkin in *The Nigger of the 'Narcissus'* who insists that 'I can look after my rights' and is prepared to 'kick up a bloomin row' to defend them is a landlubbing shirker and physically disgusting.

> a man with shifty eyes and a yellow hatchet face ... a squeaky voice ... He looked as if he had been cuffed, kicked, rolled in the mud; he looked as if he had been scratched, spat upon, pelted with unmentionable filth ... his neck was long and thin; his eyelids were red; rare hairs hung about his jaws; his shoulders were peaked and drooped like the broken wings of a bird; all his left side was caked in mud ... He stood repulsive and smiling.
>
> (Conrad, 1983, p. 20)

The prose here itself scratches, pelts and spits at a character it loathes. *The Nigger of the 'Narcissus'* is in this respect continuous with the deeply anti-egalitarian import of the sea-stories which were favourite boyhood reading of Conrad's. In Captain Marryat's *Mr Midshipman Easy*, an especial favourite, the eponymous hero is educated out of the pernicious egalitarianism he has picked up from Paine's *The Rights of Man* and transformed from spineless liberal landlubber to exemplary officer by the rigours, and rigorous

Stasis, Signs and Speculation: Nostromo *and History*

hierarchies, of naval life. We have seen how the narrator of *The Secret Agent* never tires of pointing out that Michaelis, leading light of the moribund Marxist/Anarchist cell 'The Future of the Proletariat', is grotesquely overweight. In *Nostromo* it comes as no surprise that a character described as 'an indigent, sickly, somewhat hunchbacked little photographer, with a white face' turns out also to have 'a magnanimous soul dyed crimson by a bloodthirsty hate of all capitalists, oppressors of the two hemispheres' (Conrad, 1986, p. 436).

This is all fear masquerading as loathing, and perhaps an unacknowledged sense of recognition. Conrad loathes his Communistic characters with an irrational virulency that cannot help but make the reader feel that he somewhere senses a veracity that refuses to be dismissed by uneasy sneering. One moment in *Nostromo* comes close to bringing this recognition to consciousness – significantly, given the novel's acknowledgement of capitalism's monopoly on discourse, it is conveyed via a wordless moment of connection. Alone at Nostromo's death-bed is the Communist, at whom the 'Man of the People' directs 'a glance of enigmatic and profound enquiry' (Conrad, 1986, p. 462).

There is an insistent duplicity in the presentation of Marxist ideas by this 'homo-*duplex*' – Conrad coined this famous self-definition in a letter contemporaneous with, and discussing, the composition of *Nostromo*. For example, one can place statements made by the Marxist slob Michaelis ranting to his fellow supine activists side by side with some of the most pithy and insightful political assessments voiced in *Nostromo* with all appearance of an intellectual continuity. Michaelis and *Nostromo* share classic Marxist/ materialist analyses. Capitalism spells conflict:

> 'The possessors of property had not only to face the awakened proletariat, but they had also to fight among themselves. Yes. Struggle, warfare, was the condition of private ownership. It was fatal . . .'.
>
> (Conrad, 1980 (1), p. 42)

> 'No!' interrupted the doctor. 'There is no peace and no rest in the development of material interests. They have their law, and their justice. But it is founded on expediency, and is inhuman; it is without rectitude, without the continuity and the force that can be found only in a moral principle. Mrs Gould, the time approaches when all that the Gould Concession stands for shall weigh as heavy upon the people as the barbarism, cruelty, and misrule of a few years back.'

Joseph Conrad

'How can you say that, Dr Monygham?' she cried out, as if
hurt in the most sensitive part of her soul.

(Conrad, 1986, p. 423)

History and consciousness are the product of economic relations and
not vice versa:

'History is made by men, but they do not make it in their heads.
The ideas that are born in their consciousness play an insignificant
part in the march of events. History is dominated and determined
by the tool and the production – by the force of economic
conditions.'

(Conrad, 1980 (1), p. 42)

Material changes swept along in the train of material interests.
And other changes more subtle, outwardly unmarked, affected
the minds and hearts of the workers.

(Conrad, 1986, pp. 417–18)

Nostromo, the novel of 'material interests', both depicts and, in its
own deadlocked and embattled narrative, actually enacts Conrad's
insight in 'Autocracy and War': 'Democracy, which has elected to
pin its faith to the supremacy of material interests, will have to fight
their battles to the bitter end' (Conrad, 1970, p. 85).

Descriptive deadlock

In the 'Author's Note' to *An Outcast of the Islands* Conrad described
his drained and debilitated state on completing *Almayer's Folly*. For
Conrad the completion of a novel was invariably accompanied by
a physical and mental collapse – and none more than *Nostromo*,
'Months of nervous strain have ended in complete nervous breakdown . . . the M.S. . . . lays on a table at the foot of the bed and he
lives mixed up in the scenes and holds converse with the characters'
(Conrad, 1983–90, vol. 4, p. 87). [The letter quoted, which is from
Conrad's wife Jessie to David Meldrum, is dated 6 February 1910
and refers to the period after the completion of *Under Western Eyes*,
not *Nostromo*. It is to be found, not in Conrad's *Collected Letters*, as
Reilly's reference would suggest, but in *Joseph Conrad: Letters to
William Blackwood and David S. Meldrum*, ed. William Blackburn
(Durham, North Carolina: Duke University Press, 1958), p. 192
(ed.)]. Thus Conrad's statement here can serve as one instance of a
characteristic deadlock.

Stasis, Signs and Speculation: Nostromo *and History*

Almayer's Folly had been finished and done with. The mood
itself was gone. But it had left the memory of an experience
that both in thought and emotion was unconnected with the sea,
and I suppose that part of my moral being which is rooted in
consistency was badly shaken. I was a victim of contrary stresses
which produced a state of immobility. I gave myself up to
indolence. Since it was impossible for me to face both ways I
had elected to face nothing. The discovery of new values in life
is a very chaotic experience; there is a tremendous amount of
jostling and confusion and a momentary feeling of darkness.
I let my spirit float supine over the chaos.

(Conrad, 1984, 'Author's Note', p. 7)

Conrad relishes the exactitude of technical expression, so perhaps
we can detect a metaphor drawn from the science of materials in
the formulation 'I was a victim of contrary stresses which produced
a state of immobility'. Marlow in the Congo is fascinated by his
discovery of Towson's manual on the breaking-strains of ships'
cables. Conrad's own works are about testing breaking-strains –
physical, ethical and emotional – and his metaphor here suggests an
instance from Towson of the cable stretched taut by opposed forces.
This is Conrad at 'the end of the tether'. The submerged metaphor
surfaces in *Nostromo* to evoke unforgettably Decoud's devastating
alienation alone on the *Isabel*. 'In the daytime he could look at the
silence like a still cord stretched to breaking-point, with his life, his
vain life, suspended from it like a weight' (Conrad, 1986, p. 414).

'Stillness' and 'immobility' that indicate, not repose, but the near-
tearing tautness of contrary forces – this is the characteristic tension
of *Nostromo*. The novel, like its author here, is debilitated by an
'immobility' affecting characters, setting and narrative alike. At its
heart is the contradiction that a work so obviously concerned with
the movement of historical change is everywhere mesmerised by
immobility. The word is repeatedly evoked, far more frequently
than the key-term always cited in criticism, 'material interests'.
The regularity of its reappearances both evokes an immanent inertia
and actually clogs the novel's apparent narrative and historical
movement with a congealing repetitiveness.

[Mr Gould's] face was calm with that immobility of expression
which betrays the intensity of mental struggle.

(Conrad, 1986, p. 321)

The Garibaldino – big erect, with his snow-white hair and beard –
had a monumental repose in his immobility, leaning upon a rifle.

(Conrad, 1986, p. 455)

221

Joseph Conrad

> Behind him the immobility of Mrs Gould added to the grace of her seated figure the charm of art, of an attitude caught and interpreted forever . . . Mrs Gould's face became set and rigid . . . her still and sad immobility . . .
>
> (Conrad, 1986, pp. 430–1)

> And the old man, bent forward, his head in his hand, sat through the day in immobility and solitude.
>
> (Conrad, 1986, p. 390)

> his eyes met again the shape of the murdered man suspended in his awful immobility, which seemed the uncomplaining immobility of attention . . .
>
> (Conrad, 1986, p. 365)

> Father Corbelan had remained quite motionless for a long time with that something vengeful in his immobility which seemed to characterise all his attitudes.
>
> (Conrad, 1986, p. 185)

> a great land of plain and mountain and people, suffering and mute, waiting for the future in a pathetic immobility of patience.
>
> (Conrad, 1986, p. 102)

> A big green parrot . . . screamed out ferociously '*Viva Costaguana!*' . . . and suddenly took refuge in immobility and silence.
>
> (Conrad, 1986, p. 88)

Only in one instance is immobility equated with repose – otherwise it is the grim parody of repose of the 'awful' immobility of the hanged Hirsch; it is 'sad', 'vengeful', 'pathetic', a betrayal of 'inner struggle'. *The Shadow-Line* (1917) develops a triple analogy between the dilemma of a captain whose ship languishes in a slough so absolute that the sails hang like granite, the ordeal of the contemporary generation of youth to whom the novel is dedicated bogged in the slough of the First World War and Conrad's own sense of creative impasse. Conrad would complain of being, like the ship in the novel, 'complètement embourbé' – completely stuck. In *Nostromo* also, immobility is a central metaphor implicating the novel's *action*, the *historical context* which it addresses, and the writer's own sense of *artistic deadlock*. The form of description characteristic of the novel is endless variation on an apparent 'universal repose of all visible things'.

222

Stasis, Signs and Speculation: Nostromo *and History*

All at once, in the midst of the laugh, he became motionless and silent as if turned to stone.

(Conrad, 1986, p. 373)

[Dr Monygham] sitting . . . so motionless that the spiders, his companions, attached their webs to his matted hair . . .

(Conrad, 1986, p. 318)

The solid wooden wheels of an ox-cart, halted with its shaft in the dust, showed the strokes of the axe . . .

(Conrad, 1986, p. 103)

the equestrian statue of the King dazzlingly white in the sunshine, towering enormous and motionless above the surges of the crowd with its eternal gesture of saluting . . .

(Conrad, 1986, p. 327)

For a long time even [Nostromo's] eyelids did not flutter upon the glazed emptiness of his stare.

(Conrad, 1986, p. 410)

Perfectly motionless in that pose, expressing physical anxiety and unrest, [Teresa Viola] turned her eyes alone towards Nostromo.

(Conrad, 1986, p. 224)

The Capataz frowned: and in the immense stillness of sea, islands, and coast, of cloud forms on the sky and trails of light upon the water, the knitting of that brow had the emphasis of a powerful gesture. Nothing else budged for a long time; then the Capataz shook his head and again surrendered himself to the universal repose of all visible things.

(Conrad, 1986, p. 410)

The novel's crucially developed descriptive motifs are such emphases writ large; the ever-lowering monumentality of Mount Higurota, the absolute, black, solid stillness of the aptly-named Golfo Placido, the statuesque bearing of Nostromo on horseback, the mesmerised spectators of Hirsch's statically suspended corpse, Decoud's equivalent metaphorical suspension alone on the *Isabel*.

Talking about novels within the traditions of nineteenth-century realism, Lukács argues in 'Narrate or Describe?' that the subversive potential of works apparently critical of capitalism is usually

Joseph Conrad

smothered at birth by a conservatism latent within their style. This style is characteristically a debilitating, reifying,* descriptiveness. The presence of this monumental and moribund descriptiveness indicates how these works are in fact absolutely subservient to an ideology congenial to capitalism which denies the possibility of change and hence monumentalises and eternalises capitalism itself. His instances of static, debilitating description, as opposed to the dynamic and engaging *narration* of process Scott, Balzac or Tolstoy achieve, are Flaubert and Zola. In these authors, 'the characters are merely spectators, more or less interested in the events. As a result, the events themselves become only a tableau for the reader, or, at best, a series of tableaux. We are merely observers' (Lukács, 1970, p. 130). A Marxist and a Nietzschean analysis are strikingly congruent. What Nietzsche said of the nineteenth century's experience of history – that we are no longer participants, but merely strolling spectators visiting an exhibition – is here Lukács's vision of nineteenth-century fictional characters' relation to their world and, by extension, the readers' relation to theirs – 'merely observers' of 'a series of tableaux'. Lukács also decisively echoes an assertion of Conrad's from *A Personal Record* (1912) where he describes reality as 'the sublime spectacle', even positing 'the conception of a purely spectacular universe' (Conrad, 1988, pp. 92–3). Peculiarly apposite to Decoud is the notion of a character who, a 'mere spectator', is 'more or less interested in the events'. We can recall the ironically detached 'idle boulevardier's' tangled relation to 'disinterest'.

In fact there are striking instances of congruity between Conrad's writing practice in *Nostromo* and Lukács's analysis of capitalist fiction's descriptive deadlock and delivery of the reified image of a reified world. This is essentially the argument of Kiernan Ryan in 'Revelation and Repression in Conrad's *Nostromo*'. He suggests that the immobility immanent in characters, setting and narrative structure alike qualify it as an even better model than Lukács's own instances of the densely descriptive and essentially moribund capitalist text which, while appearing to activate the subversive potential within historical change, in fact smothers history and denies even the existence of such change. One of the points on which I depart from Ryan's analysis is that I would argue that – unlike Zola and Flaubert as Lukács characterises them – Conrad foregrounds and renders self-conscious and hence problematic his leanings towards Lukácsian 'description'.

For Lukács 'Description contemporises everything. Narration recounts the past ... the contemporaneity of the observer making a description is the antithesis of the contemporaneity of the drama.

Stasis, Signs and Speculation: Nostromo *and History*

Static situations are described, states or attitudes of mind of human beings or conditions of things – still lives' (Lukács, 1970, p. 130). I am reminded of the opening page of *Nostromo* where the reader is at first invited to expect a 'narration' that 'recounts the past': 'In the time of Spanish rule, and for many years afterwards, the town of Sulaco . . . had never been commercially anything more important than a coasting port . . .'. But by the next paragraph the style has gelled into 'description' which 'contemporises everything' introducing its extended present-tense set-piece of Costaguanan geography and topography. 'On one side of this broad curve in the straight seaboard of the Republic of Costaguana, the last spur of the coast range forms an insignificant cape . . . On the other side, what seems to be an isolated patch of blue mist floats lightly on the glare of the horizon.' In fact the description lingers over an evocation of the 'prevailing calms of its vast gulf' that suggests that Costaguanan geography has ensured the preservation of Lukácsian 'static situations . . . still lives'. 'Sulaco had found an inviolable sanctuary from the temptations of a trading world in the solemn hush of the deep Golfo Placido as if within an enormous semi-circular and unroofed temple open to the ocean, with its walls of lofty mountains hung with the mourning draperies of cloud' (Conrad, 1986, all p. 39). The image captures two crucial aspects of the 'descriptive version of the world'; the denial of capitalist history – 'sanctuary from the temptations of a trading world' – and the *staged*, but not *dramatised*, aspect of reality – Sulaco here sounds like an abandoned amphitheatre.

Description for Lukács renders the world an array of discrete, reified elements with no vital connection, and the style of the descriptive novel is an equivalently bitty and scattered form of seeing such a world. In *Lord Jim* there is a descriptive passage which evokes with a startling exactness Lukács's formulation that 'The false contemporaneity of description transforms the novel into a kaleidoscopic chaos'.

> There was, as I walked along, the clear sunshine, a brilliance too passionate to be consoling, the streets full of jumbled bits of colour like a damaged kaleidoscope: yellow, green, blue, dazzlingly white, the brown nudity of an undraped shoulder, a bullock-cart with a red canopy, a company of native industry in a drab body with dark heads marching in dusty laced boots, a native policeman in a sombre uniform . . .
>
> (Conrad, 1980 (2), p. 122)

Conrad exactly reproduces Lukács's 'kaleidoscopic chaos' and actually self-consciously characterises not merely Marlow's vision

Joseph Conrad

here but his own descriptive technique as 'like a damaged kaleidoscope'. The world fractures into a neurotic scattering of momentarily arresting details, vision jerking from one detail to the next with no stepping back to see the larger composition – a lurid, unbending pointillism. Sentence structure and speaker's vision are alike slackly additive, paratactic rather than structured and syntactic. Marlow's walk anticipates the urban wanderings of later modernist protagonists – Prufrock, Mrs Dalloway, Septimus Smith and Bloom – whose perceptions are all slackly successive fragments of observation but most precisely, the vision of Decoud who, on the *Isabel*, 'beheld the universe as a succession of incomprehensible images' (Conrad, 1986, pp. 413–14).

A description of goods on display in Anzani's shop in *Nostromo* is like a realisation in miniature of another of Lukács's formulations about the descriptive style:

> The result is a series of static pictures, of still lives connected only through the relations of objects arrayed one beside the other according to their own inner logic, never following one from the other, certainly never one out of the other. The so-called action is only a thread on which the still lives are disposed in a superficial, ineffective fortuitous sequence of isolated, static pictures.
>
> (Lukács, 1970, p. 144)

> It was next to Anzani's great emporium of boots, silks, ironware, muslins, wooden toys, tiny silver arms, legs, heads, hearts (for ex-voto offerings), rosaries, champagne, women's hats, patent medicines, even a few dusty books in paper covers and mostly in the French language.
>
> (Conrad, 1986, p. 157)

The list captures in miniature the novel's 'series of static pictures . . . objects arranged one beside the other'. In fact it is almost a checklist of the novel's contents, as well as an enactment in miniature of its static array of discrete, reified elements. Limbs and hearts rendered in silver – as in further memorable instances of the novel's reification imagery Nostromo has silver welded into his veins and Mrs Gould's heart turns to silver brick – and all scattered, dismembered, dispersed, as Nostromo feels he has been dispersed, 'Nostromo here and Nostromo there – where is Nostromo?' (Conrad, 1986, p. 351). There are the 'boots' and 'ironware' of revolutionary and counter-revolutionary forces; 'rosaries' and 'offerings' which evoke the pervasive fetishism and 'purely spiritual value' of objects which trouble characters and narrator alike and of which the perverse mutability of the San Tomé silver is emblematic, and even, in the

Stasis, Signs and Speculation: Nostromo *and History*

dusty French books, something of a homage to the French fiction
to which Conrad's own style is indebted. Flaubert is both Lukács's
great instance of the debilitating descriptiveness of capitalist art,
and Conrad's acknowledged literary master.

With great acumen Conrad has used a display of shop goods
to exemplify the contents and form of his own novel. A display
of goods is the fundamental structuring principle of capitalist
expression, even its art. Captain Mitchell's tedious official account
of Sulacan 'historical events' narrates how Sulaco became 'the
Treasure-House of the world'. Henry James – with whom Conrad
disagreed over the relations between fiction and history – dubbed
Middlemarch 'a treasure-house of details' (James, 1987 (*Galaxy*, March
1873), p. 75), a perverse irony given how repulsed Dorothea is by
Rome's accumulation of cultural trophies. Under capitalism everything from states to art-works is readily translated into displays of
possessions. *Nostromo* – a succession of highly-wrought set-pieces,
brilliantly detailed – is, in perhaps a debilitating sense, another
'treasure-house of details'.

As Kiernan Ryan describes it, the novel itself is Anzani's display
of essentially unrelated objects writ large, each reified element held
in the gel of a dense descriptiveness.

> The descriptive strategy of *Nostromo* is most immediately evident
> in its meandering mode of advance through set-piece tableaux
> rendered with a lingering profusion of detailed circumstances.
> One thinks of the opening frieze of life at the Casa Viola; of the
> O.S.N. convité on the *Juno*; of the Goulds frozen silent in their
> house; the troops' embarkation under Barrios; the Goulds' party,
> with Decoud and Antonia on the balcony; Decoud alone at night
> in the Casa Viola: the hypnotic Placido Gulf scene: Nostromo and
> Monygham spellbound before the grotesque suspended corpse
> of Hirsch; Decoud lost out of time in the infinite solitude of the
> island. The novel delivers no sense of developing action emerging
> through the vital interplay of the characters with each other and
> their world. Quite the reverse. The narration does not flow, it
> coils and eddies through a configuration of still centres, congealed
> *settings for* action which, if recounted at all, is not fully narrated
> from the 'inside' as well – through the evolving subjectivity of
> active participants – but statically depicted as a ready-made
> phenomenon, a finished product.
>
> (Ryan, 1982, p. 167)

The last two phrases evoke Marx's concept of the fetishised object
of production which I shall argue finds echoes everywhere in

Joseph Conrad

the novel as well as Anzani's arrangement of goods on display. Conrad's comments on his own writing add useful evidence of the justice of Ryan's analysis, and his own acknowledgement of his descriptive impasse. Ryan quotes a letter to Garnett: 'It is evident that my fate is to be descriptive and descriptive only. There are things I *must* leave alone' (Conrad, 1983–90, vol. 4, p. 89). One could cite also the admission in the 'Author's Note' to *An Outcast of the Islands* and relating to that novel: 'The mere scenery got a great hold of me as I went on, perhaps (I may just as well confess that) the story itself was never very near my heart' (Conrad, 1984, 'Author's Note', p. 8).

'Mere scenery' overwhelming 'story itself' is exactly the disaster of capitalist prose Lukács diagnoses in 'Narrate or Describe?'. One instance in the novel seems to bring all these concerns with Lukácsian description to a head – the pivotal moment when we learn, as Charles Gould announces it to his wife, that his father has died. The death precipitates Charles's exploitation of the Gould Concession which, abandoned under Gould senior who urged his son not to take it up, becomes the transforming force in Sulacan history.

> She was the first person to whom he opened his lips after receiving the news of his father's death.
>
> 'It has killed him!' he said.
>
> He had walked straight out of town with the news, straight out before him in the noonday sun on the white road, and his feet had brought him face to face with her in the hall of the ruined *palazzo*, a room magnificent and naked, with here and there a long strip of damask, black with damp and age, hanging down on a bare panel of the wall. It was furnished with exactly one gilt armchair, with a broken back, and an octagon columnar stand bearing a heavy marble vase ornamented with sculptured masks and garlands of flowers, and cracked from top to bottom. Charles Gould was dusty with the white dust of the road lying on his boots, on his shoulders, on his white cap with two peaks. Water dripped from under it all over his face, and he grasped a thick oaken cudgel in his bare right hand.
>
> She went very pale under the roses of her big straw hat, gloved, swinging a clear sunshade, caught just as she was going out to meet him at the bottom of the hill, where three poplars stand near the wall of a vineyard.
>
> 'It has killed him!' he repeated.
>
> (Conrad, 1986, pp. 82–3)

Stasis, Signs and Speculation: Nostromo *and History*

This is, like the opening description of Sulaco, suggestive of an amphitheatre awaiting a performance, 'semi-circular and unroofed ... with its walls of lofty mountains hung with ... mourning draperies' (Conrad, 1986, p. 39). Both descriptions illustrate exactly Ryan's observation about Conrad offering *'settings for* action' which then fails to materialise. What a splendid set designer Conrad would have made on the evidence of this austerely ruined palazzo with its sculptural furnishings, fractured and monumental. The stage is set for an absent epic action, a tragedy – a Sophocles or a Racine – which fails to turn up or which swept off long ago. Only an Oedipus or a Phèdre would fail to be swamped and intimidated by such a setting, as their understudies the Goulds so evidently are. Or perhaps the formulation *'settings for* action' is inappropriate. Instead of the setting being the backdrop for action, it almost seems as if the action is mere pretext for the setting. Descriptive 'background' and dramatised 'foreground' have changed places, a great chunk of static 'scene-setting' interrupting the very articulation of Gould's crucial announcement of rupture and change.

Here we can understand Conrad's concern over the centrality of 'mere scenery' and his being 'descriptive and descriptive only'. We wait for something to happen only to have the same words of Gould's repeated as if action is congealing to become as monumental as its setting. Speeches have to be repeated, setting is precise and final – *'exactly one* gilt armchair'. As if moving over a canvas the eye is guided by compositional structures – a strip of black, a block of gilt, the central sculptural form of the urn. Here Conrad is achieving his ambition 'To make you *see'*, efficiently aping 'the plasticity of sculpture ... the colour of painting' (Conrad, 1983, 'Preface', pp. 13, 12). Conrad called *Nostromo* 'my largest canvas' (Conrad, 1980 (1), 'Author's Note', p. 8). The Classical vase, Keats's image of immemorial stillness and evocative also of Arnold's monumentally objective Classical art, is compositionally central and a metonym for the monumentality of the whole. Ornament (masks and flowers) encrusts the vase, as the Goulds (mask-like and be-flowered respectively) merely ornament their setting. Ornamentation – the term Marlow used for Kurtz's human decor of severed heads – is both repeated motif and fundamental stylistic principle in Conrad's prose. And Charles Gould – so often depicted as reified as when his 'steady poise' on horseback echoes the equestrian statue of Charles IV he passes – completes the statuesque arrangement and as such enacts another of Lukács's formulations, 'When men are portrayed through the descriptive style, they become mere still lives' (Lukács, 1970, p. 143). He is even, like the books in Anzani's shop, dust-covered.

229

Joseph Conrad

The mesmerising reification will not be shaken off. 'She was too startled to say anything; he was contemplating with a penetrating and motionless stare the cracked marble urn as though he had resolved to fix its shape forever in his memory . . . while he stood by her, again perfectly motionless in the contemplation of the marble urn' (Conrad, 1986, p. 83). The Goulds *are* Arnold's reified spectators of reification – fixing statuary with 'riveted gaze'. But as so often in Conrad, the immanent stillness and reification is evidence not of repose but of barely contained tensions, as with Conrad describing himself as 'a victim of contrary stresses which produced a state of immobility'. 'Contrary stresses' here have broken the back of the regal gilt seat and cracked the immemorial urn. The great images of authority and stasis are fractured.

This is a good point at which to part company with Ryan's Lukácsian comparison. If one's Marxist critical model was provided by Brecht/Benjamin rather than Lukács one would be more sympathetic to the possibility of critical energies within a consciously stilled representation. Benjamin explains Brecht's dramatic method in precisely these terms.

> The task of epic theatre . . . is not so much the development of actions as the representation of conditions . . . This discovery (alienation) of conditions takes place through the interruption of happenings. The most primitive example would be a family scene. Suddenly a stranger enters. The mother was just about to seize a bronze bust and hurl it at her daughter; the father was in the act of opening the window in order to call a policeman. At that moment a stranger appears in the doorway. This means that the stranger is confronted with the situation as a startling picture: troubled faces, an open window, the furniture in disarray. But there are eyes to which even more ordinary scenes of middle-class life look almost equally startling.
>
> (Benjamin, 1973, 'What is Epic Theatre?', pp. 152–3)

Benjamin's metonym of the bronze bust within the composition standing for the reification of the whole is very reminiscent of the method of *Nostromo*, a masterpiece of 'the interruption of happenings'. To return to Conradian breaking-strain imagery, where Ryan sees monumental reification everywhere in *Nostromo*, it appears rather that Conrad scrutinises, like Gould opposite the cracked urn, an utterly unstable tension – 'contrary stresses' – between reification and dissolution, atrophy and evanescence. The fractured monument – the Amarilla club, Mitchell's tedious tourist monologue observes, contains a bust of a bishop with its

230

Stasis, Signs and Speculation: Nostromo *and History*

nose broken – is a splendid image for an apparently solid surface straining against dissolution, an erection that hints at collapse. [. . .]

Works cited

Adorno, Theodor (1974) *Minima Moralia: Reflections from a Damaged Life*, trans. E. F. N. Jephcott, London: Verso.

Benjamin, Walter (1973) *Illuminations*, ed. Hannah Arendt, trans. Harry Zohn, London: Fontana.

Conrad, Joseph (1970) *Notes on Life and Letters* (first published 1921), London: J. M. Dent.

—— (1980) (1) *The Secret Agent: A Simple Tale* (first published 1907), Harmondsworth: Penguin.

—— (1980) (2) *Lord Jim: A Tale* (first published 1900), Harmondsworth: Penguin.

—— (1983) *The Nigger of the 'Narcissus', Typhoon and Other Stories* (first published 1898, 1903), Harmondsworth: Penguin.

—— (1983–90) *The Collected Letters*, 4 vols., ed. Frederick R. Karl and Laurence Davies, Cambridge: Cambridge University Press.

—— (1984) *An Outcast of the Islands* (first published 1876), Harmondsworth: Penguin.

—— (1986) *Nostromo: A Tale of the Seaboard* (first published 1904), Harmondsworth: Penguin.

—— (1988) *'The Mirror of the Sea'* and *'A Personal Record'* (first published 1906, 1912) ed. Zdislaw Najder, Oxford: Oxford University Press.

James, Henry (1987) *The Critical Muse: Selected Literary Criticism*, ed. Roger Gard, Harmondsworth: Penguin.

Lukács, Georg (1970) *Writer and Critic and Other Essays*, trans. Arthur Kahn, London: Merlin Press.

Reilly, Jim (1991) *Joseph Conrad*, Life and Works Series, Brighton: Wayland.

Ryan, Kiernan (1982) 'Revelation and Repression in Conrad's *Nostromo*', in *The Uses of Fiction: Essays in Honour of Arnold Kettle*, ed. Douglas Jefferson and Graham Martin, Milton Keynes: Open University Press.

Part Six

Modernity

13 Joseph Conrad and the Rhetoric of Enigma*

ALLON WHITE

This excerpt addresses a feature of Conrad's writing which often strikes readers on first encounter, and is sometimes a barrier to appreciation: his use of an ornate and repetitive style to create a haze of mystery around events, places and even people. White sees the function of Conrad's stylistic obscurity as the preservation of 'aura', a concept drawn from the work of the German philosopher and cultural theorist Walter Benjamin. The 'aura' of a work of art is generated by a mystical sense of its authenticity, its historical uniqueness and its ritualistic function. However, according to Benjamin the aura is eroded by modern technology which allows the mechanical reproduction of images and art works. This has the effect of clearing the way for innovation. White cites a range of Benjamin's phrases characterizing and defining 'aura' and demonstrates their close applicability to *Heart of Darkness*. So White sees Conrad's obscurity of style as a resistance to modernity, arguing later in the chapter that Conrad belongs to the 'Romantic survival' within modernism (see p. 23). He supports this by comparing elements of Conrad's style to the prescriptions of Symbolist and Impressionist painting.

[. . .]

In Conrad, mystery is everywhere and nowhere. The narratives constantly dissolve into 'the opal mystery of great distances'. The sea, the land, women, religion, nature, life, the unconscious, language itself, all present themselves to Conrad as radically unknowable. One's own personality 'is only a ridiculous and aimless masquerade of something hopelessly unknown',[1] and absolute Truth is 'like Beauty itself' and 'floats elusive, obscure, half submerged, in the silent still waters of mystery'.[2] It is not difficult to be cynical about this kind of language, and suggest that

---

* Reprinted from *The Uses of Obscurity: The Fiction of Early Modernism* (London: Routledge & Kegan Paul, 1981), pp. 110–17.

Joseph Conrad

it is used self-consciously to disguise ignorance or to give a vague mystical glow to otherwise mundane material. Indeed there is evidence in Conrad's letters to support this view. In a letter to R. B. Cunninghame Graham he wrote: 'Straight vision is a bad form . . . as you know. The proper thing is to look round the corner, because if Truth is not there, there is at any rate a something that distributes shekels.'[3]

This direct equation of commercial profit with obliqueness of vision and fictional technique can be compared to a remark made by Conrad in an essay on Guy de Maupassant: 'Nobody has ever gained the vast applause of a crowd by the simple and clear exposition of vital facts. . . .'[4] On the basis of these remarks one wonders how far Conrad himself possessed the 'Russian simplicity' of which he wrote in *Under Western Eyes*:[5]

> That propensity of lifting every problem from the plane of the understandable by means of some sort of mystic expression . . . I suppose one must be a Russian to understand Russian simplicity, a terrible corroding simplicity in which mystic phrases clothe a naive and hopeless cynicism.

Even with these fairly explicit remarks in mind, it is impossible to measure if, and how far, Conrad cynically deploys a code of enigma in his more oracular works simply to create a profitable mystical glow: if the phrases clothe cynicism, they do it successfully enough. When he writes in *Heart of Darkness* that 'the air of mystery would deepen a little over the muddle of the station', or when he ends 'The Planter of Malata' under a mysterious cloud (a favourite narrative termination in Conrad which he also uses in *Nostromo* and *Heart of Darkness*) it is impossible to read a disguised cynical intention into the words:[6]

> A black cloud hung listlessly over the high rock on the middle hill; and under the mysterious silence of that shadow Malata lay mournful with an air of anguish in the wild sunset, as if remembering the heart that was broken there.

This is magazine sentimentalism – Conrad at his worst – but it does not sound hollow or cynical. It is only by analysing the extensive network of figures and ciphers in his work which relate the narrative to an obscure interpretative domain supposedly hidden within, that the uses of the enigmatic code may be judged.

In a series of brilliant essays Walter Benjamin describes a process of change in the period from Baudelaire to Proust which he called

236

Joseph Conrad and the Rhetoric of Enigma

the elimination of the 'aura' of the work of art.[7] That which withers in the age of mechanical reproduction, he says, is the aura of the work of art. It is clearly related to secularization but not reducible to it. Benjamin writes:[8]

> The definition of the aura as a 'unique phenomenon of a distance however close it may be' represents nothing but the cult value of the work of art in categories of space and time perception. Distance is the opposite of closeness. The essentially distant object is the unapproachable one. Unapproachability is indeed a major quality of the cult image. True to its nature, it remains 'distant, however close it may be'. The closeness which one may gain from its subject matter does not impair the distance which it retains in its appearance.

It seems to me a primary function of the rhetoric of enigma in Conrad to preserve – indeed to intensify – the 'aura' of the art work. Benjamin's description of the aura in terms of a distance preserved even in closeness is fundamental to Conrad's fiction. He constructs narratives in which 'impenetrability', literal and meta-phorical, is profoundly important. There is a certain epistemological threshold which he refuses to cross, always with the disclaimer that a near approach to the matter is beyond his power: 'The essentials of this affair lay deep under the surface, beyond my reach, and beyond my power of meddling.'[9] His stories are full of boundaries, limits and thresholds which, like horizons, recede as one approaches. With characteristic insistence, the journey up river into the heart of darkness is into an 'impenetrable' realm, and Marlow remarks:[10]

> I looked around, and I don't know why, but I assure you that never, never before, did this land, this river, this jungle, the very arch of this blazing sky, appear to me so hopeless and so dark, so impenetrable to human thought, so pitiless to human weakness.

Geoffrey Renouard is exemplary of the Conradian hero in this respect, feeling like an explorer 'trying to penetrate the interior of an unknown country, the secret of which is too well defended by its cruel and barren nature'. The opposed tensions in the narratives are perfectly indexed in this simile, for his characters are often poised on the outer border of some physical or mental territory which simultaneously fascinates and repels. This unknown domain marks the limit to the narrative in that its boundaries define the ultimate horizon of expectation, the *non plus ultra** of desire and

237

Joseph Conrad

fear in the story. Within the territory we are assured that there
resides something immensely precious and immensely corrupting,
but also, inevitably, just beyond our comprehension. And this is
as much a matter of subjective interiority as physical extension.
Almayer's 'treasure', the Gould Concession, the ivory, the 'mystery
of Samburan' all have their analogues in the psychic 'treasure'
buried deep in the personality of his characters. Indeed the
'mystery' of earth and of mind are given as a unity, and Conrad's
stories often write the one in terms of the other through a symbolic
coalescence of nature and psyche. Heyst, pushed to his limits by
Mr Jones, says to Lena:[11]

> That's it. I don't know how to talk. I have managed to refine
> everything away. I've said to the Earth that bore me: 'I am I and
> you are a shadow' and, by Jove, it is so. But it appears that such
> words cannot be uttered with impunity. Here I am on a Shadow
> inhabited by Shades. How helpless a man is against the Shades!
> How is one to intimidate, persuade, resist, assert oneself against
> them?

Dissolution into shades of intangibility places the active force of
his narrative in the noumenal* margins of something approached
but never reached. This preserved distance which creates the aura
of the work is necessarily an external relationship between the
'impenetrable' core of the narrative (personality/territory) and
the outer zone of conjecture and uncertainty which envelops it.
The narrator in *Heart of Darkness* describes Marlow's story in terms
which precisely confirm Benjamin's description of aura:[12]

> The yarns of seamen have a direct simplicity, the whole meaning
> of which lies within the shell of a cracked nut. But Marlow was
> not typical . . . and to him the meaning of an episode was not
> inside like a kernel but outside, enveloping the tale which brought
> it out only as a glow brings out a haze, in the likeness of one of
> these misty halos that sometimes are made visible by the spectral
> illumination of moonshine.

In terms of the literary signs and symbols used in these stories,
this external 'haze' is the primary region of interpretative obscurity.
There are obscurities of extension as well as of compression, and
Conrad creates obscurity by simplification and extension. By
contrast, Meredith's obscurity results from compression, the need
to reduce self-exposure by condensation into ellipses and dense
tissues of metaphor. Meredith writes as though subjectivity had to

238

Joseph Conrad and the Rhetoric of Enigma

be squeezed into a single point of energy – as though the self were only secure when refined to a rapid, discontinuous movement. As he writes in 'The Empty Purse':[13]

> The plural swarm round us; ourself in the thick,
> A dot or a stop: that is our task;

But it is important to note that the multiplication of potential interpretations of signs is not to be confused with the multiplication of the number of signs themselves. A surplus of meaning is most often due, not to a concentration of signs as in Meredith, but to a lack of information, and it is the absence of a sufficient context of signs, of framing, which leaves a message open. Communication theory has convincingly shown that the relation between information and signification is in inverse ratio, and the greater the information (redundancy) the less the chance of multiple readings.

This principle is a foundation of obscurity in Conrad. It is not a density of signification which produces the sense of mystery here, but an attenuation of form and feature. Conrad effaces boundary limits so that distinctions dissolve into distances. This 'tensile' obscurity is presented as much by the topography of Conrad's fiction as by its symbolic resonance. Walter Benjamin remarks that 'Experience of the aura [thus] rests on the transposition of a response common in human relationships to the relationship between the inanimate or natural object and man.'[14]

This is amply demonstrated with respect to Conrad by a close analysis of the rhetoric of enigma in *Heart of Darkness*. Unlike James, Conrad does not obscure things by involution or the multiplication of subtle distinctions. He tends instead to remove the categorical divisions between different areas so that his prose aspires to the universalism of 'nature' represented as mute, primeval and illimitable. As Walter Benjamin suggests, a mysterious aura is generated by a transposition of interpersonal response (in this case, that of 'guarding secrets') into a relationship between men and nature. In *Heart of Darkness*, Conrad writes as if the words on the page were only 'surface markers' of some vast secret, and the following pages trace through this enigmatic code of secrecy as it appears in some of these surface markers.

Heart of Darkness opens with an image of 'maintained distance'. At the very outset of the story the reader learns that the narrative position, the place from which the story will be told, is in a suspended off-shore zone:[15]

> The *Nellie*, a cruising yawl, swung to her anchor without a flutter
> of the sails, and was at rest. The flood had made, the wind was

239

Joseph Conrad

nearly calm, and being bound down the river, the only thing for it was to come to and wait for the turn of the tide.

The position of the *Nellie* (deceptively innocuous name!) introduces us immediately to two of the five physical parameters which are to define the spatial organization of secrecy in the text. In contrast to many of Conrad's other stories, *Heart of Darkness* is curiously static, even though it deals with a journey. The moral disintegration associated with a closed and secret universe is counterposed with the open world of work and production: *Heart of Darkness* is a story of continually frustrated work, of enforced inactivity and stillness. This first marker inaugurates both of these semantic unities, stillness and frustrated activity. Stillness applies to both noise and movement, denoting their combined stasis, and it is used henceforth to cover both silence (a crucial term in the story) and lack of motion.

Another aspect of the spatial organization of secrecy introduced from the outset is the confusion of limits and boundaries. Analogous to figures of equivocation, physical barriers throughout the story will become vague, disordered, concealed or muddled. The very basis of knowledge – the clear perception of differences between things – will gradually disintegrate as land, water and sky melt untidily into each other. In this first 'marker' the changing tide holds the sailors off from finishing their journey, and initiates a spatial sequence of uncertain boundaries which will continue throughout the book. Both stillness and vagueness are thus presented in exordium* as preliminary signifiers of the dominant code: 'The sea-reach of the Thames stretched before us like the beginning of an *interminable waterway*.'[16]

The fictional world we are about to enter is not only very still, it is also vast. Sheer physical size, as it increases towards the infinite, becomes ungraspable and hence mysterious (literally beyond knowledge). Endless space has always been associated with silence, the absence of language, a suspension of communication: 'L'espace m'a toujours rendu silencieux.'[17] Much of the power of the Sphinx, the essential and eternal symbol of secrecy and enigma, comes not from the Sphinx at all, but from the desert which surrounds it. There, too, we find a space organized along the parameters of those in *Heart of Darkness*, a space in which silence, immensity and stillness, the uncertainty of boundaries and limits, the frustration of human endeavour, close round the Sphinx to form a secret geography, a terrain in which each of its qualities is a connotation of mystery. In *Heart of Darkness* the various spaces in which Marlow finds himself will be endless, immense, defying knowledge and the

240

Joseph Conrad and the Rhetoric of Enigma

symbolic dominion of language, not by labyrinthine involution (Dickens's London), but by extending itself beyond measure:[18]

A *haze* rested on the low shores and ran out to sea in *vanishing flatness*. The air was *dark* above Gravesend, and farther back still seemed condensed into a *mournful gloom*, brooding *motionless* over the *biggest*, and the *greatest* town on earth. [My italics]

'Haze' and 'vanishing flatness' recapitulate the spatial anxiety of uncertain boundaries, just as 'motionless' reinforces the signifier stillness, and 'biggest' and 'greatest' reinforce the immensity. The fourth parameter introduced here is darkness, already signified in the title of the story and condensing both evil and secrecy into a single quality. It is repeated in the phrase 'brooding gloom' in the next paragraph, and is much more directly signifying than the other terms – we can be in little doubt of the tone (providing it is not a trap) after the 'darkness' and 'gloom' of this paragraph. Here, at the beginning, the darkness is only gloomy: it will intensify to total blackness as the narrative unfolds.

The sombre lyricism of this and many similar markers in the story uses language and space in a way which recalls the early symbolist aesthetic of Gautier and Baudelaire. The obscurity is, significantly, not that of gothic fantasy but of symbolist *brume*.* Conrad occasionally derives his semantic shades from the gothic tradition (as in 'The Inn of the Two Witches') but the dominant inter-textual[19] form is undoubtedly symbolist. His procedure here matches almost word for word the aesthetic prescription which emanated from the famous 1867 salon:[20]

la clarté, de quelque manière qu'on l'entende, nuit à l'enthousiasme. Poète, parler sans cesse d'éternité, d'infini, d'immensité, du temps, de l'espace, de la Divinité, des tombeaux, des manes, des enfers, d'un ciel obscur, des mers profondes, des forêts obscures, du tonnerre, des éclairs qui déchirent la nue. Soyez ténébreux.

'Soyez ténébreux' perfectly matches Conrad's own description for writing, 'seek discourse with the Shades'. (In *Heart of Darkness* he uses *all* the symbolist elements listed above which the salon recommends!) In an excellent article,[21] Ian Watt has argued that Conrad's achievement in the story is to have combined the techniques of Impressionism and symbolism by having given 'a larger symbolic meaning to an Impressionist recording of particular experience'. Despite the strictures of Eloise Knapp Hay

241

Joseph Conrad

that Conrad's Impressionism was quite limited,[22] Watt's article
seems to me very persuasive. Impressionism, with its attention
to the subjectively received blurring or misting of clarity, is surely
very close to Conrad's technique in *Heart of Darkness*. (Monet wrote
of the critics who ridiculed his obscurity: 'poor blind idiots. They
want us to see everything clearly, even through the fog'.)[23] Watt
goes on to remark that with both Monet and Conrad, 'the difficulty
and obscurity are essential parts of what the artist is trying to say'.
By combining the interpretative openness of symbolism with the
maintained distance and misty vision of Impressionism, Conrad
achieves the perspective imprecision which is fundamental to aura:[24]

> The water shone pacifically; the sky, without a speck, was a
> benign immensity of unstained light; the very mist on the Essex
> marshes was like a gauzy and radiant fabric, hung from the
> wooded rises inland, and draping the low shores in diaphanous
> folds. Only the gloom to the west, brooding over the upper
> reaches became more sombre every minute. . . .

This sentence resumes all the previous spatial parameters, and
brings them together between the silence on board the yacht
(where the phrase 'we felt meditative, and fit for nothing except
placid staring' once more takes up the notion of inactivity) and
the setting sun, the disappearance of light and all the shades of
Götterdämmerung* which this suggests. Once again, the boundary
of sea and shore is obscured, this time by mists, which anticipate
two further 'misty passages' later in the narrative which also 'blur
distinctions'. Edges become fluid and intangible 'like a [. . .] line,
far, far away along a blue sea whose glitter was blurred by a
creeping mist'. Marlow continues: 'What greatness had not floated
on the ebb of that river into the mystery of an unknown earth! . . .'[25]

This is the first time that secrecy is openly introduced under the
metaphysical form of mystery. The spatial image which bears it is
once again that of immensity though here, through the references
to Sir Francis Drake, Sir John Franklin and to the Roman invaders,
the immensity is also historical. The rather inflated rhetoric of this
marker indicates secrecy and wonder through the distance of remote
time. Historical and cultural remoteness strengthen the connotation
of 'cult' (primitive and exotic) which is an important sub-structure
of the book. It is the nexus of cult and remoteness which forms a
key significance in a story which has 'unspeakable rites' at 'heart'
(rites which are always approached but never reached: it is this
combination of inapproachability and ritual which is distinctive in
the creation of literary aura). If aura is the 'unique manifestation

Joseph Conrad and the Rhetoric of Enigma

of a distance', this definition 'has the advantage of clarifying the ceremonial character of the phenomenon. The essentially distant is the inapproachable: inapproachability is in fact a primary quality of the ceremonial image.'[26] The 'drone of weird incantations' which Marlow finds in the *Heart of Darkness* is an interior index of the formal ceremonial structure of language which envelops it, the 'magic current of phrases' which constitute the unapproachable (because radically indeterminate) reference of the tale.

The perpetual transference effected by the text from the secrecy of human relations to the 'inscrutable' and 'infinite' surface of nature is increased by a rhetorical process of 'reciprocation'. Proust has remarked that 'Some people who are fond of secrets flatter themselves that objects retain something of the gaze that has rested upon them.' This enigmatic flattery operates like Borges's story 'The Mirror of Enigmas' in that it makes the enigmatic endlessly reflective (in both senses of this word). The transference from subject to object, inverting the relation of questioned and questioner (which becomes a familiar and pleasurable game amongst schoolchildren, each refusing to answer until his own question has been asked again) is an essential part of the structure in *Heart of Darkness*:[27]

> The smell of mud, of primeval mud, by Jove! was in my nostrils, the high stillness of primeval forest was before my eyes, . . . I wondered whether the stillness on the face of the immensity looking at us two were meant as an appeal or as a menace. What were we who had strayed in here? Could we handle that dumb thing, or would it handle us?

This is not simply the conjuring of anthropomorphic hostility from the inanimate, it is the discursive production of 'mystery' by the mirror-process. Marlow continually grants the forest eyes in a way which duplicates the most ancient act of totemic endowment. But at the same time the simple, unilateral relation of questioner and questioned, subject and object, becomes a complex process of reciprocation, an enigmatic movement. Benjamin once again is remarkably concise on this point:[28]

> The person we look at, or who feels he is being looked at, looks at us in turn. To perceive the aura of an object we look at means to invest it with the ability to look at us in return . . . (the ability, it would seem, of returning the gaze).

This gaze (which is characteristically feminine in Conrad) is the specular equivalent of narrative suspension. Like the Sphinx, the

243

Joseph Conrad

object 'holds' the subject in its gaze, which is the visual moment of expectation. In *Heart of Darkness*, the visual and the verbal become entwined in the following passage as Marlow transfers interrogative priority from himself to the forest:[29]

> There was no sign on the face of nature of this amazing tale that was not so much told to me as suggested in desolate exclamations, completed by shrugs, in interrupted phrases, in hints ending in deep sighs. The woods were unmoved, like a mask – heavy, like the closed door of a prison – they looked with their air of hidden knowledge, of patient expectation, of unapproachable silence.

The assimilation of the signs of the tale to the signs of nature is given in the first sentence of the passage, 'there was no sign on the face of nature of this amazing tale. . . .' a metonymic identification of the surfaces which indexes their perfect unity. This reciprocation is used frequently by Marlow. He recounts how, as a child, he had been fascinated by the blank spaces of unexplored territory on the map of Africa: 'It [the map] had ceased to be a blank space of delightful mystery – a white patch for a boy to dream gloriously over. It had become a place of darkness . . . one river . . . resembling an immense snake uncoiled. . . .'[30] He was enchanted by the absence of signs which indicated the presence of secrets. What Conrad gives here, in a vignette, is the perfect expression of the signifier which I have termed enigma. It is precisely the 'presence of missing signs', the blankness of the paper where geographical symbols ought to be, that signals the position of a secret, something quite literally to be discovered. Conrad uses the habitual associations of the term 'whiteness' to give this enigma a positive value – it is the innocent mystery of a child's universe, boyhood dreams of adventure in remote lands. But in a sudden reversal, Conrad then overthrows this positive valuation with its opposite, using darkness and the snake. The darkness is the now familiar physical metaphor of secrecy and evil, and the snake is the long coils of the Congo drawn on the white patch of the map. So the enigma of the blank space is 'solved', but only by replacing it with further symbols of secrecy and deception, of darkness and the serpent. The antithesis does not develop the reader's knowledge, but instead blocks that knowledge by leading from one discursive figure to another in a repertoire of deception. Blank space, full space, both signify mystery.

[. . .]

Joseph Conrad and the Rhetoric of Enigma

Notes

1. Conrad in a letter to E. Garnett (23 March 1896), *Letters from Conrad, 1895–1924*, ed. Edward Garnett (London, undated, 1928?), p. 23.

2. *Lord Jim*, chapter 20, p. 216. All references to the novels, stories and essays of Joseph Conrad are to the Dent Uniform Edition, 22 vols. (London, 1923–28).

3. Letter to R. B. Cunninghame Graham (5 August 1897), in *Joseph Conrad: Life and Letters*, ed. G. Jean-Aubry (London, 1927), 2 vols., I, p. 208.

4. J. CONRAD, 'Guy de Maupassant', *Notes on Life and Letters*, p. 27.

5. *Under Western Eyes*, Part Second, chapter 1, p. 104.

6. 'The Planter of Malata', *Within the Tides*, p. 86.

7. W. BENJAMIN, *Illuminations*, ed. and introd. H. Arendt, trans. H. Zohn (London, 1973). See 'The Work of Art in the Age of Mechanical Reproduction', pp. 222–5, and 'On Some Motifs in Baudelaire', p. 190.

8. W. BENJAMIN, op. cit., p. 245.

9. *Heart of Darkness*, p. 100.

10. Ibid., p. 127.

11. *Victory*, Part Four, chapter 8, p. 350.

12. *Heart of Darkness*, p. 48.

13. G. MEREDITH, 'The Empty Purse', *Poems*, ed. G. M. Trevelyan (London, 1912), p. 454.

14. W. BENJAMIN, op. cit., p. 190.

15. *Heart of Darkness*, p. 45.

16. Ibid.

17. JULES VALLÈS, 'L'Enfant', *Oeuvres* (Paris, 1950), vol. I, p. 238.

18. *Heart of Darkness*, p. 45.

19. 'Inter-textuality' is a term used to describe the network of texts, literary and otherwise, which inform a given work. It is not the same as allusion or 'echo-hearing', in that the discourses are transformed within the work and are often not direct quotations, but adaptations of the codes and languages available in the culture and its traditions.

20. E. J. CHARPIER and P. SEGHERS, 'L'Art poétique' (Paris, 1957), Salon de 1867, p. 182.

21. IAN WATT, 'Impressionism and Symbolism in *Heart of Darkness*', in *Joseph Conrad: A Commemoration*, ed. N. Sherry (London, 1976), pp. 37–53.

22. Conrad was initially derisive about Impressionist painting, but Eloise Knapp Hay ('Impressionism Limited', in ibid., pp. 54–64) shows that, perhaps through the influence of Brunetière, Conrad does adopt certain Impressionist ideas later in his career, when he 'began to aim for the same effects that he had earlier questioned'.

23. I. WATT, op. cit., p. 39.

24. *Heart of Darkness*, p. 46.

Joseph Conrad

25. Ibid., p. 47.
26. W. BENJAMIN, op. cit., p. 190.
27. *Heart of Darkness*, p. 81.
28. W. BENJAMIN, op. cit., p. 190.
29. *Heart of Darkness*, p. 129.
30. *Heart of Darkness*, p. 52.

14 The Failure of Textuality*

DAPHNA ERDINAST-VULCAN

Daphna Erdinast-Vulcan's book is an ambitious attempt to locate Conrad's work, his temperament and his beliefs in terms of a distinction between modern and pre-modern views of the universe. It argues that Conrad's temperamental scepticism drew him towards a philosophical stance characteristic of modernity, and presaged by the German philosopher Friedrich Nietzsche. According to this stance, both truth and morality are merely fragile human constructions, reality is chaotic and meaningless, and art is a source of sustaining illusions or lies. On the other hand, Conrad's ideology or his ethical beliefs led him to reject such scepticism and relativism in favour of a pre-modern outlook which Erdinast-Vulcan identifies as poetic, mythological and religious. She traces Conrad's development as a writer in terms of this tension, arguing that *Lord Jim*, *The Rescue* and *Nostromo* try to escape from scepticism by regressing into 'the heroic-mythical frame of reference' (Erdinast-Vulcan, p. 5), that *Heart of Darkness*, *Under Western Eyes* and *The Shadow-Line* chart unsuccessful quests for 'a metaphysical essence or a transcendental authority' (Erdinast-Vulcan p. 5) and, in the chapter excerpted here, that Conrad's late novels, *Chance*, *Victory* and *The Arrow of Gold*, embrace the view of the world as only a text or fiction, lacking any ultimate truth. Erdinast-Vulcan relates this developmental scheme to questions of genre (in the case of the late novels, the genre of romance) and finds anticipations of post-structuralist theory in the scepticism of the later Conrad. Her own ideological standpoint is reflected in her linking of radical scepticism to artistic failure, so that she not only identifies a strong strain of conservative resistance to modernity in Conrad, but implicitly identifies herself with this aspect of his work.

All the nobler aspects of our life are based upon fictions. . . . It is an error to suppose that an absolute truth, an absolute criterion of

---

* Reprinted from *Joseph Conrad and the Modern Temper* (Oxford: Clarendon Press, 1991), pp. 139–47, 172–85.

Joseph Conrad

knowledge and behaviour, can be discovered. The higher aspects
of life are based upon noble delusions.

(H. Vaihinger, *The Philosophy of 'As If'*, p. 84)

Though, strictly speaking, life is but a web of illusion and a
dream within a dream, it is a dream that needs to be managed
with the utmost discretion, if it is not to turn into a nightmare.
In other words, however much life may mock the metaphysician,
the problem of conduct remains.

(Irving Babbitt, *Rousseau and Romanticism*, p. xiv)[1]

The problem underlying this last section of the discussion is, once
again, the concept of 'life as a text'. Conrad is still concerned with,
to use Stein's words, the question of 'how to be', and with the role
of art in providing the answer to this question.[2] But the relation
between art and life is almost entirely reversed now: whereas in the
early phase of Conrad's work, the prototext is myth, which signifies
an alternative mode of perception and conduct, the prototext in
the late phase is, appropriately enough, the romance, signifying
a sense of unreality, fictionality, and illusion. In order to mark the
distinction between these two opposite conceptions of life as a text,
which represent, in fact, the two opposite meanings of myth, I
have used the term 'textuality' for the latter phase. The notion of
'textuality' is, of course, a fashionable post-modernist construct, but
its philosophical source is, not surprisingly, the radical scepticism
of Nietzsche, and the concept of 'the will of illusion'.

A systematic formulation of the Nietzschean outlook was offered
as early as 1911 by Hans Vaihinger in *The Philosophy of 'As If'*.

It must be remembered that the object of the world of ideas as
a whole is not a portrayal of reality – this would be an utterly
impossible task – but rather to provide us with an *instrument for
finding our way about more easily in this world*.[3]

Many thought-processes and thought-constructs appear to be
consciously false assumptions, which either contradict reality or
are even contradictory in themselves, but which are intentionally
thus formed in order to overcome difficulties of thought by this
artificial deviation and reach the goal of thought [i.e. To serve 'the
Will to Live and dominate'] by roundabout ways and by-paths.
These artificial thought-constructs are called Scientific Fictions,
and distinguished as conscious creations by their 'As If' character.

The 'As If' world, which is formed in this manner, the world of
the 'unreal', is just as important as the world of the so-called real

248

The Failure of Textuality

or actual (in the ordinary sense of the word); indeed *it is far more important for ethics and aesthetics. This aesthetic and ethical world of 'As If', the world of the unreal, becomes finally for us a world of values* which, particularly in the form of religion, must be sharply distinguished in our mind from the world of becoming.[4]

We encounter at the very threshold of these fictions one of the most important concepts ever formed by man, the idea of *freedom*; human actions are regarded as free, and therefore as 'responsible' ... In the course of their development men have formed this important construct from immanent necessity, because only on this basis is a high degree of culture and morality possible. ... There is nothing in the real world corresponding to the idea of liberty, though in practice it is an exceedingly necessary fiction.[5]

In the category of practical fictions a number of other moral concepts and postulates are also to be enumerated, such as the concept of duty, immortality, etc. ... Here belong all the so-called 'ideals' of ordinary life. From a logical standpoint they are really fictions, but in practice they possess tremendous value in history. The ideal is an ideational construct contradictory in itself and in contradiction with reality, but it has an irresistible power. *The ideal is a practical fiction.*[6]

True morality must always rest on a *fictional* basis. ... We must act with the same seriousness and the same scruples *as if* the duty were imposed by God, *as if* we would be judged therefore, *as if* we would be punished for immorality.[7]

In a long section entitled 'Historical Confirmations', Vaihinger acknowledges his indebtedness to Nietzsche and to other sceptics. His exposition of Nietzsche's radical scepticism is of particular relevance to the present discussion.

[Nietzsche] holds that over against the world of shifting, evanescent becoming, there is set up, in the interests of understanding and of the aesthetic satisfaction of the fantasy, a world of 'being' in which everything appears rounded off and complete ... This invented world is a justified and indispensable myth; from which it finally follows that false and true are relative concepts.

'Lying, in the extra-moral sense', is what Nietzsche ... calls the conscious deviation from reality to be found in myth, art, metaphor, etc. The intentional adherence to illusion, in spite of the

249

Joseph Conrad

realization of its nature, is a kind of 'lie in an extra-moral sense'; and 'lying' is simply the conscious, intentional encouragement of illusion.[8]

Other Nietzschean concepts are taken up by Vaihinger in the same spirit: the reference to 'all customary articles of belief and even the convictions of science' as mere 'regulative fictions',[9] the exposure of a 'philosophical mythology [which] lies hidden in language [and which] breaks through at every moment, no matter how careful we may be';[10] and the designation of the ideas of freedom and responsibility, cause and effect, means and ends, as 'fictions', i.e. non-referential and arbitrary constructions. 'When we read this sign-world into things as something really existing and mix it up with them, we are merely doing what we have always done, namely mythologizing'.[11] From Nietzsche's concept of 'mythologizing' to current structuralist and post-structuralist poetics, it is but a short distance, easily traversed by Derrida's invocation of 'the joyful Nietzschean affirmation of the play of the world and the innocence of becoming, the affirmation of a world of signs which has no truth, no origin, no nostalgic guilt, and is proffered for active interpretation'.[12]

I would suggest that the 'textual' phase in Conrad's work is marked by a Nietzschean sensibility, by a renunciation of the ideological quest for authority. The tropological* mode underlying this phase is the *aporia*, a self-engendered paradox, a logical impasse. It is no accident that this trope has gained such currency with deconstruction: the radical epistemological scepticism of deconstruction, its substitution of discourse for essence, its refusal to accept the consolations of authority, and its suspicion of rhetoric, have turned the *aporia* into a pervasive mode of authorial and critical consciousness.

> Sooner or later there is the encounter with an 'aporia' or impasse. The bottom drops out . . . The center of the work of the uncanny critics is in one way or another a formulation of this experience which momentarily and not wholly successfully rationalizes it, puts it in an image, a figure, a narrative or a myth. Here, however, the distinction between story, concept, and image breaks down, at the vanishing point where each turns into something other than itself, concept into the alogical figure into catachresis,* narrative into ironical allegory. . . . The aporia, like the chasm it opens, cannot, in fact, be mastered.

The deconstructive critic seeks to find, by this process of retracing, the element in the system studied which is alogical, the thread

The Failure of Textuality

in the text which will unravel it all, or the loose stone which will pull down the whole building. The deconstruction, rather, annihilates the ground on which the building stands by showing that the text has already annihilated that ground, knowingly or unknowingly. Deconstruction is not a dismantling of the structure of a text but a demonstration that it has already dismantled itself. Its apparently solid ground is not rock but thin air.[13]

This shibboleth of deconstruction is, of course, directly related to the scepticism of Nietzsche and Vaihinger: no rhetorical device could be more aporetic than the innocent 'as if' construction, an analogy that proclaims its own invalidity even as it is made. The 'textual' phase of Conrad's work is dominated by an aporetic consciousness closely related to that of Nietzsche and Vaihinger: his characters seem to be aware of their literariness, conscious of their own fictionality, even as they act out their self-assigned roles as knights in romances of their own making.

Conrad's affinity with the Nietzschean temperament has already been demonstrated in the first chapter of this study. But unlike Nietzsche, the prophet of modernity, or Vaihinger, his own contemporary, Conrad was already able to recognize the devastating moral implications of the philosophy of 'As If'. His letter to the *New York Times*, published on 2 August 1901, reads like a passage of Vaihinger's:

Science . . . , whatever authority it may claim, is not concerned with truth at all, but with the exact order of such phenomena as fall under the perception of the senses. Its conclusions are quite true enough if they can be made useful to the furtherance of our little schemes to make our earth a little more habitable. The laws it discovers remain certain and immovable for the time of several generations . . . The only indisputable truth of life is our ignorance. Besides this there is nothing evident, nothing absolute, nothing uncontradicted; there is no principle, no instinct, no impulse that can stand alone at the beginning of things and look confidently to the end.[14]

Theory is a cold and lying tombstone of departed truth. (For truth is no more immortal than any other delusion.)[15]

The ultimate implication of this old-new philosophical outlook, as pointed out by Gerald Graff, is that if 'the artifice is the only reality available', and if 'reality does not exist, or rather exists only in a fictionalized version', then 'everything is swallowed up in an

251

Joseph Conrad

infinite regress of textuality', and literature, like other sense-making procedures, should renounce any truth-claims that it may have once possessed.[16]

> Knowing and naming itself as fiction, literature becomes a vehicle for a nihilistic metaphysics, an anti-didactic form of preaching. In a world in which nobody can look outside the walls of the prison house of language, literature, with its built-in confession of its self-imprisonment, becomes once again the great oracle of truth, but now the truth is that there is no truth . . . Where reality has become unreal, literature qualifies as our guide to reality by de-realizing itself.[17]

Graff's poignant analysis follows the idea of 'textuality' to its ultimate and inevitable conclusion. If we accept the view that reality is ultimately unknowable or non-existent apart from our mythical (i.e. fictional) constructions of it, we will lose all power of action. The fallacy of the theories of 'As If' is only too clear: 'Somehow we are supposed to "order" our attitude to the world by making use of fictions whose lack of truth we recognize but decide to regard as irrelevant. . . . The very admission that our beliefs are founded on myths undermines their ability to generate credence.'[18]

In terms of the present analysis, the view of reality as a text reverses the concept of myth as used in the first section: in the mythical mode, as experienced by Jim, Karain, Lingard, and Nostromo, the word is endowed with the power to create a world. In the textual mode, as we shall see, the 'world' has been *reduced* to a 'mere word'. If myth, as used in the first section of this study, implies a metaphysics of presence,* textuality implies a metaphysics of absence, a void covered by a thin network of interpretations. This metaphysics of absence, the radical epistemological scepticism, the conception of life as a mere text are undoubtedly familiar to the reader at the close of the twentieth century, but they are as old as modernity itself, and closely related to the Romantic legacy and its current prophets.

Critical periodizations of Conrad's writings often relegate the works written after 1912 to the writer's 'decline', with *The Shadow-Line* as an exception to an otherwise inferior range of works. D. Hewitt, T. Moser, and A. J. Guerard are the first and most notable exponents of this view, which has by now gained such currency amongst Conrad scholars that one need hardly recapitulate it here.[19] The apparent depletion of creative energy in this last phase has been attributed to various psychological causes, such as the separation from Ford and a subsequent 'Infection-Exhaustion

252

The Failure of Textuality

Psychosis', ill-health and the mental lassitude of old age, or a 'postdepressive reaction' which activated a movement to a more 'affirmative' mood as a self-defensive mechanism.[20]

I believe that the last phase of Conrad's work does reflect a considerable decline in artistic quality and seriousness, but it seems to me that to accuse Conrad of having turned from his former scepticism to glib moralizing is a misconstruction of the dynamics of his work.[21] I would argue that the opposite is true, that Conrad's decline works his surrender to the radical scepticism of the Nietzschean outlook which he had managed to keep at bay throughout the best part of this creative career. This Nietzschean outlook, which has so far broken through only in Conrad's letters and in the peculiar thematic and structural tensions already pointed to, now emerges in full force, when both the author and his characters seem to be afflicted with an acute sense of the unreality of their world.

In a later section of this chapter, I will, of course, have to account for this question-begging last point and establish the legitimacy of the analogy between the writer and his protagonists, and the extrapolation from the moral or practical failure of the characters within a given literary work to the artistic failure of the work. I would argue that this last phase of Conrad's work is not merely *about* the failure of textuality: it is, in fact, a *symptom* of this failure.

Two of the later novels, *Chance* and *Victory*, cannot be summarily relegated to Conrad's phase of decline, in spite of the considerable diversity of critical evaluations of their artistic quality. I believe, however, that these two controversial novels already share the syndrome of textuality and should be considered as border-line cases. There is little doubt that a third novel, *The Arrow of Gold*, is, indeed, an artistic failure, but it is an extremely interesting failure for the purpose of this study, if only because its dynamics are so inextricably linked with this failure of vision which is to be demonstrated. All three works proclaim themselves as romances by a profusion of generic signals: the protagonists are a 'damsel in distress' and a knightly male figure, and the plot revolves around the rescue of the damsel from a sinister rival figure. The stories of Lena and Heyst, Flora and Captain Anthony, Rita and M. George can be, and indeed have been, read as traditional stories of Love and Adventure. The story of Edith Travers and Captain Lingard in *The Rescue*, which was completed at this late stage after an interval of twenty-three years, has also been construed – by readers as well as by some of the characters themselves – in this light.[22]

But these strong generic statements, or 'signals', are systematically questioned and eventually pre-empted in the three novels: the male protagonists, the 'knightly' figures, are all presented as essentially

253

Joseph Conrad

powerless, bewildered, and uncertain of their roles. The plot, too, does not entirely conform to the generic conventions: in *Victory* it ends with a failure; in *Chance* and in *The Arrow*, where the 'rescue' does seem to conclude with the traditional happy ending, it goes beyond the union of the lovers and ends with their eventual separation. And finally, there is a corrosive undercurrent of narrative irony and sarcasm, which exposes and challenges the naïve conventions characteristic of this genre.

The subversion or 'deconstruction' of the generic statement which the novels initially seem to make is closely related to the problem of textuality. The protagonists seem to be strangely aware of their own fictionality. They are all apparently aware that 'such a thing as character has no real existence. It is only a helpful abstraction' and that 'the subject, the *ego* is only a fiction'.[23] It is this awareness which renders them impotent, weak, and unfit for their roles.

Marlow, who, I would argue, is the real protagonist of *Chance*, is persistently calling attention to the interpretative nature of his enterprise. He never pretends to have at his disposal anything but 'bits of disconnected statements' which he is trying to 'piece together' (p. 222), and fills the gaps between these fragments with his own conjectures and constructions. His constant allusions to literature and his explicit search for the generic model of his story enhance the sense of unreality of which so many readers of the novel have complained. Heyst, the chivalrous protagonist of *Victory*, views life as 'a delusion and a snare' (p. 212), and has lost 'all belief in realities' (p. 350). Having inherited the profound philosophical scepticism of his father (who, as we shall see, is an extremely Nietzschean figure), he can only relate to Lena as to a text, which remains undecipherable to the very end. M. George, the young protagonist of *The Arrow of Gold*, is also presented as a fictional entity, a 'young Ulysses'. Both he and Rita, acting under assumed names in a ludicrous game of conspiracy with remarkably little conviction or zeal, are, as we shall see, uncomfortably conscious of their own fictionality.

This view of life as a text or a spectacle yields in all three protagonists a detached aestheticist attitude, which inhibits and undermines their performance. They all seem to obey the Nietzschean dictum 'not to measure the world by our personal feelings but as if it were a play and we were part of a play',[24] 'to regard our manner of living and acting as parts in a play, including therein our maxims and principles'.[25] The peculiar emotional aridity of Marlow, the failure of Heyst, and the eventual disillusionment of M. George are, as we shall see, directly related to their view of life as a text and of all convictions as mere illusions or precarious interpretations.

254

The Failure of Textuality

The fallacy of the philosophy of 'As If' is embodied in these literary characters who are so fatally aware of their own fictionality, and of the 'textual' quality of life, that they lose all powers of action. The only protagonist who eventually renounces this outlook, and thereby redeems both himself and the novel, is Marlow. The other two remain hopelessly locked within their respective fictions, detached spectators of their own plays, unable to act out their knightly roles with full conviction.

[. . .]

Victory

The critical controversy over the artistic merits of *Victory* and its place in Conrad's work has produced a diversity of judgements, ranging from the view that the novel is 'among those of Conrad's works which deserve to be current as representing his claim to classical standing' to the assertion that 'the time has come to drop *Victory* from the Conrad canon'.[26] It seems to me that at least some of the elements which have generated this wide divergence can be resolved by viewing the novel as a product of Conrad's 'textual' mode.

The first chapter opens with the seemingly irrelevant ruminations of the narrator on the relation between diamonds and coal. This introductory passage, atypical of the pace of the rest of the novel in its leisurely, speculative tone, has been taken by critics to establish the theme of doubling in the novel, the resemblance between ostensibly opposite beings like Heyst and 'the plain Mr Jones'.[27] I believe that the theme introduced by this somewhat incongruous opening is more complex than that: coal and diamonds are related to each other not, as one might expect after having read the opening sentence, by an elaborate explanation of the 'very close chemical relation' which links them, but by the fact that 'both these commodities *represent* wealth' (p. 3, my emphasis). The focus, then, is not on a common chemical essence but on the quality of *representation*.

But there is a major difference between these two cases of material substances representing wealth: one can easily understand the practical fascination of coal as a source of energy and heat, but the 'mystical' fascination of diamonds would be much harder to grasp, if it were not for the fact that our civilization has, for no practical reason, chosen to endow these shining pebbles with the power to signify wealth. The relation of the substance to the represented quality in the case of coal is metonymic or representative, but in

255

Joseph Conrad

the case of diamonds it is clearly semiotic, i.e. arbitrary and entirely artificial.

A similar treatment is accorded by the narrator to The Tropical Belt Company.

> The world of finance is a mysterious world in which, incredible as the fact may appear, evaporation precedes liquidation. First the capital evaporates, and then the company goes into liquidation. These are very unnatural physics . . .
>
> (p. 3)

This playful inversion of the laws of physics introduces the reader once again to the major concern of the novel: even the laws of physics – 'discovered' by science and therefore ostensibly objective and immutable – are presented as a system of signs, human constructs which function by human consent and can be inverted at will.

As we have already seen, this view of reality as a construct, or – as the post-modernists would have it – a text, is not atypical of Conrad, but in *Victory* we meet the first Conrad protagonist who is so entirely caught up in it that he cannot bring himself to act at all. An apt diagnosis of Heyst's malady has been offered by H. J. Laskowski, who rightly relates the protagonist's frame of mind to the philosophical scepticism of Berkeley and Hume, a 'denial of what may be called "self" or "mind" if by either of these terms we mean an abiding human essence' and a '"skeptical doubt" as to the continued existence of objects when they are not being perceived'. Laskowski diagnoses Heyst as 'a man beset by the skeptical doubt of Hume, a man who tries to live with a radical awareness of his own insubstantiality, and the insubstantiality of everything around him.'[28]

Heyst's 'disenchantment' (p. 65), his view of the world as 'nothing but an amusing spectacle' (p. 178), his temperamental attitude of 'a spectator' (pp. 185, 196) become not only an epistemological stance but an ethical position as well. I would suggest that this form of unbelief is an early version of post-modernist textuality, a view of the world as an infinite series of signs without an ultimate referent, and a condemnation of essentialism* as a falsified conception of life. This view, as reflected in Heyst's relativistic, textual sensibility (which renders the novel extremely vulnerable to deconstruction), is ultimately rejected in *Victory*, at least on the level of the author's conscious and explicit message, on moral grounds.[29]

Axel Heyst is the *fin de siècle* protagonist who realizes that appearances are all that one can ask for or have in this world

256

The Failure of Textuality

(p. 204); who scorns life – or rather 'what people call by that name' – for the 'fatal imperfection' of its gifts which, he believes, 'makes of them a delusion and a snare' (p. 212); who has managed to 'refine everything away' by turning the earth to 'a shadow', who has lost 'all belief in realities' (p. 350). In his admission to Lena that he is powerless to protect her (p. 347), that he has 'neither force nor conviction', 'neither strength nor persuasion' to act (p. 350), Heyst himself relates his passivity to his view of reality as a mesh of illusions. His initial response to the pending confrontation with the murderous trio is 'all this is too unreal altogether' (p. 347), a response which he reiterates later in his 'showdown' with Jones: 'you people . . . are divorced from all reality in my eyes' (p. 364). Heyst's inability to suspend his disbelief in the spectacle of life has left him entirely impotent. At the moment when he can easily overcome Jones, his very will is 'dead of weariness' and he moves 'like a prisoner captured by the evil power of a masquerading skeleton out of the grave' (p. 390). The skeleton is not necessarily the spectral figure of Jones staggering at Heyst's side, but that of his father who had, by his negation of life, rendered him unfit for it.

The nature of the Heystian frame of mind, the philosophy of total negation, has been studied in depth by various critics. S. Kahele and Howard German describe him as 'the man whose thinking was devoted to the destruction of illusion', and whose scepticism reflects Conrad's view that ideals are 'inevitably extremely subjective'. Conrad's ambivalence about the role of illusion in the human enterprise – the tension between his Heystian scepticism on the one hand and his realization that illusions are necessary for the survival of humanity on the other (p. 94) – is, they rightly maintain, one of the central dynamic principles of the novel.[30] Another notable study of the Heystian frame of mind is Bruce Johnson's analysis of the novel as an indictment of Schopenhauer's philosophy: 'there can be no doubt that Heyst's skepticism is "metaphysical" and that the elder Heyst's vision of "man's right to absolute moral and intellectual liberty" evolves out of the frightening contingency of man in a universe that has no moral plan'.[31]

The metaphysical nature of Heyst's scepticism is, indeed, irrefutable, but I would suggest that the philosophical prototype of the elder Heyst is Nietzsche rather than Schopenhauer, for while it is true that Nietzsche's metaphysical scepticism evolved out of Schopenhauer's bleak vision, it was he who embraced its logical consequences and declared the 'death of God' in an uninhibited celebration of moral 'perspectivism'.[32] Heyst Sr cuts a Nietzschean figure in his role as 'a thinker, stylist, and man of the world' (p. 92), a 'destroyer of systems, of hopes, of beliefs' (p. 175). The description

257

Joseph Conrad

of the father's style, 'the broken text of reflections, maxims, short phrases, enigmatical sometimes and sometimes eloquent' (p. 219), is closely reminiscent of the philosopher's notorious aphorisms, and some of the Heystian postulates do, indeed, sound like quotations from Nietzsche: 'the desire is the bed of dreams' (p. 219); 'men live their captivity. To the unknown force of negation they prefer the miserably tumbled bed of their servitude' (p. 220).[33]

Heyst's bleak vision of morality, postulating that 'the so-called wickedness must be, like the so-called virtue, its own reward – to be anything at all' (p. 219), sounds like an echo of Nietzschean gesture beyond Good and Evil, his denial of any transcendental or inherently valid ethical sanction. It is not surprising, therefore, that the 'plain Mr Jones' is presented as both the father's and the son's double, as it is he, rather than Heyst Jr, who takes the Heystian attitude to its ultimate conclusion.[34] The ethical relativism which emerges from the awareness of the metaphysical void, the sense that, as Johnson puts it, 'there are no sanctions in the artificial fictions of society',[35] opens up a moral abyss down which Heyst the son is forced to look. As he does so, he recognizes a caricatured reflection of himself in the image of Jones.

Another concomitant of the Nietzschean-Heystian world-view is the conception of the world in aesthetic terms, as a spectacle. This typical *fin de siècle* attitude, which finds its paragon in the languid pose of Jones, is also – albeit in a more refined and less ruthless form – at the source of Heyst's conception of the world.[36] The aestheticist dimension in the portrayal of Heyst is mostly evident in Conrad's use of sound and music, which has been largely overlooked even by critics who explore this aspect of the novel. Pater's famous formulation of the aestheticist credo that 'all art constantly aspires to the condition of music' (a reiteration of Schopenhauer's hierarchy of the arts), which reflects the attempt to break away from the concept of mimesis and to work within a perfect system which is entirely self-referential and self-contained, is curiously echoed in the description of Heyst. 'Like most dreamers, to whom it is given sometimes to hear the music of the spheres, [he] had a taste for silence which he was able to gratify for years. The islands are very quiet' (p. 66).

But Heyst is drawn despite himself out of his insular position into the sordid reality of common humanity by the noise of 'rasped, squeaked, scraped snatches of tunes' played by Zangiacomo's Ladies' Orchestra, 'an instrumental uproar, screaming, grunting, whining, sobbing, scraping, squeaking some kind of lively air' (pp. 67–8). Heyst's response to the brutish noise is significant:

258

The Failure of Textuality

In the quick time of that music, in the varied, piercing clamour of the strings ... there was a suggestion of brutality – something cruel, *sensual* and repulsive. ... But there is an unholy fascination in systematic noise. He did not flee from it incontinently as one might have expected him to do. He remained, astonished at himself for remaining, since nothing could have been more repulsive to his tastes, more painful to his senses, and, so to speak, more contrary to his genius, than this *rude exhibition of vigour*. The Zangiacomo band was not making music; it was simply murdering silence with *a vulgar, ferocious energy*.

(p. 68, my emphases)

It seems to me that the relation posited between crudeness and virility is not accidental: Heyst's hypertrophied cultured sensibility, his taste for the perfect 'music of the spheres' which sends him into a voluntary exile in the realm of silence, is seen by Conrad as a disabling disease which will eventually render the protagonist unfit for survival.

Heyst the son is 'not a fighting man' (p. 9); he is essentially a reader, a man in 'the white drill suit of civilization' (p. 227) with a book in his hand (pp. 4, 27, 28, 180). Even Lena is ultimately just another 'text' for him: her eyes are 'unreadable' (p. 219), she is 'a script in an unknown language' (p. 222, see also pp. 310, 324). And although she gives him 'a greater sense of his own reality than he had ever known in all his life' (p. 200), it is not yet sufficient for him to recover that dimension of reality which he had renounced. Lena's attempt to reverse Heyst's 'textual' view of life, begins with her request to be named by him:

They call me Alma. ... Magdelene too. It doesn't matter; you can call me by whatever name you choose. Yes, you give me a name. Think of one you would like the sound of – something quite new. How I should like to forget everything that had gone before, as one forgets a dream that's done with ...

(p. 88)

The power which she grants him to create her anew by naming her, is undoubtedly an Adamic endowment. It is the semi-divine power to create a world with the word, which has been delegated to Adam in the act of naming God's creatures. Lena later reinforces her proffered gift when she tells her lover: 'Do you know, it seems to me, somehow, that if you were to stop thinking of me I shouldn't be in the world at all ... I can only be what you think I am'

259

Joseph Conrad

(p. 187). But Heyst cannot take the gift of creation. He has lost his belief in the power of the word to create a world, and Lena seems to despair of her role as an Eve to his Adam when she asks him: 'Do you believe that I exist?' (p. 247). It seems that he does not.

Heyst's failure to take up the Adamic role is closely related to the lethal scepticism of his father who had tried to silence the 'imperative echoes' of 'the oldest voice in the world'. It is this oldest voice which had uttered the words of creation, which had fathered the 'original Adam', the 'primeval ancestor' to whom Heyst the son would like to relate himself (p. 173). The doctrine of 'universal unbelief' (p. 199) and 'universal nothingness (p. 219) embraced by Heyst Sr reverses the Adamic endowment in its view of human reality as a hollow construct. He leaves his son with a conception of a world 'perhaps not substantial enough to grasp' (p. 176), with a legacy of counterfeit coins.

In an illuminating analysis of this relationship between the Adamic voice and the voice of Heyst Sr, Tony Tanner rightly juxtaposes the imperatives of the two fathers, the 'double voice of the dual father'. The Adamic voice commands Heyst to 'copulate and multiply' and the voice of the dead father tells him to deny his sexuality, to abstain. Tanner describes the father as 'the ghost voice of books', who had tried 'to dominate and master the world with the word', and contrasts Lena's physical, literal presence, her 'living voice', with the dead 'sense' of the father's presence.[37] I believe that this juxtaposition of the father's word with Lena's voice underscores the proposed diagnosis of the pathological textuality which afflicts the protagonist.

The wider cultural implications of *Victory*, its critique of the ethical relativism and the scepticism of the post-Nietzschean world which engendered the aestheticist-decadent outlook, and its hostile anticipation of some post-modernist concepts, call for a view of the story of Axel Heyst as a study case of crumbling civilization. This aspect of the novel has been recognized by several critics.[38] The view of the sophisticated and highly civilized as foredoomed by definition, of hypercerebration and reflection as inimically hostile to instinctual life forces is, indeed, symptomatic of the age. This attitude is succinctly formulated in *The Modern Temper* by Joseph Wood Krutch who regards 'the detachment of mind from its function [i.e. physical survival] which makes philosophy possible' as a 'vital liability', because 'intelligence which is detached, skeptical, ironic . . . puts the man or the race which possess it at a disadvantage in dealing with those whose intelligence serves their purpose'. He concludes – like Nietzsche, Spengler, and other

260

The Failure of Textuality

prophets of doom – that 'civilizations die from philosophical calm, irony and the sense of fair play quite as surely as they die of debauchery'.[39]

However one may object to or wish to modify this prognosis, it is certainly true in the case of Axel Heyst, the urbane, ironic, ultra-civilized specimen of a dying race. Living amongst the overgrown ruins of the commercial Western enterprise, in the shadow of the gigantic blackboard featuring the initials of the evaporated company, he is, indeed, a 'man of the last hour' or 'the hour before last' (p. 359) rather than the 'original Adam' (p. 173). It is Wang, the man who cultivates the vegetable garden and uses his intelligence as an instrument for survival, who is the true descendent of the first man. If there is one sense in which Heyst does share something with the original Adam, it is the fact of the fall, but whereas the first fall was occasioned by the first man's need to eat of the tree of knowledge, his weary descendant is already carrying the seed of that life-denying fruit of knowledge – left to him as a legacy from his father – within him, as he tried to reinstate himself in the Garden.

Another relevant aspect of *Victory* is the plurality of its textual affinities. The novel has been successfully and convincingly shown to be related to various biblical passages, to *The Tempest*, to *Hamlet*, to *Macbeth*, and to the *Aeneid*.[40] As the literary models suggested by the critics cited below are all substantiated by weighty evidence in the novel, there emerges a baffling range of texts all claiming to be the literary progenitors of this work. Which, then, is the prototext to which *Victory* should be related? The answer, I believe, should be, 'all of them'. The blatant textuality of this novel, the fact that it parades itself as a literary text by numerous allusions to other texts, is a significant correlative of the protagonist's frame of mind. For Heyst the reader, a man who views reality as a spectacle or a mesh of appearances, is so afflicted with this textual or literary view of life, that he can never suspend his disbelief and respond to the drama of reality as if it were real indeed.

An interesting symptom of this state of mind which generates a view of reality as a system of references without referents appears in the use of the monetary analogy in the novel. Heyst explains his father's disillusionment in terms of counterfeit coins:

I suppose he began like other people; took fine words for good, ringing coin and noble ideas for valuable bank notes. . . . Later he discovered – how am I to explain it to you? Suppose the world were a factory and all mankind workmen in it. Well, he

261

Joseph Conrad

discovered that the wages were not good enough. That they were paid in counterfeit money.

(pp. 195–6)

A strikingly similar analogy has been made by Hans Vaihinger in *The Philosophy of 'As If'*.

We hardly notice that we are acting on a double stage – our own inner world (which, of course, we objectify as the world of sense-perception) and also an entirely different and external world. There are then exchange centers, where the values of one world are changed into those of the other and the active intercourse between both worlds is made possible, where the light paper currency of thought is exchanged for the heavy coin of reality, and where on the other hand the heavy metal of reality is exchanged for a lighter currency which nevertheless facilitates intercourse.

The difficulty . . . lies entirely in the reduction of one system to another, in effecting the exchange. Large quantities of false paper-money, many false ideas, that cannot be changed into material values, find their way into circulation; the nominal value of paper money is not always paid, but the price which rules on the market . . . [But] all higher speculation and the whole of our intricate system of exchange are only possible by this expedient and by these fictional values.

'Fictional value' is the name given in political economy to paper-money and such ideas as, for instance, the pound sterling, etc. The paper is regarded as if it had the value of metal . . . Our analogy thus has a real basis. . . . Concepts too are merely conventional signs. . . . In every instance it is the fictive function that is here at work.[41]

But Heyst's analogy, seemingly straightforward and simple, has yet another twist, of which he – like many professed disciples of Saussure – seems to be oblivious. If all mankind are workmen in the 'factory', then there is no sense in which one can talk of counterfeit money because the value of currency is determined by human consent. Bank notes have no intrinsic value beyond the paper they are printed on. They acquire value when a significant group of people decides that these particular pieces of paper represent something else, something tangible and 'real', like land or sheep. Language functions in much the same way, on the basis of

The Failure of Textuality

common consent. When a group of people accept a certain sound combination as a signifier, it becomes a living word.

Thus when Heyst talks of his father's 'living word' (p. 196), he is, in a sense, using the very counterfeit money he despises, for once he has decided to break through the barrier of silence in which he had cloistered himself, he must share the basic assumptions that are common to mankind, he must believe that there is something real to be represented in order for any communication to take place at all. His agony at the thought of Lena's response to Schomberg's allegations against him is also embedded in a recognition of the inevitability of representation: 'you thought that there was no smoke without fire!' For a man to whom *all* is smoke without fire, the discovery of the 'power of words' (p. 214) is shattering indeed.

This last point is related to two fault-lines which have served as the arena for the critical debate about the literary value of the novel and which, I believe, are closely related to each other. The first problem is the generic transition from the realistic mode of Part I to an allegorical mode which eventually seems to take over the rest of the work. This ambivalent generic identity has generated an opposition between two mutually exclusive approaches to the novel. Hewitt, Moser, and Guerard view the novel as a realistic work that fails partly because of the insistent allegorical dimension which precludes realistic psychological characterization, whereas Paul Wiley, John Palmer, and others celebrate the allegorical dimension and the rich symbolism of the novel.[42] There have been some attempts to accommodate the generic transition, notably by R. W. B. Lewis who modifies the allegorical element and prefers to call it an 'allegorical swelling', or Gary Geddes who argues that the pervading irony in the novel acts as a 'built-in antidote or counterweight to its allegorizing tendencies'.[43] I would suggest a different, perhaps less apologetic way of accommodating the seemingly incongruent generic mix in the novel, and relate it to the second, ostensibly technical difficulty – the narrative discontinuity.

The blatant inconsistency of the narrative mode, the abandonment of the first-person narrator of Part I, his replacement by an omniscient narrative voice in Part II, when the action moves to Samburan, and his eventual reinstatement at the very end, after Heyst's death, has been regarded by critics as yet another of the novel's failures, an awkward handling of the physical removal of the protagonists away from the first narrator's territory to an isolated island. It is only in the more recent readings of the novel (like those offered by Gary Geddes and William Bonney) that serious attempts to account for this narrative transition as a correlative of a thematic shift have been made.

263

Joseph Conrad

I believe that both these targets of critical disapproval – the generic shift and the narrative discontinuity – reflect the basic dynamism of the novel. These two 'aesthetic' ruptures should be viewed in a Bakhtinian light, as the projections of the protagonist's frame of mind, the fault-lines within his consciousness. Both the allegorical mode and the omniscient narrative voice belong to a metaphysically integrated conception of the world: the allegory depends for its viability on an a priori clear-cut conceptual system, just as the omniscient narrative voice is premised on a clear notion of authority. One can easily see why allegory as a genre and omniscience as a narrative mode are not favoured in the literature produced in the age of relativism after the disintegration of metaphysics and the death of God. What we have in Part II of the novel, then, is a transition to a different premise, or at least an attempt to suspend the radical, essentially modern scepticism of the first-person narrator which is but a reflection of the Heystian frame of mind. In Part II Heyst is given the opportunity to cast himself into the allegory, or into the Eden myth: he may be able to redeem himself by suspending his disbelief and acting out his part in the allegory.

The significant use of religious terminology can also be viewed in the same context. The volcano which is Heyst's closest neighbour and which resembles the intermittent glow of his cigar, is 'a pillar of smoke by day and a loom of fire at night' (p. 168). This is an obvious reference to the pillar of alternating smoke and fire which had led the Israelites on their way to the promised land, whose immediate significance is, of course, heavily ironic: in Heyst's world there can be no promised land, and his 'pilgrimage' is indeed 'aimless' (p. 31). Heyst's eventual choice of death by fire may, then, be construed at least as an attempt to redeem the value of that debased religious currency, to reinstate the metaphysical framework which makes the allegory viable. Heyst's references to the deluge, the destruction of a corrupt civilization (p. 191), and his playful attitude to the notion of Providence (pp. 199, 359), of 'retribution' (p. 354), can also be seen in the same light as the foredoomed attempts of the protagonist to restore the lost metaphysical dimension.

It seems to me that the transition to the allegorical mode is effective in its very crudity, for it is Heyst himself who posits the allegory in his search for a textual or literary model to his reality. It is Heyst himself who presents the trio as 'evil intelligence', 'instinctive savagery', and 'brute force' (p. 329). But the self-consciousness of the spectator-participant, who tried to define the generic category of the spectacle, divests the allegory of its primal power which depends on a system of beliefs and cannot function in the absence

The Failure of Textuality

of a coherent metaphysical view. For Heyst, the man who cannot believe, 'good' and 'evil' are but 'optical delusions' like hope or fellowship or love (see pp. 80, 82).[44] The allegory remains a quaint artistic spectacle, because Heyst cannot bring himself to act upon it as an Everyman would have done.

The discontinuity of the narrative mode can also be accounted for by this wavering of the novel between the poles of disbelief and willed belief, between the Heystian temperament and the desire to negate the 'universal nothingness' (p. 219) with an act of creation. The narrator of the first part embodies, as observed by W. Bonney, 'a placid model of Old Heyst' in his static detachment, his pervasive irony, and his refusal to commit himself and engage in an intimate contact with the protagonists.[45] He persistently – and for the most part without any apparent relevance – calls attention to his use of words: his somewhat crude puns on 'forced' and 'forcible' (p. 5), on the bald 'top' of Heyst's head and the 'tip-top' house of the Tesman Brothers (p. 7), enhance the sense of a 'free play of meaning', as does his gossipy speculative manner of introducing the protagonists. This self-reflexive quality of the narrative is yet another symptom of the 'textual' state of mind, the conception of all human enterprise as an illusory construct.

The transition to the omniscient mode, like the allegorical shift, affords the protagonist a temporary sanctuary by transporting him to Samburan, out of the relativizing voice of the first-person narrator. But Heyst's scepticism is incurable. The tentative sanctuary with which Conrad has provided him is not strong enough to withstand the corrosive voice of his father. As the story reverts to the realistic mode and the first-person narrator takes over once more, one realizes that the victory of Lena's life-giving powers, a victory which Heyst seems to have finally conceded in the verbal affirmation with which he concludes his life, is yet another illusion. The last word is 'nothing'.

There remains, of course, the question of the artistic merit of the novel. Rather than join the controversy on the side of either the realistic or the allegorical readings, I would suggest that if the novel does not 'work', it is not because of any technical or stylistic defects. The failure here is a failure of vision, the work of a writer who, like his protagonist, cannot will himself into a belief in the power of words, who, like his protagonist, has come to suspect language as counterfeit coins. When Axel Heyst tells Lena of 'the man with the quill pen in his hand' who is 'responsible for [his] existence' (p. 195), he points to the portrait of his father. But the man who has, in fact, created Heyst with the quill pen in his hand and is thus responsible for his existence is, of course, Conrad himself, the

Joseph Conrad

author of Heyst's tale. The ambivalence of the attribution, the deliberate fusion of parental authority and authorial responsibility is, I believe, at the core of *Victory*, for it is Conrad's own failure, as well as that of his protagonist, to fend off the Heystian element in himself which underlies the peculiar generic conflict in the novel, the narrative discontinuity, and the ambiguity of the denouement.

The close affinity between the Conradian temperament and that of his protagonist is evident to any reader of Conrad's letters. The most thorough discussions of this resemblance are offered by Daniel Schwarz, who rightly describes Heyst as 'a double for part of Conrad's temperament', and by Douglas D. Park, who describes Conrad's own scepticism as 'a temperamental condition', a consciousness which 'undermines all perception' and which 'ultimately turns against itself. It dissolves its own surfaces, rationalizations, impulses, emotions, until nothing is left but a paralyzed complexity.' Conrad's Heystian sensibility is evident, as Park shows, in his letters to Marguerite Poradowska and to Edward Garnett, where he confesses – like his protagonist – to having lost all sense of reality. A similar line is followed by Gary Geddes, who also quotes the letters to Garnett, Cunninghame Graham, and others in support of the correlation between Conrad's outlook and that of his protagonist, and aptly underscores some phrases that 'might have been lifted directly from the writings of Heyst's father'.[46]

The significance of Heyst Sr's attempt to silence 'the oldest voice in the world' has already been discussed. The analogy between the primal act of creation – that of the primal voice which had created the world with his word – and the creative power of the artist is obvious: had Conrad accepted the Heyst imperative to 'look on – make no sound' (p. 175), he would have been, like his protagonist, another exile in the realm of silence. His manifest disobedience is, in itself, a kind of victory, a declaration of faith in the power of the word to create a world.

Notes

1. HANS VAIHINGER, *The Philosophy of 'As If': A System of the Theoretical, Practical and Religious Fictions of Mankind.* First published in Berlin, 1911, trans. C. K. Ogden (1924; London: Routledge & Kegan Paul, 1952). IRVING BABBITT, *Rousseau and Romanticism* (Boston: Houghton Mifflin Co., 1919).

2. *Lord Jim*, p. 213. All references to Conrad's works follow the pagination of the Dent Uniform Edition (London & Toronto: J. M. Dent & Sons Ltd, 1923–25).

3. *The Philosophy of 'As If'*, p. 15. In 1919 Vaihinger founded, together with Dr Raymund Schmidt, the journal *Annalen der Philosophie* ('with particular reference to the problems of the "As If" approach').

The Failure of Textuality

4. Ibid., pp. xlvi–xlvii, my emphasis.

5. Ibid., p. 43.

6. Ibid., p. 48.

7. Ibid., p. 49.

8. Quoted in ibid., p. 342.

9. Ibid., p. 346.

10. Ibid., p. 349.

11. Ibid., p. 354.

12. Jonathan Culler, *Structuralist Poetics* (London: Routledge & Kegan Paul, 1975), p. 247.

13. J. Hillis Miller, 'Stevens' Rock and Criticism as Cure', *Georgia Review*, 30 (1976), pp. 338, 341.

14. Quoted in *The Collected Letters of Joseph Conrad*, ed. Frederick R. Karl and Laurence Davies, 5 vols. (Cambridge: Cambridge University Press, 1983–96), ii. 348.

15. Letter to Garnett on 15 March 1895, in *Collected Letters*, i. 205.

16. Gerald Graff, *Literature against Itself: Literary Ideas in Modern Society* (Chicago: University of Chicago Press, 1979), pp. 60–1.

17. Ibid., p. 179.

18. Ibid., p. 184.

19. Douglas Hewitt, *Joseph Conrad: A Reassessment* (1952; 3rd edition, London: Bowes & Bowes, 1975), pp. 103–11; Thomas C. Moser, *Joseph Conrad: Achievement and Decline* (Hamden, CT: Archon Books, 1966), pp. 116–19, 155–6, 158–9 and *passim*; Albert J. Guerard, *Conrad the Novelist* (Cambridge, MA: Harvard University Press, 1958), pp. 255–61, 272–8.

20. Bernard C. Meyer, *Joseph Conrad: A Psychoanalytic Biography* (Princeton: Princeton University Press, 1967), pp. 221–43; Frederick R. Karl, *Joseph Conrad: The Three Lives* (London: Faber & Faber, 1979), pp. 749, 764, 770–2, 797–800; Zdzisław Najder, *Joseph Conrad: A Chronicle*, trans. Carroll-Najder (Cambridge: Cambridge University Press, 1983).

21. This view is shared by most critics who accept the theory of the later decline and view Conrad's later works as informed by a 'sentimental ethic' (Guerard's term), an easy affirmation of values which had been questioned before, an exteriorization of the source of evil, etc.

22. *The Rescue* is, in many ways, similar to the novels discussed in this section, in that it reflects the tension between myth and textuality, which, as we shall see, are the two poles of the romantic outlook. This novel, begun in 1896 and finished in 1919, belongs in fact, to both these phases in Conrad's work, thematically as well as chronologically. My reasons for placing it in the 'mythical' phase are largely methodological.

23. Quoted by Vaihinger, *The Philosophy of 'As If'*, pp. 350, 357.

24. Ibid., p. 297.

25. Ibid., p. 282.

26. F. R. Leavis, *The Great Tradition* (1948; London: Chatto & Windus, 1979), p. 209; Guerard, *Conrad the Novelist*, p. 275.

Joseph Conrad

27. SHARON KAHELE and HOWARD GERMAN, 'Conrad's *Victory*: A Reassessment', *Modern Fiction Studies*, 10/1 (1964), pp. 55–72; J. DEURBERGUE, 'The Opening of *Victory*', *Studies in Joseph Conrad*, 2 (1975), pp. 239–70.

28. HENRY J. LASKOWSKI, '*Esse Est Percipi*: Epistemology and Narrative Method in *Victory*', *Conradiana*, 9/3 (1977), pp. 2725–86. For an earlier, similar view of Heyst, see DONALD A. DIKE, 'The Tempest of Axel Heyst', *Nineteenth-Century Fiction*, 17/2 (1962), pp. 95–113.

29. The word 'vulnerability' is used here advisedly, for it seems to me that an interpretation which adheres to the Heystian outlook and chooses to ignore its final condemnation, like that offered by WILLIAM W. BONNEY in 'Narrative Perspective in *Victory*: The Thematic Relevance', *The Journal of Narrative Technique*, 5/1 (1975), pp. 24–39, is a denial of the acknowledgement of moral responsibility which is at the core of Conrad's work.

30. KAHELE and GERMAN, 'Conrad's *Victory*', pp. 70, 65.

31. BRUCE JOHNSON, *Conrad's Models of Mind* (Minneapolis: University of Minnesota Press, 1971), pp. 160, 165. A similar view is taken by ARNOLD E. DAVIDSON in *Conrad's Endings: A Study of the Five Major Novels*, UMI Research Press Studies in Modern Literature (Ann Arbor, MI, 1984). Davidson equates Heyst's physical disarming, the theft of his revolver, to the process of 'metaphysical disarming' set off by Heyst Sr, a process which has robbed reality of its substance for the son (p. 94).

32. A recent, much acclaimed study of Nietzsche's work, *Nietzsche: Life as Literature*, by A. NEHAMAS (Cambridge, MA: Harvard University Press, 1986), projects an extremely Heyst-like figure which, I believe, justifies my own treatment of the haunting presence of the father.

33. For a fuller treatment of the Nietzschean outlook see the introductory section to this chapter.

34. The justice of Jones's claim to be Heyst's double has been recognized by several critics, including PAUL WILEY, *Conrad's Measure of Man* (Madison: University of Wisconsin Press, 1954), KAHELE and GERMAN, 'Conrad's *Victory*', JOHNSON, *Conrad's Models of Mind*, DIKE, 'The Tempest of Axel Heyst', DANIEL SCHWARZ, *Conrad: The Later Fiction* (London: Macmillan, 1982), and others.

35. JOHNSON, *Conrad's Models of Mind*, p. 170.

36. The relationship between Heyst's outlook and the aesthetic-decadent frame of mind has been noted and discussed in several readings of the novel. JOHNSON, *Conrad's Models of Mind*, pp. 43, 160–1; JOSEPH MARTIN, 'Conrad and the Aesthetic Movement', *Conradiana*, 3 (1985), pp. 199–213.

37. TONY TANNER, 'Joseph Conrad and the Last Gentleman', *Critical Quarterly*, 28/2 (1986), p. 133.

38. See WILEY, *Conrad's Measure of Man*, p. 151; SCHWARZ, *Conrad: The Later Fiction*, pp. 60–1, 66; STANLEY RENNER, 'The Garden of Civilization: Conrad, Huxley and the Ethics of Evolution', *Conradiana*, 7/2 (1975), pp. 61–75; GARY GEDDES, *Conrad's Later Novels* (Montreal: McGill-Queen's University Press, 1980), p. 58.

39. JOSEPH WOOD KRUTCH, *The Modern Temper* (London: Jonathan Cape, 1930), pp. 44, 43, 45.

40. WILFRED S. DOWDEN, *Joseph Conrad: The Imaged Style* (Nashville: Vanderbilt University Press, 1970), pp. 156–66; DWIGHT PURDY, *Joseph Conrad's Bible* (Norman: University of Oklahoma Press, 1984), pp. 118–44; DAVID LODGE,

The Failure of Textuality

'Conrad's *Victory* and *The Tempest*: An Amplification', *Modern Language Review*, 59 (1964), pp. 195–9; DIKE, 'The Tempest of Axel Heyst'; ADAM GILLON, 'Joseph Conrad and Shakespeare, part Four: A Reinterpretation of *Victory*', *Conradiana* 8/1 (1975), pp. 61–75; TONY TANNER, 'Gentlemen and Gossip: Aspects of Evolution and Language in Conrad's *Victory*', *L'Époque Conradienne* (May 1981), pp. 1–56; C. T. WATTS, 'Reflections on *Victory*', *Conradiana*, 15/1 (1983), pp. 73–9.

41. VAIHINGER, *The Philosophy of 'As If'*, pp. 159–60.

42. GUERARD, *Conrad the Novelist*: HEWITT, *Conrad: A Reassessment*; MOSER, *Achievement and Decline*; WILEY, *Conrad's Measure of Man*; JOHN A. PALMER, *Joseph Conrad's Fiction* (Ithaca, NY: Cornell University Press, 1968), pp. 166–97.

43. R. W. B. LEWIS, 'The Current of Conrad's *Victory*' in *Joseph Conrad: A Collection of Criticism*, ed. F. R. Karl (New York: McGraw-Hill Book Company, 1975), pp. 101–19; GEDDES, *Conrad's Later Novels*.

44. The concept of 'human optics' may have been derived from Nietzsche. 'We speak as though there were really existing things . . . But real things exist only for human optics: and from this we cannot escape' (quoted by VAIHINGER, *The Philosophy of 'As If'*, p. 348).

45. BONNEY, 'Narrative Perspectives in *Victory*', p. 30.

46. SCHWARZ, *Conrad: The Later Fiction*, p. 69; DOUGLAS B. PARK, 'Conrad's *Victory*; The Anatomy of a Pose', *Nineteenth-Century Fiction*, 31/2 (1976), pp. 151–2; GEDDES, *Conrad's Later Novels*, pp. 55–6.

Notes on authors

CHINUA ACHEBE is a novelist, poet and critic and currently teaches at Bard College, Annadale-on-Hudson, in the USA. He has published a series of novels about the modern history of Nigerian society: *Things Fall Apart, No Longer at Ease, Arrow of God, A Man of the People, Anthills of the Savannah*. His critical work includes *Morning Yet on Creation Day*, a collection of essays in the series Studies in African Literature.

CHRIS BONGIE is an Associate Professor at the College of William and Mary, Virginia, USA, in the English Department, and Director of the Literary and Cultural Studies programme. Since completing *Exotic Memories* he has been working on a study of creolisation in colonial and post-colonial literatures, with a primary focus on the French Caribbean, to be entitled *Islands and Exiles: The Creole Identities of Post/Colonial Literature*.

TERENCE CAVE is Professor of French Literature at the University of Oxford and Fellow of St John's College, Oxford. His principal publications are: *Devotional Poetry in France 1570–1613* (1969), *The Cornucopian Text: Problems of Writing in the French Renaissance* (1979), *Recognitions: A Study in Poetics* (1988) and editions of George Eliot's novels *Daniel Deronda* and *Silas Marner*. He is a Fellow of the British Academy.

DAPHNA ERDINAST-VULCAN is Senior Lecturer in English at the University of Haifa. She is the author of *Graham Greene's Childless Fathers* (1988) and *Joseph Conrad and the Modern Temper* (1991).

JEREMY HAWTHORN is Professor of Modern British Literature at the University of Trondheim, Norway. He is the author of numerous articles on Conrad's work, as well as two books, *Joseph Conrad: Narrative Technique and Ideological Commitment* (1990) and *Joseph Conrad: Language and Fictional Self-Consciousness* (1979). His other publications include *Studying the Novel* (3rd edition, 1997), *A Glossary of Contemporary Literary Theory* (1992) and *Cunning Passages: New Historicism, Cultural Materialism and Marxism in the Contemporary Literary Debate* (1996).

FREDRIC JAMESON is William Lane Professor of Comparative Literature at Duke University and the most influential Marxist critic in the United States of America. *The Political Unconscious* is his best-known work of literary criticism, but his writing ranges widely over art, architecture and other cultural forms, for example in *Postmodernism, or the Cultural Logic of Late Capitalism* (1991). Other works include *The Prison House of Language* (1972), *Late Marxism* (1990), *Signatures of the Visible* (1991) and *The Seeds of Time* (1994).

WAYNE KOESTENBAUM is a critic and poet and currently an Associate Professor of English at Yale University. His principal books include, in addition to *Double Talk, The Queen's Throat: Opera, Homosexuality, and the Mystery of Desire* (1993) and *Jackie Under My Skin: Interpreting an Icon* (1995).

PADMINI MONGIA is an Associate Professor of English at Franklin and Marshall College, Pennsylvania, where she teaches nineteenth-century British literature and post-colonial literature and theory. She has published articles on Conrad and edited *Contemporary Post-Colonial Theory: A Reader* (1996).

Notes on authors

FRANCIS MULHERN is Professor of Critical Studies at Middlesex University. He is the author of *The Moment of 'Scrutiny'* (1979), *Contemporary Marxist Literary Criticism* (1992), and *The Present Lasts a Long Time: Essays in Cultural Politics* (forthcoming).

NINA PELIKAN STRAUS is Associate Professor in Comparative Literature at Purchase College, State University of New York. She has published on Conrad, Kafka, Kundera and Feminist Philosophy and has interests in Marxist and Feminist thought. She is the author of *Doestoevsky and the Woman Question: Rereadings at the End of a Century* (1994).

JIM REILLY was a lecturer in English at Queen Mary and Westfield College, University of London, until his tragically early death in 1993. In addition to *Shadowtime: History and Representation in Hardy, Conrad and George Eliot* (1993) he published work on D. H. Lawrence, George Eliot and Alasdair Gray.

ALLON WHITE taught at the University of Sussex before his tragically early death in 1988. He was the author of *The Uses of Obscurity: The Fiction of Early Modernism* (1981) and co-author (with Peter Stallybrass) of *The Politics and Poetics of Transgression* (1986).

RAYMOND WILLIAMS, a cultural critic who has been hugely influential on the British New Left, was a Staff Tutor for Oxford University Adult Education (1946–61) and subsequently a Fellow of Jesus College, Cambridge, and Professor of Drama at Cambridge. His critical attention to 'culture', broadly defined to include the media, was a major influence on the development of the new discipline of cultural studies. His critical works include *Culture and Society 1780–1950* (1958), *The Long Revolution* (1961), *Modern Tragedy* (1966), *The Country and the City* (1973), *Keywords* (1976), *Marxism and Literature* (1977), *Politics and Letters* (1979) and *Problems in Materialism and Culture* (1980). He also wrote a series of novels about the people and history of the Welsh borders where he grew up. He died in 1988.

MARK A. WOLLAEGER is Associate Professor of English at Vanderbilt University, Tennesse. He is the author of *Joseph Conrad and the Fictions of Skepticism* (1990) and co-editor of *Joyce and the Subject of History* (1996). He has published articles on modern fiction, film, and literary theory in *English Literary History*, *Modern Language Quarterly*, *James Joyce Quarterly*, and *The Yale Journal of Criticism*. His work in progress includes a study of culture and national identity in modern British fiction.

Glossary of terms

analeptic	In narratology, analepsis is the evocation of an event from an earlier stage in the story (roughly analogous to flashback in film).
anamnesis	The recollection of past events.
anaphoral	Characterised by anaphora, a rhetorical device, consisting of repetition of a word or group of words.
anomy	Disregard of the law.
aporia	An unresolvable difficulty, contradiction or paradox. The term is used in a positive sense by deconstructive critics, with reference to the excess within every system or the undecidability within every reading of a text.
bêtise	(French) Stupidity, folly.
Bildungsroman	(German) A literary term, meaning literally 'formation novel', for a novel which is concerned with the education and development of its main character, usually from childhood onwards.
bovarysme	(French) This term, derived from the name of the heroine of Gustave Flaubert's novel *Madame Bovary*, means longing for, and attempting to live out in reality, a fantasy life based on the reading of fiction.
brume	(French) Thick haze, mist or fog.
catachresis	The inappropriate use of a word.
coup de foudre	(French) Love at first sight (literally, a flash of lightning).
deictic	Pointing.
deictics	Words such as 'it', 'this', 'here' which refer to something defined by the context.
diachronic	Involving or focusing on a process of change over time (compare synchronic).
dialogic	Term used by the Russian theorist Bakhtin, in opposition to monologic, to refer to the element of dialogue, and hence the recognition of the equality of other speakers, present within a discourse.
donnée	(French) Fundamental idea.
écriture	(French) Term employed by structuralist and post-structuralist critics to refer to writing considered, not as the expression of the mind of the author, but as an autonomous system (literally, writing).
encomiastic	An encomium is a formal (and usually elaborate) expression of praise.
epiphenomenon	Something which is secondary, a product of something else.
epistemological	Pertaining to knowledge; more strictly, pertaining to the philosophical theory of knowledge, its grounds and its methods.
epistemophilia	Love of, or desire for, knowledge.
essentialism	Belief in the existence of essences, involving the assumption that objects or people possess qualities inherently and independently of context.
êthos	(Greek; as used by Aristotle) Character.
exordium	The beginning or introductory part of a text or discourse.

Glossary of terms

extra fabulum (Latin) Outside the story; not depicted in the text.

figura (Latin) A person, event, object or action which stands for or is a sign for something beyond itself. The term derives from the medieval Christian practice of interpreting the New Testament of the Bible in terms of typological correspondences with the Old Testament (for example, Adam as a 'type' or *figura* of Christ).

Götterdämmerung (German) 'The Twilight of the Gods', the title of the last part of Richard Wagner's Ring Cycle of operas, and hence used to imply the decadence and final downfall of some great way of being or institution.

gynophobia Morbid and irrational fear and horror of women.

hamartia (Greek) In Aristotle's theory of tragic drama, *hamartia* is an error, which is committed by the tragic hero through ignorance or some moral fault, and which contributes to his downfall.

instance In narratology, a 'narrative instance' refers to the conditions under which a narrative is produced, involving factors such as time, location and person.

iterative A mode of narration which involves narrating once events which occur several times.

meta-narrative A higher level narrative; a narrative of or about other narratives.

metaphysical Relating to the ultimate conditions of existence, such as time, space, cause and being.

metaphysics of presence A term applied by the theorist Jacques Derrida to a conception of meaning which he claims has dominated the traditions of Western thought. According to this conception, meaning is present in the mind of the individual, and can therefore attain stability and determinacy. Derrida regards the metaphysics of presence as a delusion, and counters it with his own conception of meaning as unstable and decentred.

metempsychosis The movement of a soul from one body to another.

métissage (French) Cross-breeding.

metonymically Metonymy is a figure of speech based on contiguity, in which something associated with a thing is substituted for it (for example describing the monarchy as 'The Crown'). Often distinguished from metaphor, which is based on similarity.

monologic Term used by the Russian theorist Bakhtin, in opposition to dialogic, to describe a text which speaks with a single, authoritative voice, thus denying the existence of other points of view and failing to acknowledge the response of others.

mutatis mutandis (Latin) With appropriate changes being made.

mystagogue Someone who introduces others to religious mysteries or doctrines.

negative capability Phrase invented by the poet John Keats. He defined negative capability as 'when a man is capable of being in uncertainties, mysteries, doubts, without any irritable reaching after fact and reason'.

non plus ultra (Latin) The utmost limit that can be reached.

noumenal In the philosophy of Kant: relating to objects which can only be apprehended by intellectual intuition (as opposed to 'phenomenal', which means relating to immediate objects of perception).

panopticism A term used by the cultural theorist and historian Michel Foucault. Derived from Jeremy Bentham's Panopticon (a

273

Joseph Conrad

	design for a prison), it refers to the control of the individual through processes of surveillance which are internalised in the form of a self-monitoring subjectivity.
paralogical	Involving false reasoning.
phatic	A phatic utterance is one which performs a social function (such as 'nice to meet you'), rather than communicating any information.
plenitude	Fullness, with implications of presence, completion and pleasure.
proleptic	In narratology, prolepsis is the narration of an event in advance of its occurrence in the story (compare analepsis).
psychomacy	Conflict of the soul.
psychopomp	A person who acts as a spiritual guide for someone else's soul.
reifying	To reify persons or abstractions is to regard them as material objects. For Karl Marx reification involved social relations between people being thought of as if they were relations between things; in capitalism this is associated with depersonalisation, with the fetishisation of commodities and with the alienation of workers from the product of their labour. The term has been extended by critics to suggest various forms of freezing of relationships or processes into a seeming fixity.
ressentiment	(French) Word used by the philosopher Nietzsche to imply resentment and anger masquerading as morality.
signified	See signifier.
signifier	In structuralist theory a linguistic sign (a word) consists of a signifier (the sound) and a signified (the concept). This can be extended to literary signs so that an element in a novel can be described as a signifier, while the meaning of that element within the system of meaning established by the text can be described as its signified.
Strong Poet	In the theory of influence developed by the critic Harold Bloom, the Strong Poet is the writer who succeeds in destroying symbolically the power of a male predecessor while taking over his strength and authority.
synchronic	Focusing on a system as it exists at a single moment in time (compare diachronic).
trope	A rhetorical or figurative use of language, such as a metaphor.
tropological	Relating to tropes; i.e. metaphorical or figurative.
Ur	(German) Original, originating, earliest.
vraisemblable	(French) Giving the impression of truth and/or reality.

Further reading

1 General critical studies

BERTHOUD, JACQUES. *Joseph Conrad: The Major Phase*. Cambridge: Cambridge University Press, 1978.

COX, C. B. *Joseph Conrad: The Modern Imagination*. London: Dent, 1974.

FOGEL, AARON. *Coercion to Speak: Conrad's Poetics of Dialogue*. Cambridge, MA: Harvard University Press, 1985.

GUERARD, ALBERT. *Conrad the Novelist*. Cambridge, MA: Harvard University Press, 1958.

HERVOUET, YVES. *The French Face of Joseph Conrad*. Cambridge: Cambridge University Press, 1990.

KIRSCHNER, PAUL. *Conrad: The Psychologist as Artist*. Edinburgh: Oliver & Boyd, 1968.

MURFIN, ROSS C. (ed.). *Conrad Revisited: Essays for the Eighties*. Alabama: University of Alabama Press, 1985.

SAID, EDWARD. *Joseph Conrad and the Fiction of Autobiography*. Cambridge, MA: Harvard University Press, 1966.

SHERRY, NORMAN (ed.). *Joseph Conrad: A Commemoration: Papers from the 1974 International Conference on Conrad*. London: Macmillan, 1976.

WATT, IAN. *Conrad in the Nineteenth Century*. London: Chatto & Windus, 1980.

WATTS, CEDRIC. *A Preface to Conrad*. London: Longman, 1982.

2 Narrative, textuality and interpretation

ARMSTRONG, PAUL B. 'The Politics of Irony in Reading Conrad'. *Conradiana* 26.2/26.3 (Autumn 1994), pp. 85–101.

BERTHOUD, JACQUES. 'Narrative and Ideology: A Critique of Fredric Jameson's *The Political Unconscious*', in *Narrative: From Malory to Motion Pictures*, ed. Jeremy Hawthorn. London: Edward Arnold, 1985, pp. 101–15.

BROOKS, PETER. *Reading for the Plot: Design and Intention in Narrative*. Cambridge, MA, and London: Harvard University Press, 1984. See Chapter 9: 'An Unreadable Report: Conrad's *Heart of Darkness*'.

HAWTHORN, JEREMY. *Joseph Conrad: Language and Fictional Self-Consciousness*. London: Edward Arnold, 1979.

LOTHE, JAKOB. *Conrad's Narrative Method*. Oxford: Clarendon Press, 1989.

SAID, EDWARD. *The World, the Text and the Critic*. 1983; London: Faber, 1984. See Chapter 5: 'Conrad: The Presentation of Narrative'.

TANNER, TONY. ' "Gnawed Bones" and "Artless Tales": Eating and Narrative in Conrad'. *Partisan Review*, 45.1 (1978), pp. 94–107.

WATTS, CEDRIC. *The Deceptive Text: An Introduction to Covert Plots*. Brighton: Harvester, 1984.

3 Imperialism

BIVONA, DANIEL. *Desire and Contradiction: Imperial Visions and Domestic Debates in Victorian Literature*. Manchester and New York: Manchester University Press, 1990. See Chapter 3.

Joseph Conrad

BRANTLINGER, PATRICK. 'Heart of Darkness: Anti-Imperialism, Racism, or Impressionism?'. *Criticism*, 27.4 (1985), pp. 363–85.

—— *Rule of Darkness: British Literature and Imperialism, 1830–1914*. Ithaca and London: Cornell University Press, 1988.

BRISTOW, JOSEPH. *Empire Boys: Adventures in a Man's World*. London: Harper Collins Academic, 1991. See 'Conrad's Man', pp. 153–69.

FINCHAM, GAIL and MYRTLE HOOPER (eds). *Under Postcolonial Eyes: Joseph Conrad After Empire*. Rondebosch: University of Cape Town Press, 1996.

GREEN, MARTIN. *Dreams of Adventure, Deeds of Empire*. New York: Persea Books, 1979.

HAMNER, ROBERT D. (ed.). *Joseph Conrad: Third World Perspectives*. Washington DC: Three Continents, 1990.

HAWKINS, HUNT. 'Conrad's Critique of Imperialism in Heart of Darkness'. *PMLA*, 94 (March 1979), pp. 286–99.

KRENN, HELIENA. *Conrad's Lingard Trilogy: Empire, Race and Woman in the Malay Novels*. New York: Garland, 1990.

MONGIA, PADMINI. 'Imperialism and Narrative Understanding in Conrad's Lord Jim'. *Studies in the Novel*, 24 (1992), pp. 173–86.

NAIPAUL, V. S. 'Conrad's Darkness'. *New York Review of Books*, 19 October 1974, pp. 16–21. Reprinted in *The Return of Eva Peron & Other Essays*. London: Deutsch, 1980, pp. 205–27.

PARRY, BENITA. *Conrad and Imperialism: Ideological Boundaries and Visionary Frontiers*. London and Basingstoke: Macmillan, 1983.

PRATT, MARY LOUISE. 'Travel Narrative and Imperialist Vision', in *Understanding Narrative*, ed. James Phelan and Peter Raboniwitz. Columbus: Ohio State University Press, 1994.

ROBERTS, ANDREW MICHAEL. 'Economies of Empire and Masculinity in Conrad's Victory', in *Imperialism and Gender: Constructions of Masculinity*, ed. C. E. Gittings. Hebden Bridge, West Yorkshire: Dangaroo Press, 1996, pp. 158–69. Also available as *Kunapipi* 18.1 (1996).

SAID, EDWARD. *Culture and Imperialism*. London: Chatto & Windus, 1993.

TORGOVNICK, MARIANNA. *Gone Primitive: Savage Intellects, Modern Lives*. Chicago and London: University of Chicago Press, 1990. See Chapter 7: 'Travelling with Conrad' (on *Heart of Darkness*).

WATTS, CEDRIC. '"A Bloody Racist": About Achebe's View of Conrad'. *Yearbook of English Studies*, 13 (1983), pp. 196–209.

WHITE, ANDREA. *Joseph Conrad and the Adventure Tradition: Constructing and Deconstructing the Imperial Subject*. Cambridge: Cambridge University Press, 1993.

4 Gender and sexuality

BRODIE, SUSAN L. 'Conrad's Feminine Perspective'. *Conradiana*, 16.2 (1984), pp. 141–54.

DEKOVEN, MARIANNE. *Rich and Strange: Gender, History, Modernism*. Princeton: Princeton University Press, 1991.

KLEIN, KAREN. 'The Feminine Predicament in Conrad's Nostromo', in *Brandeis Essays in Literature*, ed. John Hazel Smith. Waltham, MA: Brandeis University, 1983, pp. 101–16.

LANE, CHRISTOPHER. *The Ruling Passion: British Colonial Allegory and the Paradox of Homosexual Desire*. Durham and London: Duke University Press, 1985. See Chapter 4: 'Fostering Subjection: Masculine Identification and Homosexual Allegory in Conrad's Victory'.

MOFFAT, WENDY. 'Domestic Violence: The Simple Tale within The Secret Agent'. *English Literature in Transition 1880–1920*, 37.4 (1994), pp. 465–89.

Further reading

NADELHAFT, RUTH. *Joseph Conrad.* Hemel Hempstead: Harvester Wheatsheaf, 1991. In the Harvester series 'Feminist Readings'.

ROBERTS, ANDREW MICHAEL (ed.). *Conrad and Gender.* Amsterdam and Atlanta, GA: Rodopi, 1993. Also available as *The Conradian*, 17.2 (Spring 1993).

—— 'The Gaze and the Dummy: Sexual Politics in Conrad's *The Arrow of Gold*', in *Joseph Conrad: Critical Assessments*, ed. Keith Carabine. Robertsbridge: Helm Information, 1992, pp. 528–50.

SHOWALTER, ELAINE. *Sexual Anarchy: Gender and Culture at the Fin de Siècle.* London: Bloomsbury, 1991. See pp. 95–104 on *Heart of Darkness*.

SMITH, JOANNA M. ' "Too Beautiful Altogether": Patriarchal Ideology in *Heart of Darkness*', in *Joseph Conrad: Heart of Darkness: A Case Study in Contemporary Criticism*, ed. Ross C. Murfin. New York: St Martin's Press, 1989.

STOTT, REBECCA. *The Fabrication of the Late Victorian Femme Fatale.* Basingstoke: Macmillan, 1992.

5 Class and ideology

EAGLETON, TERRY. *Criticism and Ideology: A Study in Marxist Literary Theory.* 1976; London: Verso, 1978. See pp. 130–40.

FLEISHMAN, AVROM. *Conrad's Politics.* Baltimore: The Johns Hopkins Press, 1967.

HAY, ELOISE KNAPP. *The Political Novels of Joseph Conrad.* Chicago: University of Chicago Press, 1963.

JENKINS, GARETH. 'Conrad's *Nostromo* and History'. *Literature and History*, 3.6 (Autumn 1977), pp. 138–78.

RYAN, KIERNAN. 'Revelation and Repression in Conrad's *Nostromo*', in *The Uses of Fiction: Essays in Honour of Arnold Kettle*, ed. Douglas Jefferson and Graham Martin. Milton Keynes: Open University Press, 1982.

6 Modernity, modernism, romanticism, postmodernism

BERNSTEIN, STEPHEN. 'Conrad and Postmodernism: *Under Western Eyes*'. *The Conradian*, 20.1–20.2 (Spring–Autumn 1995), pp. 31–56.

CONROY, MARK. *Modernism and Authority: Strategies of Legitimation in Flaubert and Conrad.* Baltimore and London: Johns Hopkins University Press, 1985.

DODSON, SANDRA. 'Conrad's *Lord Jim* and the Inauguration of a Modern Sublime'. *The Conradian* 18.2 (Autumn 1994), pp. 77–101.

ELAM, DIANE. *Romancing the Postmodern.* London and New York: Routledge, 1992. See Chapter 3: 'Romantic Letters and Postmodern Envelopes: Joseph Conrad and the Imperialism of Historical Representation' (on *Nostromo*).

LEVENSON, MICHAEL. *A Genealogy of Modernism: A Study of English Literary Doctrine 1908–1922.* Cambridge: Cambridge University Press, 1984.

—— *Modernism and the Fate of Individuality: Character and Novelistic Form from Conrad to Woolf.* Cambridge: Cambridge University Press, 1991. See Chapter 1.

THORBURN, DAVID. *Conrad's Romanticism.* New Haven: Yale University Press, 1974.

7 Post-structuralism and deconstruction

BONNEY, WILLIAM. *Thorns and Arabesques: Contexts for Conrad's Fiction.* Baltimore and London: Johns Hopkins University Press, 1980.

Joseph Conrad

HANSFORD, JAMES. 'Money, Language and the Body in "Typhoon"'. *Conradiana*, 26.2–26.3 (Autumn 1994), pp. 135–55.

MILLER, J. HILLIS. *Fiction and Repetition: Seven English Novels*. Oxford: Basil Blackwell, 1982. See Chapter 2: '*Lord Jim*: Repetition as Subversion of Organic Form'.

—— '*Heart of Darkness* Revisited', in *Conrad Revisited*, ed. Ross C. Murfin. Alabama: University of Alabama Press, 1985, pp. 31–50.

SAID, EDWARD. *Beginnings: Intention and Method*. Baltimore: Johns Hopkins University Press, 1975, pp. 100–37.

STEIN, WILLIAM B. '*The Secret Agent*: The Agon(ies) of the Word', in *Critical Essays on Joseph Conrad*, ed. Ted Billy. Boston, MA: G. K. Hall and Co., 1987, pp. 162–80.

8 Psychoanalytical

CREWS, FREDERICK. 'Conrad's Uneasiness – and Ours', in *Out of My System: Psychoanalysis, Ideology and Critical Method*. New York: Oxford University Press, 1975.

HAMPSON, ROBERT. *Joseph Conrad: Betrayal and Identity*. London: Macmillan, 1992.

MEYER, BERNARD. *Joseph Conrad: A Psychoanalytical Biography*. Princeton: Princeton University Press, 1967.

PACCAUD-HUGUET, JOSIANE. 'Nostromo: Conrad's Man of No Parentage'. *The Conradian*, 18.2 (Autumn 1994), pp. 65–76.

SIMPSON, DAVID. *Fetishism & Imagination: Dickens, Melville, Conrad*. Baltimore and London: Johns Hopkins University Press, 1982.

9 Biographical and contextual

BAINES, JOCELYN. *Joseph Conrad: A Critical Biography*. Westport, CT: Greenwood Press, 1975.

KARL, FREDERICK R. and LAURENCE DAVIES (eds.). *The Collected Letters of Joseph Conrad* (5 vols.). Cambridge: Cambridge University Press, 1983–96.

NAJDER, ZDZISŁAW. *Joseph Conrad: A Chronicle*. Cambridge: Cambridge University Press, 1983.

SHERRY, NORMAN. *Conrad's Eastern World*. Cambridge, Cambridge University Press, 1966.

—— *Conrad's Western World*. Cambridge, Cambridge University Press, 1971. (Together with the previous item this identifies geographical, historical and biographical sources for Conrad's fiction.)

Index

Achebe, Chinua, 4, 9–10, 11, 13, 109–23
Morning Yet on Creation Day, 109
Things Fall Apart, 110
Adorno, T. W., 212n, 214, 217, 231n
adventure stories, 2, 3, 155–70, 193–6, 202–3, 253
Aeneid, The, 261
alêtheia (unveiling), 62
alienation, 22, 59, 129, 145–6, 221
allegory, 62–3, 66, 207, 250, 263–5
Althusser, Louis, 201
ambiguity, 3, 6, 9, 79–80, 87, 93, 172, 179, 193, 196, 204, 266
anagnôrisis, 47, 51, 58, 60–3, 66, 69n
Anderson, Perry, 40
anomy, 49–50, 64, 65
apocalypse, 174–5
aporia, 127, 250–1
Arac, Jonathan, 144–5, 151n
Arendt, Hannah, 245n
Aristotle, 4, 47, 98
Arnold, Matthew, 229
Austen, Jane, 158
Northanger Abbey, 158

Babitt, Irving, 248, 266n
Rousseau and Romanticism, 248
Bakhtin, Mikhail, 4, 6, 91, 96, 101, 104n, 264
The Dialogic Imagination, 104n
Balzac, Honoré de, 67n, 201–3, 207, 213n, 224
Le Colonel Chabert, 67n
Banfield, Ann, 76, 89n
Barthes, Roland, 5, 6, 8, 26n, 47, 172
'The Death of the Author', 6
The Pleasure of the Text, 8
S/Z, 5, 6
Batchelor, John, 69n
Baudelaire, Charles, 141, 236, 241
Benjamin, Walter, 23, 28n, 214–15, 230, 231n, 235–9, 243, 245n, 246n
'The Work of Art in the Age of Mechanical Reproduction', 23
'What is Epic Theatre?', 230
Bergson, Henri, 101
Berkeley, 208, 256
Berthoud, Jacques, 19, 27n

Bhabha, Homi K., 27n, 37n
Nation and Narration, 37n
biography, 15
Blackburn, William, 220
Blackwood, William, 220
Bloom, Harold, 175
Bloomfield, Morton W., 213n
Bobrowski, Tadeusz, 16
Bongie, Chris, 4, 10–11, 21, 24, 26n, 28n, 124–51, 157, 168n
Bonney, William, 263, 265, 268n, 269n
Borges, Jorge Louis, 243
'The Mirror of Enigmas', 243
Brantlinger, Patrick, 9, 26n, 157, 168n, 169n
Rule of Darkness, 157
Brebach, Raymond, 197n
Brecht, Bertolt, 210, 230
Brodie, Susan, 178, 187n
Brooks, Peter, 67n, 70n
Bros, Addison, 27n
Bruffee, Kenneth A., 150n, 151n
Brunetière, Ferdinand, 245n

Calinescu, Matei, 28n
Camus, Albert, 209
Carabine, Keith, 169n
Cave, Terence, 2, 4, 5, 8, 47–70
Recognitions, 8, 47n
Cavell, Stanley, 105n
Charpier, E. J., 245n
Chodorow, Nancy, 158, 162, 167, 169n
Chrétien de Troyes, 67n
Yvain, 67n
Christian Science Monitor, 121–2, 123n
Clapperton, Hugh, 128
Clarke, John R., 103n
class, 3, 4, 16–20, 204
Cohn, Dorrit, 73, 88n
Transparent Minds, 73, 88n
colonialism, 9, 124, 166, 214, 216
comedy, 91–106
communism, 17, 218–19
Conan Doyle, Arthur, 105n
Connor, Steven, 3–4, 24, 25n, 28n
Theory and Cultural Value, 3
Conrad, Joseph, life of, 1–2, 16–17

279

Joseph Conrad

Conrad, Joseph, works by
  A Personal Record, 28n, 105n, 118,
    224, 231n
  Almayer's Folly, 3, 25n, 73–5, 88n,
    130–2, 134–6, 178, 213n, 220–1
  'Amy Foster', 104n
  An Outcast of the Islands, 130–1,
    135–6, 139, 143, 178, 215, 220, 228,
    231n
  'An Outpost of Progress', 137, 139
  The Arrow of Gold, 2, 3, 25n, 247,
    253–4
  'Autocracy and War', 144, 220
  'The Black Mate', 75
  Chance, 3, 13, 14, 25n, 71, 247, 253–4
  The Collected Letters of Joseph Conrad,
    25n, 27n, 150n, 197n, 231n, 267n
  The End of the Tether, 34, 67n, 72,
    207
  'Geography and Some Explorers',
    136
  'Guy de Maupassant', 245n
  Heart of Darkness, 3, 6, 8, 9–10, 12,
    13, 14, 23, 25, 34–6, 63, 64, 67n,
    70n, 72, 92, 93, 95, 105n, 109–23,
    127, 129, 136–7, 139, 142, 144, 159,
    161, 167, 170n, 171–88, 235–44,
    245n, 246n, 247
  The Inheritors, 190–1, 196, 198n
  'The Inn of the Two Witches', 241
  'Karain: A Memory', 3, 101, 137–8,
    141, 143–4
  'The Lagoon', 137, 139
  Last Essays, 127
  Letters from Joseph Conrad 1895–1924,
    197n, 245n
  *Letters of Joseph Conrad to Marguerite
    Poradowska 1890–1920*, 103n, 105n,
    106n
  Lord Jim, 3, 11, 14, 18, 19, 25, 48, 58,
    62, 63, 64, 69n, 70n, 89n, 96, 101,
    129–31, 136–7, 139, 144, 150,
    155–70, 201–2, 204, 207–8, 210–12,
    213n, 216, 225, 231n, 247
  The Mirror of the Sea, 191, 231n
  The Nature of a Crime, 190, 196–7
  The Nigger of the 'Narcissus', 16, 20,
    33, 37, 43n, 71, 130, 136–7, 143–50,
    207, 209, 216, 218, 231n
  Nostromo, 3, 7, 14, 16, 18, 19, 25, 40,
    71, 77–88, 89n, 91, 94, 96, 101, 103,
    130, 203–4, 212, 213n, 214–31,
    231n, 236, 247
  Notes on Life and Letters, 231
  'Ocean Travel', 20, 27n
  'The Planter of Malata', 236, 245n
  'The Rescuer'/*The Rescue*, 2, 134,
    137, 247, 253, 267n
  'The Return', 137, 141
  Romance, 15, 189–98
  The Rover, 13
  The Secret Agent, 2, 3, 6, 7, 12, 14, 16,
    25n, 70n, 90n, 91–106, 130, 178,
    216, 219, 231n
  'The Secret Sharer', 25, 69n
  Selected Literary Criticism, 66n
  The Shadow-Line, 58, 222, 247
  The Sisters, 25n
  'Tales of the Sea', 136
  Tales of Unrest, 130, 136–7, 143
  'Travel', 20, 27n
  Typhoon, 2, 33, 37, 41–2, 43n, 95, 207
  Under Western Eyes, 2, 5, 8, 16, 25,
    48–70, 87, 105n, 178, 220, 236,
    245n, 247
  Victory, 13, 25n, 130, 245n, 247,
    253–4, 255–66
  Within the Tides, 28n
  Youth, 67n
Conroy, Mark, 104n
Corneille, Pierre, 67n
  Don Sanche, 67n
Covino, William A., 168n
Cox, C. B., 66n, 70n
Crane, Stephen, 105n
Culler, Jonathan, 267n
Cunninghame Graham, R. B., 236,
  245n, 266
Curle, Richard, 66n, 127–8
  Into the East, 127, 130

Dante Alighieri, 98, 180, 185–6
Darwin, Charles, 102
Davidson, Arnold E., 268n
Davies, Laurence, 25n, 27n, 150n, 197n,
  231n, 267n
decadence, 125, 127, 134, 137, 141, 143,
  147–9, 260, 268n
deconstruction/ive, 4, 5, 7, 47, 125,
  136, 149, 172, 185, 212, 214, 250–1,
  254, 256
DeKoven, Marianne, 170n
Delbanco, Nicholas, 197n
Derain, André, 120
Derrida, Jacques, 5, 26n, 171, 250
  'Force and Signification', 5
Descartes, René, 91, 102
desire, 8, 47, 48, 55, 61–2, 65, 66, 124,
  126, 184
detective fiction, 2, 3, 202
Deurbergue, J., 268n
dialogic, 6–7, 91, 96

Index

Dickens, Charles, 2, 40, 67n, 241
  Great Expectations, 67n, 68n
différance, 5
difference, 10, 48, 124, 126, 128–9, 132,
  142–3, 166
Dike, Donald A., 268n, 269n
Dinnerstein, Dorothy, 158, 167, 169n
direct speech, 73, 79, 82–3, 86–7, 90
discourse, 3, 8–9, 12, 51, 53, 54, 59,
  125, 202, 211, 217, 219, 243–4,
  245n, 250
Dostoevsky, Fyodor, 2, 25n, 68n, 105n
  Crime and Punishment, 68n, 69n, 105n
Dowden, Wilfred S., 268n
Doyle, Michael W., 150n
dream-work, 8
'dual voice' theory, 75–6, 83
Dumas, Alexandre, 191
Durkheim, Emile, 50

Eagleton, Terry, 9, 17, 26n, 27n
  Criticism and Ideology, 17
Eliot, George, 40
  Middlemarch, 227
Eliot, T. S., 6, 14, 21, 189
Ellmann, Maud, 27n
empire, 12, 37, 124
Engels, Friedrich, 213n
Erdinast-Vulcan, Daphna, 4, 20–1,
  23–4, 28n, 91, 247–69
êthos, 51
eurocentrism, 11, 109
evaluation, 25
exotic(ism), 11, 24, 124–39, 142–3, 145,
  242

Fanon, Franz, 119
feminism/ist, 4, 14, 155–70, 171–88
Feuerbach, Ludwig, 208
fin-de-siècle, 10, 15, 127, 137, 140–1,
  155–7, 168n, 170, 194, 256, 258
Flaubert, Gustave, 2, 40, 134, 141, 192,
  206–7, 213n, 224, 227
  Education sentimentale, 213n
  Madame Bovary, 206, 213n
  La Tentation de Saint Antoine, 207,
    213n
  Trois Contes, 207
Fleishmann, Avrom, 16, 17, 27n
Fogel, Aaron, 25n
Ford, Ford Madox, 15, 25, 104n,
  189–97, 197n, 198n, 252
  *Joseph Conrad: A Personal
    Remembrance*, 190
foreign(ness), 12, 97, 104n
Foreman, Michael, 123n

Foucault, Michel, 4, 7, 8–9, 26n, 91,
  125, 214
France, Anatole, 2
Frankfurt School, 203, 211
Fraser, Gail, 151n
free indirect discourse (FID), 72–81, 83,
  88n
Freud, Sigmund, 6, 8, 63, 181–3, 187n,
  201, 203, 212n, 216
  Introductory Lectures, 183
  'The Poet and Day-Dreaming', 181

Galsworthy, John, 104n
Garnett, Edward, 197n, 245n, 266, 267n
Gates, Henry Louis, 9, 26n
Gauguin, Paul, 120, 130
Gautier, Théophile, 241
gay theory, 15, 37, 189–98
Geddes, Gary, 263, 266, 268n, 269n
Gee, John, 103n, 105n, 106n
Gekoski, R. A., 103n
gender, 3, 4, 12–15, 155–98
Genette, Gérard, 5, 26n, 72
genre(s), 2, 15, 155–70, 173, 193–6, 202,
  211, 247, 253–4, 263–4, 266
George, Jessie (Mrs Joseph Conrad),
  70n, 105n, 190n, 197n, 220
German, Howard, 257, 268n
ghost stories, 55
Gilber, Sandra, 178, 187n
Gillon, Adam, 269n
Gissing, George, 201–2, 214
Goethe, Johann Wolfgang von, 180
Good, Byron, 105n
Goonetilleke, D. C. R. A., 150n
Gothic, 15, 155–70, 202, 241
Graff, Gerald, 251–2, 267n
Green, Martin, 157, 168n, 170n
Gross, Seymour, 180, 187n
Guerard, Albert, 6, 13–14, 26n, 27n,
  122n, 184, 187n, 212–13n, 252, 263,
  267n, 269n
  Conrad the Novelist, 6, 13–14

Haggard, Sir H. Rider, 157, 159, 161
  Ayesha, 163
  King Solomon's Mines, 159, 161
hamartia, 4, 51
Hampson, Robert, 6, 26n, 27n
Hararl, Josue V., 187n
Hardy, Thomas, 104n, 214
Hartman, Geoffrey, 175, 187n
Hawthorn, Jeremy, 4, 7–8, 67n, 68n,
  70n, 71–90
  *Joseph Conrad: Narrative Technique
    and Ideological Commitment*, 71n

281

Joseph Conrad

Hawthorne, Nathaniel, 40
Hay, Eloise Knapp, 241–2, 245n
Hegel, G. W. F., 207, 214
Henley, W. E., 190, 197n
Hernandi, Paul, 74–5
Hervouet, Yves, 25n
Hewitt, Douglas, 252, 263, 267n
'high' culture, 202–3
historicism, 125, 135–6, 143–50
Holland, Norman, 161, 169n, 212n
Horkheimer, Max, 212n
Horney, Karen, 180, 187n
Howe, Irving, 94–5, 103n
Hueffer, Elsie, 190
humanism, 7, 17–20, 39–40, 43n, 186
Hume, David, 256
Hunter, Allan, 151n
Huxley, T. H., 102, 105n
Huysmans, Joris-Karl, 141
  À rebours, 141
hybrid(ity), 2, 3, 10, 11, 37, 133

identity politics, 4, 10, 158
ideology, 2–4, 8, 13, 16–20, 125, 201,
  204, 206–10, 224
imperialism, 4, 8–12, 15, 109–51, 155,
  168, 175, 179, 186, 192, 209
impressionism, 3, 9, 190, 203, 206, 208,
  212n, 235, 241–2, 245n
Ingram, Allan, 66n
International Socialist Association, 16
interpretation, 1, 3, 4–8, 201, 252, 254
intertextuality, 241, 245n
irony, 6, 9, 76–8, 80, 81, 83, 85–6, 92–5,
  115, 125, 131, 134, 137, 167, 174,
  179, 184, 217, 250, 254, 260–1,
  263–5

James, Henry, 22, 40, 48, 66n, 68n, 186,
  192, 227, 231n, 239
  The Ambassadors, 48, 66n
  The Golden Bowl, 68n
Jameson, Fredric, 2, 4, 19, 24, 27n,
  156–7, 168, 201–13
  The Political Unconscious, 19, 201
Jauss, Hans, 173, 187n
Jean-Aubry, G., 68n, 104n, 213n, 245n
Jefferson, Douglas, 89n, 231n
Jenkins, Gareth, 131, 150n
Jesus, 183
Johnson, Bruce, 257–8, 268n
Johnson, Samuel, 186
Jones, Charles, 89–90n
Jones, Susan, 25n
Joyce, James, 183
  Ulysses, 183

Kafka, Franz, 98
  The Penal Colony, 98
Kahele, S., 257, 268n
Kahane, Claire, 157–8, 169n
Karl, Frederick R., 25n, 27n, 136–7,
  150n, 151n, 184, 187n, 197n, 198n,
  231n, 267n, 269n
Keats, John, 229
Kenner, Hugh, 106n
Kermode, Frank, 92, 103n
Kettle, Arnold, 7
Kimbrough, Robert, 67n, 187n, 188n
Klein, Karen, 178, 187n
Kleinman, Arthur, 105n
Knowles, Owen, 169n
Koestenbaum, Wayne, 15, 189–98
Kolodny, Annette, 175, 187n
Konigsberg, Ira, 187n
Korzeniowski, Apollo, 16
Krajka, Wieslaw, 169n
Krieger, Murray, 213n
Krutch, Joseph Wood, 260–1, 268n
  The Modern Temper, 260–1, 268n

La Fayette, Marie Madeleine de la
  Vergue, comtesse de, 57
  La Princesse de Clèves, 57
La Mettrie, Julien Offroy de, 102
Langbaum, Robert, 28n
Laskowski, H. J., 256, 268n
Lawrence, D. H., 14
Leavis, F. R., 1, 2, 3, 6, 7, 23, 25n, 26n,
  37, 38–42, 43n, 112, 122n, 212n,
  267n
  The Common Pursuit, 43n
  The Great Tradition, 1, 2, 25n, 37,
    40, 122n, 212n, 267n
  Towards Standards of Criticism, 43
Leavis, Q. D., 38
Le Bon, Gustave, 140, 146–7, 151n
  La Psychologie des Foules (The
    Crowd), 140, 146
Le Carré, John, 49
  The Spy Who Came in from the Cold,
    49
Leopold, King of Belgium, 116, 120
Levenson, Michael, 20, 21, 28n
  A Genealogy of Modernism, 20
Lewis, M. G., 158
  The Monk, 158, 169n
Lewis, R. W. B., 263, 269n
liberal humanism, 17
Lodge, David, 268–9n
Lothe, Jakob, 7, 26n
  Conrad's Narrative Method, 7
Loti, Pierre, 126, 138

Index

Lukács, Georg, 214, 223–30, 231n
  'Narrate or Describe?', 223, 228
Luyat, Anne, 168n

Macherey, Pierre, 201
Marryat, Captain Frederick, 136, 218
  Mr Midshipman Easy, 218
Martin, Graham, 89n, 231n
Martin, Joseph, 268n
Marx, Karl, 205, 208, 213n, 227
  The German Ideology, 208
Marxist literary theory, 4, 6, 7, 17–20,
  37, 201–13, 214–31
masculinity, 14–15, 19, 37, 41, 166–8,
  170n, 173, 189–98
mass culture, 202–3, 211
Matisse, Henri, 120
Maupassant, Guy de, 2, 236
McClintock, Anne, 159, 169n, 170n
McHale, Brian, 74–5, 89n
Meldrum, David, 220
melodrama, 61, 63, 64, 209
Mencken, H. L., 197n
Meredith, George, 22, 238–9, 245n
  'The Empty Purse', 239
Merton, Robert K., 151n
metacommentary, 24, 203–4
Meyer, Bernard C., 106n, 118–19,
  123n, 177, 187n, 197n, 212n,
  267n
Miller, J. Hillis, 104n, 151n, 174, 179,
  187n, 212n, 213n, 267n
Millett, Kate, 27n
Minh-ha, Trinh T., 26n
Mitchell, Juliet, 177–8, 187n
Mizener, Arthur, 197n
modernism/ist, 3, 10, 20–4, 110, 156,
  168, 172, 202–4, 206–8, 211
modernity, 1, 4, 10, 20–4, 124–5, 127,
  128–30, 136, 139, 142, 144–5,
  148–9, 168, 235–69
Mohantry, Chandra Talpade, 27n
Monet, Claude, 242
Mongia, Padmini, 2, 4, 14–15, 155–70
monologic, 7, 96, 100
Mora, Gabriela, 187n
Moser, Thomas, 198n, 213n, 252, 263,
  267n
Mulhern, Francis, 2, 3, 5, 7, 8, 37–43
  The Moment of 'Scrutiny', 43n
Murfin, Ross C., 187n

Nadelhaft, Ruth, 14, 27n, 178, 187n
  Joseph Conrad, 14
Najder, Zdzislaw, 27n, 106n, 151n,
  267n

narrative, 2, 3, 4–8, 52, 53, 55, 65,
  72–88, 88n, 89n, 90n, 115, 204, 206,
  263–6
narratology, 4, 10, 71, 145
Nehamas, A., 268n
Nettels, Elsa, 168n
New Critics, 6
New York Times, 251
Nietzsche, Friedrich, 99, 105n, 175, 204,
  224, 247–51, 253–4, 257–8, 260,
  268n, 269n
Northcliffe, Lord, 105n

other(ness), 10–11, 12, 124–6, 134–5,
  146, 165–6, 206, 217
Owen, W. J. B., 150n

Paccaud, Josiane, 89
Paine, Thomas, 218
  The Rights of Man, 218
Palmer, John, 263, 269n
Park, Douglas D., 266, 269n
Park, Mungo, 128
parody, 100, 174, 179, 222
Parry, Benita, 151n
Pascal, Roy, 75–7, 89n
  The Dual Voice, 75, 89n
Pater, Walter, 190, 258
Picasso, Pablo Ruiz y, 120
Plato, 9, 74
plot, 10, 51, 53, 55, 201
Poland/Polish, 1, 16–17, 216
politics, 16
Polo, Marco, 120, 128
Poradowska, Marguerite, 94, 103n,
  105n, 106n, 266
post-colonial theory, 4, 11–12, 37, 109,
  125
postmodernism, 4, 11, 21, 124–5, 248,
  256, 260
post-structuralism/ist, 5–6, 8, 47, 201,
  213n, 247, 250
Pound, Ezra, 21, 189–90
Price, Martin, 103n, 104n
Proust, Marcel, 202, 205, 236, 243
psychoanalysis, 4, 6, 14, 22, 37, 125,
  155–70, 171, 201
Purdy, Dwight, 268n
Putnam, Hilary, 105n

queer studies, 15, 189–98

race/racism, 4, 9, 12, 13, 109–23, 124,
  135, 176, 178, 186
Racine, Jean, 53, 229
  Bajazet, 53

283

Joseph Conrad

Radcliffe, Ann, 158
 The Mysteries of Udolpho, 158, 161–2
Raskin, Jonah, 123n
reader-response criticism, 171
realism/ist, 9, 62, 202–3, 206–7, 211, 263, 265
Reilly, Jim, 2, 16, 18–19, 25n, 27n, 214–31, 231n
 Shadowtime, 2, 214n
Reiter, Rayna, 169n
Renner, Stanley, 268n
reported speech, 73, 79, 82, 84, 87, 90
reversal, 61
rhetoric, 4, 11, 12, 125, 177, 180, 185, 235, 242–3, 250–1
Richards, I. A., 6
Rimmon-Kenan, Shlomith, 74, 89n
 Narrative Fiction, 74, 89n
Roberts, Andrew Michael, 25n, 27n, 155n, 170n
romance, 2, 3, 15, 48, 155–70, 189–98, 201–3, 207, 211, 247–8, 251, 253
Romance of the Rose, 179
Romanticism, 21–2, 23, 102, 235, 252, 267n
Rousseau, Jean-Jacques, 52, 60, 68n, 105n
 Confessions, 60
Rubin, Gayle, 162, 169n
Ryan, Kiernan, 84, 89n, 224, 227, 230, 231n
 'Revelation and Repression in Conrad's *Nostromo*', 224, 227, 231n

Said, Edward, 13, 27n, 142, 151n, 173–4, 178, 187, 212n, 213n
same(ness), 10–11, 126, 134, 142, 146
Saussure, Ferdinand de, 262
Schmidt, Dr Raymund, 266n
Schopenhauer, Arthur, 93, 257–8
Schwarz, Daniel, 266, 268n, 269n
Schweitzer, Arthur, 116
Scott, Sir Walter, 224
Sedgwick, Eve Kosofsky, 170n
Segalen, Viktor, 145
Seghers, P., 245n
Sertoli, Giuseppe, 143, 149, 151n
sexism, 13, 172–3, 175–8, 185–6
sexuality, 4, 8, 12–15, 164–5, 189–98
Shakespeare, William, 40
 Hamlet, 261
 King Lear, 186
 Hamlet, 261
 Macbeth, 261
 The Tempest, 261

Sherman, Leona, 161, 169n
Sherry, Norman, 245n
Showalter, Elaine, 170n, 187n
Shweder, Richard, 105–6n
Simpson, David, 128–9, 132, 143, 150n
'single voice' theory, 75
Smith, John H., 187n
Smith, Virginia Llewellyn, 68n
Sophocles, 213n, 229
space, concepts of, 4, 125–6, 138, 155–70, 201–3, 205, 207, 210–11
Spengler, Oswald, 260
Spitzer, Leo, 76–7
Spivak, Gayatri, 171–2, 174, 176, 181, 185, 187n
spy stories, 49
Stallman, Robert W., 104n
Steiner, Joan, 157, 168n
Sterne, Laurence, 98
 Tristram Shandy, 98
Stevenson, Robert Louis, 190–1, 193–4, 202
story, 10, 51, 53, 72
Stott, Rebecca, 12, 27n, 170n
Straus, Nina Pelikan, 13, 109, 170n, 171–88
structuralism/ist, 4–5, 6, 71, 125, 204, 250
Sturm, Paul J., 103n, 105n, 106n
Swift, Jonathan, 93–4, 103n
 'A Modest Proposal', 93
 A Tale of a Tub, 93
symbolism, 3, 235, 241–2

Tadié, Jean-Yves, 67n
Taine, Hippolyte, 151n
Tanner, Tony, 50, 67n, 68n, 212n, 260, 268n, 269n
textuality, 4–8, 247–8, 252–4, 260–1, 265
Thackeray, William, 40
Thomas, Keith, 105n
Thompson, Gordon, 174, 188n
Thorburn, David, 184, 188n
 Conrad's Romanticism, 184
Times Literary Supplement, 190
Tolstoy, Leo, 224
Torgovnick, Marianna, 160–1, 169n, 170n
 Gone Primitive, 160–1
Trevelyan, G. M., 245n
Trevor-Roper, Hugh, 110
Trilling, Lionel, 186, 188n
 Sincerity and Authority, 186

Vaihinger, Hans, 247–51, 262, 266n, 267n, 269n
 The Philosophy of 'As If', 247–51, 262, 266n, 267n

284

Index

Vallès, Jules, 245n
value(s), 1–4, 5, 6, 10, 12, 13, 23, 24, 71, 125, 143, 146, 210, 249, 267n
Van Ghent, Dorothy, 70n, 212n, 213n
van Hooft, Karen S., 187n
Vartanian, Aram, 105n
Vattimo, Gianni, 124
Verne, Jules, 126, 146
Vlaminck, Maurice, 120
Vollard, Ambroise, 120

Walpole, Horace, 213n
Watt, Ian, 21–2, 28n, 103n, 133, 146, 150n, 151n, 177–8, 180, 185, 188n, 212n, 241–2
Conrad in the Nineteenth Century, 21–2
Watts, Cedric, 26n, 269n
Weiner, Philip P., 105n
Wellek, René, 38, 43n

Wells, H. G., 103, 157, 192
White, Allon, 4, 22–4, 28n, 235–46
The Uses of Obscurity, 22–4
Widmer, Kingsley, 103n
Wilcox, Stewart, 175–6, 188n
Wilde, Oscar, 15, 196
Wiley, Paul, 263, 268n, 269n
Willett, Frank, 119–20, 123n
Williams, Raymond, 7, 31–6, 211, 213n
The English Novel, 31
Wollaeger, Mark, 2, 4, 6–7, 26n, 91–106
Woolf, Virginia, 106n, 173, 188n
Wordsworth, William, 132–3, 150n
'I wandered lonely as a cloud', 133
The Prelude, 132
work, 5, 204, 207–8, 240

Yeats, W. B., 180, 185–6, 190

Zola, Emile, 224

285